Selected Papers from the Second Conference on Parallel Processing for Scientific Computing

C.W. Gear
R.G. Voigt

Library of Congress Catalog Card Number 87-60435
ISBN 0–89871–216–5

Part I

Reprinted from the SIAM Journal on Scientific and Statistical Computing
Volume 8, Number 1, January 1987.

A NOTE FROM THE EDITORS

The future of scientific computing will certainly include parallel processing. The editors of the *SIAM Journal on Scientific and Statistical Computing* (SISSC) are pleased to publish in the January and March issues of this volume selected papers from the Second Conference on Parallel Processing for Scientific Computing held in Norfolk, Virginia on November 18–21, 1985.

This conference covered a broad spectrum of issues related to parallel computing, including algorithm development and analysis, computer architecture, and programming languages in such areas as automatic detection of parallelism, performance prediction, system simulation, communication and synchronization complexity, and load balancing.

The conference program consisted of 16 invited talks that surveyed some aspect of parallel computation, 24 research papers chosen on the basis of extended abstracts, and a large number of contributed papers. (Because many of the topics addressed were outside the scope of SISSC, a number of quite good papers will not appear in this journal. We expect that additional papers from the conference will be published in journals that cover other areas of parallel computation.)

Of the papers selected for publication in SISSC, two general themes are worth noting. The first is that parallel computers are indeed a reality—results on the performance of particular algorithms on particular systems are now being reported. This experimental activity is clearly quite important to the development of scientific computing, although it is true that a strong and unifying mathematical foundation to this work is as yet lacking. Second is that new algorithms are appearing that have been motivated by parallel computing. In at least one case (the eigenvalue algorithm discussed in the Dongarra–Sorensen paper, to appear in the next issue) the algorithm appears to be superior to the best traditional methods for serial computers. This is an exciting development that vividly demonstrates the value of a new perspective.

The editors of SISSC wish to thank Jack Dongarra and Garry H. Rodrigue, who joined the regular editors A. Björck, D. Gannon, J. A. George, F. O'Sullivan, A. Sameh, D. Sorensen, P. Swarztrauber, and G. Wahba in overseeing the review of the nearly 40 papers that were submitted. Standard SIAM policy for selecting referees and making recommendations for publication were followed.

We also wish to thank the organizing committee of the conference, which consisted of Robert G. Voigt, Chairman, Institute for Computer Applications in Science and Engineering; Billy L. Buzbee, Los Alamos National Laboratory; Dennis B. Gannon, Indiana University; and Garry H. Rodrigue, Lawrence Livermore National Laboratory.

The Second Conference in Parallel Processing was sponsored by the SIAM Activity Group on Supercomputing with partial support from the Air Force Office of Scientific Research, the Army Research Office, and the National Science Foundation.

C. W. Gear
R. G. Voigt

SIAM J. SCI. STAT. COMPUT.
Vol. 8, No. 1, January 1987

THE WY REPRESENTATION FOR PRODUCTS OF HOUSEHOLDER MATRICES*

CHRISTIAN BISCHOF† AND CHARLES VAN LOAN†

Abstract. A new way to represent products of Householder matrices is given that makes a typical Householder matrix algorithm rich in matrix-matrix multiplication. This is very desirable in that matrix-matrix multiplication is the operation of choice for an increasing number of important high performance computers. We tested the new representation by using it to compute the QR factorization on the FPS-164/MAX. Preliminary results indicate that it is a very efficient way to organize Householder computations.

Key words. Householder matrices, QR factorization, vector parallelism

AMS(MOS) subject classification. 65

1. Introduction. During the past five years a great deal has been written about matrix computations in high performance "supercomputing" environments. For example, techniques have emerged for designing linear algebra codes that "squeeze" the most out of various vector pipeline architectures. The reader is referred to the excellent survey article by Dongarra, Gustavson and Karp (1984). One theme in their work is how to take an algorithm such as Gaussian elimination and organize it in such a way that the resulting code is rich in matrix-vector multiplication. The regularity of that operation allows for maximum pipelining and minimum traffic to and from memory. The papers by Dongarra and Eisenstat (1984) and Dongarra, Kaufman and Hammarling (1985) further dramatize this point.

It is now the case with some new architectures that high performance can best be achieved with algorithms that are rich in *matrix-matrix* multiplication. Such a requirement leads naturally to block algorithms. For methods such as Gaussian elimination and the Cholesky factorization the course of action is relatively straightforward. Consider the LU factorization:

$$\begin{bmatrix} A_{11} & A_{12} & A_{13} \\ A_{21} & A_{22} & A_{23} \\ A_{31} & A_{32} & A_{33} \end{bmatrix} = \begin{bmatrix} L_{11} & 0 & 0 \\ L_{21} & L_{22} & 0 \\ L_{31} & L_{32} & L_{33} \end{bmatrix} \begin{bmatrix} U_{11} & U_{12} & U_{13} \\ 0 & U_{22} & U_{23} \\ 0 & 0 & U_{33} \end{bmatrix}.$$

If we assume that the first block row of U and the first block column of L are known, then the blocks L_{22}, U_{22}, L_{32}, and U_{23} can be resolved from the equations

$$L_{22} U_{22} = A_{22} - L_{21} U_{12},$$

$$L_{22} U_{23} = A_{23} - L_{21} U_{13},$$

$$L_{32} U_{22} = A_{32} - L_{31} U_{12}.$$

Note that the right-hand sides are rich in matrix-matrix multiplication. If block dimensions are chosen properly then the overall method will be sufficiently rich in

* Received by the editors December 12, 1985; accepted for publication (in revised form) April 9, 1986. Computations associated with this research were performed on the Production Supercomputer Facility at Cornell University which is supported in part by the National Science Foundation and the IBM Corporation. Additional funding was provided by Office of Naval Research contract N00014-83-K-0640. This paper appeared in the Proceedings of the 1986 ARRAY Conference, Portland, Oregon, April 6-10, 1986.

† Department of Computer Science, Cornell University, Ithaca, New York 14853.

that operation to ensure high performance. This has been demonstrated by Steve Oslon of Floating Point Systems who has implemented the above scheme (with pivoting) on the FPS-164/MAX.

The FPS-164/MAX has an architecture that "likes" matrix–matrix multiplication and it is for this machine that we have developed a new algorithm for the QR factorization that performs extremely well. Although our technique has been tailored to the FPS-164/MAX, we suspect that our work will be of interest to users of other high performance computers such as the Cray-2 and the IBM 3090.

It should be noted that the block procedures for matrix decompositions involving orthogonal transformations are not so straightforward. Consider the QR factorization:

$$A = [A_1, A_2, A_3] = QR = [Q_1, Q_2, Q_3] \begin{bmatrix} R_{11} & R_{12} & R_{13} \\ 0 & R_{22} & R_{23} \\ 0 & 0 & R_{33} \end{bmatrix}.$$

If the first block column of Q and the first block row of R are known, then Q_2 and R_{22} can be obtained by computing the QR factorization

$$Q_2 R_{22} = A_2 - Q_1 R_{12}$$

whereupon $R_{23} = Q_2^T A_3$. These are essentially the key steps of a block version of modified Gram–Schmidt (MGS). Block MGS is certainly rich in matrix multiplication but the "Q" matrix may not be sufficiently orthonormal for certain applications. (See Golub and Van Loan (1983, pp. 151–152) for a description of MGS and its properties.) It is an open question how to organize block MGS and what its numerical properties are. We shall not treat the matter further in this paper.

Our intention is to examine how the perfectly stable Householder QR factorization procedure can be written in a form that is rich in matrix multiplications. Householder transformations underpin the eigenvalue and least squares solvers in EISPACK and LINPACK. A discussion of the algorithms in these packages may be found in Golub and Van Loan (1983).

The key to obtaining block Householder algorithms that are rich in matrix multiplication turns out to be what we call the "WY representation." It amounts to writing products of Householder matrices like

$$Q_k = P_1 \cdots P_k, \qquad P_i \in R^{m \times m}$$

in the form

(1.1) $$Q_k = I + WY^T, \qquad W, Y \in R^{m \times k}.$$

Several authors have looked at similar ways to group and generalize Householder matrices and we review this work in § 2. The basic properties of the WY representation are detailed in § 3. In § 4 we show how to compute the QR factorization using the WY representation. An implementation of our algorithm on the FPS-164/MAX is then described in § 5. The last section suggests how the WY representation can be used to compute other decompositions that involve orthogonal transformations.

2. Aggregating Householder transformations. The idea of "aggregating" Householder transformations for performance is not new. Dongarra, Kaufman and Hammarling (1985) suggest pairing Householder matrices in order to reduce the number of vector memory references. For example, they recommend that the update

$$A := (I - \alpha ww^T)(I - \beta uu^T)A$$

be computed as follows:

$$v^T := w^T A,$$
$$x^T := u^T A,$$
$$y^T := v^T - (\beta w^T u) x^T,$$
$$A := A - \beta u x^T - \alpha w y^T.$$

As the authors point out, this maneuver actually increases the number of required flops. But the resulting algorithm is faster in pipelined environments because there is less memory traffic. The WY representation (1.1) is a generalization of this pairwise grouping strategy.

Note that an orthogonal matrix of the form $I + WY^T$ can be thought of as a generalized Householder matrix, an idea that was examined by Dietrich (1976). Given an m-by-p matrix partitioned as follows

$$X = \begin{bmatrix} X_1 \\ X_2 \end{bmatrix} \begin{matrix} p \\ m-p \end{matrix},$$

Dietrich shows how to compute a full rank m-by-p matrix

$$W = \begin{bmatrix} W_1 \\ W_2 \end{bmatrix} \begin{matrix} p \\ m-p \end{matrix},$$

so that if

$$P = I - 2W(W^T W)^{-1} W^T,$$

then

(2.1)
$$P^T X = \begin{bmatrix} T \\ 0 \end{bmatrix} \begin{matrix} p \\ m-p \end{matrix}.$$

The matrix P above is clearly a block generalization of a Householder matrix. A stable method for computing W using some recent algorithmic developments is as follows:

Step 1. Compute the QR factorization:

$$X = \begin{bmatrix} Q_1 \\ Q_2 \end{bmatrix} R.$$

Step 2. Compute the CS decomposition:

$$Q_1 = U_1 C V^T, \quad C = \text{diag}(c_1, \cdots, c_p), \quad 1 \geq c_1 \geq \cdots \geq c_p \geq 0,$$
$$Q_2 = U_2 S V^T, \quad S = \text{diag}(s_1, \cdots, s_p), \quad 0 \leq s_1 \leq \cdots \leq s_p \leq 1.$$

(Here, U_1, U_2 and V are orthogonal.)
Step 3. Set

$$W = \begin{bmatrix} U_1(C+I) \\ U_2 S \end{bmatrix}.$$

The trouble with this method of aggregating Householder transformations is that some delicate SVD computations are involved in Step 2. See Stewart (1983) or Van Loan (1985) for details concerning the computation of the CS decomposition. In addition to these difficulties, the matrix T in (2.1) will not generally be upper triangular

$(T = U_1 V^T R)$. Thus, if we incorporated Dietrich's idea in a QR factorization algorithm the resulting R would be block upper triangular. True upper triangular form could easily be achieved but it is an inconvenient post-computation.

3. The WY representation. Recall that an m-by-m Householder matrix is an orthogonal matrix of the form

$$P = I + uv^T$$

where $v \in R^m$ has unit 2-norm length and $u = -2v$. Householder matrices can be used to compute all kinds of important matrix decompositions and the large number of subroutines in LINPACK and EISPACK that rely on these transformations underscores their importance.

In a typical application a sequence of Householder transformations $P_i = I + u_i v_i^T$ is applied to a given matrix. Consider the following algorithm for computing the QR factorization of

$$A = [a_1, \cdots, a_n], \qquad a_j \in R^m.$$

ALGORITHM 3.1.
For $k = 1:n$
    For $j = 1:k-1$
        $a_k := a_k + (u_j^T a_k) v_j, \qquad (a_k := P_{k-1} \cdots P_1 a_k)$
    end j
    Compute unit 2-norm v_k so that if $u_k = -2v_k$ and $P_k = I + u_k v_k^T$ then $P_k a_k$ is
        zero in components $k+1$ to m.
end k

This computation is rich in inner products and SAXPY's but not in matrix multiplication. (A "SAXPY" is the operation $y := \alpha x + y$ where x and y are vectors and α is a scalar.) The SAXPY's in the j loop cannot be performed in parallel because the a_k are different for each j.

Reversing the order of the loops in Algorithm 3.1 essentially gives the LINPACK QR factorization procedure. In this version the key computations are updates of the form $A := (I + u_j v_j^T)^T A$. The inner products associated with $u_j^T A$ can be computed in parallel as can the SAXPY's associated with $A := A + v_j(u_j^T A)$. What prevents "supervector performance" is an unfavorable ratio of vector loads and unloads to actual computation. See Dongarra, Kaufman and Hammarling (1985).

We propose a new way to represent products of Householder matrices that rectifies this problem. In particular, we exploit the fact that a product of Householders

$$Q_k = P_1 \cdots P_k$$

can be written in the form

$$Q_k = I + W_k Y_k^T$$

where W_k and Y_k are m-by-k matrices. Note that the mission of the j loop in Algorithm 3.1 is to compute $Q_{k-1}^T a_k$.

To anticipate the value of the WY representation, observe that if B is a matrix then the computation $B := Q_k^T B$ is rich in matrix multiplication:

$$B := B + Y_k(W_k^T B).$$

However, before we can pursue the algorithmic benefits of the WY representation we must establish its existence and show how it can be updated.

The WY form certainly exists for the $k=1$ case. Indeed, since $Q_1 = P_1 = I + u_1 v_1^T$ we just set $W = u_1$ and $Y = v_1$. To establish the result for general k, we show how to obtain (W_k, Y_k) from (W_{k-1}, Y_{k-1}) upon receipt of the kth Householder matrix $P_k = I + u_k v_k^T$. From the manipulations

$$Q_k = Q_{k-1}P_k = (I + W_{k-1}Y_{k-1}^T)(I + u_k v_k^T)$$
$$= I + [W_{k-1}, Q_{k-1}u_k][Y_{k-1}, v_k]^T$$
$$= I + [W_{k-1}, u_k][P_k Y_{k-1}, v_k]^T,$$

we see that there are actually two ways to accomplish this:

Method 1.
$$W_k = [W_{k-1}, Q_{k-1}u_k],$$
$$Y_k = [Y_{k-1}, v_k].$$

Method 2.
$$W_k = [W_{k-1}, u_k],$$
$$Y_k = [P_k Y_{k-1}, v_k].$$

We have used Method 1 in our implementations feeling that the matrix-vector multiplication $Q_{k-1}u_k$ is easier to optimize than the rank one update $P_k Y_{k-1}$. However, this is not a clear choice. Indeed, it may be wiser to update WY factors using Method 2 for the following reason. In many applications such as in Algorithm 3.1 the first $k-1$ components of the Householder vector v_k are zero. Thus, if Method 2 is used then a simple check reveals that *both* Y_k and W_k are lower trapezoidal. However, if Method 1 is used than *only* Y_k is lower trapezoidal.

We point out that manipulation of Householder matrices through the WY form is stable. The same favorable roundoff properties that attend "conventional" Householder algorithms apply if the computations are arranged in WY form. This claim is justified in a brief appendix to be found at the end of the paper.

Finally, we mention that the above updating formulae generalize. In particular, if $U = I + W_U Y_U^T$ and $V = I + W_V Y_V^T$ are orthogonal matrices in WY form then $Q = UV$ has its WY factors given by $W_Q = [W_U, UW_V]$ and $Y_Q = [Y_U, Y_V]$.

4. Computing the QR factorization using the WY representation. To illustrate the attractiveness of the WY representation, we show how it can be used to compute the QR factorization of a rectangular matrix $A = [a_1, \cdots, a_n] \in R^{m \times n}$. A naive (but instructive) WY implementation of Algorithm 3.1 is as follows:

ALGORITHM 4.1.
For $k = 1:n$
  $a_k := (I + WY^T)^T a_k$,   ($a_k := Q_{k-1}^T a_k$, skip if $k=1$)
  Compute unit v such that if $u = -2v$ then $(I + uv^T)a_k$ is zero in components
    $k+1$ to m.
  $W := [W, (I + WY^T)u]$,   ($W = [u]$ if $k=1$)
  $Y := [Y, v]$,   ($Y = [v]$ if $k=1$)
end k

There are three problems with this algorithm. (1) It requires $2mn^2 - n^3/2$ flops, approximately twice what is required by the usual Householder QR factorization scheme, e.g., Algorithm 3.1. (2) It requires an m-by-n workspace for W. (3) It is not rich in matrix-matrix multiplication.

The same criticisms would essentially apply if Method 2 updating was used although one could get by with $n^2/2$ fewer storage locations and $p^3/2$ fewer flops.

To obtain a successful QR factorization scheme using the WY representation it is necessary to partition A into block columns:

$$A = [A_1, \cdots, A_N]$$

where each A has p columns. (If p does not divide n then A_N may have fewer than p columns, an unimportant detail that we hereafter suppress.) The appropriate column width p depends on the underlying architecture. (For the FPS-164/MAX it will turn out to be equal to the maximum number of parallel dot products that can be performed.)

The basic idea of our procedure is as follows. At the beginning of Step k ($1 \le k \le N$) the matrix A has been overwritten with

$$P_{(k-1)p} \cdots P_1 A = \begin{bmatrix} R_{11} & R_{12} & R_{13} \\ 0 & \bar{A}_k & B \end{bmatrix} \begin{matrix} (k-1)p \\ r \end{matrix}$$
$$ (k-1)p \quad p \quad q$$

where $r = m - (k-1)p$ and $q = n - kp$. The QR factorization of $\bar{A}_k$ is then computed and the orthogonal matrix (in WY form) is applied to B.

In our formal description of this procedure we use the notation $A(i_1:i_2, j_1:j_2)$ to designate the submatrix of A defined by rows i_1 through i_2 and columns j_1 through j_2.

ALGORITHM 4.2.
For $k = 1:N$
$\quad s := (k-1)p + 1$
$\quad$ Compute W and Y such that $I + WY^T$ is orthogonal and $(I + WY^T)A(s:m, s:s+p-1)$ is upper triangular.
$\quad A(s:m, s:n) := (I + WY^T)^T A(s:m, s:n)$
end k

Upon emergence from this algorithm the matrix A is overwritten by R. The Householder vectors v_i that are generated can be stored below the diagonal in the usual manner. (See Golub and Van Loan (1983, p. 148).) It is not necessary to save the W matrices from step to step and so we just need an m-by-p workspace for W. (This is in contrast to the m-by-n workspace required by Algorithm 4.1.) Algorithm 4.2 is clearly rich in matrix–matrix multiplication. Indeed much more work is spent applying the WY factors than generating them which is good in that it implies richness in matrix multiplication. To be specific, $(2mn^2 - n^3)/N$ flops are required to generate the W's and Y's while $(mn^2 - n^3/3)$ flops are needed to apply them. Since the LINPACK QR algorithm requires $mn^2 - n^3/3$ flops we see that Algorithm 4.2 is more expensive by a factor of $(1 + 2/N)$ from the standpoint of flops. For modest (and realistic) values of N this factor is for all practical purposes equal to one. Moreover, in high performance environments just counting flops is an inadequate measure of efficiency. The number of references to memory usually has a much greater bearing on the efficiency of an algorithm. This is borne out by our experience implementing Algorithm 4.2 on the FPS-164/MAX.

5. Performance on the FPS-164/MAX system. Up to now a "flop" has meant the amount of work that is roughly associated with an operation of the form $a_{ij} := a_{ij} + a_{ik}a_{kj}$. However, manufacturers of "high performance" computers quantify speed using "high performance flops." A "high performance flop" equals two "regular" flops. Thus, n-by-n matrix multiplication requires $2n^3$ flops. In this section we will quantify speed in terms of millions of high performance flops per second as we will be reporting on the FPS-164/MAX. (Independent adder and multiplier units are what makes high performance flop rates relevant.)

The FPS-164 is an 11 Megaflop (Mflop), 64-bit general purpose scientific processor built by Floating Point Systems Inc. It is attached to the I/O system of a general purpose host computer. In a typical situation the program executing on the 164 is a subroutine called from a host FORTRAN program.

The FPS-164 can be enhanced with additional "MAX boards" that can perform selected linear algebra calculations very fast. Each board buys 22 Mflops and up to fifteen can be installed in a single 164. A fully configured FPS-164/MAX thus has a theoretical peak performance level of 341 Mflops. A nice overview of the architecture is given in Madura, Broussard and Strickland (1985). We cover just enough of its features to build an appreciation for the type of algorithm that performs efficiently in the MAX environment.

Each MAX module operates synchronously and in parallel with the 164's CPU. The modules appear as memory to the 164's CPU in that they are accessed via reads and writes to reserved addresses. The essential components of a MAX module are two fully pipelined adder/multiplier pairs and eight vector registers (length = 2047). The MAX modules have a limited repertoire of operations but by design they figure heavily in matrix computations. If n_{max} denotes the number of installed MAX boards then the system is able to perform

$$n_d = 4 + 8 \cdot n_{max}$$

parallel dot products or

$$n_v = 1 + 4 \cdot n_{max}$$

parallel SAXPY's as follows:

Parallel Dot Product.

If $V = [v_1, \cdots, v_d] \in R^{m \times d}$ $(d \leq n_d)$ resides in the MAX vector registers and $w \in R^m$ is stored in main memory, then it is possible to compute the d inner products $v_i^T w$ concurrently. If $d = n_d$ then this means that $V^T w$ can be formed at an approximate rate of $11 + 22 \cdot n_{max}$ Mflops.

Parallel SAXPY.

If $V = [v_1, \cdots, v_d] \in R^{m \times d}$ $(d \leq n)$ resides in the MAX vector registers and the vectors $z \in R^d$ and $u \in R^m$ are in main memory, then it is possible to compute the s SAXPY's $v_i := v_i + z_i u$ concurrently. If $d = n_v$ then the computation $V := V + uz^T$ can be formed at the approximate rate of $5 + 11 \cdot n_{max}$ Mflops.

FPS has extended its ANSI FORTRAN 77 to accommodate a set of subroutines that perform the above computations. This includes a set of routines for executing the required loads and unloads that are responsible for moving data between the MAX modules and main memory. (To those familiar with the FPS-164, table memory essentially acts like a half MAX board. So when we refer to "MAX boards" we really mean "MAX boards plus table memory.")

Because the overhead associated with the loading and unloading of the MAX modules can easily dominate a floating point computation, it is desirable that the vectors loaded into a MAX module be reasonably long and (more critically) that they be "re-used" as much as possible before they are returned to main memory. That way, the cost of a load (or unload) is spread over a significant amount of high speed computation.

With this review of the FPS-164/MAX we can present the MAX version of Algorithm 4.2. In the kth step of the algorithm attention is focussed on the submatrix

$$A(s:m, s:n) = [\bar{A}_k, B] \quad q$$
$$\qquad\qquad\qquad p \quad r$$

where $q = m - (k-1)p$, $r = n - kp$, and $s = 1 + (k-1)p$. The block width p is taken to be the maximum number of parallel dot products that can be performed, i.e., $p = n_d$. There are three steps to consider.

Step 1. Compute the QR Factorization of $\bar{A}_k$.

Algorithm 4.1 is used for this purpose. The MAX boards are *not* used here as the algorithm is not rich in matrix multiplication.

Step 2. Compute $Z^T = W^T B$.

Let $B = [b_1, \cdots, b_r]$ be a column partitioning of B. Noting that W entirely fits into the MAX vector registers, $Z \in R^{r \times p}$ is computed as follows:

Load W into the MAX boards.
For $i = 1:r$
    Compute $z(i:i, 1:p) := b_i^T W$ (Parallel Dot Product)
end i

Note that W is reused $r = n - kp$ times. Except at the very end of the algorithm this portion of the computation can proceed at close to peak parallel dot product speed.

Step 3. Overwrite B with $B + YZ^T$.

This is a parallel SAXPY operation. For clarity, assume that s divides r and that $t = r/s$. Partition B, Y, and Z as follows:

$$B = [B_1, \cdots, B_t], \qquad B_i \in R^{q \times s},$$
$$Y = [y_1, \cdots, y_p], \qquad y_i \in R^q,$$
$$Z = \begin{bmatrix} z_{11} & \cdots & z_{1p} \\ \vdots & & \vdots \\ z_{t1} & \cdots & z_{tp} \end{bmatrix}, \qquad z_{ij} \in R^s.$$

With this partitioning the update $B := B + YZ^T$ can be computed as follows:

For $i = 1:t$
    Load B_i into the MAX vector registers.
    For $j = 1:p$
        $B_i := B_i + y_j z_{ji}^T$ (Parallel SAXPY)
    end j
    Unload B_i into main memory.
end i

The re-use factor for this portion of the algorithm is p.

The MAX algorithm just described has been tested on Cornell's FPS-164/MAX system. Currently, this is a one MAX Board installation implying 33 Mflop peak dot product performance and 15 Mflop peak SAXPY performance.

We point out that the fraction of the overall computation that is performed on the MAX boards is $N/(N+2)$ where $N = n/n_d = n/12$. For the various values of n

represented in the table, this fraction ranges from .71 to .97. Of all the MAX computations in our implementation half are parallel dot products and half are parallel SAXPY's. Table 1 indicates the megaflop rates that our code has achieved for problems of varying dimension. An optimized "LINPACK QR" code running on the 164 without MAX boards would perform in the vicinity of 6 Mflops. We feel that these benchmarks confirm that the WY representation is a viable way of organizing Householder computations on the FPS-164/MAX.

TABLE 1
Performance in Megaflops (Mflops).

m	$n = .25m$	$n = .50m$	$n = .75m$	$n = m$
250	7	9	11	11
500	10	13	14	15
750	13	14	16	17
1000	14	15	17	18

6. Other factorizations. Householder matrices are traditionally used in the computation of the following decompositions:

$$Q^H A Q = T \quad (A \text{ symmetric}, T \text{ tridiagonal}),$$
$$Q^H A Q = H \quad (H \text{ Hessenberg}),$$
$$U^T A V = B \quad (B \text{ bidiagonal}).$$

When one contemplates WY versions of these algorithms some new difficulties arise that are not present in the QR factorization. These problems stem from the fact that the above decompositions involve both left and right transformations. This makes "delayed" application of the Householder matrices problematical. In the QR scheme we can reduce a subset of columns without touching the "rest" of the matrix. This is because the Householders are applied from just one side. However, in Householder tridiagonalization (for example) this is not possible. The second Householder P_2 is a function of *all* the matrix elements because it is based on the second column of

$$P_1^T A P_1 = \begin{bmatrix} x & x & 0 & 0 & 0 \\ x & x & x & x & x \\ 0 & x & x & x & x \\ 0 & x & x & x & x \\ 0 & x & x & x & x \end{bmatrix}.$$

In particular, n^2 flops are required to compute this column. This is *not* an order of magnitude less work than performing the entire update $A := P_1^T A P_1$ which costs $2n^2$ flops. Thus, unlike in the QR factorization method, nothing is gained by aggregating Householders and *then* applying them in WY form.

One way out of this jam is to strive for block tridiagonalization. Partition A as follows:

$$A = \begin{bmatrix} A_{11} & A_{21}^T \\ A_{21} & A_{22} \end{bmatrix} \begin{matrix} p \\ n-p \end{matrix}.$$
$$\quad\quad p \quad n-p$$

If we compute the QR factorization

$$A_{21} = QR, \qquad Q = I + WY^T,$$

then update

$$B = Q^T A_{22} Q = (I + WY^T)^T A_{22} (I + WY^T)$$

we obtain

$$A := \text{diag}\,(I_p, Q)^T A \,\text{diag}\,(I_p, Q) = \begin{bmatrix} A_{11} & R^T \\ R & B \end{bmatrix}.$$

This illustrates the basic step of the algorithm. Although it is rich in matrix multiples it leaves us with a bandwidth p eigenproblem. One possibility would be to reduce the resulting matrix to tridiagonal form using the method of Schwartz (1968). The overall success of this procedure in the MAX environment is the next item on our agenda and will be reported elsewhere along with some related procedures for bidiagonalization and Hessenberg reduction.

Appendix. Roundoff properties of the WY representation. In this Appendix we have opted for an "$O(\mathbf{u})$" analysis feeling that complete rigor would add only tedium to an otherwise simple argument. For further comments on the "philosophy" of roundoff analysis, see Golub and Van Loan (1983, p. 32 ff).

Suppose $\mathbf{u}$ is the unit roundoff and A and B are floating point matrices. If $\text{fl}(AB)$ denotes the computed product of A and B then

$$\text{fl}(AB) = AB + E$$

where

$$\|E\|_2 = O(\mathbf{u}) \|A\|_2 \|B\|_2.$$

Likewise, if A and B are compatible for addition, then

$$\text{fl}(A + B) = A + B + E$$

with

$$\|E\|_2 = O(\mathbf{u})(\|A\|_2 + \|B\|_2).$$

Repeated use will be made of these well-known facts.

We begin with a definition. Suppose W and Y are m-by-k matrices with floating point entries. We say that

$$Q = I + WY^T$$

$\mathbf{u}$-orthogonal if the following three properties hold:

(A1) $$\|W\|_2 = O(1),$$

(A2) $$\|Y\|_2 = O(1),$$

(A3) $$\|Q^T Q - I\|_2 = O(\mathbf{u}).$$

If we apply Q to a floating point matrix A then

$$\text{fl}(QA) = QA + F$$

where

$$\|F\|_2 = O(\mathbf{u})\|A\|_2.$$

Since (A3) implies that the singular values σ_i of Q are all of the form $\sigma_i = 1 + O(\mathbf{u})$, it follows that

(A4) $$\mathrm{fl}(QA) = Q(A + Q^{-1}F) = Q(A + E)$$

where

(A5) $$\|E\|_2 = \|Q^{-1}F\|_2 = O(\mathbf{u})\|A\|_2.$$

Thus, if (A1), (A2), and (A3) hold then manipulations with Q in WY form are stable because it allows for a favorable inverse error analysis.

A corollary of this result is that

$$P = I + uv^T$$

is **u**-orthogonal provided the floating point vectors v and u satisfy

(A6) $$\|v\|_2 = 1 + O(\mathbf{u})$$

and

(A7) $$u = -2v.$$

This can be used to confirm the stability of conventional Householder matrix manipulations.

What we must show is that when the WY representation is updated (say by Method 1) then properties (A1)–(A3) remain in force. To this end, suppose

$$W_+ = [\, W,\ \mathrm{fl}(Qu)\,],$$

$$Y_+ = [\, Y,\ v\,],$$

$$Q_+ = I + W_+ Y_+^T$$

where u and v satisfy (A6) and (A7) and (W_+, Y_+) is the computed WY representation of the approximate orthogonal matrix QP. Setting $A = u$ in (A4) and (A5) gives

(A8) $$\mathrm{fl}(Qu) = Qu + e$$

with

(A9) $$\|e\|_2 = O(\mathbf{u})\|u\|_2 = O(\mathbf{u}).$$

Here we used the fact that $\|u\|_2 = 2 + O(\mathbf{u}) = O(1)$. It follows from (A1), (A3), (A8), (A9), and the definition of W_+ that

$$\|W_+\|_2 \le \|W\|_2 + \|\mathrm{fl}(Qu)\|_2 = O(1).$$

Likewise, (A2), (A6), and the definition of Y_+ imply that

$$\|Y_+\|_2 \le \|Y\|_2 + \|v\|_2 = O(1).$$

All that remains for us to show is that Q_+ satisfies (A3). Using (A8) and the definition of Q_+ we have

$$Q_+ = I + W_+ Y_+^T = I + WY^T + \mathrm{fl}(Qu)v^T$$
$$= Q + (Qu + e)v^T = Q(I + uv^T) + ev^T = Q(P + Q^{-1}ev^T).$$

Using (A9) it is easy to show that if

$$\bar{P} = P + Q^{-1}ev^T$$

then

$$\|\bar{P}^T\bar{P} - I\|_2 = O(\mathbf{u}).$$

This coupled with (A3) ensures that $\|Q_+^T Q_+ - I\|_2 = O(\mathbf{u})$.

We mention that if W and Y are updated using Method 2, then a similar error analysis goes through.

Acknowledgments. We are indebted to Steve Oslon of Floating Point Systems who kindly shared his MAX expertise with us as we developed our code. We are also obliged to Gene Golub of Stanford University for calling our attention to the reference Dietrich (1976).

REFERENCES

G. Dietrich (1976), *A new formulation of the hypermatrix Householder-QR decomposition*, Comput. Meth. Appl. Mech. Engrg., 9, pp. 273–280.

J. Dongarra, J. D. Bunch, C. B. Moler and G. W. Stewart (1979), *Linpack User's Guide*, Society for Industrial and Applied Mathematics, Philadelphia, PA.

J. Dongarra and S. Eisenstat (1984), *Squeezing the most out of an algorithm in Cray Fortran*, ACM Trans. Math. Software, 10, pp. 216–230.

J. Dongarra, F. G. Gustavson and A. Karp (1984), *Implementing linear algebra algorithms on dense matrices on a vector pipeline machine*, SIAM Rev., 26, pp. 91–112.

J. Dongarra, L. Kaufman and S. Hammarling (1985), *Squeezing the most out of eigenvalue solvers on high-performance computers*, Technical Memorandum 46, Mathematics and Computer Science Division, Argonne National Laboratory, Argonne, IL 60439.

G. H. Golub and C. Van Loan (1983), *Matrix Computations*, The Johns Hopkins University Press, Baltimore, MD.

D. Madura, R. Broussard and D. Strickland (1985), FPS-164 MAX: *parallel multiprocessing for linear algebra operation*, Proc. 1985 Array Processing Conference, New Orleans, pp. 33–50.

H. R. Schwartz (1968), *Tridiagonalization of a symmetric band matrix*, Numer. Math., 12, pp. 231–241.

B. T. Smith, J. M. Boyle, Y. Ikebe, V. C. Klema and C. B. Moler (1970), *Matrix Eigensystem Routines: EISPACK Guide*, 2nd ed., Springer-Verlag, New York.

G. W. Stewart (1983) *An algorithm for computing the CS decomposition of a partitioned orthonormal matrix*, Numer. Math., 40, pp. 297–306.

C. Van Loan (1985), *Computing the CS and the generalized singular value decomposition*, Numer. Math., 46, 479–491.

SIAM J. SCI. STAT. COMPUT.
Vol. 8, No. 1, January 1987

A DOMAIN-DECOMPOSED FAST POISSON SOLVER ON A RECTANGLE*

TONY F. CHAN† AND DIANA C. RESASCO†

Abstract. We present a new domain decomposed fast Poisson solver on a rectangle divided into parallel strips or boxes. The method first performs uncoupled fast solves on each subdomain, and then the interface variables are computed exactly by Fast Fourier Transform, without computing or inverting the capacitance matrix explicitly. Finally, the solution on the interior of the subdomains can be computed by one more fast solve on each subdomain. This method is especially suited for parallel implementation, since the independent problems in the subdomains can be solved in parallel, and the communication involves the interface variables only.

Key words. domain decomposition, substructuring, capacitance matrix, elliptic partial differential equations, preconditioning, fast Poisson solvers, parallel computation

AMS(MOS) subject classification. 65

1. Introduction. We consider the solution of the Poisson equation in a rectangular region partitioned into strips. By the method of Domain Decomposition, the solution of the algebraic equations resulting from the discretization on a regular grid is reduced to the solution of problems in the subdomains and a linear system for the interface unknowns, given by the *capacitance matrix*. This is an important tool in the solution of elliptic partial differential equations. There are several reasons why these techniques might be attractive:

- The method is suited for the solution of very large problems on machines with limited storage.
- Special solution techniques might exist to solve the problems on the subdomains that cannot be applied efficiently to the entire domain. This is often the case, for example, when the domain has irregular geometry, but it can be broken up into regular subdomains, like rectangles.
- The equations in the different subdomains might have different parameters or even be of different nature, in which case the idea of substructuring comes very naturally.
- The idea is attractive for parallel processing, since the problem can be decoupled in independent subproblems and the communication needed will be only for the interface values.

The capacitance matrix is expensive to compute or invert explicitly, while it is relatively simple to compute the product of such a matrix with an arbitrary vector. For that reason the interface system is usually solved by conjugate gradient methods instead of a direct method. In order to improve the convergence of the method, several preconditioning techniques have been given in the literature [7], [8], [2], [3].

For the problem considered in this paper, we present a fast direct method for the solution of the capacitance matrix that does not require the computation of the elements of the matrix. This method is related to the k-reduction method, a technique proposed by Bank and Rose [1] in order to improve the stability of the marching algorithm. In

---

*Received by the editors August 26, 1985; accepted for publication (in revised form) March 7, 1986. This work was supported in part by the Department of Energy under contract DE-AC02-81ER10996 and by a BID-CONICET fellowship from Argentina.

† Department of Computer Science, Research Center for Scientific Computing, Yale University, New Haven, Connecticut 06520.

fact, the k-reduction method can be interpreted as a particular implementation of the domain decomposition algorithm, where the number of strips is chosen to fulfill the stability constraints. In the case of uniform sized strips, the eigenvectors and eigenvalues of the capacitance matrix can be derived explicitly. This gives not only a direct method to solve the interface system, but also a framework to analyse other preconditioners.

In § 2, we apply the method of Domain Decomposition to the solution of the Poisson equation in a rectangular domain subdivided into strips, and derive a system for the interface unknowns and the capacitance matrix. In § 3, we analyze the capacitance matrix, giving its eigenvectors and eigenvalues. Based on this, we derive a fast direct method for the solution of the interface system. The eigen-decomposition of the capacitance matrix also provides a clear way of analyzing some other preconditioners. In § 4, we analyze the preconditioners given by Golub and Mayers, Dryja and Proskurowski, and Bjorstad and Widlund. Finally, in §§ 5 and 6, we discuss extensions of the method to rectangular domains subdivided into boxes, and more general variable coefficient operators and summarize the results, giving some concluding remarks.

2. Domain decomposition. We consider the Poisson equation

(2.1)
$$\Delta u = f \quad \text{on } \Omega$$

with boundary conditions

$$u = u_b \quad \text{on } \partial\Omega$$

where the domain Ω is as illustrated in Fig. 1.

We partition Ω into $k+1$ strips Ω_i, $i = 1, \cdots, k$ of sizes 1 by l_i and denote the interfaces between $\mathcal{N}_i$ and Ω_{i+1}, by Γ_i, $i = 1, \cdots, k$. We use a uniform mesh with grid

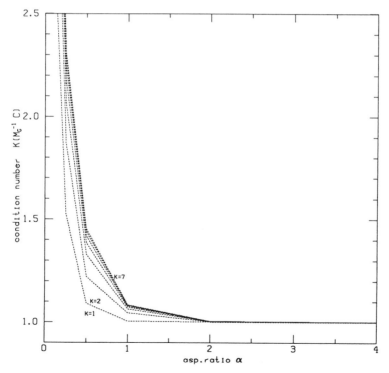

FIG. 1. *The domain Ω and its partition.*

size h on Ω with n internal grid points in the x-direction, i.e.

$$h = \frac{1}{n+1}$$

and m_i internal grid points in Ω_i in the y-direction, i.e. for $i = 1, \cdots, k+1$,

$$l_i = (m_i + 1)h.$$

Let us consider a standard 5-point centered difference approximation to (2.1). If we order the unknowns for the internal points of the subdomains first and then those in the interfaces Γ_i, then the discrete solution vector $u = (u_\Omega, u_\Gamma)$ satisfies a linear system that can be expressed in block form as

$$(2.2) \qquad \begin{pmatrix} Q_\Omega & P \\ P^T & Q_\Gamma \end{pmatrix} \begin{pmatrix} u_\Omega \\ u_\Gamma \end{pmatrix} = \begin{pmatrix} f_\Omega \\ f_\Gamma \end{pmatrix},$$

where the right-hand side depends on f and u_b and

$$(2.3) \qquad Q_\Omega = \begin{pmatrix} L_1 & & & \\ & L_2 & & \\ & & \ddots & \\ & & & L_{k+1} \end{pmatrix},$$

$$(2.4) \qquad Q_\Gamma = \begin{pmatrix} L_{k+2} & & \\ & \ddots & \\ & & L_{2k+1} \end{pmatrix}$$

where L_i corresponds to the discrete Laplacian on Ω_i for $i \le k+1$, and L_i for $i > k+1$ is the tridiagonal matrix tridiag$(1, -4, 1)$. The matrix P has the following block bi-diagonal form:

$$(2.5) \qquad P = \begin{pmatrix} P_{1,1} & & & \\ P_{2,1} & P_{2,2} & & \\ & \ddots & \ddots & \\ & & P_{k,k-1} & P_{k,k} \\ & & & P_{k+1,k} \end{pmatrix},$$

where P_{ij} corresponds to the coupling between the unknowns in the subdomain Ω_i with those in the interface Γ_j.

By applying block Gaussian elimination to (2.2), we obtain the following system for the interface unknowns:

$$(2.6) \qquad\qquad\qquad\qquad Cu_\Gamma = g$$

where

$$(2.7) \qquad\qquad\qquad\qquad g \equiv f_\Gamma - P^T Q_\Omega^{-1} f_\Omega,$$

and

$$(2.8) \qquad\qquad\qquad\qquad C \equiv Q_\Gamma - P^T Q_\Omega^{-1} P.$$

C is sometimes called the *capacitance matrix*. Since Q_Ω is block diagonal, the right-hand side of (2.6) given by (2.7) can be evaluated by solving a problem like (2.1) on each subdomain Ω_i, with zero Dirichlet boundary conditions on the interfaces Γ_{i-1} and Γ_i,

$i = 1, \cdots, k+1$. Once (2.6) is solved, the problem is decoupled and the solution u_{Ω_i} at the subdomains can be computed by solving $k+1$ independent subproblems:

$$L_i u_{\Omega i} = f_{\Omega i} - P_{i,i-1} u_{\Gamma i-1} - P_{i,i} u_{\Gamma i}$$

for $i = 1, \cdots, k+1$. This is nothing more than solving for $u_{\Omega i}$ on each subdomain Ω_i with the computed $u_{\Gamma i-1}$ and $u_{\Gamma i}$ as boundary conditions.

This technique of reducing the problem on Ω to the solution of decoupled problems on the subdomains and a smaller system for the interface is usually called *domain decomposition* or *substructuring*.

3. The capacitance system. By substituting (2.3), (2.4) and (2.5) in (2.8), we can see that the matrix C has the following block tridiagonal form:

$$(3.1) \qquad C = \begin{pmatrix} C_1 & B_2 & & \\ B_2 & C_2 & & \\ & & \ddots & \ddots & B_k \\ & & & B_k & C_k \end{pmatrix},$$

where C_i is the capacitance matrix corresponding to the interface Γ_i, i.e.

$$(3.2) \qquad C_i = L_{k+1+i} - P_{i,i}^T L_i^{-1} P_{i,i} - P_{i+1,i}^T L_{i+1}^{-1} P_{i+1,i},$$

and

$$(3.3) \qquad B_i = -P_{i,i-1}^T L_i^{-1} P_{i,i}.$$

The matrix C is expensive to compute explicitly, since the computation of the blocks C_i and B_i requires the solution of $2n$ subproblems on each Ω_i. Also, the resulting blocks are dense n by n matrices, and therefore, the solution to (2.6) by Gaussian elimination would require $\mathcal{O}(n^3)$ operations, which may overcome the $\mathcal{O}(n^2 \log(n))$ complexity of the fast solvers for the subdomains, when $m \approx n$.

Instead of using a direct method to solve the system (2.6), preconditioned conjugate gradient (PCG) methods can be applied, where only matrix-vector products of the form Cw for a given vector w are needed. From (3.2), we can see that the evaluation of $C_i w$ for each i requires the solution of two subdomain problems. For example, the product $-P_{2,2}^T L_2^{-1} P_{2,2} w$ can be computed by solving the discretized version of (2.1) on Ω_2 with homogeneous right-hand side (i.e., the Laplace equation) and boundary conditions $u = w$ on Γ_2, $u = 0$ on the rest of the boundary, and then taking the solution on the first row of grid points above Γ_2. Similarly, $B_2 w$ corresponds to taking the same solution on the first row below Γ_1.

Each iteration of the PCG method requires the solution of at least one problem at each subdomain. Therefore, it is important to keep the number of iterations low. A number of preconditioners for the matrix C have been given in the literature in order to improve the convergence [7], [8], [2], [3].

It turns out that for the problem we are considering, an exact decomposition for the capacitance matrix is possible. This fact was first pointed out by Dryja [7], who noticed that, in the uniform strip case, the same matrix C appears in the context of the Generalized Marching Algorithm in [1], where a decomposition of C is given in terms of Chebyshev polynomials. We give a different derivation of the eigenvalues and eigenvectors of the blocks C_i and B_i in (3.1) based on an extension of the two strips case given in [5]. The system (2.6) can then be solved by Fast Fourier Transforms or cyclic reduction [4], [9].

We will show that the matrices C_i and B_i in (3.1) have the same eigenvectors. Let us define the orthogonal matrix W as the matrix whose columns are

$$(3.4) \qquad w_j = \sqrt{\frac{2}{n+1}} (\sin j\pi h, \sin 2j\pi h, \cdots, \sin nj\pi h)^T$$

for $j = 1, \cdots, n$,

$$(3.5) \qquad \sigma_j = 4 \sin \frac{2j\pi h^2}{2},$$

and

$$(3.6) \qquad \gamma_j = \left(1 + \frac{\sigma_j}{2} + \sqrt{\sigma_j + \frac{\sigma_j^2}{4}}\right)^2.$$

Then, we have the following

LEMMA 3.1. *The matrices C_i and B_i have the same eigenvectors (3.4). For $i = 1, \cdots, k$, we have*

$$(3.7) \qquad W^T C_i W = \Lambda_i = \mathrm{diag}(\lambda_{i1}, \cdots, \lambda_{in}),$$

and for $i = 2, \cdots, k$, we have

$$(3.8) \qquad W^T B_i W = D_i = \mathrm{diag}(\delta_{i1}, \cdots, \delta_{in})$$

where

$$(3.9) \qquad \lambda_{ij} = -\left(\frac{1+\gamma_j^{m_i+1}}{1-\gamma_j^{m_i+1}} + \frac{1+\gamma_j^{m_{i+1}+1}}{1-\gamma_j^{m_{i+1}+1}}\right)\sqrt{\sigma_j + \frac{\sigma_j^2}{4}},$$

and

$$(3.10) \qquad \delta_{ij} = \sqrt{\gamma_j^{m_i}}\left(\frac{1-\gamma_j}{1-\gamma_j^{m_i+1}}\right).$$

Proof. We will compute the three terms of $C_i w_j$ in (3.2) separately. As we stated before, the product $-P_{i,i}^T L_i^{-1} P_{i,i} w_j$ can be computed by solving the problem

$$(3.11) \qquad \begin{aligned} \Delta_h v &= 0 &&\text{in } \Omega_i, \\ v &= 0 &&\text{on } \partial\Omega_i \cap \partial\Omega, \\ v &= 0 &&\text{on } \Gamma_{i-1}, \\ v &= w_j &&\text{on } \Gamma_i, \end{aligned}$$

and taking the values of the solution at the first row of grid points above Γ_i. By using separation of variables, it can be shown [5] that the solution to (3.11) at each grid point (s, t) is given by:

$$(3.12) \qquad v(sh, th) = (c_1 r_+^t + c_2 r_-^t) \sin sj\pi h$$

where r_+ and r_- are the roots of the characteristic polynomial corresponding to substituting (3.12) in (3.11), namely,

$$(3.13) \qquad \begin{aligned} r_+ &= 1 + \frac{\sigma_j}{2} + \sqrt{\sigma_j + \frac{\sigma_j^2}{4}}, \\ r_- &= 1 + \frac{\sigma_j}{2} - \sqrt{\sigma_j + \frac{\sigma_j^2}{4}}, \end{aligned}$$

with σ_j given by (3.5). The constants c_1 and c_2 are determined by the boundary conditions and they are given by

$$c_1 = -\frac{r_-^{m_1+1}}{r_+^{m_1+1} - r_-^{m_1+1}}, \qquad c_2 = \frac{r_+^{m_1+1}}{r_+^{m_1+1} - r_-^{m_1+1}}.$$

Therefore, we can compute the product $-P_{i,i}^T L_i^{-1} P_{i,i} w_j$ by taking $t=1$ in (3.12), i.e.

(3.14) $$-P_{i,i}^T L_i^{-1} P_{i,i} w_j = \left(\frac{r_- - r_+ \gamma^{m_i+1}}{1 - \gamma^{m_i+1}}\right) w_j$$

where

(3.15) $$\gamma_j = \frac{r_-}{r_+}.$$

Since $r_+ r_- = 1$, $\gamma_j = r_-^2$ and, therefore, (3.6) and (3.15) are equivalent. By a similar computation we can prove that

(3.16) $$-P_{i+1,i}^T L_{i+1}^{-1} P_{i+1,i} w_j = \left(\frac{r_- - r_+ \gamma_j^{m_{i+1}+1}}{1 - \gamma_j^{m_{i+1}+1}}\right) w_j.$$

Finally, it can also be verified that

(3.17) $$L_{k+1+i} w_j = (-2 - \sigma_j) w_j.$$

Combining (3.14), (3.16) and (3.17), we have

$$C_i w_j = \lambda_{ij} w_j$$

where

$$\lambda_{ij} = -2 - \sigma_j + \left(\frac{r_- - r + \gamma_j^{m_1+1}}{1 - \gamma_j^{m_1+1}}\right) + \left(\frac{r_- - r_+ \gamma_j^{m_2+1}}{1 - \gamma_j^{m_2-1}}\right),$$

which, after some simplifications, leads to the expression (3.9).

By similar arguments, $B_i w_j$ requires the computation of the solution to (3.11) at the m_ith row away from Γ_i and we can prove that:

$$B_i w_j = v(\cdot, m_i h) = -\delta_{ij} w_j$$

where

$$\delta_{ij} = c_1 r_+^{m_i} + c_2 r_-^{m_i}$$

$$= \sqrt{\gamma_j^{m_i}} \left(\frac{1 - \gamma_j}{1 - \gamma_j^{m_i+1}}\right). \qquad \square$$

Let us partition the vectors u_Γ and g in (2.6) as:

$$u_\Gamma = \begin{pmatrix} u_{\Gamma_1} \\ u_{\Gamma_2} \\ \vdots \\ u_{\Gamma_k} \end{pmatrix}, \qquad g = \begin{pmatrix} g_{\Gamma_1} \\ g_{\Gamma_2} \\ \vdots \\ g_{\Gamma_k} \end{pmatrix}$$

where, for $i = 1, \cdots, k$,

$$u_{\Gamma_i} = \begin{pmatrix} u_{1i} \\ u_{2i} \\ \vdots \\ u_{ni} \end{pmatrix}, \qquad g_{\Gamma_i} = \begin{pmatrix} g_{1i} \\ g_{2i} \\ \vdots \\ g_{ni} \end{pmatrix}.$$

The system (2.6) may be written

$$C_1 u_{\Gamma_1} + B_2 u_{\Gamma_2} = g_{\Gamma_1},$$

(3.18) $$\qquad B_i u_{\Gamma_{i-1}} + C_i u_{\Gamma_i} + B_{i+1} u_{\Gamma_{i+1}} = g_{\Gamma_i}, \qquad i = 2, \cdots, k-1,$$

$$B_k u_{\Gamma_{k-1}} + C_k u_{\Gamma_k} = g_{\Gamma_k}.$$

Using (3.7) and (3.8), the system (3.18) becomes

(3.19)
$$\begin{pmatrix} \Lambda_1 & D_2 & & \\ D_2 & \ddots & \ddots & \\ & \ddots & \ddots & D_k \\ & & D_k & \Lambda_k \end{pmatrix} \begin{pmatrix} \hat{u}_{\Gamma_1} \\ \hat{u}_{\Gamma_2} \\ \vdots \\ \hat{u}_{\Gamma_k} \end{pmatrix} = \begin{pmatrix} \hat{g}_{\Gamma_1} \\ \hat{g}_{\Gamma_2} \\ \vdots \\ \hat{g}_{\Gamma_k} \end{pmatrix}$$

where, for $i \leq k$,

(3.20) $$\hat{g}_{\Gamma_i} = W^T g_{\Gamma_i},$$

and

(3.21) $$u_{\Gamma_i} = W \hat{u}_{\Gamma_i}.$$

By reordering the equations in (3.19), the system can be reduced to the solution of n tridiagonal systems of dimension k and u_Γ can then be computed by the expression (3.21). Note that Fast Fourier Transforms can be used in computing $\hat{g}$ and u_Γ. An outline of the algorithm follows:

ALGORITHM DDFPS (Domain-Decomposed Fast Poisson Solver)

Step 1:   Compute right-hand side g by (2.7). This requires the solution of $k+1$ decoupled problems of the form (2.1) on Ω_i, $i = 1, \cdots, k+1$, namely

$$\Delta_h v_i = f \quad \text{in } \Omega_i,$$

$$v_i = u_{b_i} \quad \text{on } \partial\Omega_i \cap \partial\Omega,$$

$$v_i = 0 \qquad \text{on } \Gamma_{i-1},$$

$$v_i = 0 \qquad \text{on } \Gamma_i,$$

and then compute

$$g_{\Gamma_i} = f_{\Gamma_i} - v_i(\cdot, m_i) - v_{i+1}(\cdot, 1).$$

Step 2:   Obtain new right-hand side $\hat{g}$ by (3.20) using Fast Fourier Transforms.

Step 3:   For $j = 1, \cdots, n$, solve

(3.22)
$$\begin{pmatrix} \lambda_{1j} & \delta_{2j} & & \\ \delta_{2j} & \ddots & \ddots & \\ & \ddots & \ddots & \delta_{kj} \\ & & \delta_{kj} & \lambda_{kj} \end{pmatrix} \begin{pmatrix} \hat{u}_{j1} \\ \hat{u}_{j2} \\ \vdots \\ \hat{u}_{jk} \end{pmatrix} = \begin{pmatrix} \hat{g}_{j1} \\ \hat{g}_{j2} \\ \vdots \\ \hat{g}_{jk} \end{pmatrix}.$$

Step 4:   Fast Fourier Transform the resulting $\hat{u}_{\Gamma_i}$'s to obtain u_{Γ_i} by (3.21).

Step 5:   Solve the following problem in each subdomain

$$\Delta_h u_i = f \quad \text{on } \Omega_i$$

with boundary conditions

$$u_i = u_{b_i} \qquad \text{on } \partial\Omega_i \cap \partial\Omega,$$

$$u_i = u_{\Gamma_{i-1}} \qquad \text{on } \Gamma_{i-1},$$

$$u_i = u_{\Gamma_i} \qquad \text{on } \Gamma_i.$$

3.1. Uniform size strips. When $m_i = m$ for all i, i.e. all strips have identical dimensions, all the blocks C_i in (3.1) are identical, as well as the blocks B_i. In this case, the eigenvalues and eigenvectors of C can be explicitly computed.

LEMMA 3.2. *If $m_i \equiv m$, $1 \le i \le k+1$, then the capacitance matrix has the form*

$$C = \begin{pmatrix} C_1 & B & & \\ B & C_1 & \ddots & \\ & \ddots & \ddots & B \\ & & B & C_1 \end{pmatrix},$$

and the eigenvalues of C are given by

$$\alpha_{ij} = \lambda_j + \delta_j \cos \frac{i\pi}{k+1}$$

for $i = 1, \cdots k$ and $j = 1, \cdots n$, where λ_j are the eigenvalues of C_1 and δ_j are the eigenvalues of B. The eigenvectors v_{ij} are the direct product of the vectors w_j defined in (3.4) and

$$z_i = \left(\sin \frac{\pi i}{k+1}, \sin 2\frac{\pi i}{k+1}, \cdots, \sin k\frac{\pi i}{k+1} \right)^T,$$

i.e.,

$$v_{ij} = z_i \otimes w_j = \begin{pmatrix} \left(\sin \frac{\pi i}{k+1} \right) w_j \\ \left(\sin \frac{2\pi i}{k+1} \right) w_j \\ \vdots \\ \left(\sin \frac{k\pi i}{k+1} \right) w_j \end{pmatrix}.$$

Proof. It can be verified that

$$Cv_{ij} = \alpha_{ij} v_{ij}$$

by simple substitution and using the fact that z_i and α_{ij} are the eigenvectors and eigenvalues of the tridiagonal matrix:

$$T_j = \begin{pmatrix} \lambda_j & \delta_j & & \\ \delta_k & \ddots & \ddots & \\ & \ddots & \ddots & \delta_j \\ & & \delta_j & \lambda_j \end{pmatrix}. \qquad \Box$$

As an improvement over the plain Fourier Analysis method, which has complexity $\mathcal{O}(kn \log_2 n)$, block-cyclic reduction techniques can be combined with Fast Fourier Transforms to get an algorithm for solving the interface system for the regular sized strips case, which has asymptotic complexity $\mathcal{O}(kn \log_2 \log_2 n)$ [4], [10].

4. Analysis of some preconditioners. For more general operators and domains, the system (3.1) is solved by the preconditioned conjugate gradient method. Several preconditioners have been proposed in order to improve the convergence of the method. For the case where there is only one interface ($k = 1$), Dryja [7] proposed as preconditioner for C the square root of the one-dimensional discrete Laplacian. This matrix, which will be denoted by M_D, can be inverted by Fast Fourier Transform, since it has the following decomposition:

$$(4.1) \qquad M_D = W \operatorname{diag} (\lambda_1^D, \lambda_2^D, \cdots, \lambda_n^D) W^T$$

where the columns of W are given by (3.4) and

$$(4.2) \qquad \lambda_j^D = -2\sqrt{\sigma_j}$$

with σ_j given by (3.5). Golub and Mayers [8] improve Dryja's results with a preconditioner given by

$$(4.3) \qquad M_G = W \operatorname{diag} (\lambda_1^G, \lambda_2^G, \cdots, \lambda_n^G) W^T$$

where

$$(4.4) \qquad \lambda_j^G = -2\sqrt{\sigma_j + \frac{\sigma_j^2}{4}}.$$

For the two strips case, Bjorstad and Widlund [2] give the following approximation to C as a preconditioner:

$$M_B = L_3 - 2P_{1,1}^T L_1^{-1} P_{1,1}.$$

When the two strips have the same dimensions, this preconditioner is exact, although their method involves an extra solve in the subdomain Ω_1 in order to invert M_B, as opposed to solving by only one Fast Fourier Transform on the interface.

In [6], Dryja and Proskurowski propose an algorithm for the case of multiple strips. By ignoring the off-diagonal blocks B_i in (3.1) and using the preconditioners for the two-strips case on the diagonal, they propose using either the block-diagonal matrix $\operatorname{diag}(M_D)$ or $\operatorname{diag}(M_G)$.

Using the results of the previous section, we can analyze these preconditioners. It is a well-known fact that the rate of convergence of the preconditioned conjugate gradient method depends on the condition number of the matrix $M^{-1}C$, where M is the preconditioner, being close to one. We will use the 2-norm condition number in this paper, and for simplicity, we will only consider the case of regular sized strips, with $m_i = m$. In [5], Chan shows for the two-strips case that $K(M_G^{-1}C)$ and $K(M_G^{-1}C)$ depend on the aspect ratio

$$(4.5) \qquad \alpha = \frac{m+1}{n+1}$$

and in particular,

$$(4.6) \qquad \lim_{h \to 0} K(M_G^{-1}C) = \frac{1+e^{-2\pi\alpha}}{1-e^{-2\pi\alpha}}.$$

The asymptotic expression (4.6) is plotted in Fig. 2. As we can see, the condition number will be large for small α.

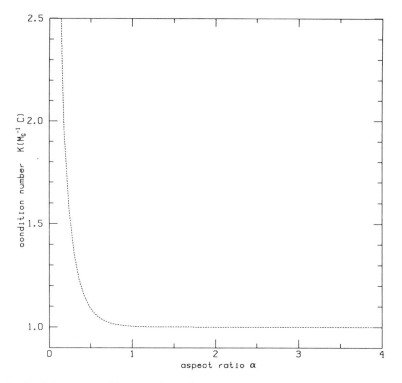

FIG. 2. *Condition number of the preconditioned capacitance matrix with Golub and Mayers' preconditioner* (*asymptote for* $h \to 0$).

For the case of multiple strips, we have to analyze the effect of dropping the blocks B_i's. Note that when the eigenvalues of B_i, namely δ_j, are small compared to λ_j, the system (3.22) becomes diagonal and therefore, it can be trivially solved. We will see that the values of δ_j are small compared to λ_j when the aspect ratio (4.5) is large. This can be derived from Lemma 3.2, where we give an asymptotic expression for the ratio δ_j/λ_j in terms of the aspect ratio α when $h \to 0$.

By computing (3.10) and (3.9) for the regular strips case, we can see that

(4.7)
$$\frac{\delta_j}{\lambda_j} = \frac{\gamma_j^{(m+1)/2}}{1 + \gamma_j^{m+1}},$$

which is a decreasing function of j. Therefore,

$$\frac{\delta_1}{\lambda_1} = \max_{1 \le j \le n} \frac{\delta_j}{\lambda_j}.$$

Moreover, we have:

LEMMA 4.1.

$$\lim_{h \to 0} \frac{\delta_1}{\lambda_1} = \frac{1}{e^{\alpha\pi} + e^{-\alpha\pi}}.$$

Proof. Since $\sigma_1 \to 0$ when $h \to 0$, we have

$$\lim_{h \to 0} (\log \gamma_1^{m+1}) = \alpha \lim_{h \to 0} \frac{1}{\gamma_1} \frac{d\gamma_1}{dh} = -2\alpha\pi.$$

Therefore,

(4.8)
$$\lim_{h \to 0} \gamma_1^{m+1} = e^{-2\alpha\pi}.$$

By (4.7) and (4.8), we have

$$\lim_{h \to 0} \frac{\delta_1}{\lambda_1} = \frac{e^{-\alpha\pi}}{1 + e^{-2\alpha\pi}} = \frac{1}{e^{\alpha\pi} + e^{-\alpha\pi}}. \qquad \square$$

When α is large enough, the δ_j's can be ignored, so that the system (3.1) becomes block-diagonal and moreover, for α large, the eigenvalues λ_{ij} approach (4.4) and in that case, (4.3) is a good approximation to C. For α small, the condition number of the preconditioned capacitance matrix becomes large. Figure 3 shows the dependence of the condition number on the aspect ratio α for different numbers of strips.

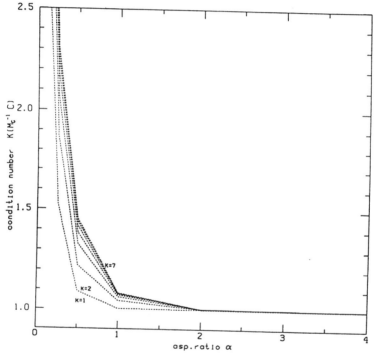

FIG. 3. *Condition number of the preconditioned capacitance matrix with Golub and Mayers' preconditioner for two, three, and up to eight strips (k is the number of interfaces).*

5. Dividing the domain into boxes. In the parallel implementation of domain decomposition, the ratio between the amount of communication and the amount of computation required grows as the strips become narrower. For this reason, it seems natural to divide the domain into boxes.

Boxes introduce a new difficulty, the cross points. Cross points are more difficult to handle, since they represent a strong coupling between interfaces. We refer the interested reader to [3].

One way around cross points is to use algorithm DDFPS recursively. We can, for example, apply algorithm DDFPS to the domain Ω divided into horizontal strips Ω_i, and then solve the subproblems in Steps 1 and 5 by subdividing each strip Ω_i in vertical strips Ω_{ij}. Another approach is given by nested dissection, which can be described recursively as follows: the domain Ω is divided in two strips Ω_1 and Ω_2. We will call this partition P_1, and given a partition P_i, P_{i+1} is obtained by subdividing each subdomain of P_i into two (vertical or horizontal) strips. An example of the partition procedure is given in Fig. 4. Algorithm DDFPS with $k=1$ is applied to P_1, and it is applied recursively in Steps 1 and 5 to solve for the problems in the subdomains. Conventional fast solvers are used for the subproblems in the finest partition.

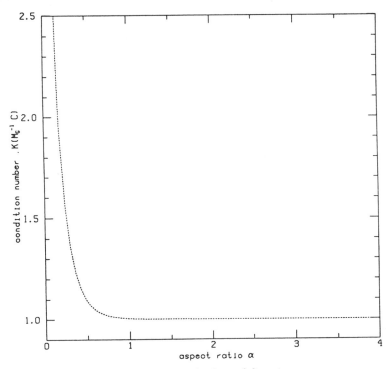

FIG. 4. *An example of nested dissection.*

6. Concluding remarks. We present a fast direct Poisson solver on a rectangle divided into parallel strips or boxes. The method is especially suited for parallel implementation, since the independent problems in the subdomains can be solved in parallel, and the communication can be reduced to k vectors of length n, where n is the number of points in the interface.

Since the method is based on the fact that C can be solved by FFT's, it can be generalized to other separable operators with coefficients which are constant in the x or y direction, and other boundary conditions. Similar arguments can be used to derive a fast solver for the Poisson equation in three dimensions. The expressions obtained for the corresponding eigenvalues λ's and δ's show that the preconditioners $\sqrt{K}$ and $\sqrt{K^2/4+K}$ have natural extensions to the three-dimensional case, where K is now the two-dimensional Laplacian operator. These results will be presented in a forthcoming report.

It appears that domain decomposition requires more computation than a conventional fast solver on the whole domain, since the algorithm requires two solves on each subdomain, namely Steps 1 and 5. Many operations can be saved, however, since only one row of the solution is needed in Step 1 for the computation of the right-hand side (2.7). Also, some of the computations in Step 1 can be saved for Step 5, since the right-hand side for the subproblems in Steps 1 and 5 differ only at one or two rows of the grid points. With these savings, algorithm DDFPS can be made computationally equivalent to the fast Poisson solver on a rectangle using FFT's in the x-direction and solving n tridiagonal systems in the y-direction.

Acknowledgment. The authors would like to thank Professor M. Dryja for pointing out the relationship between the generalized marching algorithms of Bank and Rose and the fast domain decomposed fast Poisson solver presented in this paper.

REFERENCES

[1] R. BANK AND D. ROSE, *Marching algorithms for elliptic boundary value problems. I: The constant coefficient case*, SIAM J. Numer. Anal., 14 (1977), pp. 792–828.

[2] P. BJORSTAD AND O. WIDLUND, *On some trends in elliptic problem solvers*, in Elliptic Problem Solvers, G. Birkhoff and A. Schoenstadt, eds., Academic Press, New York, 1984.

[3] J. H. BRAMBLE, J. E. PASCIAK AND A. H. SCHATZ, *Preconditioners for interface problems on mesh domains*, Math. Comp., to appear.

[4] B. L. BUZBEE, G. H. GOLUB AND C. W. NIELSON, *On direct methods for solving Poisson's equations*, SIAM J. Numer. Anal., 7 (1970), pp. 627–656.

[5] T. F. CHAN, *Analysis of preconditioners for domain decomposition*, SIAM J. Numer. Anal. (1986), to appear.

[6] M. DRYJA AND W. PROSKUROWSKI, *Capacitance matrix method using strips with alternating Neumann and Dirichlet boundary conditions*, in Advances in Computer Methods for Partial Differential Equations – V, R. Vichnevetsky and R. S. Stepleman, eds., IMACS, 1984, pp. 360–368.

[7] M. DRYJA, *A capacitance matrix method for Dirichlet problem on polygonal region*, Numer. Math., 39 (1982), pp. 51–64.

[8] G. H. GOLUB AND D. MAYERS, *The use of pre-conditioning over irregular regions*, 1983. Lecture at Sixth International Conference on Computing Methods in Applied Sciences and Engineering, Versailles, France, December 1983.

[9] P. N. SWARZTRAUBER, *A direct method for the discrete solution of separable elliptic equations*, SIAM J. Numer. Anal., 11 (1974), pp. 1136–1150.

[10] ——, *A direct method for the discrete solution of separable elliptic equations*, SIAM Rev., 19 (1976), pp. 490–501.

SIAM J. SCI. STAT. COMPUT.
Vol. 8, No. 1, January 1987

MULTIPROCESSOR FFT METHODS*

WILLIAM L. BRIGGS†, LESLIE B. HART†, ROLAND A. SWEET† AND ABBIE O'GALLAGHER‡

Abstract. Proceeding first by experiment and then by analysis, the problem of implementing FFT algorithms on a shared memory multiprocessor is investigated. Several algorithms for performing a single FFT and multiple FFTs are implemented and compared on the Denelcor HEP computer. These algorithms are then analyzed using performance models which reproduce the experimental timing curves. For both the single and multiple FFT a clear choice of superior algorithms can be made. These algorithms are expected to be useful and to preserve their performance characteristics on other shared memory multiprocessors.

Key words. fast Fourier transform multiple FFTs, multiprocessor

AMS(MOS) subject classifications. 65N30, 68B05

1. Introduction. The fast Fourier transform (FFT) is certainly one of the most widely used and thoroughly studied numerical algorithms in existence. Among its many uses in science, engineering, and applied mathematics are signal and image processing, time series and spectral analysis, and the solution of partial differential equations such as Poisson's equation by fast direct methods. Sequential FFT algorithms (those for conventional, serial computers) have been highly refined during the twenty years since the FFT was first introduced [4]. The early FFT papers [1], [2], [3], [6] offer good reading from an historical point of view and reflect both the variety of FFT algorithms and the different ways in which they may be developed.

As computers have evolved, there has been a corresponding adaptation of FFT algorithms to fit the new architectures. For example, the appearance of vector computers led to new implementations of the FFT [10], [13]-[16], [19]. The FFT proved to be highly amenable to vector or SIMD (single instruction stream-multiple data stream) computation and significant improvements in performance have been realized for this class of computers. Now, as multiprocessing and distributed computing systems become available, there is a continued interest in the FFT and its implementation on this class of MIMD (multiple instruction stream-multiple data stream) computers. This paper is a part of this latter effort, namely the study of FFT algorithms on computers which possess many processors which are capable of working independently on different sets of data. As will be seen, the inherent parallelism of the FFT can be exploited on MIMD computers, but often in very different ways than it is on vector computers.

All computations described in this study were carried out on the Denelcor HEP-1 (Heterogeneous Element Processor) computer. Briefly, the HEP is a shared memory MIMD computer in which both the arithmetic units and the instruction stream are pipelined. The one PEM (Process Execution Module) system which was used for these computations has a maximum execution rate of 10 million instructions per second and can support up to 50 independent user-created processes [11]. All programs were written in a parallel version of FORTRAN which allows for inter-process communication through the use of semaphored (or asynchronous) variables. The HEP has a

* Received by the editors August 19, 1985; accepted for publication (in revised form) March 12, 1986. This work was supported by National Bureau of Standards Cooperative Agreement 70NANB4H0008 and National Science Foundation grant DMS-8504350.

† Mathematics Department, University of Colorado, Denver, Colorado 80202.

‡ Scientific Computing Division, National Bureau of Standards, Boulder, Colorado 80202. (Contribution of the National Bureau of Standards. Not subject to copyright in the U.S.A.)

relatively low degree of parallelism, particularly when compared to vector computers and many array processors. For this reason, its parallelism is best used on a rather coarse level. As opposed to many vector algorithms, parallelism on the HEP (which has no vector capabilities) is generally introduced on the outermost levels of an algorithm. This principle will be applied throughout this study.

The demise of Denelcor as a commercial venture does not diminish the many novel features of the HEP. It is a highly versatile, general purpose computer and has served well as a laboratory for parallel algorithm development. While it is only one expression of shared memory MIMD architecture, it is viewed as a representative of many shared memory or tightly coupled systems. Although the algorithms of this paper were developed for the HEP, the ideas underlying these algorithms and much of their structure should be directly transferable to other multiprocessor environments. It is our intent to minimize HEP specificity as much as possible and to draw some general conclusions about FFTs on shared memory MIMD systems in general.

This study proceeds first in a rather experimental way to develop parallel algorithms for performing a single FFT (§ 2) and multiple FFTs (§ 3). Performance curves for these algorithms are presented which suggest the superior algorithms. In § 4, which unavoidably deals with the features of HEP architecture, the performance of the single and multiple FFT algorithms is modeled using the ideas of Hockney [7], [9]. This allows for a further comparison of the algorithms both within and outside the parameter ranges of the experiments. The paper concludes with a summary and some remarks on the applicability of these results to other multiprocessors.

2. Parallel algorithms for a single FFT. There are many different FFT algorithms and there are several different ways to derive and present them. In the interest of brevity and clarity, we will use the splitting algorithm to present one of the Cooley-Tukey versions of the FFT. In all that follows we will confine ourselves to the problem of transforming complex sequences of length N where $N = 2^m$. The problem of transforming sequences of fairly arbitrary length (the mixed radix case) can be treated by sequential algorithms and the necessary generalizations can also be applied to the parallel algorithms which will be discussed here.

Given a sequence $\{x_n\}$ of length $N = 2^m$, the discrete Fourier transform (DFT) is a sequence $\{X_k\}$, also of length N, given by

$$(2.1) \qquad X_k = \sum_{n=0}^{N-1} x_n w_N^{nk}, \qquad 0 \le k \le N-1,$$

where $w_N = e^{i2\pi/N}$. The inverse transform takes a very similar form. Given the transform sequence $\{X_k\}$, the original sequence may be recovered by

$$(2.2) \qquad x_n = \frac{1}{N} \sum_{k=0}^{N-1} X_k w_N^{-nk}, \qquad 0 \le n \le N-1.$$

Notice that both (2.1) and (2.2) amount to a complex matrix-vector multiplication. Hence, the computation of the DFT or its inverse requires roughly N^2 complex additions and multiplications. Successive applications of the splitting algorithm result in a progressive improvement in this operation count.

Splitting $\{x_n\}$ into its odd and even parts and letting

$$y_n = x_{2n} \quad \text{and} \quad z_n = x_{2n+1} \quad \text{for } 0 \le n \le \frac{N}{2} - 1,$$

the DFT may be written

$$X_k = \sum_{n=0}^{(N/2)-1} y_n w_N^{2nk} + z_n w_N^{(2n+1)k}.$$

The crucial symmetry of the complex exponential now enters. Noting that $w_N^2 = w_{N/2}$, the transform may now be written as

$$X_k = \sum_{n=0}^{(N/2)-1} y_n w_{N/2}^{nk} + w_N^k \sum_{n=0}^{(N/2)-1} z_n w_{N/2}^{nk}.$$

However, the two sums on the right side are simply the $N/2$-point transforms of the sequences $\{y_n\}$ and $\{z_n\}$ which we call $\{Y_k\}$ and $\{Z_k\}$, respectively. Therefore, for $0 \leq k \leq (N/2) - 1$,

$$X_k = Y_k + w_N^k Z_k.$$

For indices between $N/2$ and $N-1$, note that the sequences $\{Y_k\}$ and $\{Z_k\}$ have period $N/2$. Therefore,

$$X_{k+(N/2)} = Y_k + w_N^{k+(N/2)} Z_k.$$

Using the fact that $w_N^{N/2} = -1$, we have the two fundamental relations

(2.3)
$$\begin{aligned} X_k &= Y_k + w_N^k Z_k, \\ X_{k+(N/2)} &= Y_k - w_N^k Z_k, \end{aligned} \qquad 0 \leq k \leq \frac{N}{2} - 1,$$

which give the N-point transform $\{X_k\}$ in terms of the two associated $N/2$-point transforms $\{Y_k\}$ and $\{Z_k\}$. It is useful to note the savings that can be realized by a single splitting. If $\{Y_k\}$ and $\{Z_k\}$ are computed by matrix multiplication, the cost is $2(N/2)^2$ complex additions and multiplications. The combine step (2.3) costs N complex additions and $N/2$ complex multiplications which is negligible. Therefore, one application of the splitting algorithm reduces the operation count of the N-point transform from roughly N^2 to $N^2/2$.

The full FFT results by noting that the splitting algorithm may also be applied to the $N/2$-point transforms $\{Y_k\}$ and $\{Z_k\}$ and again to the resulting $N/4$-point transforms and so on. After $m = \log_2 N$ halvings, the problem reduces to computing N 1-point transforms which is trivial. The operation count is straightforward. At each of $\log_2 N$ stages, $N/2$ pairs must be computed using (2.3). Each pair requires one complex multiplication (assuming that the powers of w are available) and two complex additions. This gives a total of $N/2 \log_2 N$ complex multiplications and $N \log_2 N$ complex additions.

One consequence of the splitting procedure is that at each stage the input sequence is divided into its even and odd components. After $\log_2 N$ such splittings, the original sequence $\{x_n\}$ no longer appears in its natural order, but rather in a scrambled or bit-reversed order. The nuisance of reordering the input sequence before doing the combine phase is offset by the fact that the algorithm may be carried out "in-place" with no additional storage requirements. Furthermore, in many applications the forward transform is ultimately followed by an inverse transform. By an appropriate choice of FFT algorithms, the recordering of the data may be effectively avoided.

It should be mentioned that there are versions of the FFT (the Stockham version and its variants) which avoid the reordering of either the input or output sequence. The price which is paid for this convenience is an extra array of storage, a price which could become prohibitive in higher dimensional problems. A more recent development is the class of prime factor FFTs [17], [18]. These algorithms avoid all reordering of data and are also in-place. They are most effective on sequences whose length is highly composite and, in this sense, they complement the classical FFT algorithms. Neither the self-sorting nor prime factor FFTs will be considered in this paper.

The splitting procedure just described gives one version of the original Cooley-Tukey algorithm. The combine phase consists of $m = \log_2 N$ stages. Each stage involves $N/2$ pairwise combinations of the form (2.3). At stage k, $1 \leq k \leq m$, the pairs reside in 2^{m-k} blocks each of length 2^k. Each pairwise combination requires a particular power of w and, at stage k, 2^{k-1} different powers of w are required. These observations begin to suggest strategies for a parallel implementation of the FFT. The fundamental unit of work in the FFT is the pairwise combination. Within each stage each pairwise combination can be done in place and independently of all others. It is on this level that the algorithm will be parallelized initially. There is no parallelism on a coarser level because the $\log_2 N$ stages themselves must be done sequentially.

With these considerations in mind, two strategies for the evaluation of a single FFT were implemented in HEP-FORTRAN and compared. The first strategy will be called *scheduling-on-pairs* since each process is assigned independent pairwise combinations to perform. At the top of the algorithm, p independent processes are created and each process is given a unique integer tag j, where $1 \leq j \leq p$. At each stage of the algorithm, the jth process executes a loop of the form DO 10 $i = j$, $N/2$, p which distributes the $N/2$ pairwise combinations over the p processes. Before doing a pairwise combination, the appropriate power of w must be computed, which involves some modular arithmetic and a complex exponentiation to an integer power. At the end of each of the $\log_2 N$ stages, each process is suspended in a synchronizing barrier until all processes have finished the stage. Thus, at each stage, each of the p processes does roughly $N/2p$ complex exponentiations, $N/2p$ complex multiplications, N/p complex additions, and $N/2p$ index calculations which involve some modular arithmetic.

At this point, a remark should be made concerning the ground rules for these numerical experiments. It has been decided, somewhat arbitrarily, that all algorithms will compute powers of w while in progress. This is not as efficient as pre-computing powers of w and storing them, but it does give a uniform set of conditions under which the algorithms may be compared. In § 4, an attempt will be made to estimate the savings which would result from replacing complex exponentiations by fetches to data memory.

Improvements on the scheduling-on-pairs algorithm can be realized only if the overall computational load is reduced. All good sequential FFT codes recognize the fact that once a power of w is computed it should be used immediately throughout the stage rather than recomputing it for each pair. Furthermore, complex exponentiations can be minimized if powers of w are updated by multiplications. While this idea is easily written into a sequential code, there are genuine subtleties in incorporating it into a parallel code, especially for arbitrary p. The algorithm which results will be called *scheduling-on-w*. The difficulty in implementing scheduling-on-w lies in the fact that the number of distinct powers of w which are needed changes at each stage of the algorithm. At stage k, there are 2^{k-1} distinct powers of w which must be computed. Thus in the early stages of the computation, when $2^{k-1} < p$, several processes may share the same power of w and the pairwise combinations associated with that power of w. However, during the later stages when $2^{k-1} > p$, each process may be assigned to more than one power of w and the pairwise combinations associated with each power of w. Clearly the scheduling and the structure of the algorithm change at the point when $2^{k-1} > p$. Some additional logic is required to accomplish this change in scheduling.

The question is whether this additional overhead pays for the savings in complex exponentiations. Figure 1 shows an example of scheduling-on-w for the case $N = 32$, $p = 5$.

Stage $k = 1$
    Powers of w_{32}:   0
                                $p_1 p_2 p_3 p_4 p_5$

Stage $k = 2$
    Powers of w_{32}:   0   8
                          $p_1 p_3 p_5$ $p_2 p_4$

Stage $k = 3$
    Powers of w_{32}:   0   4   8   12
                          $p_1 p_5$ p_2 p_3 p_4

Stage $k = 4$
    Powers of w_{32}:   0   2   4   6   8   10   12   14
                          p_1 p_2 p_3 p_4 p_5 p_1 p_2 p_3

Stage $k = 5$
    Powers of w_{32}:   0   1   2   3   4   5   6   7   8   9   10   11   12   13   14   15
                          p_1 p_2 p_3 p_4 p_5 p_1 p_2 p_3 p_4 p_5 p_1 p_2 p_3 p_4 p_5 p_1

FIG. 1. *Assignment of five processors, p_1, p_2, p_3, p_4, and p_5, in the scheduling-on-w algorithm for an $N = 32$ point transform.*

The scheduling-on-pairs and the scheduling-on-w algorithms were both implemented in HEP FORTRAN and applied to a wide range of problem sizes with $1 \leq p \leq 20$ processes. Figure 2 shows a sample of these experiments for the cases $\log_2 N = 6, 10, 12, 16$. The most significant result is that economizing the powers of w computation by scheduling-on-w has a dramatic effect on computation times. The scheduling-on-w algorithm ran faster than the scheduling-by-pairs algorithm by 25% (for small N) to 80% (for large N). Since the cost of doing pairwise combinations is the same for both algorithms, this difference is due primarily to the cost of computing powers of w. These differences will be quantified in § 4.

The implementation of the scheduling-on-w algorithm relies on no special features of the HEP. Furthermore, its success could also be expected to transfer to other shared memory systems in which complex exponentiation requires a significant number of floating point operations. (On the HEP, the cost is 10–50 flops, depending on the arguments.)

The timing curves also show that the maximum speed-up and the number of processes which gives the maximum speed-up both increase with the problem size. This is due, in part, to the increase in the fraction of fully parallel code which can be executed between process synchronizations. Said differently, as N increases, the amount of time spent in synchronizing barriers becomes insignificant. Because of features of the HEP hardware (discussed in § 4), speed-ups level off with increasing N at about 10 and are generally achieved with 15–18 processes. When more than the optimal number of processes is used, the execution times show a slow rise due to contention among processes during the synchronization phases. These qualitative features are not unique to the HEP. Any tightly coupled multiprocessor executing a program which contains some fraction of sequential code will have an optimal configuration in which speed-up and interprocessor contention are balanced.

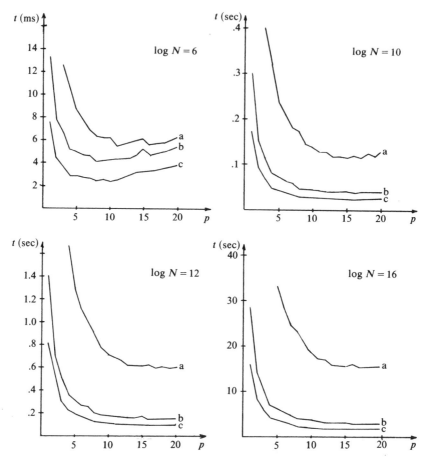

FIG. 2. *Execution times for* (a) *scheduling-on-pairs,* (b) *scheduling-on-w and* (c) *Edson's algorithm for a single* FFT *of length* $N = 256$; 1,024; 4,096; 65,536.

In a large percentage of applications, the input sequence consists of real numbers. In this case, it is not difficult to show that the transform $\{X_k\}$ of a real sequence has the property of conjugate symmetry; i.e., $X_k = \bar{X}_{N-k}$. Furthermore, the partial transforms of length 2^k which are computed at stage $1 \le k \le \log_2 N$ also have conjugate symmetry. This fact may be used to do the entire transform in real arithmetic which reduces both the operation count and the storage requirement by a factor of two. The resulting method is generally referred to as Edson's algorithm [1]. The scheduling issues discussed for the complex FFT also pertain to the real FFT. Given the superiority of the scheduling-on-w approach, Edson's algorithm was implemented using this strategy. As a point of reference, the execution times for this version of Edson's algorithm are also given in Fig. 2. These times are consistently 60% of the execution times for the corresponding complex FFT. This is due to the fact that while the overhead for the scheduling-on-w remains the same, the pairwise combinations cost half as much for Edson's algorithm as they do for the complex FFT. Additional symmetries of the input sequence (e.g., even, odd, quarter wave even and odd) could also be exploited to give even further savings.

Having determined a clearly preferable method for performing a single FFT, we turn to the problem of doing multiple FFTs. As will be seen, the benefits of the scheduling-on-w strategy can also be applied to this problem to give significant savings.

3. Parallel algorithms for multiple FFTs. Many applications require not a single FFT, but rather multiple FFTs. For example, the Fourier analysis of a two-dimensional field of data may be computed through one-dimensional FFTs along the rows of the grid followed by a sweep of FFTs along the columns of the grid. Similarly, the solution of a two-dimensional boundary value problem can be carried out by transforming (i.e., doing FFTs) along grid lines in one coordinate direction and then possibly (depending upon the algorithm) transforming in the orthogonal direction. These forward transforms are eventually followed by inverse transforms in both directions. Therefore, it is important to have parallel algorithms for performing multiple FFTs across either the rows or columns of a two-dimensional grid.

Consider the problem of computing M FFTs of length N, where again N is a power of two. Three strategies have been considered, implemented in HEP FORTRAN, and compared.

(a) *Parallel calls to sequential* FFTs. This approach elevates the level of parallelism one degree by imbedding a sequential N-point FFT algorithm within each process. The M sequences are then distributed over the processes. This method, which will be called the *parallel calls algorithm*, is probably the most obvious way to do a multiple FFT in parallel, but it is not the only way.

(b) *Parallel FFT with inner loop.* This version uses the best algorithm from the previous section (scheduling-on-w) for doing a single FFT. However, each component of the input sequence $\{x_n\}$ is now considered to be an M-vector. Each pairwise combination is done within a loop which runs over all M components. Although the HEP cannot vectorize this new, innermost loop, the method can still be expected to be competitive. This method will be called the *inner loop algorithm.*

(c) *Truncated parallel* FFT. As a serial method, this idea was first presented by Korn and Lambiotte [13] and is discussed further by Swarztrauber [14] and Temperton [16]. Assume that the M input sequences are individually bit-reversed and then concatenated to form a sequence of length MN. If an algorithm for a single FFT is applied to this long sequence and terminated after $m = \log_2 N$ stages, then the M transform sequences are produced in the locations originally held by the respective input sequences. As with the single FFT, the bit reversals may be avoided if inverse transforms are eventually done. The parallel form of the truncated algorithm simply uses scheduling-on-w to perform the MN-point transform of the concatenated sequence. For these experiments, M is also assumed to be a power of two. Most of the classical FFT algorithms have a truncated version; however the position of the transformed sequences may vary from one method to another.

Hockney and Jesshope [10] give an extensive presentation and analysis of multiple FFT methods for vector and array processors. Of the five methods discussed there, only one has a clear analogue in this study. The $(A+B)_{par}$ and $(PARAFT)_{par}$ methods require a machine parallelism which far exceeds that of the HEP or most current MIMD computers. The $(A+B)_{seq}$ and $(PARAFT)_{seq}$ methods, in which the best parallel algorithm is applied successively to each input sequence, really have no analogue. Hockney and Jesshope's MULTFT algorithm is reflected in the parallel calls algorithm in which a serial FFT is applied in parallel across the M input vectors.

Figure 3 shows the results of applying these three algorithms to M FFTs of length N where $M = N$ and $\log_2 N = 5, 6, 7, 8$. The performances of the truncated FFT and the inner loop algorithm are indistinguishable over all problem sizes and levels of parallelism. This fact might have been anticipated since both algorithms have identical computational loads and synchronization overheads. The only difference in the two algorithms is in the DO LOOP structure and the use of a doubly-subscripted array in

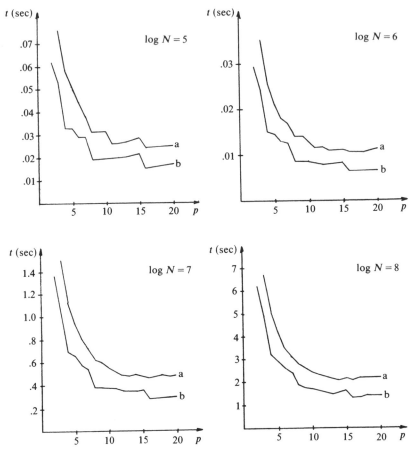

FIG. 3. *Execution times for* (a) *parallel calls and* (b) *inner loops and truncated* FFT *algorithms for M complex sequences of length N with M = N = 32, 64, 128, 256 with 1 to 20 processes.*

the inner loop algorithm as opposed to a singly subscripted array in the truncated FFT. These differences become negligible with large problems. However, there are applications in which the inner loop algorithm could have some advantages. For problems in which transforms along rows are followed by transforms along columns, the inner loop algorithm can be easily modified to avoid transposition of the data. A problem which requires the transform of every qth row of an array $(q>1)$ is difficult to handle with the truncated FFT, while the inner loop algorithm requires only a minor modification.

The parallel calls algorithm runs 55–60% slower than the inner loop and truncated FFT algorithms over all problem sizes. This difference will be quantified in the following section. It can be explained by the fact that in the parallel calls algorithm all of the overhead for a single FFT (computation of sines and cosines, DO LOOP set-up) must be repeated for each of the M/p transforms which each process performs. The other two algorithms minimize the computation of powers of w through scheduling-on-w. In addition, the overhead which *is* necessary in the inner loop and truncated FFT algorithms is used on roughly M times as many pairwise combinations which makes much more efficient use of the overhead. The parallel calls algorithm does have the attribute that it requires no synchronizing barriers. With these experimental results and qualitative observations, we now turn to a more analytical investigation of these algorithms.

4. Models of performance. In this section, a quantitative analysis of the algorithms of the previous two sections is given. Models of performance will be developed which can be used to reproduce the experimental timing curves and to predict algorithm performance outside of the experimental parameter ranges. The models make extensive use of the ideas proposed by Hockney for vector computers [7] and for the HEP [9]. This analysis does require some specific discussion of HEP architecture which has been minimized until this point.

Of particular importance to the following analysis is the fact that the HEP achieves its parallelism through an instruction pipeline that has eight segments. When this pipeline is filled, an instruction can be executed every clock cycle (100 ns). One can imagine that each of the p active processes successively inserts an instruction into the pipeline. Therefore, a given process will wait 8 clock cycles between instructions if $p \leqq 8$ or p clock cycles between instructions if $p > 8$. However, the HEP rarely operates in this idealized mode. While most instructions can be executed in 8 clock cycles, delays typically occur. One source of delay is the storing and fetching of data in the main memory. If data are not available or if there is contention for asynchronous variables, the pending instruction is temporarily suspended. Delays also occur when an instruction requires the result of a floating point divide. Because the divide unit requires 1700 ns per result, subsequent instructions are "waved off" until the results are available. The effect of these delays is that the effective length of the instruction pipeline is not 8, but somewhere between 12 and 16 segments, varying with the instruction mix of the program being run.

In Hockney's benchmark experiments [9] which involve a single floating point operation (flop) per process and a single type of synchronization, the effective pipeline length, L, can be identified as the number of processes which gives the minimum execution time. If we let P denote the average time between the instructions of a single process, it follows that if $p \leq L$, then $P = L$ cycles, whereas if $p > L$, then $P = p$ cycles.

As will be shown below, when a program involves a variety of different operations and more than one type of synchronization, it is no longer possible to identify an effective pipeline length L which is constant for all values of p. This makes it difficult to determine, a priori, values for the parameter P. The timing models which will be developed depend critically upon having good estimates of P for various values of p. These estimates of P will be determined experimentally which leads to some modifications of Hockney's model. Figure 4 shows schematically how P varies with p in Hockney's benchmark model and in a model of a more general algorithm.

With these remarks, we now turn to the modeling of the various FFT algorithms. Figure 5 shows schematically the form of the algorithms which have been developed in this study. They all consist of a fan-in stage in which processes are created, followed by the execution stage in which all processes are active, terminated by a fan-out phase in which the processes die. The execution stage itself generally consists of several (usually $\log_2 N$) substages which are separated by synchronizing barriers. After each of these barriers there is also a fan-in phase in which processes are successively released from the barrier.

Let process 1 initially be the main calling program. Process 1 creates $p - 1$ processes and then itself becomes the pth independent process. Therefore the total execution time for the algorithm is simply the total time that process 1 is working. It should be mentioned that HEP programs have a nondeterministic character and at some point

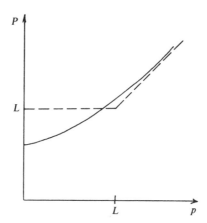

FIG. 4. *The variation of P, the average time in clock cycles between the instructions of an individual process, with p, the number of active processes. Dashed line shows an idealized model with a fixed effective pipeline length L. Solid line shows a more typical situation for a program with a mix of instructions.*

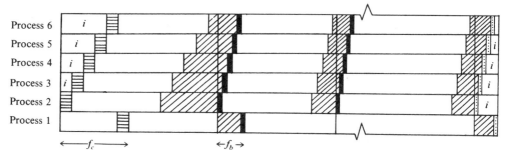

FIG. 5. *Schematic time line of a multistage algorithm showing the scheduling of 6 processes through the phases of creation, computation and barrier synchronization. The times f_c and f_b (see text) are indicated. The execution time for the algorithm is the total time that process 1 is active. ▤: creation of process, □: computation, ▨: barrier, ■: fan-out from barrier, ▨: final fan-out, i: idle time.*

the identity of specific processes cannot be followed. This fact does not affect the following analysis. Another simplification which will be made concerns the divisibility of work. As suggested by Fig. 1, Q independent units of work cannot always be spread evenly over p processes. At least one process must do $[Q/p]$ units of work, which gives the irregular peaks in the timing curves. No attempt will be made to account for these effects which do become insignificant for large problems. Jordan [12] discusses divisibility effects and is able to model them quite accurately.

The following quantities will be used in the performance models. The parameter values were determined from separate timing experiments.

i_0 = number of instructions to create a process = 29.

i_1 = number of instructions to enter a synchronizing barrier = 9.

i_2 = number of instructions to exit from a synchronizing barrier = 2.

i_3 = average number of instructions/flop.

i_4 = number of instructions to set up a DO LOOP = 33.

i_5 = number of flops per INT or MOD operation = 4.

i_6 = number of flops per complex exponential = 11.

i_7 = number of flops per integer divide = 4.

i_8 = number of flops per complex multiply = 6.

i_9 = number of flops per floating point divide = 2.

i_{10} = number of flops per SIN or COS = 20.

B = number of flops for a pairwise combination (one complex multiply and two complex adds) = 10.

p = number of active processes created.

P = average time between the instructions of an individual process.

$m = \log_2 N$.

$l = \lceil \log_2 p \rceil$.

τ = clock cycle = 100 ns.

The values of i_6 and i_{10} vary depending on the arguments of the function. The given values are averages which give accurate estimates for the flop count. The parameter i_3 also varies with the instruction mix, but values between 5.4 and 6.5 fit these algorithms very closely. Finally, the pairwise combinations of the first stage are simpler (since $w^0 = 1$) and require only 4 flops. While these savings are incorporated into the programs, it will be neglected to simplify the analysis. With these preliminaries, the execution times of the various FFT algorithms may be described.

Each algorithm involves an initial fan-in stage for the creation of p processes. The time required for this phase is $f_c = pPi_0$ (a departure from Hockney's expression since P is defined differently). At the end of this fan-in stage, all p processes are active and will remain active either doing work or waiting in a barrier until the computation is finished. After each synchronizing barrier, there is a fan-in stage as processes are successively released from the barrier. This phase requires a time of $f_b = pPi_2$. At the end of the computation, there is a final fan-out phase as the processes retire. This fan-out requires a time of f_b in cases in which the processes were last synchronized in a barrier.

The execution times for each of the FFT algorithms may now be described. In each case, the total computation time is determined as the amount of time that process 1 is active (see Fig. 5).

(a) *Single transform by scheduling-on-pairs.* In this algorithm all $m = \log_2 N$ stages require essentially the same amount of work. Therefore,

$$(4.1) \qquad \frac{T_0}{\tau} = f_c + m \left[i_3 P \left(\frac{N}{2p} (2i_5 + i_6 + i_7 + B) + i_9 + 2i_{10} \right) + P(i_1 + i_4) + f_b \right].$$

The quantity multiplied by i_3 represents the cost of floating point operations. Of that cost, the quantity multiplied by $N/2p$ reflects each processes' share of the pairwise combinations. The overhead for DO LOOPS and barrier synchronization must be paid m times.

(b) *Multiple FFTs by parallel calls.* In this algorithm there are no intermediate barrier synchronizations. The M input sequences are simply distributed over p processes. The time required is

$$(4.2) \qquad \frac{T_1}{\tau} = f_c + P \left[i_3 \frac{M}{p} \left(m \left(\frac{NB}{2} + i_9 + 2i_{10} \right) + N i_8 \right) + i_4 \frac{M}{p} (N + m) \right].$$

Each process bears the full expense of M/p sequential FFTs, each of which has a floating point cost (the term multiplied by i_3) and an overhead for DO LOOPs. On the other hand, inter-process synchronization is negligible.

(c) *Truncated FFT for M sequences.* This analysis with $M = 1$ will give the model for scheduling-on-w for a single FFT. Recall that the structure of this algorithm changes at stage k, where $k > l = \lceil \log_2 p \rceil$. With this in mind, the time required for this algorithm is given by

$$\frac{T_{2,M}}{\tau} = f_c + P \sum_{k=1}^{l} \left[i_3 \left(\frac{MNB}{2p} + 2i_5 + i_6 + 3i_7 \right) + i_1 + i_4 \right]$$

$$+ P \sum_{k=l+1}^{m} \left[i_3 \left(\frac{MN}{2p} B + 2i_6 + i_7 + \left(\frac{2^{k-1}}{p} \right) i_8 \right) + i_1 + i_4 (1 + 2^{k-1}) \right] + mf_b$$

(4.3)

$$\approx f_c + P \left[i_3 \left(\frac{mMNB}{2p} + 2li_5 + (2m-1)i_6 + (m+2l)i_7 + \frac{N}{p} i_8 \right) \right.$$

$$\left. + \left(\frac{N}{p} + m \right) i_4 + mi_1 \right] + mf_b.$$

(d) *Parallel* FFT *on vector components.* As discussed in the previous section, this algorithm performs almost identically to the truncated FFT. The differences cannot be captured in these timing models. Therefore, expression (4.3) will be taken as the model for this algorithm also.

Each of the timing models (4.1), (4.2), and (4.3) can be expressed in terms of Hockney's generic formula

$$T = r_\infty^{-1}(s + s_{1/2}),$$

where r_∞ is the maximum flop rate of the computer with p active processes, s is the *total* flop count for all processes, and $s_{1/2}$ is the overhead of fan-ins, fan-outs, DO LOOPs and barriers, measured in flops. In this case, $r_\infty = (p/P)1/i_3\tau$ and therefore as p approaches P, the computer nears its maximum possible execution rate, $(10/i_3)M$ flops. The difference between p and P is a measure of the inefficiency or lack of utilization in the instruction pipeline.

The timing models (4.1), (4.2), and (4.3) each lead to generic expressions of the form

$$T = r_\infty^{-1}(\underbrace{Q + pR}_{s} + \underbrace{U + Vp + Wp^2}_{s_{1/2}}).$$

The term Q represents flops which are distributed over the processes. This work is reduced per process as p increases. The term including R represents redundant computations which all processes must do independent of p. This term does not appear in the parallel calls algorithm (4.2). The term U represents overhead which is reduced as processes are added and appears in (4.2) and (4.3) as DO LOOP set-ups. The term involving V represents fixed overhead in DO LOOP set-ups and synchronization barriers which affect all processes independent of p. Finally, the term Wp^2 represents the cost of fan-in and fan-out phases which appear in all three algorithms. Clearly these algorithms include some additional costs which do not appear in Hockney's benchmark model.

A comparison of model times may now be made. Equations (4.1) and (4.3) for a single FFT show that the cost of doing pairwise combinations, $mNB/2p$, is identical. The primary difference arises in the auxiliary arithmetic terms i_5, i_6, i_7, i_8, i_9, and i_{10}. For fixed p, these terms are weighted by mN in (4.1) and by m and N in (4.3), which accounts for much of the difference in computation times. Equating T_0 and $T_{2,1}$ indicates that there is no equal performance curve for the two algorithms that lies in a feasible region of the (N, p) parameter plane. As suggested by the experiments of § 2, the scheduling-on-w algorithm is superior to the scheduling-on-pairs algorithm over a wide range of problem sizes and levels of parallelism.

A comparison of timing expressions (4.2) and (4.3) for multiple FFTs indicates that the work involved in pairwise combinations is identical. Once again the difference in the performance curves arises in the cost of doing auxiliary arithmetic. In the parallel calls algorithm, the expense of computing sines, cosines, and complex multiplications must be repeated for each of M sequences each of length N. In the truncated FFT algorithm, these auxiliary computations are minimized to begin with and once they are done, they may be used over M sequences. Equating (4.2) and (4.3) shows that the only possible equal performance curve occurs in the limit of large p and small M, a regime which fits neither useful applications nor current MIMD architectures. Therefore, the performance models support the conclusion of § 3 that the truncated FFT and the inner loops algorithms are superior to the parallel calls algorithm.

In Fig. 6, the timing models (4.2) and (4.3) are used to fit the experimental timing curves for the case of 256 256-point transforms. Table 1 gives the values of P which were used for each value of p as well as the flop rate which was achieved for each value of p. Both the values of P and the flop rates were determined from a system timing routine which resides on the HEP. The timing curves fit the data very closely. In particular, the point of minimum execution time is resolved very well, indicating that the models capture the effects of process contention fairly accurately. Both algorithms reach almost 100% utilization of the instruction pipeline (10 million instructions/second) with 16 processes. However, the truncated FFT algorithm attains a higher

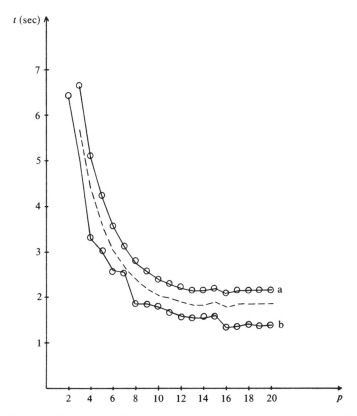

FIG. 6. *Execution times for the* (a) *parallel calls and* (b) *inner loops and truncated* FFT *algorithms for 256 complex sequences of length 256. Open circles give predicted times from the performance models. The dashed line gives the projected performance curve of the parallel calls algorithm when computation of powers of w is replaced by data fetches.*

TABLE 1
$M = 256$ FFTs *of length* $N = 256$.

p	Parallel calls ($i_3 = 6.5$)		Truncated FFT ($i_3 = 5.4$)	
	P (cycles)	r_∞ (Mflop)	P (cycles)	r_∞ (Mflop)
1	9.4	0.16	9.7	0.20
2	9.5	0.32	9.8	0.38
3	9.6	0.47	11.4	0.49
4	9.8	0.62	9.9	0.74
5	10.1	0.74	11.5	0.80
6	10.2	0.88	11.9	0.93
7	10.5	1.00	13.5	0.95
8	10.7	1.12	11.2	1.31
9	11.1	1.20	12.7	1.30
10	11.5	1.30	13.5	1.36
11	12.1	1.35	14.0	1.45
12	12.7	1.41	14.4	1.53
13	13.3	1.46	15.3	1.57
14	14.4	1.46	16.6	1.55
15	15.9	1.41	18.4	1.50
16	16.0	1.50	16.0	1.84
17	17.5	1.46	17.2	1.82
18	18.4	1.46	19.6	1.43
19	19.4	1.46	19.6	1.79
20	20.1	1.49	20.7	1.77

P is the average time (in clock cycles) between instructions of an individual process. r_∞ is the flop rate attained with p active processes.

flop rate, because of the mix of instructions. For the truncated FFT, $i_3 = 5.4$ instructions/flop, while for the parallel calls algorithm, $i_3 = 6.5$ instructions/flop.

It has become clear that the computation of powers of w is an important factor in determining the relative performance of the various FFT algorithms. The models of this section may be used to estimate the effect of this expense. If powers of w are pre-computed and stored in the main data memory, then complex exponentiations/multiplications and sine/cosine evaluations may be replaced by data fetches. Making this modification in the truncated FFT model results in a 1% reduction in computation time, fairly uniformly across all problem sizes and levels of parallelism. A similar modification in the parallel calls model results in a uniform 15% reduction in computation times (see Fig. 6). The truncated FFT algorithm experiences little improvement since auxiliary arithmetic in computing powers of w has been minimized to a great degree. While the parallel calls algorithm shows a noticeable improvement, it still runs 35% slower than the truncated FFT on a 256×256 problem (compared to 55% slower when computing powers of w). It is difficult to predict the further improvement if powers of w could be stored in a high speed cache memory (which does not exist on the HEP) or partially in registers. However, within the bounds of these models the truncated FFT (and the inner loop algorithm) appear to have a comfortable margin of superiority over the parallel calls algorithm.

5. Summary and conclusions. Proceeding first in an experimental manner and then analytically, the problem of implementing single and multiple FFT algorithms on an MIMD computer has been investigated. For computing a single transform, the strategy of scheduling-on-w minimizes the expense of computing powers of w and leads to significant savings over the alternate scheduling-on-pairs algorithm. The scheduling-on-w approach was also applied to Edson's algorithm for transforming a real sequence and could also be applied to other symmetric transforms.

Of the three algorithms studied for transforming multiple sequences, two algorithms, the truncated FFT and the inner loops algorithm, performed almost identically and significantly better than the parallel calls algorithm. The two superior algorithms are both based on the scheduling-on-w idea. The inner loops algorithm is preferable for applications in which alternate rows or columns of an array must be transformed.

The performance of all of these algorithms was modeled using the ideas of Hockney. The model equations support the conclusions of the experiments and can be used to fit the experimental timing curves very closely. The models also suggest that the algorithms which emerge superior in the experiments remain superior over all reasonable ranges of problem size and levels of parallelism. The models were also used to estimate the improvements which would result if powers of w were precomputed and stored rather than computed in progress. This modification would lead to a 15% improvement in the parallel calls algorithm for multiple FFTs, but still does not make it competitive with the inner loops and truncated FFT algorithms.

The HEP is admittedly just one representative of the class of MIMD computers. Nevertheless, it would be useful to extract some conclusions which might apply to other multiprocessors. Like the HEP, most shared memory systems which are available today have a fairly low degree of parallelism. Computers like the CRAY-XMP, CRAY-2, the ETA-10, and the Alliant have ten or fewer processors which work in an MIMD fashion. It is felt that the algorithms which were developed in this study can be implemented on such tightly coupled, shared memory systems and that the performance characteristics of the algorithms would remain qualitatively unchanged. The algorithms would require modification to account for system-specific synchronization mechanisms, the possible existence of high speed cache memory and the availability of vector capabilities. In this latter regard, the inner loops algorithm for multiple FFTs holds yet another advantage in that it possesses a high degree of inner parallelism which could be exploited by vector processors.

Within the domain of loosely coupled or distributed MIMD systems, it would be difficult to apply the results of this study. In such systems, the cost of communication between processors and their local memories becomes significant and cannot be neglected in comparison to computation costs. It is possible that the implementation and performance of the algorithms of this study could be significantly different for such systems. Models which explicitly include communication costs [5] are necessary to make any comparisons.

The algorithms which have been described will be implemented on other shared memory systems to investigate their generality and applicability. Furthermore, in a project just completed on the HEP, these FFT methods have been incorporated into the FACR (ℓ) algorithm [8] for the direct solution of Poisson's equation. The results of this study are forthcoming.

Acknowledgments. We are grateful to Harry Jordan and Paul Swarztrauber for several valuable discussions during the course of this work. The referees of this paper offered many valuable suggestions which have been incorporated with much appreciation. Denelcor and Los Alamos National Laboratory provided computer time on their HEPs, without which this research would have been impossible. In addition, the staff of both facilities gave generously of their time and expertise. The students of the Spring 1984 and Fall 1984 CU-Denver Math Clinic made many contributions to the early stages of this work.

REFERENCES

[1] G. D. BERGLAND, *A fast Fourier transform for real-valued series*, Comm. ACM, 11 (1968), pp. 703–713.

[2] E. O. BRIGHAM, *The Fast Fourier Transform*, Prentice-Hall, Englewood Cliffs, NJ, 1974.

[3] W. T. COCHRAN ET AL., *What is the fast Fourier transform?* IEEE Trans. Audio. Electroacoustics, An-15 (1967), pp. 45–55.

[4] J. W. COOLEY AND J. W. TUKEY, *An algorithm for the machine calculation of complex Fourier series*, Math. Comp., 19 (1965), pp. 297–301.

[5] D. B. GANNON AND J. VAN ROSENDALE, *On the impact of communication complexity on the design of parallel numerical algorithms*, IEEE Trans. Comput. (1984), pp. 1180–1194.

[6] W. M. GENTLEMAN AND G. SANDE, *Fast Fourier transforms for fun and profit*, 1966 Fall Joint Computer Conference, AFIPS Proc., 29 (1966), pp. 563–578.

[7] R. W. HOCKNEY, *Characterizing computers and optimizing the FACR (ℓ) Poisson-solver on parallel unicomputers*, IEEE Trans. Comput. (1983), pp. 933–941.

[8] ———, *A fast direct solution of Poisson's equation using Fourier analysis*, J. Assoc. Comput. Mach., 12 (1965), pp. 95–113.

[9] ———, *Performance characterization of the HEP*, in Parallel MIMD Computation: HEP Supercomputer and Its Applications, J. S. Kowalik, ed., MIT Press, Cambridge, MA, 1985, pp. 59–90.

[10] R. W. HOCKNEY AND C. R. JESSHOPE, *Parallel Computers—Architecture, Programming and Algorithms*, Adam Hilger, Bristol, 1981.

[11] H. F. JORDAN, *Experience with pipelined multiple instruction streams*, Report CSDG 83-4, Dept. Electrical Comput. Enging., Univ. Colorado, Boulder, CO, 1983.

[12] ———, *Interpreting Parallel Processor Performance Measurements*, Report CSDG 85-1, Dept. Electrical Comput. Enging., Univ. Colorado, Boulder, CO, 1985.

[13] D. G. KORN AND J. J. LAMBIOTTE, *Computing the fast Fourier transform on a vector computer*, Math. Comput., 33 (1979), pp. 977–992.

[14] P. N. SWARZTRAUBER, *FFT algorithms for vector computers*, Parallel Computing, 1 (1984), pp. 45–63.

[15] ———, *Vectorizing the FFT's*, in Parallel Computations, G. Rodrigue, ed., Academic Press, New York, 1982.

[16] C. TEMPERTON, *Fast mixed-radix real Fourier transforms*, J. Comput. Phys., 52 (1983), pp. 340–350.

[17] ———, *Implementation of a self-sorting in-place prime factor FFT algorithm*, J. Comput. Phys., 58 (1985), pp. 283–299.

[18] ———, *A note on the prime factor FFT algorithm*, J. Comput. Phys., 52 (1983), pp. 198–204.

[19] ———, *Self-sorting mixed-radix fast Fourier transforms*, J. Comput. Phys., 52 (1983), pp. 1–23.

SIAM J. SCI. STAT. COMPUT.
Vol. 8, No. 1, January 1987

ASYNCHRONOUS RELAXATIONS FOR THE NUMERICAL SOLUTION OF DIFFERENTIAL EQUATIONS BY PARALLEL PROCESSORS*

DEBASIS MITRA†

Abstract. We consider asynchronous relaxations for the numerical solution by parallel processors of initial value problems involving a class of ordinary differential equations. The differential equations may be nonlinear, nonautonomous and nonhomogeneous. The proposed algorithms have several advantages in the parallel processing context, and these apply irrespective of the number of processors and the architecture of the computing system. The form of the given equations is as a partitioned system which closely corresponds to the composition of physical systems from subsystems. The algorithms iterate asynchronously on functions. We prove that the computed functions uniformly converge at a geometric rate to the unique solution of the given equations. The assumption on the asynchronous aspects of the algorithm are that delays are uniformly bounded and that a nonstarvation condition applies. In practice these are not burdensome. The assumptions on the differential equations are dominance conditions. For linear autonomous equations the assumption is that a certain matrix is an M-matrix.

Key words. parallel processing, asynchronous relaxations, waveform relaxations, differential equations

AMS(MOS) subject classifications. 65L05, 65W05

1. Introduction. We propose asynchronous relaxations for obtaining, by parallel processing, the solutions of initial value problems on ordinary differential equations. The differential equations may be nonlinear, nonautonomous and nonhomogeneous; the results of this paper apply when various restrictions are placed on the equations. Relaxation algorithms can be devised with various degrees of asynchronism, and an asynchronous computational model is proposed in this paper for their unified specification and analysis. The generality of the asynchronous computational model is derived from the presence of its various parameters. A particular limiting case, which is obtained by appropriate selections of the parameters, is synchronous relaxations. At the other extreme, we obtain a purely asynchronous algorithm of particular interest. This algorithm is characterized by the absence of essentially all synchronization or coordination on the processors. Other algorithms with intermediate degrees of asynchronism are also described by the model. The asynchronous computational model is precisely described in § 2.2.

Asynchronous algorithms have been previously proposed [1]-[5] and analyzed for use in parallel processors for the solution of various problems other than the solution of differential equations. Certain advantages are obvious: first, the reduction in synchronization between processors yields reduced idle times for the processors; contentions over communication recources and memory accesses are reduced; task management and programming are simplified. On the crucial question of algorithmic efficiency there is evidence that, in certain interesting cases, asynchronous algorithms outperform their synchronous counterparts on account of the different nature of information flow during computations. For instance, [5] gives experimental data which shows over an interesting range of parameters the improvement in performance gained from asynchronism. An important goal, then, is to be able to recognize problems which can be solved by asynchronous relaxations. The analysis in this paper is devoted to that end.

---

* Received by the editors November 26, 1985; accepted for publication (in revised form) March 19, 1986.

† AT&T Bell Laboratories, Murray Hill, New Jersey 07974.

We prove convergence results for the asynchronous computational model. Let $\|\mathbf{x}\|$ denote a norm of $\mathbf{x} \in \mathbb{R}^N$ and X the set of all N-vector functions which are continuous in the interval $[0, t']$. Define the norm of any function $\mathbf{x}$ in X to be

$$\|\mathbf{x}\| = \sup_{0 \leq t \leq t'} \|\mathbf{x}(t)\|.$$

We prove that $\|\mathbf{x}^{(i)} - \mathbf{x}\| \leq cR^i, 0 \leq R < 1, c < \infty$, where $\mathbf{x}^{(i)}$ is the vector function available after the ith update in the asynchronous relaxations, and $\mathbf{x}$ is the unique vector function solution of the given initial value problem. Thus uniform convergence at a geometric rate is proven. See § 6.2 for a discussion and summary.

There are two sets of assumptions made to arrive at the above results. The first specifically concerns the asynchronous aspects and the second concerns the differential equations. Roughly, the first set (see § 2.3) requires that the delays in the implementation are bounded by a finite constant and that every type of task is guaranteed at least one completion in all sequences of task completions of an arbitrary, but fixed, length. These requirements are generally easy to satisfy. The assumptions on the differential equations (see §§ 4.1 and 5.1 for the linear and nonlinear equations, respectively) are all related to dominance conditions. In the special case where the homogeneous part of the equation is autonomous and linear, the only assumption is that a certain matrix, $\mathbf{M} - \mathbf{N}$, is an M-matrix [8]. In this case the rate of convergence is given in part by the spectral radius of $\mathbf{M}^{-1}\mathbf{N}$.

The iteration in the algorithm is on functions. From the point of view of this paper, the primitive tasks consist primarily of the computation of functions which are solutions of nonhomogeneous, initial value problems. The method of numerical integration used to solve the problem is not discussed in this paper.

The purely asynchronous algorithm, which we have mentioned before as a limiting case of the asynchronous computational model, is characterized by each processor successively executing the following cycle until termination, independently of the state of the other processors: read the functions of the task allocated to it, solve the initial-value problem associated with the task, and finally disseminate the solution functions by either writing into shared memory or by sending messages to the appropriate processors. Note that this form of asynchronous computations is compatible with the use of a scheduler to order the tasks. Typically such a scheduler is required to parallelize Gauss–Seidel schemes in which a single processor performs the tasks in some specific order [12].

The asynchronous properties of the relaxations are derived primarily from two sources. First, the times taken to perform tasks are allowed to vary unpredictably within large bounds, and, second, great latitude is allowed in the sequencing of tasks. The convergence result is for a computational model which accommodates major differences in the number and speed of processors, memory, communications and synchronization primitives. These differences are reflected in the values of parameters of the computational model, i.e. the delays and the compositions of the update sets.

The synchronous version of the algorithm, see § 2.2, has sometimes been called "waveform relaxations" [6], and these have been successfully applied to the solution of VLSI circuit-equations by uniprocessors. It is shown below that the synchronous algorithm is a special case of the asynchronous computational model described in § 2.2.

The paper is organized as follows. In § 2.1 we describe the equations, and in §§ 2.2 and 2.3 we give the computational model and the accompanying assumptions. Section 3 is mainly concerned with differential inequalities, which are used throughout the paper. Sections 4 and 5 analyze, in turn, linear and nonlinear equations. We feel that such a separation benefits the exposition. Section 6 picks up the qualitatively similar results obtained at the ends of §§ 4 and 5, to prove uniform convergence for both types of equations. Concluding remarks are contained in § 7.

2. Model of asynchronous relaxations. We give, first, a preliminary description of a class of differential equations and, second, a model of the asynchronous relaxations for numerically solving the equations.

2.1. A class of differential equations. The most general equations that are considered in this paper are nonlinear, nonautonomous and nonhomogeneous. The initial value is given and a unique solution is known to exist for the interval of interest, say $0 \le t < t'$. The value of t' is ignored here since our analysis applies for all t'; however, it is recognized that t' may be an important parameter in the implementation since storage requirements alone may cause the interval of interest to be partitioned into several smaller intervals [12].

The equations are of the form

(2.1)
$$\frac{d}{dt}\mathbf{x}(t) + \mathbf{F}(\mathbf{x}, t) = \mathbf{G}(\mathbf{x}, t) + \mathbf{u}(t), \qquad t \ge 0,$$

$$\mathbf{x}(0) = \mathbf{x}_0,$$

in which $\mathbf{x}$, $\mathbf{u}$, $\mathbf{F}$, and $\mathbf{G}$ are elements of $\mathbb{R}^N$ for each value of t. In addition, it is assumed that $\mathbf{F}$ has a special structure:

(2.2)
$$\mathbf{F}(\mathbf{x}, t) = \{\mathbf{F}_1(\mathbf{x}_1, t), \mathbf{F}_2(\mathbf{x}_2, t), \cdots, \mathbf{F}_n(\mathbf{x}_n, t)\}'.$$

$\mathbf{G}$ may not have this special structure. Thus (2.1) allows the following partitioning into n subsystems which are indexed by j.

(2.3)
$$\frac{d}{dt}\mathbf{x}_j(t) + \mathbf{F}_j(\mathbf{x}_j, t) = \mathbf{G}_j(\mathbf{x}_1, \mathbf{x}_2, \cdots, \mathbf{x}_n, t) + \mathbf{u}_j(t), \qquad t \ge 0, \quad 1 \le j \le n,$$

$$\mathbf{x}_j(0) = \mathbf{x}_{j,0}.$$

In (2.2) and (2.3); $\mathbf{x}_j$, $\mathbf{u}_j$, $\mathbf{F}_j$ and $\mathbf{G}_j$ are elements of $\mathbb{R}^{N_j}$ for each value of t, and $\sum_{j=1}^{n} N_j = N$.

The assumed structure is naturally associated with physical systems composed of subsystems, in which case the internal dynamical relations of the jth subsystem are incorporated in the function $\mathbf{F}_j$, while the cross-couplings between variables of the jth subsystem and the variables in the other subsystems are reflected in the function $\mathbf{G}_j$. The function $\mathbf{G}_j$ is allowed to have $\mathbf{x}_j$ as an argument because in certain nonlinear physical systems a complete separation of variables may not be possible without defining very large subsystems.

The solution of the nonlinear equations (2.3) is considered in § 5, while in § 4 the simpler, linear counterpart of the equation and its solution are considered and the necessary techniques developed.

2.2. The model for asynchronous computations. In order to describe the computational model we need to first introduce a set of primitive tasks, $\{T_j\}$, of various types. The subscript gives the type, of which there are as many as there are subsystems in the system of differential equations, namely, n. As this suggests, there is a close connection between tasks T_j and the jth subsystem in (2.3).

For a task T_j to be completely defined, its arguments $(\mathbf{z}_1, \mathbf{z}_2, \cdots, \mathbf{z}_n)$ must be specified. These arguments are continuous vector functions of t, $t \ge 0$, and $\mathbf{z}_j \in \mathbb{R}^{N_j}$,

$1 \leq j \leq n$, for each value of t. We say that $\mathbf{y} = T_j(\mathbf{z}_1, \mathbf{z}_2, \cdots, \mathbf{z}_n)$ if $\mathbf{y}(t)$, $t \geq 0$, is the unique solution of the following initial value problem:

$$\frac{d}{dt}\mathbf{y} + \mathbf{F}_j(\mathbf{y}, t) = \mathbf{G}_j(\mathbf{z}_1, \mathbf{z}_2, \cdots, \mathbf{z}_n, t) + \mathbf{u}_j(t), \qquad t \geq 0,$$

(2.4)

$$\mathbf{y}(0) = \mathbf{x}_{j,0}.$$

Thus apart from its arguments, the task T_j is tied to the jth subsystem in (2.3). For this reason we sometimes refer to the completion of a task T_j as an update of the jth subsystem.

In the following description of the model for asynchronous computations, the symbol i is reserved for indexing the updates, i.e., task completions. Typically, but not always, the completion of only one task comprises an update. To allow the more general case, $U(i)$, a subset of $\{1, 2, \cdots, n\}$, denotes the types of tasks (or subsystem indices) whose completion comprise the ith update. If the ith update is due, perhaps in part only, to a task T_j being completed, i.e., $j \in U(i)$, then we denote the result of this completed task by $\mathbf{x}_j^{(i+1)}$.

The computational model is

(2.5) $$\mathbf{x}_j^{(i+1)} = \begin{cases} T_j(\mathbf{x}_1^{(i-d(i,j,1))}, \mathbf{x}_2^{(i-d(i,j,2))}, \cdots, \mathbf{x}_n^{(i-d(i,j,n))}) & \text{if } j \in U(i), \\ \mathbf{x}_j^{(i)} & \text{if } j \notin U(i) \end{cases}$$

for $i = 0, 1, 2, \cdots$.

The terms $\{d(i, j, k)\}$ are referred to as delays. The delays are not assumed to be known in advance, and in fact, they will have many components, such as numerical integration time, communication delays, memory access delays and software delays. The substantial extent to which the implementation is allowed to be asynchronous in the model is due to the allowed dependence of the delays on their three arguments, and the minimal nature of the restriction placed on delay values. The only restriction that will be placed on the delay values, see A2 in § 2.3, is one of uniform boundedness.

Synchronous relaxations are obtained from (2.5) in the special case where $d(i, j, k) \equiv 0$ and $U(i) = \{1, 2, \cdots, n\}$ for each i. The synchronous relaxations have also been called "waveform relaxations" in the literature [6] on VLSI circuit-equations solution techniques. Also, the relaxations in which $U(i) = \{(i \bmod n) + 1\}$, $i \geq 0$, and $d(i, j, k) \equiv 0$, may reasonably be called Gauss–Seidel; these relaxations may be implemented by only 1 processor.

To start the relaxations, we require the continuous vector functions $\mathbf{x}_j^{(0)}(t)$, $t \geq 0$, $1 \leq j \leq n$, which are arbitrary except that their initial values match the given initial values for the subsystems, i.e. $\mathbf{x}_j^{(0)}(0) = \mathbf{x}_{j,0}$. We assume that

(2.6) $$\mathbf{x}_j^{(0)}(t) = \mathbf{x}_j^{(i)}(t), \quad t \geq 0, \quad 1 \leq j \leq n \quad \text{for } i < 0.$$

This convenient assumption places no additional restrictions on the implementation.

The tasks as defined here have not previously been considered in the literature on asynchronous algorithms. The model for asynchronous computations given in (2.5), augmented by appropriate definitions of the tasks, gives models closely related to those in [1]–[5].

2.3. Assumptions on the asynchronous relaxations. While additional assumptions will be made, in the course of the analysis on the differential equations given in § 2.1, there are only two assumptions on the model in (2.5) for asynchronous computations.

ASSUMPTION A1. There exists a finite d which uniformly bounds the delays, i.e.,

(2.7) $$0 \leq d(i, j, k) \leq d < \infty, \quad i \geq 0, \quad 1 \leq j \leq n, \quad 1 \leq k \leq n.$$

ASSUMPTION A2. There exists an integer s, $s < \infty$, such that every subsystem is updated at least once in every s consecutive updates.

In connection with Assumption A1 note that $d(i, j, k)$ is not greater than the total number of updates that occur between the ith update and the prior update which marks the beginning of the integration which results in the ith update. Therefore the bound d in A1 exists in the typical case where a given number of processors, working at possibly different positive speeds, implement in some arbitrary order the integrations of the subsystems, the associated workloads being possibly unequal. A naive value for d is obtained from the lower and upper bounds of the speeds and workloads.

Assumption A2 is a nonstarvation condition. Since each update concerns at least one subsystem, violations of A2 can only occur if the ratio of updates for some pair of subsystems is allowed to become unbounded.

Different versions of A1 and A2 have been assumed in previous work on asynchronous numeric algorithms [1]–[5].

3. Preliminaries.
3.1. Differential inequalities.
The subsequent analysis makes considerable use of differential inequalities. For this reason we collect here certain well-known results related to differential inequalities; for additional information the reader is referred to the excellent text by Coppel [7].

Observe that where $x(t)$ is continuously differentiable, the derivative of $|x(t)|$ may not exist at points where $x(t) = 0$. However, the right derivative, $(d^+/dt)|x(t)|$, which is defined below, does exist,

(3.1) $$\frac{d^+}{dt}|x(t)| \triangleq \lim_{h \to +0} \frac{|x(t+h)| - |x(t)|}{h}.$$

To calculate $(d^+/dt)|x(t)|$ it is helpful to have the function $\operatorname{sgn}(x)$ where

(3.2) $$\operatorname{sgn}(x) = 1 \quad \text{if } x > 0; \quad = -1 \text{ if } x < 0; \quad = 0 \text{ if } x = 0.$$

It then follows that

(3.3i) $$\frac{d^+}{dt}|x(t)| = \operatorname{sgn}(x(t)) \frac{d}{dt} x(t) \quad \text{if } x(t) \neq 0,$$

(3.3ii) $$\frac{d^+}{dt}|x(t)| = \left| \frac{d}{dt} x(t) \right| \quad \text{if } x(t) = 0.$$

The main result on differential inequalities that we will need is a result from Coppel [7]. This theorem applies to differential inequalities in which the right-hand side is restricted to be of type K (after Kamke). A vector function $\mathbf{f} = (f_1, f_2, \cdots)$ of a vector variable $\mathbf{x} = (x_1, x_2, \cdots)$ is of type K in a set S if for any two vectors in S, $\mathbf{a}$ and $\mathbf{b}$,

(3.4) $$\left. \begin{array}{l} a_p = b_p \\ a_q \leq b_q, \ q \neq p \end{array} \right\} \quad \text{implies } f_p(\mathbf{a}) \leq f_p(\mathbf{b}).$$

For the example

(3.5) $$\mathbf{f}(\mathbf{x}, t) = \mathbf{M}(t)\mathbf{x} + \mathbf{v}(t)$$

where $\mathbf{M}$ is a continuous, matrix function of t and $\mathbf{v}(t)$ is a continuous vector function of t, $\mathbf{f}(\mathbf{x}, t)$ is of type K for each fixed value of t if and only if all off-diagonal elements of $\mathbf{M}$ are nonnegative. In the analysis to follow we shall be concerned with differential inequalities involving vector functions of the above kind.

Coppel [7] proves, in particular, that the following holds. Let $\mathbf{z}(t)$ be the unique solution on an interval $[a, b]$ of the equation

$$(3.6) \qquad \frac{d}{dt}\mathbf{z}(t) = \mathbf{f}(\mathbf{z}, t)$$

where $\mathbf{f}(\mathbf{z}, t)$ is continuous in an open set, satisfies the Lipschitz condition [7], and is of type K for each fixed value of t. If $\mathbf{x}(t)$ is continuous on $[a, b]$, satisfies the differential inequality

$$(3.7) \qquad \frac{d^+}{dt}\mathbf{x}(t) \leq \mathbf{f}(\mathbf{x}, t)$$

on (a, b) and $\mathbf{x}(a) \leq \mathbf{z}(a)$, then $\mathbf{x}(t) \leq \mathbf{z}(t)$ for $a \leq t \leq b$.

3.2. Notation. All vectors are assumed to be column vectors. Vector transposition is denoted by the superscript $'$. For $\mathbf{x}$ a vector with a typical element denoted by x_p, let $|\mathbf{x}|$ denote the vector in which $|\mathbf{x}|_p = |x_p|$ for each p. In particular

$$\frac{d^+}{dt}|\mathbf{x}(t)| = \left\{ \frac{d^+}{dt}|x_1(t)|, \frac{d^+}{dt}|x_2(t)|, \cdots \right\}'.$$

We employ the inequality convention between vectors in which $\mathbf{x} \leq \mathbf{y}$ is equivalent to $x_p \leq y_p$ for each p.

The above conventions are extended to matrices in the natural way. Thus $|\mathbf{M}|$ denotes the matrix obtained from the matrix $\mathbf{M}$ by replacing elements by their absolute values. Also, we let $\mathbf{I}$ denote the identity matrix and $\mathbf{e}_q$ the qth column of $\mathbf{I}$. The vector $\mathbf{1}$ is defined to have unity for all its elements.

4. Linear differential equations. The problem that we will consider here is the numerical computation of the unique solution $\mathbf{x}(t)$, $t \geq 0$, of a linear counterpart of the equations described in § 2.1. If we let $\mathbf{F}_j(\mathbf{x}_j, t) = \mathbf{D}(j; t)\mathbf{x}_j$, and $\mathbf{G}_j(\mathbf{x}_1, \mathbf{x}_2, \cdots, \mathbf{x}_n, t) = \sum_{k=1}^{n} \mathbf{B}(j, k; t)\mathbf{x}_k(t)$ for $1 \leq j \leq n$, then we obtain from (2.3) the following system of partitioned differential equations:

$$(4.1) \qquad \frac{d}{dt}\mathbf{x}_j(t) + \mathbf{D}(j; t)\mathbf{x}_j(t) = \sum_{k=1}^{n} \mathbf{B}(j, k; t)\mathbf{x}_k(t) + \mathbf{u}_j(t), \qquad t \geq 0, \quad 1 \leq j \leq n,$$

$$\mathbf{x}_j(0) = \mathbf{x}_{j,0}.$$

The constituents of the given quantities, $\mathbf{D}$, $\mathbf{B}$, and $\mathbf{u}$, are continuous in t, $t \geq 0$, and bounded. The matrices $\mathbf{D}(j; t)$ and $\mathbf{B}(j, k; t)$ are, respectively, N_j by N_j and N_j by N_k.

We let $D_{pq}(j; t)$, $1 \leq p \leq N_j$, $1 \leq q \leq N_j$ denote the components of $\mathbf{D}(j; t)$. Similarly, $B_{pq}(j, k; t)$, $1 \leq p \leq N_j$, $1 \leq q \leq N_k$ denote the components $\mathbf{B}(j, k; t)$.

4.1. Assumption. We let $\mathbf{M}(j; t)$ denote the N_j by N_j matrix derived from $\mathbf{D}(j; t)$ in the following manner:

$$(4.2) \qquad M_{pq}(j; t) \triangleq \begin{cases} D_{pq}(j; t), & p = q, \\ -|D_{pq}(j; t)|, & p \neq q. \end{cases}$$

The N by N matrix $\mathbf{M}(t)$ is then defined in the natural way:

$$(4.3) \qquad \mathbf{M}(t) = \mathbf{M}(1; t) \oplus \mathbf{M}(2; t) \oplus \cdots \oplus \mathbf{M}(n; t).$$

Thus $\mathbf{M}(t)$ is block-diagonal with nonpositive off-diagonal elements for each t.

The N_j by N_k matrix $\mathbf{N}(j, k; t)$ is derived from $\mathbf{B}(j, k; t)$: for $1 \leq j \leq n$, $1 \leq k \leq n$, $1 \leq p \leq N_j$, $1 \leq q \leq N_k$,

$$(4.4) \qquad N_{pq}(j, k; t) = |B_{pq}(j, k; t)|.$$

Finally, the N by N matrix $\mathbf{N}(t)$ is defined to have $\mathbf{N}(j, k; t)$ as its (j, k)th block constituent.

In the analysis of linear differential equations we will need the following.

ASSUMPTION L1. There exists a constant N-vector $\boldsymbol{\pi}$ with all components finite and positive, and a positive constant ε such that

$$(4.5) \qquad [\mathbf{M}(t) - \mathbf{N}(t)]\boldsymbol{\pi} \geq \varepsilon \mathbf{1}, \qquad t \geq 0.$$

COROLLARY 1. *There exists a constant r, $0 \leq r < 1$, such that*

$$(4.6) \qquad \mathbf{N}(t)\boldsymbol{\pi} \leq r\mathbf{M}(t)\boldsymbol{\pi}, \qquad t \geq 0.$$

Proof. From the prior assumption of boundedness of the constituent functions of the matrices appearing in (4.1), it follows that there exists some b, $b < \infty$, such that

$$(4.7) \qquad \mathbf{M}(t)\boldsymbol{\pi} \leq b\mathbf{1}, \qquad t \geq 0.$$

Let $r = 1 - \varepsilon/b$, so that $0 \leq r < 1$. With this identification it is straightforward to verify (4.6). $\square$

COROLLARY 2. *Suppose that in (4.1), $\{\mathbf{D}(j; t)\}$ and $\{\mathbf{B}(j, k; t)\}$ are constant. Then Assumption L1 is equivalent to the condition*

$$(4.8) \qquad (\mathbf{M} - \mathbf{N}) \text{ is an } M\text{-matrix.}$$

Proof. $(\mathbf{M} - \mathbf{N})$ is a matrix with all off-diagonal elements nonpositive. The assertion is a well-known property of such matrices [8]. (The reader will find in [9] a variety of other equivalent properties.) $\square$

When (4.1) is autonomous, it is possible to obtain a sharp estimate of the important constant r which appears in (4.6).

COROLLARY 3. *If $\{\mathbf{D}(j; t)\}$ and $\{\mathbf{B}(j, k; t)\}$ in (4.1) are independent of t, then*

$$(4.9\text{i}) \qquad \text{(i) } \rho < 1, \text{ where } \rho \text{ is the spectral radius of } \mathbf{M}^{-1}\mathbf{N}.$$

(ii) *For any $r > \rho$, there exists a positive vector $\boldsymbol{\pi}$ such that*

$$(4.9\text{ii}) \qquad \mathbf{N}\boldsymbol{\pi} < r\mathbf{M}\boldsymbol{\pi}.$$

Proof. The proof of (i) is in [8]. The proof of (ii) follows from well-known properties of M-matrices: $\{r\mathbf{I} - \mathbf{M}^{-1}\mathbf{N}\}$ and $\mathbf{M}$ are M-matrices and consequently their inverses exist and are nonnegative; hence the inverse of $(r\mathbf{M} - \mathbf{N})$ exists and is nonnegative. Let $\boldsymbol{\pi} = (r\mathbf{M} - \mathbf{N})^{-1}\boldsymbol{\mu}$, where $\boldsymbol{\mu}$ is any positive vector. Clearly $\boldsymbol{\pi}$ is itself positive and also (4.9ii) holds. $\square$

Note that in (ii) of the above corollary, r may be taken to be arbitrarily close to ρ.

4.2. Asynchronous relaxations. Recall that the symbol i is used to index updates, $U(i)$ denotes the set of indices of subsystems which are updated in the ith update, and $\{\mathbf{x}_j^{(i+1)}(t), t \geq 0, 1 \leq j \leq n\}$ are the computed function values on completion of the *i*th update. From (2.4), (2.5) and (4.1) we see that these functions are the solutions of the equations

(4.10i)

$$\frac{d}{dt}\mathbf{x}_j^{(i+1)}(t) + \mathbf{D}(j;t)\mathbf{x}_j^{(i+1)}(t) = \sum_{k=1}^{n} \mathbf{B}(j,k;t)\mathbf{x}_j^{(i-d(i,j,k))}(t) + \mathbf{u}_j(t), \quad t \geq 0 \quad \text{if } j \in U(i),$$

$$\mathbf{x}_j^{(i+1)}(0) = \mathbf{x}_{j,0},$$

(4.10ii) $$\mathbf{x}_j^{(i+1)}(t) \equiv \mathbf{x}_j^{(i)}(t), \quad t \geq 0 \quad \text{if } j \notin U(i).$$

It is easy to see that a unique solution exists to the initial value problem in (4.10i). The N_j-vector function $\mathbf{x}_j^{(i+1)}(t)$, $t \geq 0$, is the estimate of $\mathbf{x}_j(t)$, as given by (4.1), after the *i*th update.

4.3. Analysis.
4.3.1. Comparison system. Define the N_j-vector $\mathbf{y}_j^{(i)}(t)$ thus:

(4.11) $$\mathbf{y}_j^{(i)}(t) \triangleq \mathbf{x}_j^{(i)}(t) - \mathbf{x}_j(t), \quad t \geq 0, \quad 1 \leq j \leq n, \quad i = 0, 1, \cdots.$$

From (4.1) and (4.10) it is clear that

(4.12) $$\mathbf{y}_j^{(i)}(0) = \mathbf{0}, \quad 1 \leq j \leq n, \quad i = 0, 1, \cdots.$$

Also, from (4.1) and (4.10),

(4.13i) $$\frac{d}{dt}\mathbf{y}_j^{(i+1)}(t) + \mathbf{D}(j;t)\mathbf{y}_j^{(i+1)}(t) = \sum_{k=1}^{n} \mathbf{B}(j,k;t)\mathbf{y}_k^{(i-d(i,j,k))}(t) \quad \text{if } j \in U(i),$$

(4.13ii) $$\mathbf{y}_j^{(i+1)}(t) \equiv \mathbf{y}_j^{(i)}(t), \quad t \geq 0 \quad \text{if } j \notin U(i).$$

4.3.2. Differential inequalities. Let $y_{j,p}^{(i+1)}(t)$ denote the *p*th constituent of the N_j-vector $\mathbf{y}_j^{(i+1)}(t)$. From (4.3i), for $j \in U(i)$,

(4.14)

$$\{\operatorname{sgn} y_{j,p}^{(i+1)}(t)\}\frac{d}{dt}y_{j,p}^{(i+1)}(t) + D_{pp}(j;t)|y_{j,p}^{(i+1)}(t)|$$

$$+ \sum_{q:q \neq p} D_{pq}(j;t)[\{\operatorname{sgn} y_{j,p}^{(i+1)}(t)\}y_{j,q}^{(i+1)}(t)]$$

$$= \sum_{k=1}^{n}\sum_{q=1}^{N_q} B_{pq}(j,k;t)[\{\operatorname{sgn} y_{j,p}^{(i+1)}(t)\}y_{k,q}^{(i-d(i,j,k))}(t)], \quad t \geq 0.$$

It follows that

(4.15i)

$$\{\operatorname{sgn} y_{j,p}^{(i+1)}(t)\}\frac{d}{dt}y_{j,p}^{(i+1)}(t) + D_{pp}(j;t)|y_{j,p}^{(i+1)}(t)| - \sum_{q:q \neq p}|D_{pq}(j;t)||y_{j,q}^{(i+1)}(t)|$$

$$\leq \sum_{k=1}^{n}\sum_{q=1}^{N_q}|B_{pq}(j,k;t)||y_{k,q}^{(i-d(i,j,k))}(t)|, \quad t \geq 0.$$

Also, when $y_{j,p}^{(i+1)}(t) = 0$ it follows directly from (4.13i) that

(4.15ii) $$\left|\frac{d}{dt}y_{j,p}^{(i+1)}(t)\right| - \sum_{q:q \neq p}|D_{pq}(j;t)||y_{j,q}^{(i+1)}(t)| \leq \sum_{k=1}^{n}\sum_{q=1}^{N_q}|B_{pq}(j,k;t)||y_{k,q}^{(i-d(i,j,k))}(t)|.$$

Hence, from the definition of the right derivative, see (3.3) in § 3.1, it follows from (4.2), (4.3) and (4.4) that

(4.16) $$\frac{d^+}{dt}|\mathbf{y}_j^{(i+1)}(t)| + \mathbf{M}(j;t)|\mathbf{y}_j^{(i+1)}(t)| \leq \sum_{k=1}^{n}\mathbf{N}(j,k;t)|\mathbf{y}_k^{(i-d(i,j,k))}(t)|, \quad t \geq 0.$$

In summary, if $j \in U(i)$ then (4.16) augmented by the initial condition $|\mathbf{y}_j^{(i+1)}(0)| = \mathbf{0}$ holds, and if $j \notin U(i)$ then

$$(4.17) \qquad |\mathbf{y}_j^{(i+1)}(t)| = |\mathbf{y}_j^{(i)}(t)|, \qquad t \geq 0.$$

4.3.3. Bounds. Making use of (4.6) in Corollary 1 to Assumption L1, the right-hand side of (4.16) may be upper bounded thus:

$$(4.18) \qquad \sum_{k=1}^{n} \mathbf{N}(j, k; t)|\mathbf{y}_k^{(i-d(i,j,k))}(t)| \leq [r\{\max_{1 \leq k \leq n} w_k^{(i-d(i,j,k))}\}]\mathbf{M}(j; t)\boldsymbol{\pi}_j,$$

for $t \geq 0$, where

$$(4.19) \qquad w_j^{(i)} \triangleq \sup_{t \in [0,\infty)} \max_{1 \leq p \leq N_j} \{|y_{j,p}^{(i)}(t)|/\pi_{j,p}\}, \qquad 1 \leq j \leq n, \quad i \geq 0.$$

From (4.16) and (4.18) we then have, for $j \in U(i)$, $t \geq 0$,

$$(4.20) \qquad \begin{aligned} &\frac{d^+}{dt}\{|\mathbf{y}_j^{(i+1)}(t)| - s_j^{(i+1)}\boldsymbol{\pi}_j\} + \mathbf{M}(j; t)\{|\mathbf{y}_j^{(i+1)}(t)| - s_j^{(i+1)}\boldsymbol{\pi}_j\} \leq 0, \qquad t \geq 0, \\ &\{|\mathbf{y}_j^{(i+1)}(0)| - s_j^{(i+1)}\boldsymbol{\pi}_j\} = -s_j^{(i+1)}\boldsymbol{\pi}_j \end{aligned}$$

where

$$(4.21) \qquad s_j^{(i+1)} \triangleq r\{\max_{1 \leq k \leq n} w_k^{(i-d(i,j,k))}\}.$$

Now, if the differential inequality in (4.20) is stated in the form

$$(4.22) \qquad \frac{d^+}{dt}\mathbf{z}(t) \leq \mathbf{f}(t, \mathbf{z}), \qquad t \geq 0$$

then $\mathbf{f}$ is of type K for each t, see § 3.1. The prime reason for this is that the off-diagonal terms of $\mathbf{M}(j; t)$ are nonpositive. An application of the main result on differential inequalities stated in § 3.1 then yields

$$(4.23) \qquad |\mathbf{y}_j^{(i+1)}(t)| - s_j^{(i+1)}\boldsymbol{\pi}_j \leq \mathbf{z}(t), \qquad t \geq 0$$

where $\mathbf{z}(t)$ is the unique solution of the following initial value problem:

$$(4.24) \qquad \begin{aligned} &\frac{d}{dt}\mathbf{z}(t) + \mathbf{M}(j; t)\mathbf{z}(t) = 0, \qquad t \geq 0, \\ &\mathbf{z}(0) = -s_j^{(i+1)}\boldsymbol{\pi}_j. \end{aligned}$$

Since $\mathbf{z}(0) \leq \mathbf{0}$, it is easy to see that

$$(4.25) \qquad \mathbf{z}(t) \leq \mathbf{0}, \qquad t \geq 0.$$

Hence, from (4.23) and (4.25),

$$|\mathbf{y}_j^{(i+1)}(t)| \leq s_j^{(i+1)}\boldsymbol{\pi}_j, \qquad t \geq 0.$$

From the definitions of $w_j^{(i+1)}$ and $s_j^{(i+1)}$ in (4.19) and (4.21), we obtain the result which is summarized now.

PROPOSITION 1. *For the linear differential equations in* (4.1) *subject to Assumption* L1, *the asynchronous relaxations in* (4.10) *satisfy the following: for* $i = 0, 1, 2, \cdots$

$$(4.26i) \qquad w_j^{(i+1)} \leq r\{\max_{1 \leq k \leq n} w_k^{(i-d(i,j,k))}\} \quad if\ j \in U(i),$$

$$(4.26ii) \qquad w_j^{(i+1)} = w_j^{(i)} \quad if\ j \notin U(i)$$

where (see (4.6)) $0 \leq r < 1$, *and*

$$w_j^{(i)} = \sup_{t \in [0,\infty]} \max_{1 \leq p \leq N_j} \{|y_{j,p}^{(i)}(t)|/\pi_{j,p}\},$$

and

$$y_{j,p}^{(i)}(t) = x_{j,p}^{(i)}(t) - x_{j,p}(t). \qquad \square$$

We will return to this result in § 6.

5. Nonlinear differential equations. We consider the equations given in (2.3), namely

$$\frac{d}{dt}\mathbf{x}_j + \mathbf{F}_j(\mathbf{x}_j, t) = \mathbf{G}_j(\mathbf{x}_1, \mathbf{x}_2, \cdots, \mathbf{x}_n, t) + \mathbf{u}_j(t), \qquad t \geq 0, \quad 1 \leq j \leq n,$$

(5.1)

$$\mathbf{x}_j(0) = \mathbf{x}_{j,0},$$

and analyze the convergence properties of the asynchronous relaxations described in § 2.2. In § 5.2 we give some examples of systems of equations satisfying the assumptions made on them.

5.1. Assumptions. In the notation we employ, $\mathbf{F}_j = (F_{j,1}, F_{j,2}, \cdots, F_{j,N})'$. The constituents functions in $\mathbf{G}_j$ are similarly represented.

ASSUMPTION N1. The function $\mathbf{F}(\mathbf{x}, t)$ is continuous for $t \geq 0$ and for $\|\mathbf{x}\| < \infty$ ($\|\mathbf{x}\|$ any norm in $\mathbb{R}^N$). Furthermore, for $1 \leq j \leq n$, all $\mathbf{u} \in \mathbb{R}^{N_j}$ and all $\mathbf{v} \in \mathbb{R}^{N_j}$, there exist nonnegative, uniformly bounded functions $D_{pq}(j; t)$, $1 \leq p \leq N_j$, $1 \leq q \leq N_j$, continuous in t, $t \geq 0$, such that, for $t \geq 0$

(5.2i) $\{\text{sgn}\,(u_p - v_p)\}\{F_{j,p}(\mathbf{u}, t) - F_{j,p}(\mathbf{v}, t)\} \geq D_{pp}(j; t)|u_p - v_p| - \sum_{q:q \neq p} D_{pq}(j; t)|u_q - v_q|,$

and, if $u_p = v_p$, then

(5.2ii) $$|F_{j,p}(\mathbf{u}, t) - F_{j,p}(\mathbf{v}, t)| \leq \sum_{q:q \neq p} D_{pq}(j; t)|u_q - v_q|.$$

Note that (5.2ii) is expected from (5.2i) if $(u_p - v_p)$ is perturbed about a small neighborhood of 0.

ASSUMPTION N2. The function $\mathbf{G}(\mathbf{x}, t)$ is continuous for $t \geq 0$ and for $\|\mathbf{x}\| < \infty$. Furthermore, there exist nonnegative, continuous functions $\phi_{j,p}(t)$ such that for all $\mathbf{u} \in \mathbb{R}^N$ and all $\mathbf{v} \in \mathbb{R}^N$,

(5.3) $$|G_{j,p}(\mathbf{u}, t) - G_{j,p}(\mathbf{v}, t)| \leq \phi_{j,p}(t)\|\mathbf{u} - \mathbf{v}\|, \qquad t \geq 0.$$

In (5.3), the norm is the weighted L_∞-norm in $\mathbb{R}^N$, i.e., for $\mathbf{x} \in \mathbb{R}^N$,

(5.4) $$\|\mathbf{x}\| = \max_{1 \leq j \leq n} \max_{1 \leq p \leq N_j} |x_{j,p}|/\pi_{j,p}$$

where π is a fixed, positive, weight vector.

ASSUMPTION N3. There exists a constant ε, $\varepsilon > 0$, such that for $t \geq 0$

(5.5) $$\mathbf{M}(t)\pi - \phi(t) \geq \varepsilon \mathbf{1},$$

where the matrix function $\mathbf{M}(t)$ is constituted from the functions $D_{pq}(j, t)$ as specified before in (4.2) and (4.3), § 4.1.

This completes the assumptions that we will need in connection with the analysis of the asynchronous relaxations for nonlinear, nonautonomous differential equations.

Since $\mathbf{u}(t)$ is continuous in t, the continuity and the Lipschitz condition are satisfied in the initial-value problem in (5.1), and thus a unique solution exists [7].

Note that if we identify $\boldsymbol{\phi}(t)$ in (5.5) with $\mathbf{N}(t)\boldsymbol{\pi}$ in (4.5), the two inequalities are identical. We may therefore conclude the following, as in the first corollary to Assumption L1 in § 4.1.

COROLLARY. *There exists a constant* r, $0 \le r < 1$, *such that*

$$(5.6) \qquad\qquad \boldsymbol{\phi}(t) \le r\mathbf{M}(t)\boldsymbol{\pi}, \qquad t \ge 0. \qquad\qquad \Box$$

5.2. Examples. We briefly consider some simple and typical examples of the N-vector function $\mathbf{F}(\mathbf{x}, t)$, and investigate the requirements for Assumption N1 to be satisfied and the specification of the functions $\{D_{pq}(j; t)\}$ which appear in the statement of the assumption.

5.2.1. A simple example is

$$(5.7) \qquad\qquad \mathbf{F}(\mathbf{x}, t) = \mathbf{A}\mathbf{x}$$

where $\mathbf{A}$ is a constant matrix. In this case (5.2) requires that

$$(5.8) \qquad\qquad A_{pp}(j) \ge 0$$

in which case we may satisfy (5.2) by taking

$$(5.9) \qquad D_{pp}(j; t) = A_{pp}(j) \quad \text{and} \quad D_{pq}(j; t) = |A_{pq}(j)|, \quad p \ne q.$$

5.2.2. Another example is

$$(5.10) \qquad\qquad \mathbf{F}_j(\mathbf{x}_j, t) = [f_{j,1}(x_{j,1}), f_{j,2}(x_{j,2}), \cdots, f_{j,N_j}(x_{j,N_j})]'$$

for $1 \le j \le n$, in which for each p, $f_{j,p}(x_{j,p})$ is continuously differentiable. In this case, in (5.2) we may take $D_{pq}(j; t) \equiv 0$ for $p \ne q$, and the requirement in (5.2) then translates to

$$(5.11) \qquad \{\text{sgn}\,(u - v)\}\{f_{j,p}(u) - f_{j,p}(v)\} \ge D_{pp}(j; t)|u - v|,$$

for all real u and v, where $D_{pp}(j; t) \ge 0$. Thus $f_{j,p}(u)$ must be monotonic, nondecreasing with increasing x, but note that it is not necessary that $f_{j,p}(0) = 0$. When the monotonicity condition holds, (5.2) is satisfied if we take

$$(5.12) \qquad\qquad D_{pp}(j; t) = \inf_x f'_p(x) \ge 0.$$

5.2.3. In the final example, for $1 \le j \le n$,

$$(5.13) \qquad \mathbf{F}_j(\mathbf{x}_j, t) = \mathbf{A}(j)[f_{j,1}(x_{j,1}), f_{j,2}(x_{j,2}), \cdots, f_{j,N_j}(x_{j,N_j})]',$$

in which $f_{j,p}$ for each p is continuously differentiable and satisfies the Lipschitz condition, and $\mathbf{A}(j)$ is a constant matrix. It is easy to see that (5.2) is satisfied if

$$(5.14\text{i}) \qquad A_{pp}(j)\{\text{sgn}\,(u - v)\}\{f_{j,p}(u) - f_{j,p}(v)\} \ge D_{pp}(j; t)|u - v|$$

and, for $p \ne q$,

$$(5.14\text{ii}) \qquad |A_{pq}(j)||f_q(u) - f_q(v)| \le D_{pq}(j; t)|u - v|$$

for all real u and v.

In considering (5.14i) first, we note that $A_{pp}(j)$ may have either sign. However, necessarily, (a) if $A_{pp}(j) \ge 0$ then $f_{j,p}(x)$ must be monotonic, nondecreasing with increasing x; (b) if $A_{pp}(j) \le 0$ then $f_{j,p}(x)$ must be monotonic, nonincreasing with increasing x. That is,

(5.15) $$A_{pp}(j)f'_{j,p}(x) \geq 0 \quad \text{for all } x \text{ and } p.$$

If this condition is satisfied then, it is quite easy to see that (5.14i) and (5.14ii), and therefore (5.2), are satisfied with the following choices:

$$D_{pp}(j; t) = |A_{pp}(j)|S_{j,p} \quad \text{where } S_{j,p} \triangleq \inf_x |f'_{j,p}(x)|,$$

(5.16) and, for $p \neq q$,

$$D_{pq}(j; t) = |A_{pq}(j)|L_{j,q} \quad \text{where } L_{j,q} \triangleq \sup_x |f'_{j,q}(x)|.$$

5.3. Asynchronous relaxations. From (2.3), (2.4) and (2.5) we have, for $i = 0, 1, \cdots$ and $1 \leq j \leq n$,

$$\frac{d}{dt}\mathbf{x}_j^{(i+1)}(t) + \mathbf{F}_j(\mathbf{x}_j^{(i+1)}, t) = \mathbf{G}_j(\mathbf{x}_1^{(i-d(i,j,1))}, \cdots, \mathbf{x}_n^{(i-d(i,j,n))}, t) + \mathbf{u}_j(t), \quad t \geq 0,$$

(5.17i)

$$\mathbf{x}_j^{(i+1)}(0) = \mathbf{x}_{j,0} \quad \text{if } j \in U(i),$$

(5.17ii) $$\mathbf{x}_j^{(i+1)}(t) = \mathbf{x}_j^{(i)}(t), \quad t \geq 0 \quad \text{if } j \notin U(i).$$

Note that by our earlier assumptions, continuity and the Lipschitz condition are satisfied in the initial-value problem (5.17i) and thus a unique solution exists.

5.4. Analysis.
5.4.1. Comparison system. Define, as in (4.11)

(5.18) $$\mathbf{y}_j^{(i)}(t) \triangleq \mathbf{x}_j^{(i)}(t) - \mathbf{x}_j(t), \quad t \geq 0, \quad 1 \leq j \leq n, \quad i = 1, 2, \cdots.$$

Clearly

$$\mathbf{y}_j^{(i)}(0) = \mathbf{0}.$$

From (5.1), (5.17) and (5.18),

$$\frac{d}{dt}y_{j,p}^{(i+1)}(t) + [F_{j,p}(\mathbf{x}_j^{(i+1)}, t) - F_{j,p}(\mathbf{x}_j, t)]$$

(5.19i)

$$= [G_{j,p}(\mathbf{x}_1^{(i-d(i,j,1))}, \cdots, \mathbf{x}_n^{(i-d(i,j,n))}, t) - G_{j,p}(\mathbf{x}_1, \cdots, \mathbf{x}_n, t)],$$

$$t \geq 0, \quad y_{j,p}^{(i+1)}(0) = 0, \quad 1 \leq p \leq N_j \quad \text{if } j \in U(i)$$

(5.19ii) $$\mathbf{y}_j^{(i+1)}(t) = \mathbf{y}_j^{(i)}(t), \quad t \geq 0 \quad \text{if } j \notin U(i).$$

We proceed to examine the case of $j \in U(i)$ and to obtain, with the aid of Assumptions N1 and N2, a differential inequality for $|y_j^{(i+1)}(t)|$. The right-hand side of (5.19i) may be bounded by using Assumption N2:

$$|G_{j,p}(\mathbf{x}_1^{(i-d(i,j,1))}, \cdots, \mathbf{x}_n^{(i-d(i,j,n))}, t) - G_{j,p}(\mathbf{x}_1, \cdots, \mathbf{x}_n, t)|$$

(5.20)

$$\leq \phi_{j,p}(t)[\max_{1 \leq k \leq n} w_k^{(i-d(i,j,k))}], \quad t \geq 0,$$

where, as in (4.19),

(5.21) $$w_j^{(i)} \triangleq \sup_{t \in [0,\infty]} \max_{1 \leq p \leq N_j} |y_{j,p}^{(i)}(t)|/\pi_{j,p}, \quad 1 \leq j \leq n, \quad i \geq 0.$$

By multiplying (5.19i) by $\{\operatorname{sgn} y_{j,p}^{(i+1)}(t)]$ and taking note of Assumption N1, and also by evaluating $|(d/dt)y_{j,p}^{(i+1)}(t)|$ when $y_{j,p}^{(i+1)}(t)=0$, we obtain, analogously to (4.15),

$$
\frac{d^+}{dt}|y_{j,p}^{(i+1)}(t)|+D_{pp}(j;\,t)|y_{j,p}^{(i+1)}(t)|-\sum_{q:q\neq p}D_{pq}(j;\,t)|y_{j,q}^{(i+1)}(t)|
$$

(5.22)

$$
\leq\phi_{j,p}(t)[\max_{1\leq k\leq n}w_k^{(i-d(i,j,k))}],\qquad t\geq 0.
$$

To recapitulate, if $j\in U(i)$ then we have (5.22), and if $j\notin U(i)$ then

$$
|y_j^{(i+1)}(t)|=|y_j^{(i)}(t)|,\qquad t\geq 0.
$$

5.4.2. Bounds. We may now make use of (5.6), a corollary to Assumption N3, which bounds $\phi(t)$, to state the right-hand side of (5.22) in a more convenient form. Thus,

(5.23) $\phi_{j,p}(t)\left[\displaystyle\max_{1\leq k\leq n}w_k^{(i-d(i,j,k))}\right]\leq s_j^{(i+1)}\left[D_{pp}(j;\,t)\pi_{j,p}-\displaystyle\sum_{q:q\neq p}D_{pq}(j;\,t)\pi_{j,q}\right]$

where

(5.24) $s_j^{(i+1)}\triangleq r\{\displaystyle\max_{1\leq k\leq n}w_k^{(i-d(i,j,k))}\}.$

From (5.22) and (5.23),

$$
\frac{d^+}{dt}\{|y_{j,p}^{(i+1)}(t)|-s_j^{(i+1)}\pi_{j,p}\}+D_{pp}(j;\,t)\{|y_{j,p}^{(i+1)}(t)|-s_j^{(i+1)}\pi_{j,p}\}
$$

$$
-\sum_{q:q\neq p}D_{pq}(j;\,t)\{|y_{j,q}^{(i+1)}(t)|-s_j^{(i+1)}\pi_{j,q}\}\leq 0,\qquad t\geq 0,
$$

which in vector form is

(5.25) $\dfrac{d^+}{dt}\{|\mathbf{y}_j^{(i+1)}(t)|-s_j^{(i+1)}\boldsymbol{\pi}_j\}+\mathbf{M}(j;\,t)\{|\mathbf{y}_j^{(i+1)}(t)|-s_j^{(i+1)}\boldsymbol{\pi}_j\}\leq 0,\qquad t\geq 0.$

This differential inequality is identical to (4.20) and we may therefore conclude that

$$
|\mathbf{y}_j^{(i+1)}(t)|\leq s^{(i+1)}\boldsymbol{\pi}_j,\qquad t\geq 0
$$

and, thereby,

$$
w_j^{(i+1)}\leq r\{\max_{1\leq k\leq n}w_k^{(i-d(i,j,k))}\},
$$

where $w_j^{(i+1)}$ is as defined in (5.21). In summary we have

PROPOSITION 2. *For the nonlinear differential equations in* (5.1) *subject to Assumptions* N1, N2 *and* N3, *the asynchronous relaxations in* (5.17) *satisfy the following: for* $i=0,1,2,\cdots$

$$
w_j^{(i+1)}\leq r\{\max_{1\leq k\leq n}w_k^{(i-d(i,j,k))}\}\quad\text{if }j\in U(i),
$$

$$
w_j^{(i+1)}=w_j^{(i)}\quad\text{if }j\notin U(i),
$$

where $0\leq r<1$ (*see* (5.6)), *and*

$$
w_j^{(i)}=\sup_{t\in[0,\infty]}\max_{1\leq p\leq N_j}\{|y_{j,p}^{(i)}(t)|/\pi_{j,p}\}
$$

and,

$$
y_{j,p}^{(i)}(t)=x_{j,p}^{(i)}(t)-x_{j,p}(t).\qquad\qquad\square
$$

6. Convergence of the asynchronous relaxations. The end results of the two preceding sections on, respectively, linear and nonlinear differential equations differ only in the values that may be attached to the parameter r. These results rely only on assumptions on the respective differential equations and not at all on those aspects of the asynchronous process which have to do with the relative frequencies of updates and the delays in the updates. Here we introduce these aspects and, by making use of Assumptions A1 and A2 given in § 2, give a unified proof of uniform convergence.

6.1. Convergence of the discrete, asynchronous process. From Propositions 1 and 2,

$$w_j^{(i+1)} \le r\{\max_{1 \le k \le n} w_k^{(i-d(i,j,k))}\} \quad \text{if } j \in U(i),$$

$$w_j^{(i+1)} = w_j^{(i)} \quad \text{if } j \notin U(i).$$

Hence from Assumption A1,

(6.1) $$w_j^{(i+1)} \le r[\max_{0 \le \delta \le d} \max_{1 \le k \le n} w_k^{(i-\delta)}] \quad \text{if } j \in U(i).$$

By recalling that $r < 1$ we have, in particular,

(6.2) $$\max_{0 \le \delta \le d} \max_{1 \le j \le n} w_j^{(i'-\delta)} \le \max_{0 \le \delta \le d} \max_{1 \le j \le n} w_j^{(i-\delta)}, \quad 0 \le i \le i'-1.$$

We also have

PROPOSITION 3.

(6.3) $$\max_{1 \le j \le n} w_j^{(i')} \le r[\max_{0 \le \delta \le d} \max_{1 \le j \le n} w_j^{(i-\delta)}], \quad 0 \le i \le i'-s.$$

Proof. From Assumption A2, subsystem j must be updated at least once in the series of consecutive updates with indices in $[i'-s, i'-1]$. Say that the last update of subsystem j in this series is indexed τ.

$$w_j^{(i')} = w_j^{(\tau+1)} \le r[\max_{0 \le \delta \le d} \max_{1 \le k \le n} w_k^{(\tau-\delta)}], \quad \text{from (6.1)},$$

$$w_j^{(i')} = w_j^{(\tau+1)} \le r[\max_{0 \le \delta \le d} \max_{1 \le k \le n} w_k^{(i-\delta)}], \quad i \le \tau \le i'-s, \quad \text{from (6.2)}. \qquad \square$$

The above proposition has the following corollary in the form of a recursive inequality:

(6.4) $$[\max_{0 \le \delta \le d} \max_{1 \le j \le n} w_j^{(i'-\delta)}] \le r[\max_{0 \le \delta \le d} \max_{1 \le j \le n} w_j^{(i-\delta)}], \quad 0 \le i \le i'-(d+s).$$

We now state the main result, in which the norm $\| \; \|$ in $\mathbb{R}^N$ is

$$\|\mathbf{x}\| = \max_{1 \le j \le n} \max_{1 \le p \le N_j} |x_{j,p}|/\pi_{j,p}.$$

PROPOSITION 4. *For $i = 0, 1, 2, \cdots$*

(6.5) $$\sup_{t \in [0,\infty]} \|\mathbf{x}^{(i)}(t) - \mathbf{x}(t)\| \le Cr^l,$$

where $0 \le r < 1$, $l = \lfloor i/(d+s) \rfloor$ and $C = \max_{1 \le j \le n} w_j^{(0)}$.
Proof. Equation (6.4) yields

(6.6) $$[\max_{0 \le \delta \le d} \max_{1 \le j \le n} w_j^{(i-\delta)}] \le Cr^l$$

where

$$C = \max_{0 \leq \delta \leq d} \max_{1 \leq j \leq n} w_j^{(-\delta)} = \max_{1 \leq j \leq n} w_j^{(0)}.$$

The statement in the proposition is implied by (6.6). □

6.2. Discussion. We may conclude from the last proposition that the long-term average rate of geometric convergence (per update) is not less than $r^{1/(d+s)}$.

We have proven uniform convergence for the proposed asynchronous relaxations under different conditions for three variants of the differential equations in (2.1):

(6.7i)
$$\frac{d}{dt}\mathbf{x}(t) + \mathbf{D}\mathbf{x}(t) = \mathbf{B}\mathbf{x}(t) + \mathbf{u}(t),$$

(6.7ii)
$$\frac{d}{dt}\mathbf{x}(t) + \mathbf{D}(t)\mathbf{x}(t) = \mathbf{B}(t)\mathbf{x}(t) + \mathbf{u}(t),$$

(6.7iii)
$$\frac{d}{dt}\mathbf{x}(t) + \mathbf{F}(\mathbf{x}, t) = \mathbf{G}(\mathbf{x}, t) + \mathbf{u}(t).$$

We have assumed A1 and A2, see § 2.3, in all cases. In case (i) uniform convergence at a geometric rate occurs when $\mathbf{M}^{-1}\mathbf{N}$ is an M-matrix; in this case the parameter r in the bound on the rate of convergence may be chosen to be arbitrarily close to ρ, the spectral radius or $\mathbf{M}^{-1}\mathbf{N}$, where $\mathbf{M}$ and $\mathbf{N}$ are obtained from $\mathbf{D}$ and $\mathbf{B}$ as in (4.2) and (4.4). In particular, if $\mathbf{D}$ has nonpositive off-diagonal elements and $\mathbf{B}$ is nonnegative, the $\mathbf{M} = \mathbf{D}$ and $\mathbf{N} = \mathbf{B}$.

The uniform convergence for case (ii) requires Assumption L1, see § 4.1, and case (iii) requires Assumptions N1, N2 and N3, see § 5.1. The result for case (iii) subsumes the result for case (ii).

7. Concluding remarks. We have proven convergence results for an asynchronous computational model. This model has several parameters and, by appropriate selections of these parameters, it can be made to describe algorithms with various degrees of asynchronism. Similarly, architectural differences giving rise to varying rates of execution of the primitive tasks are also tolerated in the model.

Algorithmic efficiency, synchronization penalty, the software overhead for coordination and communication congestion are major factors which will contribute towards greater use of asynchronism in algorithms. These factors become more pronounced as the number of processors is increased. The Ultracomputer [10] and the CHOPP [11] are examples of designs in which ultimately thousands of processors are proposed to be used. The asynchronous computational model and results for it should therefore prove useful in the future.

We mention that [12] describes implementations of asynchronous relaxations on a parallel processor[1] for systems with up to 64,000 tightly coupled, linear differential equations which describe the evolution with time of the state probabilities of Markov processes. The Markov processes model manufacturing lines with random service times and finite buffers. The procedure employed in [12] consists of first obtaining a good Gauss–Seidel-like relaxation for uniprocessors and then obtaining parallel asynchronous versions of it. Also described are competing implementations and related experimental results on the scheduling of tasks, the use of "windows" related to finite integration intervals, distributed convergence tests and termination, and the distributed

---

[1] The BALANCE™ (trademark of Sequent Computer Systems, Inc.) 8000.

computation of statistics of the Markov process. Finally, a result is given which bounds the effect of independent error functions which are introduced in the execution of each of the primitive tasks.

REFERENCES

[1] D. CHAZAN AND W. MIRANKER, *Chaotic Relaxation*, Linear Algebra Appl., 2 (1969), pp. 199–222.

[2] G. M. BAUDET, *Asynchronous iterative methods for multiprocessors*, J. Assoc. Comput. Mach., 25 (1978), pp. 226–244.

[3] D. P. BERTSEKAS, *Distributed asynchronous computation of fixed points*, Math. Programming, 27 (1983), pp. 107–120.

[4] ———, *Distributed dynamic programming*, IEEE Trans. Automat. Control, AC-27 (June 1982), pp. 610–616.

[5] B. LUBACHEVSKY AND D. MITRA, *A chaotic, asynchronous algorithm for computing the fixed point of a nonnegative matrix of unit spectral radius*, J. Assoc. Comput. Mach., 33 (1986), pp. 130–150.

[6] E. LELARASMEE, A. E. RUEHLI AND A. L. SANGIOVANNI-VINCENTELLI, *The waveform relaxation method for time-domain analysis of large scale integrated circuits*, IEEE Trans. Computer-Aided Design of Integrated Circuits and Systems, CAD-1 (July 1982), pp. 131–145.

[7] W. A. COPPEL, *Stability and asymptotic behavior of differential equations*, Heath Mathematical Monographs, Boston, MA, 1965.

[8] R. S. VARGA, *Matrix Iterative Analysis*, Prentice-Hall, Englewood Cliffs, NJ, 1962.

[9] M. FIEDLER AND V. PTAK, *On matrices with nonpositive off-diagonal elements and positive principal minors*, Czechoslovak. Math. J., 12 (1962), pp. 382–450.

[10] A. GOTTLIEB, R. GRISHMAN, C. P. KRUSKAL, K. P. MCAULIFFE, L. RUDOLPH AND M. SNIR, *The NYU ultracomputer—designing an MIMD shared memory parallel computer*, IEEE Trans. Comput., C-32 (Feb. 1983), pp. 175–189.

[11] L. A. COHN, *A conceptual approach to general purpose parallel computer architecture*, Ph.D. dissertation, Columbia University, New York, 1983.

[12] D. MITRA, *Implementations of asynchronous relaxations for the solution of linear differential equations on a parallel processor and related theoretical results*, in preparation.

SIAM J. Sci. Stat. Comput.
Vol. 8, No. 1, January 1987

SOLVING EQUATIONS OF MOTION ON A VIRTUAL TREE MACHINE*

W. W. ARMSTRONG†, T. A. MARSLAND†, M. OLAFSSON† AND J. SCHAEFFER†§

Abstract. The dynamic equations of motion for rigid links connected at hinges to form a tree are amenable to a parallel solution. Such a solution can potentially provide a real-time simulation of the dynamic behavior of a broad class of objects used in animation and robotics even when the number of links is large. However, the design of a parallel algorithm poses problems not encountered in the sequential, one-processor case, such as assignment of links to processes, allocation of processes to physical processors, synchronization of processes, and the reduction of communication losses. The computation time using a parallel algorithm and an unlimited number of processors is shown to grow with the height of the tree rather than with its number of links. Increased communication costs degrade performance by a factor at most equal to the fanout. The facility used to investigate these problems is a Virtual Tree Machine (VTM) multi-computer implemented on a network of autonomous VAX-11/780 computers and SUN-2 workstations, each running a UNIX operating system.‡ Although the VTM is physically connected via a local area network, its performance in this study reflects what would occur in a point-to-point interconnection of processors in a tree configuration which would be much more expensive to build and test.

Key words. dynamics of open chains, equations of motion, animation, robotics, parallel computation, ordinary differential equations

AMS(MOS) subject classifications. 65L99 70-04 70-08 70-09

1. Introduction. Recent papers have discussed the use of dynamics for purposes of graphical simulation or animation. The thesis of Wilhelms gives a general overview of the area [1]. It has been noted that the computation time required to solve the equations of motion of a collection of rigid links, connected at hinges, by techniques such as that of Gibbs-Appel can grow as the cube or fourth power of the number of links in the system [2], making such techniques inappropriate when the number of links is large. Recently, the equations of motion of such tree linkages have been formulated in hinge-centered coordinates, and solved by a method requiring time growing linearly with the number of links [3]. In addition, this new algorithm allows a significant amount of parallelism. Indeed, the exploitation of parallel execution on several processors has the potential to reduce the growth of the computation time to being linear in the height of the tree, rather than in its number of links.

The improved performance due to parallel processing should make possible applications of dynamics to graphical simulation and animation which have heretofore been beyond the capacity of existing general-purpose computers. For example, the use of dynamics to generate frame-to-frame motions of animated characters, under real-time control of an animator, can possibly add realism and reduce costs of animation, as well as allowing some exploration of alternative possibilities by the animator. The addition of numerous "sensor" links to the dynamic system, no longer an impediment to real-time operation, has been suggested as a way to control the shape of deformable surfaces. Again, this could remove considerable burden from the animator. There are applications of the parallel simulation to computer-aided manufacturing. For example, the graphical simulation of a robot manipulator in real-time can be useful during its design as well as for the training of operators. Recently, methods of using

---

* Received by the editors November 25, 1985; accepted for publication (in revised form) May 14, 1986.
† Department of Computing Science, University of Alberta, Edmonton, Alberta, Canada, T6G 2H1.
§ Funding for this work was provided by the Natural Sciences and Engineering Research Council of Canada.
‡ VAX is a trademark of Digital Equipment Corporation, SUN is a trademark of Sun Microsystems, Inc., and UNIX is a trademark of AT&T Bell Laboratories.

parallel processing for manipulator control have been proposed which depend on solving a scheduling problem [4], however that work takes the desired motion as input and produces joint forces and torques to realize the motion as output. In animation, the forces and torques (or control information from which they can be derived) are the inputs, and the motion is the output. In this way, built-in limitations on forces and torques constrain the animator to create a motion which could realistically be produced by muscular action.

The main thrust of our paper is to describe a parallel solution for determining the motion of tree linkages. In § 2 the equations are given and a solution is outlined which imposes an order on the computations reflecting the interconnection of links. In § 3 we show how these computations can be mapped to a tree of processes. Details of these computations are deferred to the Appendix. The Virtual Tree Machine multicomputer which supports the parallel implementation is described in § 4. Experimental and analytical results follow.

2. The equations of motion and their solution. The linkage trees considered consist of rigid links connected at hinges. The hinges allow three rotational degrees of freedom. This corresponds to a ball and socket joint. The reason for using this type of joint is the greater ease of formulating the equations of motion without the constraints which reduce the rotational degrees of freedom. Prismatic joints, which allow translations, are not considered. A typical linkage is shown in Figure 1.

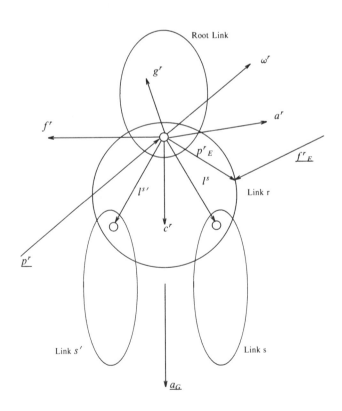

FIG. 1. *Quantities associated with link r.*

The following representations are used for physical quantities, whereby vectors, unless otherwise noted, are here represented in a frame attached to link r and moving with it: m_r is the mass of link r; a_G is the acceleration of gravity (in an inertial frame); f_E^r is an external force (inertial frame) acting on link r at the point p_E^r; g_E^r is an external torque (inertial frame) acting on link r; a^r is the acceleration of the proximal (parent) hinge of link r; ω^r is the angular velocity of link r; c^r is the vector from the proximal hinge to the center of mass of link r; f^r and g^r are the force and torque which link r exerts on its parent at the proximal hinge; l^s is the vector from the proximal hinge of link r to the proximal hinge of child s of link r. R^r converts vector representations in the frame of link r to the representations in the frame of the parent link; R_I^r converts to representations in the inertial frame; J^r is the 3×3 moment of inertia matrix of link r about its proximal hinge; S_r is the set of all links having link r as parent.

The first equation of motion, giving the rate of change of ω^r as a result of various torques, is:

$$J^r \, \dot{\omega}^r = g_\Sigma^r - m_r \, c^r \times a^r + \sum_{s \in S_r} l^s \times R^s \, f^s \tag{1}$$

where

$$g_\Sigma^r = - \omega^r \times (J^r \, \omega^r) - g^r + \sum_{s \in S_r} R^s \, g^s + R_I^{r \ T} g_E^r \tag{2}$$

$$+ \, m_r \, c^r \times R_I^{r \ T} a_G + p_E^r \times R_I^{r \ T} f_E^r.$$

The next equation of motion gives the constraint force which link r exerts on its parent at the proximal hinge:

$$f^r = f_\Sigma^r - m_r \, a^r + m_r \, c^r \times \dot{\omega}^r + \sum_{s \in S_r} R^s \, f^s \tag{3}$$

where

$$f_\Sigma^r = - m_r \, \omega^r \times (\omega^r \times c^r) + R_I^{r \ T} (f_E^r + m_r \, a_G). \tag{4}$$

The last equation comes from the hinge constraints:

$$R^s \, a^s = a_c^s + a^r - l^s \times \dot{\omega}^r \tag{5}$$

where

$$a_c^s = \omega^r \times (\omega^r \times l^s). \tag{6}$$

The hypothesis which aids in solving the equations is that there exist linear relationships

$$\dot{\omega}^r = K^r \, a^r + d^r \tag{7}$$

$$f^r = M^r \, a^r + f'^r. \tag{8}$$

In solving the equations of motion at each time step, we set the external forces f_E^r, the external torques g_E^r and the hinge torques g^r according to the control parameters, then we solve for K^r, d^r, M^r, and f'^r, starting at the leaves of the tree of links and proceeding towards the root. Intuitively, the solution method can be understood as follows. Suppose some agent accelerates a certain point on a rigid body r by an amount a^r. Then there will be a certain change of the angular velocity vector (represented in the frame of link r) given by the derivative $\dot{\omega}^r$. At the same time, there will be a force f^r (represented in frame r) acting upon the agent. Here the agent is the parent link of link r. In the absence of any child links, the equations of motion will suffice to determine $\dot{\omega}^r$ and f^r as a function of a^r. The function will be linear as expressed in equations (7) and (8) through the coefficients K^r, d^r, M^r, and $f^{\prime r}$. If there are child links, then link r will act as an agent to accelerate them. Assuming that the coefficients of (7) and (8) for the child links are known, and without knowing any of the accelerations, the coefficients for link r can be computed [3]. In this manner the coefficients for all links can be computed in an *inbound* pass towards the root link. Then, since the root is not subject to forces and torques from any parent body in the tree, we can solve the equations to get the linear and angular accelerations of all the links in an *outbound* pass toward the leaves.

3. Parallel implementation. The design of a parallel solution to these equations poses problems not encountered in the sequential case. Difficulties such as synchronizing processes, process to processor allocation, and communication overhead must be addressed [5], [6]. Synchronization overhead occurs any time a processor becomes idle, waiting for others to complete their tasks. Processor allocation deals with the problem of minimizing the possibility of two or more processes trying to use the same processor at the same time. Communication overhead is the additional burden incurred by sending messages between processes.

For example, in real-time animation of the human body, the problem can be represented by a tree-like process structure with each process representing a link. In Figure 2, processes are assigned in a one-to-one fashion to each link in the stick-figure. If two processes which are neighbors in the tree are assigned to different processors (*single-link-per-process*), there is overhead involved in their exchange of data, but only slightly more than if they are assigned to the same processor. Alternatively, this overhead can be minimized by assigning several interconnected links to the same process (*multiple-links-per-process*). Both of these approaches are examined, but for simplicity the single-link-per-process model is used to explain the distributed implementation, unless otherwise stated.

No matter whether a single-link-per-process or multiple-links-per-process model is used, each cycle (time step) of the computation proceeds in three phases. In a first outbound phase, a process waits for control information from its parent, processes it, passes it on to all its descendants, and then waits. In the following inbound phase, a process must receive data from all its descendants before it can perform its

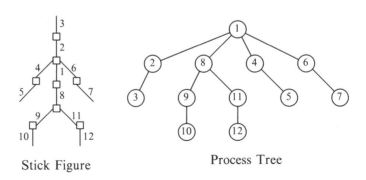

Stick Figure   Process Tree

Fig. 2. *Stick figure and the corresponding process tree.*

computations and send the results back to the parent. In particular, the computation of the quantities K^r, d^r, M^r, and f'' is done in this phase. The second outbound phase calculates the linear and angular accelerations of the links and performs part of their integration. Since not all nodes can be computing at the same time, the processes should be allocated to processors so that two processes that may be active at the same time are not on the same processor.

During initialization, the data from a non-distributed version of the dynamics program are read in and converted into the corresponding data for the distributed version. Following initialization, the dynamic equations are solved using a time step δt, whereby certain quantities are updated only every ν time steps. The functions which update the latter quantities belong to what we shall call the "slowband" computations, and the rest will be said to belong to the "fastband." The state of the simulation is graphically displayed every μ cycles.

It is worth noting at this point that the difference of execution times during fast- and slowband cycles means that an assignment of links to processes and processes to processors which is optimal for execution of the fastband may cause synchronization problems for the slowband, and vice versa. This would considerably complicate an attempt to formulate and solve the mathematical performance optimization problem.

A complete simulation cycle during the step δt, including the slowband functions and a display call, which are really only done periodically, consists of the following sequence of calls by each link process:

Outbound control pass	Inbound pass	Outbound pass
slowband_control_out fastband_control_out send_control_out	receive_data_in slowband_integration_in slowband_in fastband_in send_data_in	receive_data_out fastband_out fastband_integration_out send_data_out

An optional pass can be done during initial testing runs to verify the correctness of the solution of the equations by using the fastband_check procedure.

The control functions transmit data from a control process through the root to the various links. Again some "control" quantities may be updated in the slowband: slowband_control_out. For example there can be certain external forces and torques on links which vary slowly (like wind pressure). Other "control" quantities vary quickly (relative to δt), such as the forces of contact with the earth or other objects, and the torques generated by muscular action. These are updated in fastband_control_out. We can model contacts with the earth or with fixed or moving objects using springs and dampers. In this way the contact does not need to be considered as a constraint, which would require reformulation of the equations of motion, and perhaps loss of the efficient solution technique. In order to compute contact forces and to display the links, the root must have the orientations of all links as determined by the rotation matrices. The latter can be used to compute accurate positions and orientations of all links with respect to the root link. Passing such information inward is done by receive_data_in.

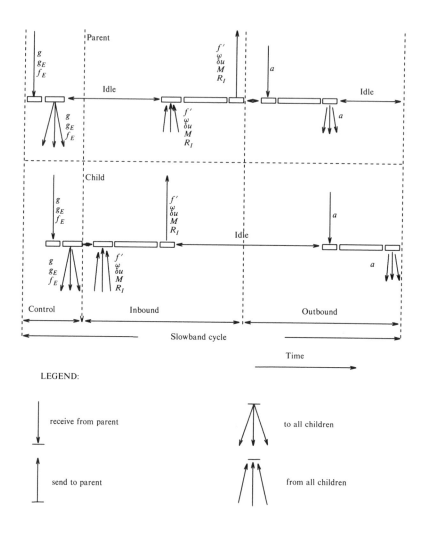

FIG. 3. *Quantities communicated between links.*

The three functions *slowband_in*, *fastband_in* and *fastband_out* perform the algebraic solution of the equations of motion. Given control forces and torques applied externally and the torques at the hinges generated by the muscles or motors, the linear accelerations of the hinges and the rates of change of the components of the angular velocity vectors of the links are determined. The *fastband_check* function determines whether the solution performed by those three functions is correct or not. The current simple integration technique in *fastband_integration_out* assumes that the previously mentioned linear and angular accelerations will be constant over the next time step. The accelerations are multiplied by δt and added to the current angular and linear velocities to get the new ones, and then the velocities are integrated again to get infinitesimal rotation vectors and positions. The *slowband_integration* call converts the infinitesimal rotation vectors into rotation matrices. To prevent accumulation of errors, the positions of the links are all derived from the root position using the rotation matrices. However, if positions are needed in the fastband for control purposes, this can be done using the results of *fastband_integration_out*. Figure 3 is a schematic view of the communications between an arbitrary interior node in the process tree, and one of its children.

4. The virtual tree machine. The facility used to solve the equations of motion is a *multi-computer* called the Virtual Tree Machine [7]. It is implemented on a network of autonomous VAX-11/780's and SUN-2 processors each running the 4.2BSD UNIX operating system [8]. The Virtual Tree Machine consists of processes under operating system control and communication paths implemented as virtual connections between processes over a local area network. The experimenter views the machine as a collection of processors (interconnected to form a tree) - each with its own local memory and peripherals. In reality, a VTM is a collection of procedures, callable from application programs, and a collection of servers, responsible for the creation of the nodes in the tree-machine according to the description provided by the user. From this description the environment is created automatically with no intervention by the user. No restriction is placed on the mapping between virtual processing elements and physical processors. During development, the whole machine might reside on one physical processor before being distributed over the selected physical machines for productive use.

The Virtual Tree Machine makes it possible to investigate issues such as synchronization, allocation and communication overhead and thus can provide valuable insight into the behavior of unavailable real machines. For example, one such machine has tree structure and high parallelism and may prove suitable for the dynamics computations [9]. Algorithms for execution on these architectures can be developed, tested and debugged using this facility, and their synchronization and communication delay properties can be studied.

5. Experimental results. Several 10-second simulations of the man-like stick figure depicted in Figure 2 were carried out. Both the *single-link-per-process* and the *multiple-link-per-process* implementations were tried. The single-link-per-process model assigns each link to its own process and then assigns processes on a path to a leaf to the same processor P_i. One such assignment is shown in Figure 4. The advantage of this method is that it ensures that information necessary for calculations within each link is made available as soon as possible. Thus, the flow of data up and down the longest path from root to leaf of the process tree determines the length of the computation cycle. The disadvantage is that the cost of communicating all the needed information between processes is high.

The solid line of Figure 5 depicts the time needed for simulation of the 12 link figure. The figure's "torso" is selected as the root of the process tree to minimize the depth of the tree and execution starts with the root reading the control information and passing it on down the tree. The children are idle until this information arrives. When the control information has propagated down to the leaves (the head and lower arms and legs of the figure) the inbound pass is started. Calculations for the inbound pass are made first in the leaf nodes and the results passed up to their parents which begin their inbound calculations only after receiving the inbound data from all their children. Once the root link has received all the inbound data from its subtrees and performed its own inbound calculations the outbound pass is started by calculating the outbound data and sending it to all the child links. Refer to Figure 3 for a graphical

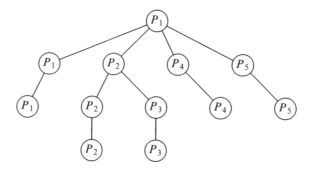

FIG. 4. *Assignment of links to twelve processes on five processors.*

representation of the communication and synchronization characteristics of this implementation.

In our simulation the time-step is set to 0.01 second. The execution time is plotted against various degrees of parallelism, from all processes assigned to one physical machine to the highest degree of useful parallelism (5 processors). For the optimal configuration of 5 processors, the execution time is reduced to 148 seconds from 227 seconds in the sequential case. It is not clear from these results whether it is the synchronization overhead or the communication overhead that plays the major role in the total overhead experienced. (The total overhead is over 100 seconds, comparing the sequential case to the single-link-per-process case when all processes run on a single machine.)

The multiple-links-per-process model eliminates the need for communication between links on the same branch by allowing each process to handle more than one link. Several links are assigned to each process, and each process is assigned to a different processor. Figure 6 shows one such assignment. Links are grouped into five processes and each process is assigned to a separate processor P_1 through P_5. Thus, only the solid lines in Figure 6 represent actual communication links. Here,

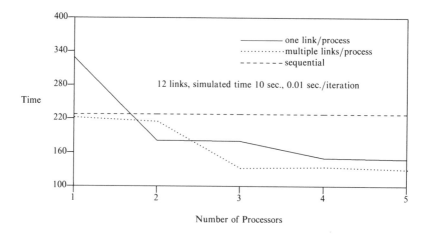

FIG. 5. *Execution time vs. number of physical processors.*

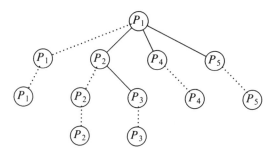

FIG. 6. *Assignment of links to five processes on five processors.*

calculations are done for all links assigned to a process before any information is sent on to its child processes or its parent. Although this reduces the communication overhead, the synchronization overhead increases as each link must wait slightly longer for the data from its parent or its children (if assigned to a different processor). The results from the multiple-links-per-process implementation are shown as the dotted line in Figure 5. The reason for the small drop in speed going from one process to two, is the fact that calculations for all links that share a process with the root link are done before any results are sent to the process handling the remaining links, resulting in almost sequential execution. For the 3 process case, the root link is given to a separate process and the remaining links are divided between the other two processes, resulting in close to parallel execution for all but one link.

Comparison of the results from these two implementations shows that the synchronization overhead rather than communication overhead is the principal cause for the lack of performance of the parallel implementations. (Eliminating much of the communication does not result in significantly better performance.) We expect that simulating several similar stick figures at once, as would be required for certain animated sequences, would reduce the effect of the synchronization overhead and permit better speedup with nearly full processor utilization. In the next section we will analytically derive formulas for estimating the maximum speedup. This will lead to a better understanding of how to use parallelism.

6. A simple model for estimating maximum speedup. To obtain an upper bound on the possible relative improvement of the VTM implementation over the sequential implementation (the "speedup"), given arbitrarily many processors, we shall consider a simple case: balanced trees of height h and fanout f. We suppose that the first control pass is nonexistent, and that the inbound pass mirrors the outbound pass as far as time is concerned, so that we can limit consideration to just the outbound pass. The speedups for the two passes are different in our case, but dealing with the synchronization of communications in both passes at once is more complex, and so we shall use the more expensive of the two passes for our estimate. We assume further that the execution time for one link is equal for all links and is t_E. Similarly all communications from a link to a child take time $t_C \leq t_E$.

Computation in the outbound pass of a tree of height $h + 1$ starts at the root link, and takes time t_E. Then the root successively communicates to $f - 1$ of its f children the information they require, taking time $(f - 1) t_C$ to do it. The same processor goes on to compute one of the subtrees of height h, while the other subtrees of height h either have started, or are just starting. If an upper bound on the total time to complete the computation for a tree of height h and fanout f is denoted by $T(h, f)$, then we have

$$T(h + 1, f) = t_E + (f - 1) t_C + T(h, f).$$

Since $T(1, f) = t_E$, we get the general formula

$$T(h, f) = t_E + (h - 1)(t_E + (f - 1) t_C).$$

The number of nodes in the tree is $(f^h - 1) / (f - 1)$, and in a sequential version the computation time would be that number times t_E. Thus the speedup resulting

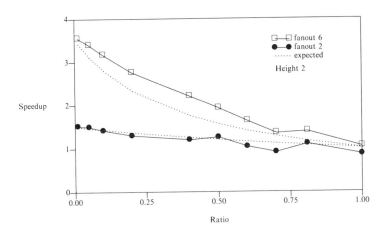

FIG. 7. *Observed speedup vs. communication to execution time ratio* (t_C/t_E).

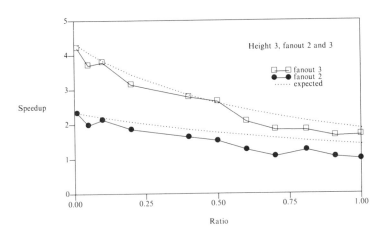

FIG. 8. *Observed speedup vs. communication to execution time ratio* (t_C/t_E).

from parallel computation is given by

$$\frac{f^h - 1}{(f - 1)\,[\,1 + (h - 1)(1 + (f - 1)\,t_C\,/\,t_E\,)]}\,.$$

For zero communication time, this becomes

$$\frac{(f^h - 1)}{(f - 1)\,h}\,.$$

When $t_C = t_E$, we get the maximum speedup

$$\frac{(f^h - 1)}{(f - 1)[\,1 + (h - 1)f\,]}\,.$$

If $h = 2$, there is no speedup at all in the latter case.

The computation time using the parallel algorithm and an unlimited supply of processors is thus theoretically shown to grow with the height of a balanced linkage tree rather than with its number of links. Considering communication times between links even as large as the execution times for the links worsens this improvement by a factor at most equal to the fanout.

Experiments were done on balanced trees using the VTM. The execution time was varied by adjusting a waiting time t_E, while t_C was measured. The observed speedups shown in Figures 7 and 8 are close to the above theoretical predictions. If we examine the speedup which could be obtained with the tree representing our stick-figure (Figure 2) by using parallelism, we get $12t_E$ compared to $4(t_E + t_C)$, for a speedup of $3/(1 + t_C/t_E)$. Averaged over both the in- and the outbound pass for the stick figure, the ratio t_C/t_E is about 0.7 which, according to the above formula, gives maximum speedup of 1.76 with five processors. This is also in close conformity to our observations.

For animation purposes, we may want to simulate several stick-figures at once, say four of them. Then t_C/t_E would be reduced by a factor of four, assuming that the cost of communication were unchanged. Then the speedup, by the above, would be 2.55, much closer to the theoretical limit of three. The synchronization overheads causing the nonlinear speedup (of three using five processors) remain, and could be dealt with by running several stick figures out of phase, so that the idle times of one stick-figure are used by others. For example, for two-stick figures on six processors, the synchronization overhead disappears if the link execution times are equal.

7. Conclusions. The parallel solution of the equations of motion of a tree-linkage using the VTM has been successful in providing a significant speedup. The speedup is a function of the tree size and configuration. The computation time using the parallel algorithm was shown to grow with the height of a balanced linkage tree rather than with its number of links. Considering communication times between links even as large as the execution times for the links worsens this exponential speedup by a factor at most equal to the fanout.

Two steps were taken which subsequently proved to be beneficial in reducing the effects of communication overheads: 1) several links were handled by a single Unix process, avoiding interprocess as well as interprocessor communications, and 2) information was not sent as soon as it became available within a process but was accumulated and sent in a single communication at the end of an iteration cycle (even though this runs counter to a dataflow philosophy).

The example of the 12-link human stick-figure which has low fanout, a height of four, and communication times which are comparable to the execution times, illustrates a case of poor speedup due to both communication and synchronization overheads. The simultaneous, in-phase simulation of several stick-figures at once would give a speedup near the maximum of three using five processors, since this reduces the ratio of communication time to execution time. To reduce synchronization overhead and approach linear speedup, several figures could be simulated out of phase so the idle times for one are used by the others.

The VTM implementation was, of course, much easier to implement and test than a physical network of processors would have been; yet the kinds of communication and synchronization problems closely reflected what could be expected in a "real" tree machine. Because there is negligible contention in the local area network while solving this problem, the VTM emulates a multiprocessor machine with point-to-point connections except for the time to form packets in the processes and ship them off serially. With more voluminous computations in the processes, and communications which better utilize the packet size, the approximation to point-to-point communications would be much closer than has been observed in the case of the stick-figure.

Many computing facilities currently use a local area network similar to the one on which the VTM is based, and hence, with the aid of VTM software, or its equivalent, it becomes possible to study parallel algorithms on networks of processors without resorting to actual construction of hardware.

Appendix: Details of the dynamics computations. The details of the dynamics computations for the VTM implementation are outlined here. No attention is paid to the control pass, since that could vary considerably depending on how control is to be achieved. In the following, the unit 3-by-3 matrix will be denoted by $\mathbf{I}$. The tilde operation on a 3-vector v, with components $v1$, $v2$, $v3$, produces a 3-by-3 matrix V such that for any 3-vector w, the vector $v \times w$ is equal to the product of V and the column-vector w.

$$\tilde{v} = V = \begin{bmatrix} 0 & -v3 & v2 \\ v3 & 0 & -v1 \\ -v2 & v1 & 0 \end{bmatrix}.$$

The following variables are also introduced in the solution since they appear as common subexpressions or are computed in the slowband and used in the fastband: W^r, T^r, Q^r, a_c^r, f'''^r.

The *receive_data_in* function gets f'^s, δu^s (which is an infinitesimal rotation vector), and ω^s from all children s of link r. In addition, during a slowband pass, *receive_data_in* gets M^s, and R_l^s. The force f'^s is the part of the force exerted by the child s on the proximal hinge which is independent of the child's acceleration. The difference between δu^s and δu^r (converted to frame s) can be used in determining a torque due to rapid changes in the angles at hinge s deriving from hinge stiffness. The difference between the omegas (the parent one converted) is similarly used for computing a frictional torque at that hinge. These quantities are treated as fast-varying, although ω, whose rate of change depends on a physical inertia, should vary slowly and could probably be placed in the slowband. (N. B. This points out a need for careful study of the rates of change of various quantities which could lead to improved simulations involving more than two bands. In such simulations, one might also determine, either beforehand or adaptively, that certain terms in our solution can be entirely neglected.)

The *slowband_integration_in* computation takes the infinitesimal rotation vector δu^r and uses it to update the rotation matrix R_I^r, resulting in a new link orientation. The result must be orthonormalized to prevent accumulation of errors.

The *slowband_in* computation for link r proceeds as follows:

Compute $a_c^s = \omega^r \times (\omega^r \times l^s)$ for $s \in S_r$. $\hfill$ (9)

Compute $Q^s = R^s M^s R^{s\,T}$ for $s \in S_r$. $\hfill$ (10)

Compute $W^s = \tilde{l}^s Q^s$ for $s \in S_r$. $\hfill$ (11)

Compute $T^r = (J^r + \sum_{s \in S_r} W^s \tilde{l}^s)^{-1}$. $\hfill$ (12)

Compute $K^r = T^r (\sum_{s \in S_r} W^s - m_r \tilde{c}^r)$. $\hfill$ (13)

Compute $M^r = (m_r \tilde{c}^r) K^r - m_r I + \sum_{s \in S_r} Q^s (I - \tilde{l}^s K^r)$. $\hfill$ (14)

Compute $g_\Sigma^{1r} = -\omega^r \times (J^r \omega^r) + R_I^{r\,T} g_E^r$ $\hfill$ (15)

$\qquad + p_E^r \times R_I^{r\,T} f_E^r + (m_r c^r) \times R_I^{r\,T} a_G$

(assuming f_E^r and g_E^r are slowly-varying).

Compute $f_\Sigma^r = -\omega^r \times (\omega^r \times (m_r c^r)) + R_I^{r\,T} (f_E^r + m_r a_G)$ $\hfill$ (16)

(assuming f_E^r is slowly-varying).

The *fastband_in* computation proceeds as follows:

Compute $f''^s = R^s f'^s$ for $s \in S_r$. $\hfill$ (17)

Compute $g_\Sigma^r = g_\Sigma^{1r} - g^r + \sum_{s \in S_r} R^s g^s$. $\hfill$ (18)

Compute $d^r = T^r (g_\Sigma^r + \sum_{s \in S_r} l^s \times (f''^s + Q^s a_c^s))$. $\hfill$ (19)

Compute $f''^r = f_\Sigma^r + (m_r c^r) \times d^r$ $\hfill$ (20)

$\qquad + \sum_{s \in S_r} (f''^s + Q^s (a_c^s - l^s \times d^r))$.

The *send_data_in* function, which occurs last in the inbound pass, provides the data to the parent for its *receive_data_in* function. In the multiple-links-per-process version, this data is, of course, not sent or received, but merely written to and accessed from the shared memory possible when only one process is involved.

Now we turn our attention to the outbound pass. The first function there is *receive_data_out*. All it does for link r is get a^r from the parent. If r is the root, this quantity must instead be computed, which is done in the following computation (equation 21). The *fastband_out* computation for link r proceeds as follows:

If r is the root then compute $a^r = -(M^r)^{-1} f''^r$. $\hfill$ (21)

Compute $\dot{\omega}^r = K^r a^r + d^r$. $\hfill$ (22)

Compute $a^s = R^{s\,T} (a_c^s + a^r - l^s \times \dot{\omega}^r)$ $\hfill$ (23)

for all children of link r.

In *fastband_integration_out*, $\dot{\omega}^r$ is multiplied by δt and the result added to ω. Then δu^r is obtained from a further integration step. The velocity and position of the root link are similarly determined by integration starting from a^1. Recall that other links have their positions determined by the root's position and link orientations. This integration technique is not stable, and development of some efficient "implicit" technique would be very useful. For animated figures, accuracy is not the goal, only realism, and the present method should be satisfactory. In an interactive system, the animator will correct for inaccuracies. Applications in robotics or biomechanics require better accuracy and stability. To the best of our knowledge, how to achieve this is an open question.

The *send_data_out* procedure merely sends a^s to all children of r. The *fastband_check* procedure goes as follows:

Receive f^s from all children.

Compute $f^r = M^r a^r + f^{\prime r}$. (24)

Compute $\dot{\omega}^r$ from equations 1 and 2, and check that it agrees with the solution value.

Compute f^r from equations 3 and 4, check that it agrees with the value computed in (24), and send it to the parent link.

REFERENCES

[1] J. WILHELMS, *Graphical simulation of the motion of articulated bodies such as humans and robots, with particular emphasis on the use of dynamic analysis*, Ph.D. Thesis, Computer Science Division, Department of Electrical Engineering and Computer Sciences, Univ. California, Berkeley, 1985.

[2] J. WILHELMS and B. BARSKY, *Using dynamic analysis to animate articulated bodies such as humans and robots*, Proc. Graphics Interface '85, Montreal (May 1985), pp. 97-104.

[3] W.W. ARMSTRONG and M.W. GREEN, *The Dynamics of articulated rigid bodies for purposes of animation*, The Visual Computer, 1 (1985), pp. 231-240 .

[4] H. KASAHARA and S. NARITA, *Parallel processing of robot-arm control computation on a multimicroprocessor system*, IEEE Journal of Robotics and Automation, RA-1 (1985), pp. 104-113 .

[5] J. MOHAN, *A Study of parallel computations - the traveling salesman problem*, Tech. Rep. CMU-CS-82-136, Dept. Comput. Sci. Carnegie Mellon Univ. (1982).

[6] T.A. MARSLAND and F. POPOWICH, *Parallel game-tree search*, IEEE Transactions on Pattern Analysis and Machine Intelligence, PAMI-7 (1985), pp. 442-452 .

[7] M. OLAFSSON and T.A. MARSLAND, *A UNIX based virtual tree machine*, CIPS Congress '85, Montreal (June 1985), pp. 176-181.

[8] D. M. RITCHIE and K. THOMPSON, *The UNIX time-sharing system*, Bell Sys. Tech. J., 57 (1978), pp. 1905-1929 .

[9] *Myrias 4000 System Description*, Myrias Research Corporation, Edmonton, February 1986.

SIAM J. SCI. STAT. COMPUT.
Vol. 8, No. 1, January 1987

DESIGN AND ANALYSIS OF PARALLEL MONTE CARLO ALGORITHMS*

V. C. BHAVSAR† AND J. R. ISAAC‡

Abstract. This paper demonstrates that the potential of intrinsic parallelism in Monte Carlo methods, which has remained essentially untapped so far, can be exploited to implement these methods efficiently on SIMD and MIMD computers. Two basic static and dynamic computation assignment schemes are proposed for assigning the primary estimate computations (PECs) to processors in a parallel computer. These schemes can be used to design parallel Monte Carlo algorithms for many applications. The time complexity analyses of static computation assignment (SCA) schemes are carried out using some results from order statistics, whereas those of dynamic computation assignment (DCA) schemes are carried out using results from order statistics, renewal and queueing theories. It is shown that for smaller number of processors, linear speedup can be achieved with the SCA schemes and the speedup almost equal to the number of processors can be achieved with the DCA schemes. Some computational results for Monte Carlo solutions of Laplace's equation are given to illustrate the performance of the various SCA and DCA schemes.

Key words. Monte Carlo methods, parallel algorithms, parallel computers, analysis of algorithms, order statistics, renewal theory, pseudorandom number generators, partial differential equations

AMS(MOS) subject classifications. 35J05, 60J15, 60K05, 60K10, 62E25, 62G30, 65C05, 65W05, 68Q25

1. Introduction. Monte Carlo methods are widely used in many scientific and engineering applications [11], [12], [18], [19], [36], [37]. In these methods, the solution of a problem is represented as a parameter of a hypothetical population. Then, a random sequence of numbers is used to construct a sample of that population from which statistical estimates of the parameter are obtained [18]. The solution estimates converge slowly (expected error is proportional to $(1/\sqrt{K})$, where K is the sample size) to the exact solution and therefore a large sample size (K equal to 10^3 to 10^5 is quite common) is required to obtain a reasonable accuracy. The estimate computations often involve random walk processes, with some random walks consisting of a large number of steps. As a consequence of these two characteristics, these methods require large computing time when implemented on sequential computers and they have not been very attractive. In this paper, we present some techniques of implementing these methods on parallel computers with a motivation to reduce their execution time and we hope that this will make these techniques more attractive in the future. Recently, Monte Carlo simulation has been identified as one of the most challenging areas for the application of parallel computers [20].

Parallel algorithms can be developed by exploiting the intrinsic parallelism in sequential algorithms. Intrinsic parallelism in Monte Carlo methods at the level of primary estimate computations (PECs) was first indicated, surprisingly, as early as in 1949 by Metropolis and Ulam in their paper defining the Monte Carlo method [30]. Parallelism at this level, as also within the computations of primary estimates, was exploited only to some extent in [33], [34] to solve partial differential equations (PDEs) on special purpose parallel computers. Thus, the potential of intrinsic parallelism in Monte Carlo methods had remained essentially untapped in their implementation on parallel computers, until our recent work [2]-[10]. Recently, the application of ICL

---

* Received by the editors November 20, 1985; accepted for publication (in revised form) March 28, 1986.

† School of Computer Science, University of New Brunswick, Fredericton, New Brunswick, Canada E3B 5A3.

‡ Department of Computer Science and Engineering, Indian Institute of Technology, Bombay, 400076, India.

DAP in solving some problems in solid-state and elementary particle physics has been reported [12].

In [2], we suggested the use of an SIMD computer, based on bit-slice microprocessors, to implement Monte Carlo methods for solving PDEs. In [3] simulation results about the effectiveness of SIMD and MIMD computer architectures for solving PDEs by Monte Carlo methods were presented. We have given some parallel algorithms for Monte Carlo solutions of linear equations in [4]. The Monte Carlo methods for solving PDEs were reconsidered in [5] and the simulation results of a parallel algorithm based on an idea by Rosin [33] were presented. This preliminary work culminated in the development of a unified treatment for the design and analysis of parallel Monte Carlo algorithms given in [6]. Recently, we have also considered the problem of implementing Monte Carlo algorithms with VLSI technology [9], [10]. In this paper, we detail some of the ideas presented in earlier papers and present the unified treatment given in [6].

This paper is organized as follows. In § 2, we briefly discuss the computational characteristics of Monte Carlo methods and show that the primary estimate computation (PEC) times are independent and identically distributed (i.i.d.) random variables. This crucial result is shown to have significant influence on the design and analysis of parallel Monte Carlo algorithms in § 3. We propose two basic schemes for assigning PECs to processors in a parallel computer: static computation assignment (SCA) and dynamic computation assignment (DCA) schemes. These schemes can be used to design parallel algorithms for any Monte Carlo method. In § 4, we describe the various SCA schemes. The details of the parallel algorithms are not included for the sake of brevity and they are given in [6]. The time complexity analyses of parallel Monte Carlo algorithms based on these schemes are carried out using some results from order statistics. Two DCA schemes are presented in § 5. The time complexity analyses of these schemes are carried out using results from order statistics, renewal and queueing theories. In § 6, we consider the standardized exponentially distributed PEC times and derive the time complexity results for the SCA and DCA schemes. We consider the problem of solving Laplace's equation by a Monte Carlo method in § 7. Some computational results illustrating the performance of the various schemes are presented. Concluding remarks are given in § 8.

2. Sequential Monte Carlo algorithms.

2.1. The Monte Carlo method. The Monte Carlo method is generally defined as representing the solution of a problem as a parameter of a hypothetical population, and using a random sequence of numbers to construct a sample of the population, from which statistical estimates of the parameter can be obtained [18]. In practice, usually, the required solution consists of a real number, which is expressed as the expected value of some random variable X with finite variance on a probability space. A set of points $\zeta_1, \zeta_2, \cdots, \zeta_K$ are sampled *independently* from the probability space, commonly using pseudorandom or quasirandom number generators. In our discussion, we will assume that "ideal" random number generators are used. A set of primary estimates, $X(\zeta_1), X(\zeta_2), \cdots, X(\zeta_K)$ are obtained. The secondary estimate of the solution is obtained by the arithmetic mean

$$(1) \qquad Y = Y(\zeta_1, \zeta_2, \cdots, \zeta_K) = \frac{1}{K} \sum_{i=1}^{K} X(\zeta_i),$$

which converges to the required solution in quadratic mean, in probability, and with probability one, as $K \to \infty$. The sampling of each point ζ_i from the population of the probability space often involves lengthy computations, such as tracing a random walk in an intricate and highly inhomogeneous space. In these cases, determination of a primary estimate usually consists of a run through either an absorbing or an ergodic Markov chain. For example, such computations are involved in Monte Carlo solutions of linear algebraic equations [18], partial differential equations [34], and many other applications [11], [12], [37].

2.2. Time complexity of sequential Monte Carlo algorithms. In general, the primary estimate computations (PECs) have the following characteristics.

C1. They are essentially *independent* of each other because $\zeta_1, \zeta_2, \cdots, \zeta_K$ are sampled independently from the probability space using ideal random number generators.

C2. They consist of the execution of *identical* steps.

C3. Their execution times are, in general, random variables because: (i) they may consist of a run through an absorbing Markov chain (i.e., a random walk) and the number of state transitions determines their execution times, and (ii) the number of comparisons required to make decisions based on a sample from random number generators is variable.

LEMMA 1. *The PEC execution times are independent and identically distributed (i.i.d.) random variables.*

Proof. The PEC execution times are random variables due to C3. The property of independency follows from C1 and identicalness follows from C2. □

This is a very crucial result in the design and analysis of parallel Monte Carlo algorithms, as discussed in § 3.

Now, let μ and σ^2 denote the mean and variance of the i.i.d. PEC times. Also, let $T(1, K)$ denote the time complexity of a sequential Monte Carlo algorithm in computing K primary estimates. Since in many applications of the Monte Carlo method the secondary estimate computation time turns out to be much smaller than the PEC times, in the ensuing analysis we will not take into account this time; if this time is not negligible in some cases, the time complexity results given in this paper can be trivially modified, as shown in [6].

THEOREM 1. *The time complexity of a sequential Monte Carlo algorithm carrying out K PECs, $T(1, K)$, has the expectation $E[T(1, K)] = K.\mu$, and the variance Var $[T(1, K)] = K.\sigma^2$.*

Proof. Follows directly from Lemma 1. □

Thus, it is seen that a sequential Monte Carlo algorithm has $O(K)$ expected time complexity and also $O(K)$ time complexity variance. In practice, it is required to choose a large value of K (10^3 to 10^5 is not uncommon) in order to attain a reasonable accuracy and hence by the Central Limit theorem it follows that $T(1, K)$ will tend to follow a normal distribution with mean $(K.\mu)$ and variance $(K.\sigma^2)$. The cumulative distribution function of a sequential Monte Carlo algorithm can be easily found out by using Theorem 1 and the techniques discussed in [6], [32].

3. Design and analysis of parallel Monte Carlo algorithms—approach and assumptions. In this section, we discuss our approach for the development of parallel Monte Carlo algorithms. First, we detail the intrinsic parallelism in Monte Carlo methods, identified in our earlier papers [2]–[5] and discuss its implications in the design of the parallel algorithms and formulate our approach. We introduce two basic schemes for the development of parallel Monte Carlo algorithms. Finally, we state the assumptions which are used in the time complexity analysis of parallel algorithms.

3.1. Intrinsic parallelism. We identify the intrinsic parallelism in Monte Carlo methods at four levels as follows.

(1) *Parallelism between computations of variables.* In Monte Carlo methods for problems involving many variables, the estimates of each of the variables can usually be obtained *independently* of the remaining variables and consequently their computations can be executed in parallel. For example, the estimates of each of the unknowns in a set of linear algebraic equations can be obtained independently of the other unknowns [18], [4]. The complete independence of the computations of variables implies that the computational modules' granularities will be large and therefore these computations are very well suited for implementation on MIMD computer architectures.

Further, the computational algorithms of each of these variables are usually *identical*, but use different data. As a result, these computations are also very well suited for implementation on SIMD computer architectures.

We have for the first time exploited the intrinsic parallelism at this level and used it in solving a set of linear algebraic equations [4].

(2) *Parallelism in secondary estimate computation.* As defined in § 2, the secondary estimate of the desired solution is usually obtained by averaging the values of K primary estimates. In an SIMD computer, this summation can obviously be carried out in $\lceil \log_2 K \rceil$ time steps, if required interprocessor communication network is available. In an MIMD computer, some part of the summation time may be overlapped with other computations, as shown in ensuing sections. We have exploited the parallelism at this level in solving linear algebraic equations [4] and partial differential equations [5].

(3) *Parallelism between different PECs.* The required K PECs to be carried out for a variable are completely independent of each other (the characteristic C1). Consequently, these PECs can be executed in parallel. Since each of the PECs often involves a lengthy computation, the computational module granularities are large enough to make these computations suitable for implementation on MIMD computers. Moreover, the PECs are also very well suited for implementation on SIMD computers due to the characteristic C2.

The parallelism at this level was hinted at as early as in 1949, by Metropolis and Ulam [30], in their paper defining the Monte Carlo method. However, its use was first suggested in [33] and subsequently it was also exploited in [34] for solving PDEs with special purpose computers. In [33] the use of a drum array processor was suggested, whereas in [34] a macro-modular computer was used. Recently, we have exploited the parallelism at this level in solving linear algebraic equations and PDEs on SIMD and MIMD computers.

(4) *Parallelism in a PEC.* In general, a PEC involves: (i) multidimensional random number generation, (ii) updating the value of a primary estimate based on a sample from random number generators, and (iii) determination of the value of a termination condition for the computation. The intrinsic parallelism exists in all these steps.

The generation of each of the components in multidimensional random number generation can be carried out in parallel. In updating the value of a primary estimate, the intervals in which a random number sample falls has to be determined and this involves many decision operations, which can be executed in parallel. Finally, the step (iii) also involves many comparison operations, which can be carried out in parallel.

In [34] pipelining has been used to reduce the execution time, whereas in [2] we have suggested the use of hardware random number generators.

3.2. Design approach. From the above discussion, it is now evident that Monte Carlo methods have a large potential for intrinsic parallelism, which has remained almost untapped so far. Further, this intrinsic parallelism can be exploited equally well for implementation on SIMD as well as MIMD computers.

In our design and analysis of parallel Monte Carlo algorithms, we consider the intrinsic parallelism only between the computations of different PECs for a variable, because these computations primarily determine the order of the time complexities of these algorithms. The results given in this paper can be trivially extended for problems involving the estimation of more than one variables, because such computations are independent of each other. If the intrinsic parallelism within each of the PECs is exploited, this usually changes the time complexity only by some constant, its order remaining unchanged.

We view the problem of designing parallel Monte Carlo algorithms exploiting the intrinsic parallelism between the PECs, as that of the assignment of PECs to processors in a parallel computer, the PEC times being i.i.d. random variables. Alternatively, each PEC can be considered as a task with random execution time. Then, we will have tasks with i.i.d. execution times and the problem can be considered as basically the scheduling of independent tasks onto multiple processors with task execution times as i.i.d. random variables.

Although the problem of scheduling a set of tasks on multiple processors has been discussed in literature, much of it assumes constant execution times (see e.g. [13], [16], [25]), and only the treatment in [1], [26], [32] is with the task execution times as random variables. Motivated by the problem decomposition strategies proposed in [32], we propose two basic schemes, static and dynamic, for the assignment of PECs to processors in a parallel computer. In a static computation assignment (SCA) scheme, a *fixed* number of PECs are assigned to each of the processors *before* any PECs are initiated. In contrast, in a dynamic computation assignment (DCA) scheme, the number of PECs carried out by each processor is determined *during* the computations, based on some global criteria.

In the SCA schemes, very small (if at all) time overheads are incurred to make the computation assignment decisions during the computations. The parallel algorithms based on these schemes cannot adapt to the variations in the PEC times (which are random variables), in the sense that the computation time is minimized based on the run-time behavior. In DCA schemes, since the assignment of PECs to processors is done during execution, the execution time of a parallel algorithm can be minimized based on its run-time behavior. Obviously, a larger time overhead is incurred in making the computation assignment decisions. It should be noted that these schemes can be used for developing parallel algorithms for almost any Monte Carlo method and hence are fundamental in nature. The various SCA and DCA schemes for parallel Monte Carlo algorithms are discussed in §§ 4 and 5.

Since usually a large number of primary estimates are used, parallel Monte Carlo algorithms may involve simultaneous operation of a large number of pseudorandom number (PRN) generators. Obviously, PRN sequences of smaller lengths will be used on each of the processors, compared to the corresponding sequential algorithms. Thus, the PRN generators should be such that the PRN sequences generated exhibit desired statistical properties for smaller lengths. In addition, the PRN sequences generated in various processors, pooled together, should satisfy the desirable properties, e.g., small cross-correlation. These and other issues related to the pseudo-random number generation are discussed in [28], [29].

3.3. Analysis of parallel Monte Carlo algorithms. In many Monte Carlo applications, PEC time distributions cannot be determined a priori. In some cases, even if it may be possible to determine the distributions, the computations involved may be too time consuming. For example, the determination of the expectation of PEC times in solving an elliptic PDE itself involves the solution of another elliptic PDE, i.e., the problem of determining the expectation has the same order of time complexity as that of the problem being solved with the Monte Carlo method [6]. Therefore in the analysis of parallel Monte Carlo algorithms we obtain the time complexity results which are independent of the probability distributions of the PEC times (i.e. distribution-free) and in closed forms.

As in sequential Monte Carlo algorithms, we assume that the secondary estimate computation time is negligible. Further, we assume, as usual in literature (see e.g. [21], [26], [32]): (i) the use of identical processors, (ii) the register load/store and communication costs as negligible, (iii) no memory or data alignment penalties, and (iv) any one of the four arithmetic operations being performed in one time unit. Further in the analysis of MIMD algorithms, we assume, as in [32]: (i) for any runnable process a processor is always assigned, and (ii) initially all runnable processes start execution at the same time. Finally, to enable easier comparison of the performance of various algorithms we assume that, in a parallel algorithm the PEC time characteristics (e.g. their mean, variance, etc.) remain exactly same as in the corresponding sequential algorithm. This implies that, for example, the possible increase in the PEC times due to conditional branches in a SIMD algorithm (see [27]) is considered as negligible. Also, the consequences of multiprocessor system characteristics, as discussed in [1], [32], are neglected. However, such changes in the PEC times can be *implicitly* taken into account by suitably modifying the statistical characteristics of the PEC times. As a consequence of the stated assumptions, the computational time behavior and the time complexities of the SIMD and MIMD algorithms corresponding to a sequential algorithm, will turn out to be the same.

Since the PEC times are random variables, in the analysis of parallel Monte Carlo algorithms we have to employ the techniques of order statistics, queueing theory, and renewal theory, as discussed in §§ 4 and 5.

4. Static computation assignment (SCA) schemes. In SCA schemes for parallel Monte Carlo algorithms, we assign a fixed number of PECs to the processors before any PECs are initiated, as discussed in § 3. We propose four SCA schemes for the development of SIMD and MIMD algorithms, dependent upon the number of processors (P) used:

    (i) SCA Scheme 1: $P \ll K$,
    (ii) SCA Scheme 2: $K/P \sim 10$,
    (iii) SCA Scheme 3: $P = K$,
    (iv) SCA Scheme 4: $P > K$.

In the Schemes 1 and 2, we assign K PECs among P processors in such a way that their sum is equal to K and each processor is assigned the same number of PECs, as far as possible; obviously, if P divides K exactly then we will assign (K/P) PECs to each of the processors. In Scheme 3, we assign only one PEC to each of the processors. In Scheme 4 also we assign one PEC to each of the processors, but terminate the computations in all active processors once K PECs are completed. The first three schemes can be considered to be as the mere special cases of a single scheme. However, we have chosen to treat them separately because the SIMD and MIMD algorithms based on them differ (see [6] for details) and moreover their analyses have to be carried out differently.

4.1. SCA Scheme 1. Assume that $M = (K/P)$, where M is an integer. Then, in this scheme we would obtain K primary estimates when all the processors complete M PECs assigned to each of them. The expected time complexity of SIMD and MIMD algorithms based on this scheme is given in the following.

THEOREM 2. *The expected time complexity of parallel Monte Carlo algorithms based on* SCA *Scheme* 1 *is given as*

(2)
$$\frac{K\mu}{P} \leq E[T(P, K)] \leq \frac{K\mu}{P} + \frac{\sqrt{K}.\sigma}{2}.$$

Proof. The execution time of the ith processor in carrying out M PECs, say t_i, is given by the sum of the execution times of each of the PECs. By Lemma 1, the PEC times are i.i.d. random variables and therefore the computation times $t_1, t_2, \cdots, t_P$ will also be i.i.d. random variables. Since $P \ll K$, M will be a large number and then by the Central Limit theorem it follows that t_i's will follow a normal distribution with mean $(M.\mu)$ and variance $(M.\sigma^2)$.

The execution time of the parallel algorithms, $T(P, K)$, is given by the random variable

$$T(P, K) = \max [t_1, t_2, \cdots, t_P].$$

Thus $T(P, K)$ represents the extreme order statistic of the i.i.d. normal random variables, $t_1, t_2, \cdots, t_P$. Since a closed form expression is not available for such an order statistic, we use the upper bound on the extreme order statistic for any symmetrically distributed i.i.d. random variables given in [17, p. 62] and obtain the upper bound given in the theorem.

The lower bound on the time complexity follows from the fact that $E[\max (t_1, t_2, \cdots, t_P)] \geq \max [E(t_1), E(t_2), \cdots, E(t_P)] = M.\mu$, which is true for any set of random variables. $\square$

Thus, SCA Scheme 1 parallel Monte Carlo algorithms have $O(K)$ expected time complexity and, comparing with the time complexity of sequential Monte Carlo algorithms, they achieve $O(P)$ speedup, i.e. linear speedup.

If $P = 2$, then the expected time complexity of these parallel algorithms can be given as [26]

(3)
$$E[T(P, K)] \cong \frac{K\mu}{P} + \sqrt{\frac{K}{\pi P}} . \sigma \quad \text{as } K \to \infty.$$

4.2. SCA Scheme 2. In this scheme, we have $(K/P) = M \sim 10$ and we assign K PECs among P processors, as in Scheme 1. In Scheme 1, since M is large, the i.i.d. random variables $t_1, t_2, \cdots, t_P$ were considered as normal, whereas in this scheme, since M is smaller, such an approximation may not be acceptable.

THEOREM 3. *The SIMD and MIMD algorithms based on Scheme 2 have the expected time complexity*

(4)
$$\frac{K\mu}{P} \leq E[T(P, K)] \leq \frac{K\mu}{P} + \frac{(P-1)\sqrt{K}}{\sqrt{(2P-1)P}} . \sigma.$$

Proof. The upper bound follows from the distribution-free upper bound on the extreme order statistic of i.i.d. random variables given in [15, pp. 46–47] and the lower bound remains same as in Theorem 2. $\square$

In practice, K is usually a large number (10^3 to 10^5 is not uncommon) and since $K/P \sim 10$, we will usually have $P \gg 1$. In this case, the upper bound in (4) can be simplified to the following:

$$E[T(P, K)] \leq \frac{K\mu}{P} + \sqrt{\frac{K}{2}} \cdot \sigma.$$

It can be easily seen that the lower bound on the speedup for SCA Scheme 2 parallel algorithms will be $O(\sqrt{P})$.

4.3. SCA Scheme 3. In this scheme, we assign one PEC to each processor. Thus the execution time of the parallel algorithms based on this scheme will be given by the extreme order statistic of K i.i.d. random variables represented by PEC times and we have the following.

THEOREM 4. *The SCA Scheme 3 parallel Monte Carlo algorithms have the expected time complexity*

$$(5) \qquad\qquad \mu \leq E[T(P, K)] \leq \mu + \frac{(K-1) \cdot \sigma}{\sqrt{(2K-1)}}.$$

Proof. Follows directly by using the distribution-free upper bound on the extreme order statistic given in [15]. □

The asymptotic time complexity of these parallel algorithms will be given as

$$(6) \qquad\qquad \mu \leq E[T(P, K)] \leq \mu + O(\sqrt{K})$$

with asymptotic speedup over the corresponding sequential algorithms as

$$O(\sqrt{K}) \leq S(K, K) \leq K.$$

In a Scheme 3 SIMD algorithm, we would use a global counter to keep track of the completed PECs. The global counter will be updated by only one processor at a time and the remaining processors in the SIMD computer will be idle. Consequently, the time complexity result would get modified to the following:

$$(7) \qquad\qquad \mu + K\tau \leq E[T(K, K)] \leq \mu + \frac{(K-1)\sigma}{\sqrt{(2K-1)}} + K\tau$$

where τ is the time required to update the global counter by a processor. Thus, the expected time complexity will turn out to be $O(K)$, whereas by neglecting such an updating time, the lower bound is a constant and the upper bound is $O(\sqrt{K})$. This demonstrates that the sequential program segments in an SIMD algorithm may increase the order of time complexity. In Scheme 3 MIMD algorithms, the global counter updating time may not contribute much time overhead, because this time will be overlapped with the PEC times of active processors.

It is interesting to compare the cumulative distribution function (cdf) of the time complexity of sequential Monte Carlo algorithms with the Scheme 3 parallel algorithms. In the sequential algorithms, the cdf will be given by the *K-fold convolution*, whereas in the parallel algorithms it is given by the Kth *power* [6]. Consequently, the variance of the time complexity of parallel Monte Carlo algorithms will turn out to be much smaller than that of the corresponding sequential algorithms. This is an attractive feature of these parallel algorithms.

4.4. SCA Scheme 4. In this scheme, we have $P > K$. We assign one PEC to each processor with a motivation to minimize the execution time of the parallel Monte Carlo algorithms by terminating the execution soon after we have K PECs completed out of the initiated P PECs. Unfortunately, this may result in a *biased* estimate of the desired solution as discussed below.

In Monte Carlo methods, the execution time of PECs is usually related to either the number of terms considered from a finite or an infinite series (e.g. Neumann series used in solving linear equations [18]), or the lengths of random walks (e.g. studies in nuclear physics [37], molecular chemistry [19]). As a result, the execution time is related to the accuracy of the estimates obtained. In the present scheme, since we always choose the earliest completing K PECs, we are effectively limiting the number of terms from a series or truncating lengths of random walks. Consequently, in this scheme we may obtain *biased* estimates.

In [6], we have given an SIMD algorithm based on this scheme. We have also given two MIMD algorithms, one with and the other without interruption of processes, as suggested in [26].

The time complexity of Scheme 4 parallel Monte Carlo algorithms is represented by the Kth order statistic of P i.i.d. PEC times, with $P > K$. Unfortunately, distribution-free closed form expressions are not possible for such an order statistic. However, tables are available for normal distribution (see [15, p. 28]), gamma distribution, logistic distribution, etc. (see [15, pp. 226–227]). In § 6 we give the expected time complexity results for Scheme 4 parallel algorithms, when the PEC times are exponentially distributed i.i.d. random variables.

5. Dynamic computation assignment (DCA) schemes. In DCA parallel Monte Carlo algorithms, whenever a PEC (or a set of PECs) is completed on a processor, the decision as to whether or not to initiate another PEC (or another set of PECs) on that processor is made during the execution, based on some global criteria. The main motivation is to minimize their execution time. Here, we propose two basic schemes for such parallel algorithms. Scheme 1 can be used in the development of parallel Monte Carlo algorithms employing arbitrary number of processors. Scheme 2 is designed specifically for implementations with $P < K$. The closed form distribution-free time complexity results for these parallel algorithms can be obtained only when $P \ll K$ and hence we consider here only such cases in the time complexity analysis.

5.1. DCA Scheme 1. In this scheme, given P processors, first we initiate P PECs in parallel. Whenever a PEC is completed on a processor, we initiate another PEC on that processor, if K PECs have not already been completed. Obviously, in this scheme we will initiate more than the required K PECs. The details of the parallel Monte Carlo algorithms are given in [6].

Figure 1 illustrates a possible execution time profile for DCA Scheme 1 parallel algorithms (under various assumptions stated in § 3) in obtaining nine primary estimates with three processors, P1, P2, and P3. The time $t_j^{(i)}$ represents the time instant at which the jth PEC is completed by the ith processor. The behavior of the parallel algorithms, taking into account computations on all the three processors, is represented by the virtual processor P^*. For P^*, time t_i represents the time instant at which the ith PEC is completed. It is seen that, when the required number of PECs are completed, the incomplete PECs on the remaining $(P-1)$ processors get aborted. Consequently, in this scheme (as in SCA Scheme 4) we may obtain biased estimates. The aborted computation time is significant only in MIMD algorithms; in SIMD algorithms this time is not significant, because if these $(P-1)$ processors did not carry out the computations which later got aborted, any way they would have been idle. In order to eliminate the wasteful computations in the DCA Scheme 1 MIMD algorithms, we give DCA Scheme 2 in the next subsection.

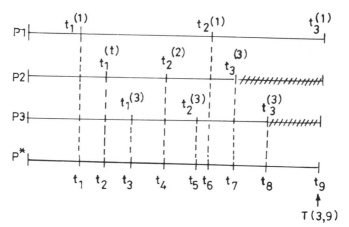

FIG. 1. *A possible execution time profile for* DCA *Scheme* 1 *parallel Monte Carlo algorithms.* P1, P2, P3: *Processors.* P*: *Virtual processor representing the execution time behavior of the parallel algorithms.* ⸺ PEC *times.* ⫫ *aborted computation time.*

THEOREM 5. *The* DCA *Scheme* 1 *parallel Monte Carlo algorithms, carrying out K complete PECs with P processors, have the expected time complexity*

(8)
$$E[T(P, K)] \cong \frac{K\mu}{P} + \frac{(P-1)(\mu^2 - \sigma^2)}{2P\mu}.$$

Proof. The time $t_j^{(i)}$, as shown in Fig. 1, represents the sum of j i.i.d. PEC times. Hence, the computational behavior of the ith processor is an ordinary renewal process [14, p. 25].

Since all the PEC times are i.i.d. random variables, a DCA Scheme 1 parallel algorithm consists of P independent ordinary renewal processes in simultaneous operation, all with the same probability distribution. Therefore, the behavior of the parallel algorithm, represented by P*, can be considered as the behavior of the superposition of the constituent P ordinary renewal processes. Then, the theorem follows by using the result in [14, pp. 73–75]. □

Thus, DCA Scheme 1 parallel Monte Carlo algorithms have $O(K)$ expected time complexity and comparing with the time complexity of sequential algorithms, they achieve speedup approximately *equal* to P, i.e., ideal speedup. If K is large, as usually it will be, then the computing time on each processor can be considered as normally distributed and then by using the result in [14, p. 73] we have

(9) $\text{Var}[T(P, K)] = \text{Var}[T(1, K)]/P^2.$

Again, this shows that the variance of the time complexity of parallel algorithms may be much smaller than that of corresponding sequential algorithms.

In DCA Scheme 1 MIMD algorithms, we will have a critical region to update the global counter for keeping track of completed PECs and to update the secondary estimate. If the critical region execution time for the constituent processes in such parallel algorithms is not to be neglected and the contention among them to execute the critical region is considered, then behavior of these algorithms can be modelled as a queueing system, similar to the models of time shared computer systems as shown in Fig. 2. Such a queueing system has been extensively studied as a model of single processor time shared computer systems (see [35, pp. 27–31], [23, pp. 144–154]), when

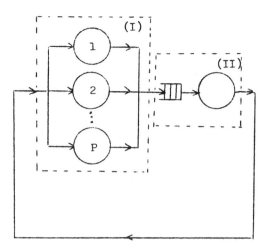

FIG. 2. *A queueing system model for DCA Scheme 1 MIMD algorithms. A. P Customers in the whole system: P processes. B. P Servers in system* I: *PECs on P processors. C.* 1 *Server in system* II: *the critical region execution. D. At most P servers active at the same time in the entire system.*

the probability distributions of all the servers are exponential. Assuming that the mean critical region execution time is equal to τ_c, the steady-state probability that no process will be executing the critical region is given by

(10) $$\pi_0 = \frac{1}{\sum_{j=0}^{P} (P! \, r^j / (P-j)!)} \quad \text{where } r = (\tau_c / \mu).$$

Since $P \ll K$, each process will execute a large number of PECs and therefore the steady-state solution is justifiable. Then, the expected time complexity of DCA Scheme 1 MIMD algorithms will be given as

(11) $$E[T(P, K)] = \frac{\tau_c \cdot K}{(1 - \pi_0)}.$$

5.2. DCA Scheme 2. This scheme is designed specifically for MIMD algorithms. In this scheme, given P processors, first we initiate P PECs in parallel. Whenever a PEC is complete, we initiate another PEC on that processor only if the required K PECs have not been already initiated. Thus, in this scheme we initiate only K PECs and therefore no PECs get aborted as in DCA Scheme 1.

Figure 3 illustrates a possible execution time profile the DCA Scheme 2 parallel Monte Carlo algorithms, assuming that nine primary estimates are to be computed using three processors. It is seen that, when the ninth PEC is initiated at time t_9^*, six PECs are already complete and two are in progress. When the longest of these three PECs completes at time t_9, we obtain the required nine primary estimates. Thus, in general, when Kth PEC is initiated, $(K-P)$ PECs are already complete and $(P-1)$ PECs are in progress. When the largest of these P PECs terminates, we obtain the required K primary estimates.

THEOREM 6. *The DCA Scheme* 2 MIMD *algorithms, carrying out K PECs with P processors* (P $\ll$ K) *have the expected time complexity*

(12) $$\tau \lesssim E[T(P, K)] \lesssim \tau + \frac{(P-1) \cdot \sigma}{\sqrt{(2P-1)}}$$

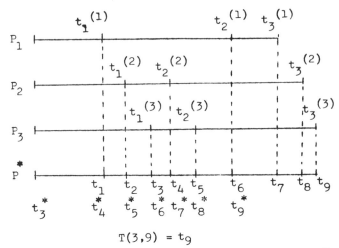

$$T(3,9) = t_9$$

FIG. 3. *A possible execution time profile for DCA Scheme 2 MIMD algorithms.* $t_j^{(i)}$: *time at which jth PEC is completed by the ith processor.* t_i: *time at which ith PEC is completed in the parallel algorithm.* t_i^*: *time at which ith PEC is initiated in the parallel algorithm.*

where

$$\tau \cong \frac{K\mu}{P} + \frac{(P-1)(\mu^2 - \sigma^2)}{2P\mu}.$$

Proof. When the Kth PEC is initiated, $(K-P)$ PECs are complete, say at time $t_{(P-K)}$. The time $t_{(P-K)}$ is a random variable representing the time instant at which $(K-P)$ renewals are completed in the superposed renewal process of the constituent P ordinary renewal processes, each ordinary renewal process comprising the i.i.d. PEC times. Therefore, by using the result in [14, p. 75], the expectation of $t_{(P-K)}$ will be given as

(13) $$E[t_{(P-K)}] \cong \frac{(K-P)\mu}{P} + \frac{(P-1)(\mu^2 - \sigma^2)}{2P\mu}.$$

Immediately after $t_{(P-K)}$, we have one new PEC and $(P-1)$ PECs already in progress. Then, the additional time required after $t_{(P-K)}$ to complete these P PECs, say t_P, will be given as

(14)
$$t_P = \max\,[\text{residual times of } (P-1) \text{ PECs, lifetime of new PEC}]$$
$$= \max\,[t_r^{(1)}, t_r^{(2)}, \cdots, t_r^{(P-1)}, t_m]$$

where $t_r^{(i)}$ is a random variable representing the residual lifetime of ith PEC, and t_m is the random variable representing the lifetime of the new PEC. The time t_P is the extreme order statistic of independent, but *not* identically distributed, P random variables. Since distribution-free closed form expressions are not possible for the expectation of the right-hand side of (14), we obtain the upper bound on the expectation of t_P as

(15)
$$E[t_P] \leq \max\,[\text{lifetimes of } P \text{ PECs}]$$
$$= \mu + \frac{(P-1) \cdot \sigma}{\sqrt{(2P-1)}}.$$

The lower bound on $E[t_P]$ is given as follows.

$$E[t_P] = E[\max\{t_r^{(1)}, t_r^{(2)}, \cdots, t_r^{(P-1)}, t_m\}]$$

(16)
$$\geq \max \{E[t_r^{(1)}], E[t_r^{(2)}], \cdots, E[t_r^{(P-1)}], E[t_m]\}$$

$$\geq \mu.$$

Now, the theorem follows from (14), (15) and (16). $\square$

Thus, the DCA Scheme 2 MIMD algorithms have $O(K)$ time complexity and, comparing with sequential algorithms, they achieve speedup approximately equal to P.

The time complexity results for the various SCA and DCA schemes are summarized in Table 1.

6. An example. In this section, we illustrate the performance of the sequential and parallel Monte Carlo algorithms, when the PEC times are standardized i.i.d. exponential random variables; i.e. their mean $\mu = 1$, standard deviation $\sigma = 1$, and their probability distribution function (pdf) given by

(17)
$$f(t) = e^{-t} \qquad (t \geq 0).$$

Then the pdf of the time complexity of sequential Monte Carlo algorithms will be given by

(18)
$$F_{(1,K)} = K\text{-fold convolution of } f(t)$$
$$= \frac{t^{(K-1)} \cdot e^{-t}}{(K-1)!}.$$

Since in practice usually K is large, the random variable $T(1, K)$ will be asymptotically normally distributed. Further, we have

(19)
$$E[T(1, K)] = K, \quad \text{and}$$

(20)
$$\text{Var}[T(1, K)] = K.$$

6.1. Performance of SCA schemes. The performance of Schemes 1 and 2 found out by using (2), (4), and (5) is given in Table 1.

In Scheme 3, the cdf of the execution time of the parallel algorithms will be given by

(21)
$$F_{(K,K)} = [1 - e^{-t}]^{(K-1)}$$

and their pdf as

(22)
$$f_{(K,K)} = K e^{-t} [1 - e^{-t}]^{(K-1)}.$$

Further, it can be easily derived that

$$E[T(K, K)] = \sum_{i=1}^{K} i^{-1}$$

(23a)
$$= H_K$$

(23b)
$$\cong \log_e K \qquad (\text{if } K \text{ is very large})$$

where H_K is the Kth harmonic number. Also, we would obtain

(24)
$$\text{Var}[T(K, K)] = \sum_{i=1}^{K} i^{-2}$$

TABLE 1
PEC (*primary estimate computation*)*-time distribution-free time complexity results for the various schemes for parallel Monte Carlo algorithms.*

Scheme	Expected time complexity
SCA Scheme 1 $\quad P \ll K$	$\dfrac{K^\mu}{P} \leq E[T(P, K)] \leq \dfrac{K\mu}{P} + \dfrac{\sqrt{K} \cdot \sigma}{2}$ If $P = 2$, $E[T(P, K)] \cong \dfrac{K\mu}{P} + \sqrt{\dfrac{K}{\pi P}} \cdot \sigma \;$ as $K \to \infty$
SCA Scheme 2 $\quad \dfrac{K}{P} \sim 10$	$\dfrac{K\mu}{P} \leq E[T(P, K)] \leq \dfrac{K\mu}{P} + \dfrac{(P-1)\sqrt{K}}{\sqrt{(2P-1)P}} \cdot \sigma$
SCA Scheme 3 $\quad P = K$	$\mu \leq E[T(P, K)] \leq \mu + \dfrac{(K-1)}{\sqrt{2K-1}} \cdot \sigma$
SCA Scheme 4 $\quad P > K$	PEC-time distribution-free time complexity results are not possible.
DCA Scheme 1	$E[T(P, K)] \cong \dfrac{K\mu}{P} + \dfrac{(P-1)(\mu^2 + \sigma^2)}{2P \cdot \mu}$
DCA Scheme 2	$\tau \leq E[T(P, K)] \leqslant \tau + \dfrac{(P-1)}{\sqrt{2P-1}} \cdot \sigma \;$ where $\tau \cong \dfrac{K\mu}{P} + \dfrac{(P-1)(\mu^2 - \sigma^2)}{2P\mu}$

K = The desired total number of primary estimates of a problem variable.
M = mean of i.i.d PEC times, σ = standard deviation of i.i.d. PEC times.
P = number of processors.
Note. The time complexity of a sequential Monte Carlo algorithm is given as $E[T(1, K)] = K \cdot \mu$.

and if K is very large, we can use the result in [22, p. 75] and obtain

$$(25) \qquad \qquad \text{Var}\,[T(K, K)] = \frac{\pi^2}{6}.$$

Thus for SCA Scheme 3, the expected time complexity increases logarithmically as against linear increase in sequential Monte Carlo algorithms. Moreover, the variance of the parallel Monte Carlo algorithms is bounded for large values of K, whereas it increases linearly for the sequential Monte Carlo algorithms.

For SCA Scheme 4, we had noted that distribution-free time complexity results are not possible. However, we can determine the expected time complexity for the present example. It can be easily shown that the Kth order statistic of P i.i.d. PEC times considered here is given as

$$E[T(P, K)] = \sum_{i=(P-K+1)}^{P} i^{-1}$$

$$(26) \qquad \qquad = H_P - H_{(P-K)}$$

$$(27) \qquad \qquad \cong \log_e P - \log_e (P - K) \quad \text{if } (P - K) \gg 1.$$

The variance of the time complexity will be given by

$$(28) \qquad \qquad \text{Var}\,[T(P, K)] = \sum_{i=(P-K+1)}^{P} i^{-2}.$$

Thus, it is seen that the expectation as well as the variance of the time complexity of SCA Scheme 4 parallel Monte Carlo algorithms can be reduced by increasing the number of processors.

6.2. Performance of DCA schemes. The performance of DCA Scheme 1 using (8) will be given as

$$(29) \qquad\qquad E[T(P, K)] = \frac{K}{P}.$$

This implies that we can achieve speedup exactly equal to P, the one which is always desired and rarely achieved in practice.

It can be easily proved that the expected time complexity of DCA Scheme 2 will be given by

$$(30) \qquad\qquad E[T(P, K)] = \frac{K}{P} + H_P.$$

The expected time complexity results given in this section are summarized in Table 2.

7. Computational results. In this section, we present some computational results illustrating the performance of the schemes for parallel Monte Carlo algorithms given in §§ 4 and 5. We consider the Laplace's equation defined on a rectangle,

$$(31) \qquad\qquad \frac{\partial^2 U}{\partial x^2} + \frac{\partial^2 U}{\partial y^2} = 0, \qquad 0 < x < 6, \quad 0 < y < 10,$$

TABLE 2

Expected time complexity of parallel algorithms based on various SCA and DCA schemes, when PEC-times are i.i.d. exponential random variables with $\mu = 1$ and $\sigma = 1$. Time complexity of sequential algorithm $= K$.

Scheme		Time complexity
SCA Scheme 1	$P \leq K$	$\dfrac{K}{P} \leq E[T(P, K)] \leq \dfrac{K}{P} + \dfrac{\sqrt{K}}{2}$
		If $P = 2$, $E[T(P, K)] \cong \dfrac{K}{2} + \dfrac{\sqrt{K}}{\sqrt{2\pi}}$.
SCA Scheme 2	$\dfrac{K}{P} \sim 10$	$\dfrac{K}{P} \leq E[T(P, K)] \leq \dfrac{K}{P} + \dfrac{(P-1)\sqrt{K}}{\sqrt{(2P-1)P}}$
		If $P \gg 1$, then $\dfrac{K}{P} \leq E[T(P, K)] \leq \dfrac{K}{P} + \sqrt{\dfrac{K}{2}}$
SCA Scheme 3	$P = K$	$E[T(P, K)] = H_K \cong \log_e K$
SCA Scheme 4	$P > K$	$E[T(P, K)] = H_P - H_{(P-K)}$
		$\cong \log_e P - \log_e (P - K)$
DCA Scheme 1	$P \ll K$	$E[T(P, K)] = \dfrac{K}{P}$
DCA Scheme 2	$P \ll K$	$E[T(P, K)] = \dfrac{K}{P} + H_P$

Note. H_n represents the nth harmonic number.

with boundary conditions

$$U(x, 0) = 10, \qquad U(x, 10) = U(0, y) = U(6, y) = -10.$$

This problem is selected for two reasons: (i) the analytic solution to this problem can be easily obtained and the Monte Carlo solutions could be compared, and (ii) the same equation has been considered in [34].

In solving PDEs by Monte Carlo methods, the solution at a point in the given region can be obtained independently of the solution at other points [2], [34]. We have selected three representative points in the region given in (31): the first point as (1, 1) near the boundary, the second point (3, 5) at the centre of the region and the third point (2, 3) in between these two points. In the method described in [34], the given region is replaced by a square mesh, as in a finite-difference method. Figure 4 shows the given region divided into a mesh, with mesh size $h = \frac{1}{4}$. Now a set of random walks are defined on the set of states comprising [10]: (i) one transient state corresponding to each of the internal nodes (i.e. the unknowns), and (ii) one absorbing state for each of the boundary nodes. In solving (31), the state transition probabilities for a step from any one internal node to its four neighboring nodes turns out to be equal to 0.25. Equation (31) was solved on a sequential computer for obtaining solutions at

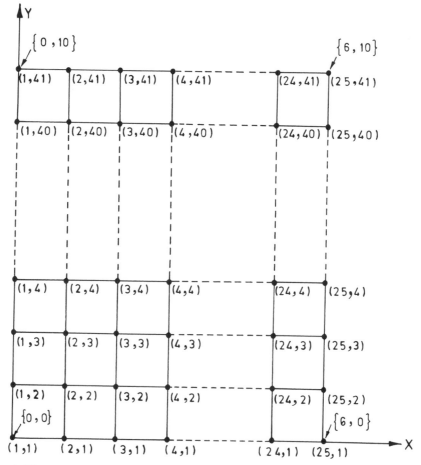

FIG. 4. *The region for Laplace's equations with mesh, mesh size* $h = \frac{1}{4}$. (m, n): *mesh points.* {x, y}: *co-ordinates.*

the selected three points and the Monte Carlo solutions were in good agreement with the analytic and numerical solutions when 2048 primary estimates were used (see [6]). The random walk duration statistics were collected for solutions at each of the selected points. Since parallel computers were not accessible, we have used the statistics collected for estimating the performance of various schemes for parallel algorithms. We consider the computational times of 2048 primary estimates on parallel computers, with the number of processors varying from 2, 4, 8, $\cdots$, 2048 in logarithmic steps, the computational time being in terms of the number of random walk steps (i.e. the duration of random walks) in a primary estimate computation.

7.1. SCA schemes. The first three SCA schemes discussed in § 4 are considered to be as follows:

1. Scheme $(P \ll K)$: for $P = 2, 4, 8, \cdots, 128$.
2. Scheme $(K/P \sim 10)$: for $P = 128, 256, 512$, and 1024.
3. Scheme $(P = K)$: for $P = 2048$.

Now, we use the sample mean and the standard deviation of the durations of random walks to obtain the bounds on the speedup of the above three schemes, using the results in Theorems 2, 3 and 4. Figures 5, 6 and 7 depict the upper and lower bounds on the speedup expected in solving (31) at points $(1, 1)$, $(2, 3)$, and $(3, 5)$, respectively, on a log-log scale. It is seen that until about $P = 64$ there is no significant difference between the upper and lower bounds. The difference increases rapidly as the number of processors are increased beyond this point. At $P = 128$, the lower bounds obtained by Scheme 1 and Scheme 2 are indicated by points A and B, respectively.

We estimate the performance of SCA parallel algorithms based on the following. It is known that given N i.i.d. random processes operating in parallel, the characteristics of the ensemble can be derived from successive observations on a single source, due to the ergodicity principle. In the present case, we use the data generated during Monte Carlo solutions on a sequential computer and estimate the performance of SCA schemes as follows. We divide the data about random walk durations into P disjoint sets with only M *successive* samples in each set. The execution time on a sequential computer is represented by the sum of the durations of all 2048 random walks in a run, whereas the execution time on a parallel computer is given by the maximum of the sum of the durations of random walks for each of the P sets. The speedup estimated for Monte Carlo solutions at the chosen three points using by the various SCA schemes is given in Figs. 5, 6, and 7, for two runs.

We make the following observations from Figs. 5, 6 and 7. The estimated speedup follows closely the lower bound, until about $P = 32$, but being always less than this bound. Here, it may be expected that the estimated performance should lie between the upper and lower bounds. However, it may be recalled that the speedup is defined as the ratio of the *expectations* of the execution times on sequential and parallel computers [32], and here we have presented the results only for two runs. From $P = 64$ to $P = 2048$, the estimated speedup is almost always within the upper and lower bounds. In many cases, the slope of the estimated speedup decreases as the number of processors increases, as expected.

7.2. DCA schemes. The speedup using the two DCA schemes from § 5 is computed using Theorems 5 and 6 by substituting the sample mean and the standard deviation of the durations of random walks, and the results are shown in Figs. 5, 6 and 7. It is seen that for Scheme 1 the speedup closely follows a linear speedup. Further, for the solution at point $(1, 1)$ the speedup is *greater* than P, due to the fact that in this case $\mu < \sigma$ (refer to (8)). For Scheme 2, the upper bound on the speedup is the same as

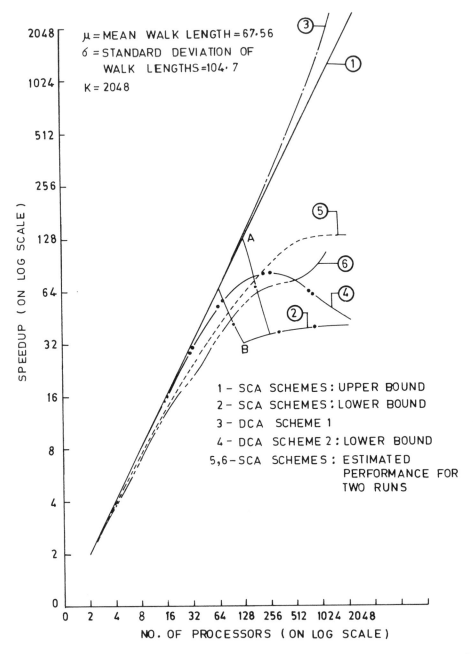

FIG. 5. *Performance of various schemes for parallel Monte Carlo algorithms for solving Laplace's equation at point* (1, 1) *in the given region.*

that of Scheme 1 by Theorem 6. The lower bound on the speedup starts dropping after about $P > 256$, due to the denominator expression in (8).

In order to estimate the performance of a DCA scheme, it should be noted that the behavior of each processor can be simulated properly only by considering successive PECs and the last PEC in these PECs may be an aborted PEC. Consequently, the completed K PECs on P processors, which determine the execution time of a simulated

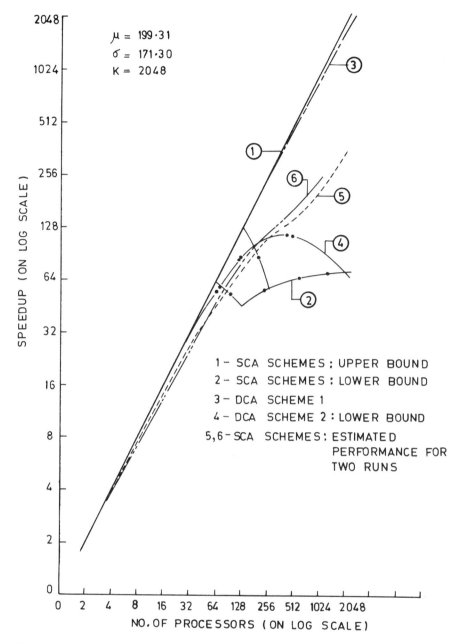

FIG. 6. *Performance of various schemes for parallel Monte Carlo algorithms for solving Laplace's equation at point* (2, 3) *in the given region.*

DCA scheme, may not necessarily be consecutive. However, the execution time of a sequential Monte Carlo algorithm has to be obtained by using only the data for consecutive K PECs. Thus, the requirements for estimating the execution time of sequential Monte Carlo algorithm and its corresponding DCA parallel algorithm are incompatible. Hence, the performance of DCA schemes for a given run cannot be estimated.

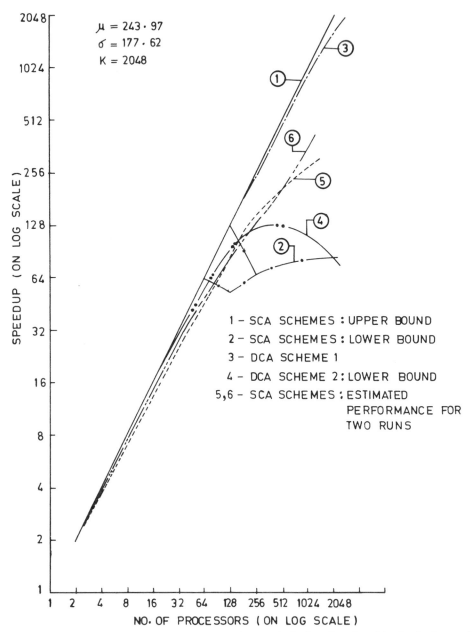

FIG. 7. *Performance of various schemes for parallel Monte Carlo algorithms for solving Laplace's equation at point* (3, 5) *in the given region.*

8. Conclusion. In this paper, we have demonstrated that the potential of intrinsic parallelism in Monte Carlo methods, which had remained essentially untapped so far, can be exploited for implementing these methods efficiently on parallel computers.

We have shown that the primary estimate computation (PEC) times in these methods turn out to be independent identically distributed random variables. This crucial result is shown to greatly influence the design and analysis of parallel Monte Carlo algorithms.

We have identified the intrinsic parallelism in these methods at four levels. The potential of this intrinsic parallelism is shown to be equally well suited for exploitation on SIMD as well as MIMD computer architectures. The computations involved have large module granularity, little concurrency control requirement and they do not demand specialized interprocessor interconnection networks.

Since the PEC times primarily determine the time complexity of a Monte Carlo method, we have proposed two basic schemes for developing parallel Monte Carlo algorithms utilizing intrinsic parallelism between PECs. In static computation assignment (SCA) schemes we assign a fixed number of PECs to the processors before any PECs are initiated, whereas in dynamic computation assignment (DCA) schemes the decision as to whether or not to initiate another PEC on a processor, whenever it completes a PEC, is made during the execution based on some global criteria. The DCA parallel Monte Carlo algorithms are more adaptable to the variations in the PEC times. The SCA and DCA schemes for parallel Monte Carlo algorithms can be applied for almost any Monte Carlo methods. In [6], we have illustrated their application in developing parallel algorithms for Monte Carlo methods used in solving linear algebraic equations and partial differential equations, and the details of the parallel algorithms are also given. In this paper, we have derived the time complexity results of these schemes. The analyses of SCA schemes were carried out using some results from order statistics, whereas those of DCA schemes were carried out using these results as well as some results from queueing theory and renewal theory. The time complexity results obtained for these schemes are independent of PEC time distributions and therefore are universal. The importance of such distribution-free results stems from the fact that for many Monte Carlo methods it is almost impossible to obtain the PEC time distributions a priori (see [6, pp. 92–165]). These schemes are shown to achieve either $O(P)$ or almost equal to P speedup, when the number of processors (P) is much smaller than the required number of primary estimates. However, as P approaches K this is no longer the case; the slope of the speedup decreases as the number of processors increases. We have shown that when the PEC times are standardized exponential random variables, it is possible to obtain exact time complexity results, rather than bounds.

Finally, we have illustrated the performance of the various schemes for parallel Monte Carlo algorithms with the solution of Laplace's equation.

The treatment in the paper assumes that "ideal" random number generators are used to drive Monte Carlo computations. However, since pseudorandom number generators are usually employed in practice, we have discussed some problems in pseudorandom number generation in parallel computations in [14], [15], [36].

We hope that the results in this paper, in [6], and our recent work [8]-[10] generates interest in the design and analysis of parallel Monte Carlo algorithms.

Acknowledgments. The authors would like to thank Dr. S. P. Nawathe, Prof. M. N. Vartak, Prof. S. L. Mehndiratta and Prof. S. Arunkumar of the Indian Institute of Technology, Bombay, for their helpful suggestions during this research work. The authors would also like to thank the referees for useful comments.

REFERENCES

[1] G. M. BAUDET, *The design and analysis of algorithms for asynchronous multiprocessors*, Ph.D. dissertation, Carnegie-Mellon University, Pittsburgh, 1978.

[2] V. C. BHAVSAR AND V. V. KANETKAR, *A multiple microprocessor system* (MMPS) *for the Monte Carlo solution of partial differential equations*, in Advances in Computer Methods for Partial Differential Equations, vol. 2, R. Vichnevetsky, ed., IMACS, New Brunswick, Canada, 1977, pp. 205–213.

[3] V. C. BHAVSAR AND A. J. PADGAONKAR, *Effectiveness of some parallel computer architectures for Monte Carlo solution of partial differential equations*, in Advances in Computer Methods for Partial Differential Equations, vol. 3, R. Vichnevetsky and R. S. Stepleman, eds. IMACS, New Brunswick, Canada, 1979, pp. 259-264.

[4] V. C. BHAVSAR AND J. R. ISAAC, *Some parallel algorithms for Monte Carlo solution of linear equations*, in Proc. 15th Annual Convention of Computer Society of India, Bombay, Feb. 8-11, 1980, vol. III, pp. 3.76-3.81.

[5] V. C. BHAVSAR, *Some parallel algorithms for Monte Carlo solutions of partial differential equations*, in Advances in Computer Methods for Partial Differential Equations, vol. 4, R. Vichnevetsky and R. S. Stepleman, eds. IMACS, New Brunswick, Canada, 1981, pp. 135-141.

[6] ———, *Parallel algorithms for Monte Carlo solutions of some linear operator problems*, Ph.D. thesis, Department of Electrical Engineering, Indian Institute of Technology, Bombay, Nov. 1981.

[7] V. C. BHAVSAR AND J. R. ISAAC, *Design and analysis of parallel algorithms for Monte Carlo methods*, in Proc. 10th IMACS World Congress on "System Simulation and Scientific Computation," Montreal, Canada, Aug. 8-13, 1982, IMACS, New Brunswick, Canada, 2, pp. 323-325.

[8] V. C. BHAVSAR, *VLSI algorithms for Monte Carlo solution of linear equations*, presented at the APICS Annual Computer Science Seminar, St. Francis Xavier Univ., Antigonish, N.S., Canada, 4-5, Nov. 1983.

[9] ———, *VLSI algorithms for Monte Carlo solutions of partial differential equations*, in Advances in Computer Methods for Partial Differential Equations, vol. 5, R. Vichnevetsky and R. S. Stepleman, eds., IMACS, New Brunswick, Canada, 1984, pp. 268-276.

[10] V. C. BHAVSAR AND U. G. GUJAR, *VLSI architectures and their applications to Monte Carlo simulation*, in Proc. IEEE International Conference on "Computers, Systems and Signal Processing," Indian Institute of Science, Bangalore, India, 3 (1984), pp. 1252-1255.

[11] K. BINDER, ed., *Monte Carlo Methods in Statistical Physics*, Springer-Verlag, Berlin, 1979.

[12] K. C. BOWLER AND G. S. PAWLEY, *Molecular dynamics and Monte Carlo simulations in solid-state and elementary particle physics*, Proc. IEEE, 72, 1 (1984), pp. 42-55.

[13] E. G. COFFMAN, JR., ed., *Computer and Job-Shop Scheduling Theory*, John Wiley, New York, 1976.

[14] D. R. COX, *Renewal Theory*, Methuen, London, 1962.

[15] H. A. DAVID, *Order Statistics*, John Wiley, New York, 1970.

[16] M. J. GONZALEZ, JR., *Deterministic processor scheduling*, ACM Computing Surveys, 9 (1977), pp. 173-204.

[17] E. J. GUMBEL, *Statistical theory of extreme values (main results)*, as Chapter 6 in Contributions to Order Statistics, A. E. Sarahan, and B. G. Greenberg, eds., John Wiley, New York, 1962.

[18] J. H. HALTON, *A retrospective and prospective survey of the Monte Carlo method*, SIAM Rev., 12 (1970), pp. 1-63.

[19] J. M. HAMMERSLEY AND D. C. HANDSCOMB, *Monte Carlo Methods*, Methuen, London, 1964.

[20] L. S. HAYNES, R. L. LAU, D. P. SIEWIOREK AND D. W. MIZELL, *A survey of highly parallel computing*, Computer, 15, 1 (1982), p. 9-24.

[21] D. HELLER, *A survey of parallel algorithms in numerical linear algebra*, SIAM Rev., 20 (1978), pp. 740-777.

[22] D. E. KNUTH, *The Art of Computer Programming*, vol. 1, *Fundamental Algorithms*, Addison-Wesley, Reading, MA, 1968.

[23] H. KOBAYASHI, *Modeling and Analysis: An Introduction to System Performance Evaluation Methodology*, Addison-Wesley, Reading, MA, 1978.

[24] E. V. KRISHNAMURTHY AND S. K. SEN, *Computer-Based Numerical Algorithms*, Affiliated East West Press, New Delhi, 1976.

[25] D. J. KUCK, *A survey of parallel machine organization and programming*, Computing Surveys, 9, 1 (1977), pp. 29-59.

[26] H. T. KUNG, *Synchronized and asynchronous parallel algorithms for multiprocessors*, in Algorithms and Complexity: New Directions and Recent Results, J. F. Traub, ed., Academic Press, New York, 1979, pp. 153-200.

[27] ———, *The Structure of Parallel Algorithms*, Dept. of Computer Science, Carnegie-Mellon Univ., Pittsburgh, CMU-CS-79-149, 1979. Also in Advances in Compters, M.C. Yovits, ed., Academic Press, New York, vol. 19, 1980.

[28] L. LAMBROU, V. C. BHAVSAR, AND U. G. GUJAR, *On the discrepancy of pseudo-random number sequences generated by the linear congruential method*, in Proc. Annual APICS Computer Science Seminar, Dept. of Mathematics, Statistics and Computing Science, Dalhousie University, Halifax, N.S., Canada, Nov. 1985, pp. 53-68.

[29] L. A. LAMBROU, *Pseudo-Random Number Sequences for Parallel Computers*, School of Computer Science, Univ. of New Brunswick, Fredericton, N.B., Canada, M.Sc. Project Report, TR86-033, Feb. 1986.

[30] M. METROPOLIS AND S. M. ULAM, *The Monte Carlo method*, J. Amer. Statist. Assoc., 44 (1949), pp. 335–341.

[31] H. NIEDERREITER, *Quasi-Monte Carlo methods and pseudorandom numbers*, Bull. Amer. Math. Soc., 84 (1978), pp. 957–1041.

[32] J. T. ROBINSON, *Some analysis techniques for asynchronous multiprocessor algorithms*, IEEE Trans. Software Engrg., SE-5, 1 (1979), pp. 24–31.

[33] R. F. ROSIN, *An Algorithm for concurrent random walks on highly parallel machines*, Cooley Electronics Lab., Univ. Michigan, Ann Arbor, TR 151, 1964.

[34] E. SADEH AND M. A. FRANKLIN, *Monte Carlo solution of partial differential equations by special purpose digital computer*, IEEE Trans. Comput., C-23 (1974), pp. 389–397.

[35] A. L. SCHERR, *An Analysis of Time-Shared Computer Systems*, MIT Press, Cambridge, 1966.

[36] YU. A. SCHREIDER, ed., *The Monte Carlo Method*, Pergamon Press, Oxford, 1966.

[37] J. SPANIER AND E. M. GELBARD, *Monte Carlo Principles and Neutron Transport Problems*, Addison-Wesley, Reading, MA, 1969.

SIAM. J. SCI. STAT. COMPUT.
Vol. 8, No. 1, January 1987

ADAPTING A NAVIER–STOKES CODE TO THE ICL–DAP*

CHESTER E. GROSCH†

Abstract. This is a report of the results of an experiment: to adapt a Navier-Stokes code, originally developed on a serial computer, to concurrent processing on the ICL D̲istributed A̲rray P̲rocessor (DAP). In this paper the algorithm used in solving the Navier-Stokes equations is briefly described. The architecture of the DAP and DAP Fortran is also described. The modifications of the algorithm so as to fit the DAP are given and discussed. Finally, performance results are given and conclusions are drawn.

Key words. Navier-Stokes, parallel computing, ICL–DAP

AMS(MOS) subject classifications. 76D05, 35Q10, 68C25

1. Introduction. The objective of the research reported here was to adapt a Navier-Stokes code, originally developed on a serial computer, to concurrent processing on the ICL–DAP and to measure the performance of the concurrent version of the code.

Despite the fact that the most powerful existing computers can perform several hundred MFLOPS (million floating point operations per second), they are clearly inadequate for many important applications. In part, this inadequacy is due to the fact that it is generally rather difficult to fully use the vector capabilities of these "supercomputers." In practice, average processing rates for many codes are in the range of ten to twenty MFLOPS (see, for example, [2]). Even if the average processing efficiency could be increased so as to more nearly reflect the potential processing power of the vector processors, the processing rates would still be inadequate for many fluid dynamic applications.

Computational fluid dynamics requires both very large amounts of fast primary storage, even larger amounts of slow, secondary storage and high average processing rates. Different individuals and groups have independently estimated that current needs for some fluid dynamic calculations are, on average, 10^3 MFLOPS processing rates, 32×10^6 words of fast primary storage, and 2.56×10^8 words of slow secondary storage. Even higher average processing rates and larger primary and secondary storage will be needed in the near future.

It appears that future supercomputers will be multiprocessors; in fact some have already appeared. There are a number of important, unresolved questions concerning these multiprocessor computers. Among these issues are: should they consist of a few, rather powerful processors or many, very much less powerful processors, or something in between? Should the new computers be SIMD or MIMD? There is a natural expectation that the multiprocessors with a few, powerful processors will have an MIMD architecture and that the others will have SIMD architectures. It seems sterile at this point to argue what, taking into account total processing power, cost, ease of programming, etc., is the "best" combination of number of processors and power per processor. Rather, carrying out experiments with existing multiprocessor computers would appear to be of greater value.

---

* Received by the editors December 2, 1985; accepted for publication (in revised form) April 10, 1986.

† Old Dominion University, Norfolk, Virginia 23508; British Maritime Technology, Teddington TW11 0JJ, England; Institute for Computer Applications in Science and Engineering, Hampton, Virginia 23665-5225. This research was supported by the National Aeronautics and Space Administration under NASA contracts NAS1-17070 and NAS1-18107 while the author was in residence at ICASE, NASA Langley Research Center, Hampton, Virginia 23665-5225.

One approach to concurrent processing for computational fluid dynamics could be to develop highly parallel algorithmic modules or kernels to perform certain computational tasks. Complete computational fluid dynamic algorithms would then be built by combining these modules. This approach has the advantage that "good," highly parallel algorithms well suited to the architecture would be used. It has the disadvantage that much of the algorithmic and code development effort of the past would be unusable and existing production codes would have to be abandoned. It would, conceivably, be many years before new production codes would be available.

An alternate approach could be to translate effective algorithms, now embodied in codes for single processor computers, onto the multiprocessor computer. This has the advantage of using existing, tested algorithms. The disadvantage is that, because the algorithm may not "fit" the multiprocessor architecture, this may be very difficult or even impossible. If such translation is possible, the algorithm may not execute effectively on the multiprocessor, that is the computational cost may be very high.

There have been a substantial number of theoretical studies of the performance of algorithms on parallel computers but far fewer actual experimental studies (see [11] for a comprehensive, up-to-date review). Most of the experimental studies of applications discussed by Ortega and Voigt (see [11, § 5]) are in the area of fluid dynamics. Apart from some early studies using Illiac IV, nearly all of this work has concentrated on the use of the Cyber 200 and Cray series of computers. The ICL-DAP is one of the few working, both in software as well as hardware, SIMD computers in existence. The MPP is another, with an architecture very similar to that of the DAP. Another large, parallel SIMD architecture is that of the Connection Machine computer. Both of these computers have a large number of single bit processors. The MPP has the same nearest neighbor connection as the DAP. The Connection Machine computer has a variable interconnection network, with a nearest neighbor connection as one possibility. It appears that there are no studies of the implementation of Navier-Stokes algorithms on either of these computers. Insofar as MIMD computers are concerned, there are even fewer actual studies of the implementation of Navier-Stokes algorithms. The exceptions are some applications using the Denelcor HEP cited by Ortega and Voigt [11].

Given the paucity of studies of complex applications to physical problems using parallel computers, it seems reasonable to carry out some now in order to measure the performance of these parallel architectures. Although there has been increasing interest in MIMD architectures and the appearance of a number of them, it is by no means clear that they are intrinsically superior to SIMD architectures for fluid dynamic applications. Both SIMD and MIMD architectures have intrinsic bottlenecks which can be revealed by experimental studies of their use in applications as well as by theoretical analysis. In view of these considerations, it seems worthwhile to measure the actual performance of an application code on a working SIMD computer. Even if one agrees that measured performance on an actual parallel processor is the true measure of computing power, there can be disagreements as to what performance is to be measured.

The time to perform a single arithmetic operation, together with the number of processors, can be used to calculate an upper bound on performance. Such a measure is widely held to be unrealistic because it does not include any of the omnipresent overhead. A different approach is to use, as a test problem, the evaluation of a slightly more complex expression such as a vector dyad, the sum or product of two vectors or a vector triad, the sum of a vector and the product of two vectors, etc. (see Hockney and Jesshope [7] and Hockney [8] for examples). While certainly more realistic than using the single operation time, the use of these test problems can be criticized because they fail to measure the overhead associated with a complex algorithm and its embodiment in a specific program in a particular programming language. Thus, these types of tests can be said to give only a measure of the maximum performance of a microsegment of a code. The average performance of a complex scientific code is probably quite different, and less than that of some microsegment. Another approach is to run a specific algorithm on a particular computer. Despite the fact that this is a very specific experiment this approach has some advantages; namely it allows an objective measurement of the performance of a complete algorithm, albeit a specific one, expressed in a specific parallel language, and executed on a specific parallel processor; and it can also yield subjective evidence as to how well an algorithm fits the architecture, how difficult it was to program in the parallel language, and so on.

The work reported here was just such an experiment. A Navier–Stokes code, embodying a compact, finite difference form of a vorticity, velocity formulation of the Navier–Stokes equations (Gatski, Grosch and Rose [3]) was reprogrammed in DAP Fortran and run on the ICL DAP. The Navier–Stokes formulation and algorithm are nonstandard but appear to be about as complicated as the standard ones. In order for this to be a realistic study, the entire code was implemented. This includes initialization, input/output, calculation of the time-dependent boundary conditions, calculation of energy, vorticity and enstrophy norms, as well as the solution for the velocity and vorticity fields. This was done so as not to overlook any hidden bottlenecks. Although the numerical scheme and the DAP have been described elsewhere, they are briefly described in §§ 2 and 3 for the sake of completeness. The implementation is described in § 4. The results are given in § 5. Finally, § 6 contains some concluding remarks.

2. The algorithm. The basic algorithm used here to solve the Navier–Stokes equations was first described, along with the results of some test cases, by Gatski, Grosch and Rose [3]. It has since been used by McInville, Gatski and Hassan [10] to study the instability and subsequent nonlinear evolution of a shear layer; by Gatski and Grosch [4] to study the flow past an open cavity in a boundary; and finally is being used to study the separating flow past a backward-facing step and the impulsive start of elliptic cylinders [5]. As mentioned above, it is briefly described here for the sake of completeness.

The Navier–Stokes equations for the two-dimensional, time-dependent flow of a viscous, incompressible fluid may be written, in dimensionless variables, as:

$$(2.1) \qquad u_x + v_y = 0,$$

$$(2.2) \qquad v_x - u_y = \zeta,$$

$$(2.3) \qquad \zeta_t + u\zeta_x + v\zeta_y = \text{Re}^{-1}(\zeta_{xx} + \zeta_{yy}),$$

where $\bar{u} = (u, v)$ is the velocity, ζ is the vorticity and Re is the Reynolds number.

The finite difference scheme used to approximate these equations is based on a compact difference method described by Rose [13] and Philips and Rose [12]. These schemes involve only variables within and on the boundaries of a single cell and are second order accurate, with the accuracy independent of the local cell Reynolds number. Apart from the independence of the accuracy on the magnitude of the cell Reynolds number, these compact schemes have certain other advantages in that it is quite simple and straightforward to use nonuniform grids and to impose boundary conditions.

The compact difference approximation to equations (2.1) to (2.3) can be briefly described. Consider a rectangular cell, centered at (x_i, y_j), with length Δx and height

Δy, see Fig. 1, and let $U_{ij}^n \equiv u(i\Delta x, j\Delta y, n\Delta t)$, for i, j, and n integers. The variables shown on cell faces of Fig. 1 are the averages of the continuous variable over that face and that at the center of a cell is the average over the entire cell. Define the difference and average operators by:

(2.4a)
$$\delta_x U_{i,j}^n \equiv (U_{i+1/2,j}^n - U_{i-1/2,j}^n)/\Delta x,$$

(2.4b)
$$\mu_x U_{i,j}^n \equiv (U_{i+1/2,j}^n + U_{i-1/2,j}^n)/2.$$

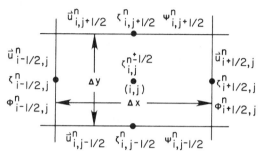

FIG. 1. *Typical computational cell and the data values associated with it.*

Then (2.1) to (2.2), hereafter the velocity equations, are replaced by:

(2.5)
$$\delta_x U_{i,j}^n + \delta_y V_{i,j}^n = 0,$$

(2.6)
$$\delta_x V_{i,j}^n - \delta_y U_{i,j}^n = \zeta_{i,j}^{n-1/2},$$

(2.7)
$$\mu_x U_{i,j}^n = \mu_y U_{i,j}^n,$$

(2.8)
$$\mu_x V_{i,j}^n = \mu_y V_{i,j}^n.$$

Assuming that ζ is known, the boundary conditions for the Cauchy-Riemann equations (2.1) and (2.2) are that one, and only one, component of the velocity is specified at each point of the boundary. For the discrete equations (2.5)-(2.8) it is easy to see that if there are N by M cells, the number of unknowns is $2(2NM + N + M)$, the number of equations is $4NM$, and the number of boundary conditions is $2(N + M)$ so that the algebraic system is determined.

The vorticity transport equation (2.33) is approximated by the system:

(2.9)
$$[\delta_t + (\mu_x U_{i,j}^n)\delta_x + (\mu_y V_{i,j}^n)\delta_y]\zeta_{i,j}^n = \mathrm{Re}^{-1}[\delta_x \phi_{i,j}^n + \delta_y \psi_{i,j}^n],$$

(2.10)
$$\delta_x \zeta_{i,j}^n = (\mu_x - \tfrac{1}{2}\Delta x q(\theta_x)\delta_x)\phi_{i,j}^n,$$

(2.11)
$$\delta_y \zeta_{i,j}^n = (\mu_y - \tfrac{1}{2}\Delta y q(\theta_y)\delta_y)\psi_{i,j}^n,$$

(2.12)
$$\mu_t \zeta_{i,j}^n = \mu_x \zeta_{i,j}^n = \mu_y \zeta_{i,j}^n.$$

Here, θ_x and θ_y are local cell Reynolds numbers given by

(2.13)
$$\theta_x = U_{i,j}^n \, \mathrm{Re} \, \Delta x/2,$$

(2.14)
$$\theta_y = V_{i,j}^n \, \mathrm{Re} \, \Delta y/2,$$

(2.15)
$$q(\theta) \equiv (\coth \theta) - (1/\theta).$$

As was shown by Gatski et al. [3], the parameter $q(\theta)$ serves to reduce the truncation error. Of course $q(\theta)$ is not computed using the definition, equation (2.15), as that would be prohibitively expensive because of the cost of calculating $\coth(\theta)$.

Instead the approximation

(2.16a) $q(\theta) = \theta/3$ for θ small,

(2.16b) $q(\theta) = (\text{sgn } \theta) - (1/\theta)$ for θ large,

is used, with sgn $\theta \equiv \theta/|\theta|$.

The solution procedure for these finite difference equations is

Step (1). Assume that $\zeta_{i,j}^{n-1/2}$ is known. Then, with one component of $\vec{u}$ prescribed on the boundary, solve (2.5) to (2.8) by relaxation.

Step (2). Determine the vorticity boundary conditions. At inflow boundaries ζ is prescribed. At solid boundaries, an increment of vorticity is created so that the tangential velocity component will equal the speed of the boundary. At outflow and freestream boundaries the vorticity is determined by the flux condition,

(2.17) $$\frac{D\zeta}{Dt} \equiv \frac{\partial \zeta}{\partial t} + (\vec{u} \cdot \nabla)\zeta = 0.$$

Step (3). Solve (2.9) to (2.11) using an ADI scheme, described in detail by Gatski et al. [3]. Then use equation (2.12) to advance ζ in time, yielding $\zeta_{i,j}^{n+1/2}$.

Further details, as needed, will be given in § 4, below, wherein the implementation on the DAP is described.

3. The ICL–DAP and DAP FORTRAN. A brief description of the DAP architecture is given here in order to clarify the way in which the Navier–Stokes code, described in § 2, was adapted to the DAP architecture. Both the hardware and software are described in order that one can appreciate some of the most important features of the DAP that contribute to its limitations and advantages. These features include, among others, the use of the control unit, the advantages and disadvantages of a bit level instruction set to implement high level instructions, the data storage scheme, and the local and global communication paths. Particular emphasis is put on the software. The Fortran functions have some rather surprising performance rates; particularly the data movement and global reduction functions. As will be seen, this large suite of efficient high level software is the major reason that the DAP can be routinely used for scientific applications rather than remain an experimental architecture. A detailed description of the DAP is given by Hockney and Jesshope [7] and in the ICL references which they cite.

The DAP is an SIMD computer with a processor array, a control unit, and an access control unit, see Fig. 2. The complete processor is embedded within an ICL 2900 system and can be used as a conventional storage unit by the 2900. Access to the DAP is through the DAP access control unit. The 2900 initiates the execution of a DAP program by passing control to the DAP master control unit. Once this is done, the DAP retains control; the 2900 cannot interrupt program execution.

The DAP control unit is similar to the control unit of a conventional serial computer. There is an instruction counter, instruction register, instruction buffer, modifier register, and eight control registers. The instruction buffer can hold up to 60 instructions, each of which is 32 bits long. The modifier register acts as a base register for memory references and the control registers are used for data and/or instruction modifications. The DAP processes data in a bit serial mode. A 200 ns fetch cycle, in which two instructions are fetched, and a 200 ns execute cycle are required for an operation on a single bit. More complex operations such as integer addition, floating point addition, etc. are microprogrammed using the primitive hardware operations. This is facilitated by the use of a hardware loop capability, through the instruction

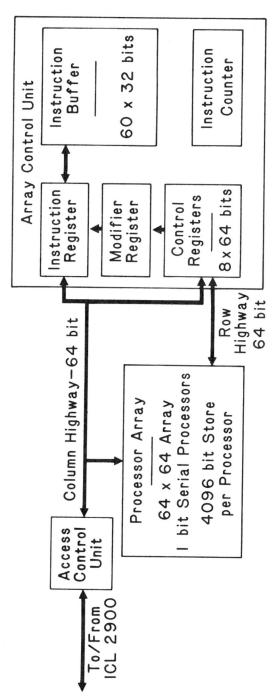

FIG. 2. Schematic diagram of the DAP architecture.

buffer, which permits the rate of instruction execution to be reduced, asymptotically, to one per cycle. The execution time for typical high level instruction such as a floating point addition is quite long, requiring from about ten to several hundred microseconds. The computational power of the DAP results from the fact that the arithmetic is performed in a processor array, not a single processor.

The DAP processor array consists of 4096 single bit processors arranged in a 64 by 64 array. Each processor has a one bit full adder, three one bit registers, an input multiplexer, an output multiplexer, as well as a 4096 bit memory. Thus the processor array has a total of two megabytes of memory. This memory is used to store both data and DAP code, so that in practice the theoretical maximum of 128 words, each of 32 bits, per processor is usually reduced to about 100 words of 32 bit data per processor. The DAP has three basic data modes; matrices which are 64 by 64 arrays, vectors having 64 or more elements, and scalars.

The storage of instructions and data can be easily visualized by considering the DAP memory as a three-dimensional array of 64 rows, 64 columns, and 4096 planes. The 32 bit instructions are stored in planes with two per row. Matrices are stored on end, so to speak, with each plane containing one bit of the words. Thus matrices of 32 bit floating point words require 32 planes but logical matrices only a single plane. Vectors with 64 elements are, on the other hand, stored in one plane with one element per row. Scalars are treated similarly to vectors.

The DAP array has both global and local communication paths. The global paths are one bit wide row and column highways (buses). The single bit column highways interface with the DAP access controller and thus provide the data paths connecting the DAP to the 2900 host. The column highways are also connected to the instruction register and master control registers. Instructions are fetched from the DAP memory along the column highways and are sent to the instruction register. Data and instructions can also be moved along the column highways to the master control registers where they can be modified. In contrast the one bit wide row highways are only connected to the master control registers and are only used to transmit data.

Apart from the data paths internal to the processor, each processor in the array is connected by four, one bit wide data paths to the four nearest neighbor processors. Thus instructions may refer to data elements in nearest neighbor processors. The edge connections can be defined by software in two ways: planar or cyclic. With a planar connection, data passed out at an edge is lost and input at an edge is defined to be zero. The cyclic connection defines, as nearest neighbors, the first and last elements of rows or columns or both.

ICL provides a DAP assembly language and a DAP Fortran, see ICL Manual, DAP: Fortran Language [1]. DAP Fortran is an extension of standard Fortran and incorporates matrix and vector instructions. There is usually very little advantage to using the assembly language instead of DAP Fortran, as the Fortran routines are highly optimized and the overhead associated with them is only of the order of 10%. Some typical Fortran statements, their execution times, and processing rates are listed in Table 1.

The processing rate is found by dividing the number of operations, 4096 for matrices and 64 for vectors, by the execution time. Although this is quite straightforward for a simple arithmetic operation, such as the addition of two matrices, there is a difficulty when we consider data transfer operations. Traditional complexity analysis, that is operation counting, has ignored the cost (time) of data movement. While this may be justified for conventional architectures, it is certainly not always true for processor arrays such as the DAP. For example, Grosch [6] has shown that the data

TABLE 1

Examples of DAP Fortran statements, execution times, and the corresponding processing rates. Here X, Y, and Z are 64 by 64 matrices of 32 bit floating point numbers; L is a 64 by 64 single bit logical matrix, i.e. a mask; V is a 64 element vector of 32 bit floating point numbers; S is a 32 bit floating point scalar.

DAP Fortran statement	Execution time (microseconds)	Processing rate (MFLOPS)
$Z = X$	17	241
$Z = X + Y$	175	23
$Z(L) = X + Y$	179	23
$Z = X * Y$	274	15
$Z = X / Y$	386	11
$Y = SQRT(X)$	194	21
$Y = EXP(X)$	414	10
$Y = SIN(X)$	862	5
$Y = TRAN(X)$	714	6
$X = MATC(V)$	31	132
$X = MATR(V)$	31	132
$Z = MERGE(X, Y, L)$	50	82
$Y = SHEP(X, 32)$	227	577
$Y = X(,-)$	23	178
$Y = SHEC(X)$	23	178
$Z = X(+,) + Y(,-)$	221	56
$Z = X(+,+) + Y(-,+)$	267	77
$S = MAXV(X)$	56	73
$S = MAXV(X, L)$	57	72
$S = SUM(X)$	450	9
CALL CONVFME(X)	2252	2

transfer cost (time) can be the major portion of the cost in the implementation of relaxation and direct Poisson solvers on processor arrays with architectures similar to the DAP. Because of the importance, and possible dominance, of the data transfer cost, all data transfers are counted as floating point operations and the time to complete them is included in the total operation time. Thus, the first Fortran statement, a matrix transfer, is counted as 4K floating point operations with an execution time of 17 μs, yielding a processing rate of 241 MFLOPS.

Logical matrices may be used as masks in arithmetic operations. The third Fortran statement in Table 1 is an example of this capability. The index, L, is a 64 by 64 logical matrix of one bit elements. The results of the right-hand side arithmetic operation, here an addition, are stored in those elements of Z for which the corresponding elements of L are true.

DAP Fortran provides an extensive set of built-in functions, which belong to one of three types: computational, aggregate, and error management. The computational functions include most of the standard Fortran functions, ABS, SQRT, EXP, SIN, and so forth. The execution times and processing rates for some of these are listed in Table 1. These timings show the advantages of bit level processing. For example, a SQRT is calculated in only about 111% of an addition time because a bit level Newton iteration scheme is used. Similarly, the EXP is evaluated in little more than one divide time. Although only examples of matrix functions are given in Table 1, the arguments of the computational functions may be of any mode (matrix, vector, or scalars) and the result will be of the same mode.

The aggregate functions perform nonnumeric operations, that is data manipulations, on vectors or matrices. Although generally not considered in standard complexity analysis, efficient implementation of the aggregate functions can be the "sine qua non" for efficient use of processor arrays. The implementation of this class of functions on the DAP is very efficient, for example the TRAN function, which transposes a matrix, is completed in about four addition times.

Mixed mode expressions, containing scalars and vectors or scalars and matrices, are permitted in DAP Fortran. The scalars are expanded to either vectors or matrices in context. The vector-matrix combination is invalid because of the ambiguity in interpretation; the vector could be expanded either as a matrix of column vectors or of row vectors. The programmer must, in order to have a vector-matrix combination, use either MATC which generates a matrix of column vectors or MATR which generates a matrix of row vectors.

The MERGE function sets the elements of matrix Z equal to the corresponding elements of X, for those elements of L which are true, and to the corresponding elements of Y, for those elements of L which are false. This function can be used to implement conditional, data dependent calculations. For example, a branch instruction with two branches can be implemented by (1) calculating the results of the first branch and storing them in matrix X; (2) calculating the results of the second branch and storing them in Y; (3) generating the mask using the data test with, say, true denoting the first branch and false the second branch; (4) finally, calling MERGE.

By convention the first index of a matrix, the I of $X(I, J)$, labels the rows and the second labels the columns, see Fig. 3. The DAP convention labels the first row of the array as the North and the first column as the West. These conventions are used in the shifting functions, SHEP(X, N) for example. This function shifts (SH) the X matrix N columns to the East (E), i.e., the first column of X becomes the $N+1$ column. The P denotes a planer shift so that the last N columns of X are shifted out of the array and the first N columns are filled with zeros. If N is not given it will be

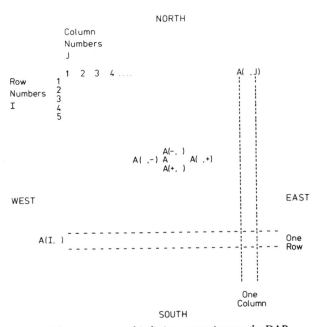

FIG. 3. *Matrix storage and indexing conventions on the DAP.*

taken to be one, and if N is greater than or equal to 64, the shift will be modulo 64. The SHEC function performs a cyclic shift in the East-West direction on the matrix. Single row or column shifts can also be accomplished by using the $+$ or $-$ notation. For example, $X(,-)$ is equivalent to SHEP(X). When using the $\pm$ notation the shifts are planer by default, but a GEOMETRY declaration can be used in any subroutine to declare the East-West or North-South shifts, or both, to be cyclic.

The MAXV function returns the maximum element of X, with an option to test only those elements of X for which the corresponding elements of L are true. The use of bit level processing yields high efficiency for this function. Finally, the SUM function calculates the sum of all of the elements of X. It is noteworthy that this requires an execution time which is slightly less than two addition times, rather than the 12 $(4096 = 2^{12})$ that might have been expected.

Figure 4 shows in block form the structure of a typical program. There can be more than one DAP entry subroutine in a Fortran program, as is shown in this figure. The call to the DAP entry subroutine must not have any arguments; all data is transferred via COMMON blocks. Immediately after entering the DAP entry routine and, again, before returning to the calling routine, the data in COMMON must be converted. This is because the data storage of standard Fortran is different from that of the DAP, as described above. The conversion routines, for example CONVFME (see Table 1), are extremely expensive in time and so the number of transfers between standard and DAP Fortran should be minimized. In particular, this affects the way in which input

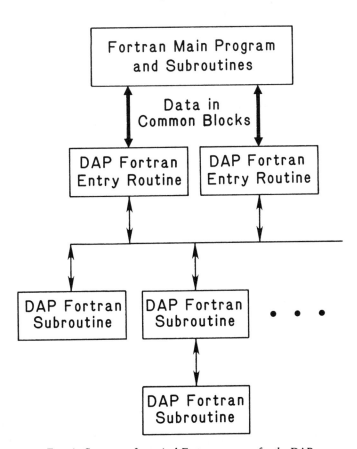

FIG. 4. *Structure of a typical Fortran program for the DAP.*

and output must be handled. Because of the difference in data storage format, there is no input or output from the DAP. The program must return from the DAP segment, at the cost of a conversion, perform the input and/or output and return to the DAP, at the cost of another conversion. Because of this overhead cost of conversion, input and output calls must be minimized. The data can be stored and output, say, done after final return from the DAP.

4. Implementation. The data structure of this algorithm, as presented in § 2, does not quite fit the DAP architecture. This is because the difference scheme is a compact one with the dependent variables defined on the cell edges rather than at the corners of a cell as in more familiar schemes. For an N by N array of cells there are N by $N+1$ cell sides and $N+1$ by N cell tops. So with the velocity, for example, defined on the cell edges the data arrays do not map directly onto an N by N array of processors.

On the other hand, there are certain advantages to using the compact difference scheme on the DAP. First, the application of boundary conditions is quite simple. There is no need to introduce "ghost" points outside of physical boundaries. Second, all derivatives are evaluated using variables which can be seen to be nearest neighbors on the computational grid (see § 2). Thus, the amount of long range communication is minimized.

The adaptation of this algorithm to the DAP architecture can be simplified by the introduction of box variables to represent the velocity field. The center of a cell is at (i, j). The box variables, $\vec{P}$, are defined at the corners of the cells, points $(i \pm 1/2, j \pm 1/2)$. They are related to the velocity $\vec{U}$ by

$$(4.1) \qquad \vec{U}_{i,j\pm1/2} = (\vec{P}_{i+1/2,j\pm1/2} + \vec{P}_{i-1/2,j\pm1/2})/2,$$

$$(4.2) \qquad \vec{U}_{i\pm1/2,j} = (\vec{P}_{i\pm1/2,j+1/2} + \vec{P}_{i\pm1/2,j-1/2})/2.$$

The (P, Q) variables are not components of the velocity, $\vec{U} = (U, V)$. They are simply auxiliary variables related to the velocity field, averaged over the cell sides, by (4.1) and (4.2). In the vorticity equations, (2.9) to (2.15), these equations, (4.1) and (4.2), are used to calculate the velocity field.

It is obvious that (2.7) and (2.8) are satisfied identically for any set of box variables. For the cell (i, j), (2.5) and (2.6) are

$$(4.3) \qquad\qquad AP = Z$$

where

$$(4.4) \qquad\qquad \vec{P}_{ij} = (P_{ij}, Q_{ij})^T,$$

and

$$(4.5a, b) \qquad P = \begin{pmatrix} \vec{P}_{i+1/2,j-1/2} \\ \vec{P}_{i+1/2,j+1/2} \\ \vec{P}_{i-1/2,j+1/2} \\ \vec{P}_{i-1/2,j-1/2} \end{pmatrix}, \qquad Z \equiv \begin{pmatrix} 0 \\ 2(\Delta y)_i \zeta_{i,j}^{n-1/2} \end{pmatrix},$$

$$(4.6) \qquad A = \begin{pmatrix} \lambda_{i,j} & -1 & \lambda_{i,j} & 1 & -\lambda_{i,j} & 1 & -\lambda_{i,j} & -1 \\ 1 & \lambda_{i,j} & -1 & \lambda_{i,j} & -1 & -\lambda_{i,j} & 1 & -\lambda_{i,j} \end{pmatrix},$$

$$(4.7) \qquad\qquad \lambda_{i,j} \equiv (\Delta y)_i/(\Delta x)_j$$

is the aspect ratio of cell (i, j).

The box variables lie at the vertices of the computational grid. The storage pattern used on the DAP is to store $\vec{P}_{i-1/2,j+1/2}$, $\zeta_{i,j}$, and $\lambda_{i,j}$ in memory of processor (i, j).

Thus with a 64×64 array of processors there is an array of 63×63 cells and for each cell we have (4.3).

The set of equations is solved by an iteration scheme which was originally proposed by Kaczmarz [9] and generalized by Tanabe [14]. If $P^{(k)}$ is the value after the kth iteration, then the residual after the kth iteration, $R^{(k)}$, is given by

(4.8)
$$R^{(k)} = AP^{(k)} - Z.$$

The next iteration is

(4.9)
$$P^{(k+1)} = P^{(k)} - \omega A^T (AA^T)^{-1} R^{(k)},$$

which, if $\omega \equiv 1$, would give

(4.10)
$$R^{(k+1)} \equiv 0.$$

For $\omega \neq 1$, this is an SOR scheme. On a serial computer the array of computational cells is swept over, applying (4.9) to each, until the maximum residual is reduced to the desired level.

The key to the adaptation of this relaxation scheme to the DAP is the realization that each $\vec{P}$ is updated four times in a sequential sweep over the array of cells. For example, see Fig. 5, if the sweep is across the columns and then down the rows, $\vec{P}_{i+1/2,j+1/2}$ is changed during the relaxation of cell (i, j) first, then of cell $(i, j+1)$, then cell $(i+i, j)$, and finally cell $(i+1, j+1)$. In each of these cases $\vec{P}_{i+1/2,j+1/2}$ lies at a different corner of the cell being relaxed. It is therefore clear that the cell iteration scheme for the box variables is a four "color" scheme.

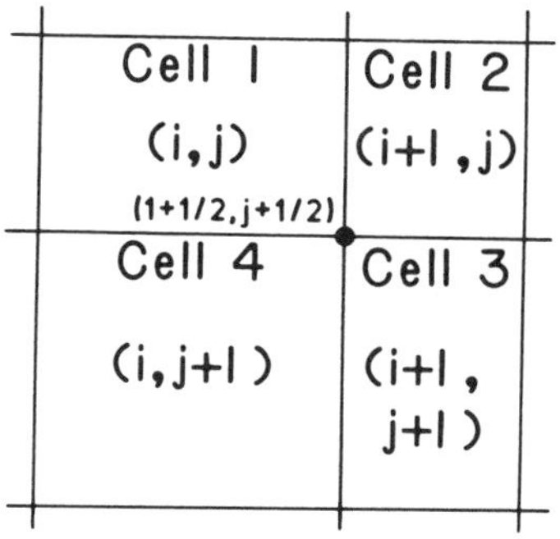

Cell 1	Cell 2
(i,j)	(i+1,j)
(1+1/2,j+1/2)	
Cell 4	Cell 3
(i,j+1)	(i+1, j+1)

FIG. 5. *Computational cells bordering the grid point* $(i+\frac{1}{2}, j+\frac{1}{2})$.

The DAP scheme is therefore to relax all of the $\vec{P}$'s four times; in the first pass a particular $\vec{P}$ is treated as lying in the lower right-hand corner of the cell and is labelled 1; in the next pass, labelled 2, as lying in the lower left-hand corner; in the third, labelled 3, as lying in the upper left-hand corner; and finally in the last pass, labelled 4, as being in the upper right-hand corner of the cell.

In detail, the DAP algorithm is implemented by

(1) Computing the residuals, $R^{(k)}$, for all cells using (4.8).
(2) Computing the correction to $P^{(k)}$ for all cells, as given in (4.9). Note that the coefficients in the matrices A and

(4.11)
$$B \equiv A^T (AA^T)^{-1}$$

are precomputed once and for all and are stored.
(3) Correct and restore the P's.

This sequence must be completed four times in order to complete a sweep. The only difference between these sequences is the assignment of the data in a particular processor memory to one of the four logical positions in a computational cell. This is easily done using logical masks which also mask out boundary values. The overhead caused by these data transfer is about 7% of the total.

Extensive experiments, using test problems with known solutions, have been carried out on serial and vector computers and on the DAP. Constant grid sizes in both directions were used and the acceleration parameter, ω, was varied in order to find the value of ω giving a minimum spectral radius. The Kaczmarz iteration scheme was applied to the original set of equations, (2.5)–(2.8), and the box scheme, (4.3) to (4.7). On the serial computers both the original and box variable forms were relaxed using lexographic, red-black, and four color orderings. A vectorized version of the original scheme using red-black ordering was implemented on a CYBER 205. Only the four color scheme with box variables was implemented on the DAP. In all cases the results were nearly identical; the minimum spectral radius is approximately 0.96 and occurs at $\omega \approx 1.95$ for $\Delta x = \Delta y = 1/63$.

Figure 6 shows the kernel of the DAP relaxation routine. The subroutine call statement, COMMON statements, declaration of temporary arrays, shifts of the data into temporary arrays, etc. are not shown in this figure. The TP's, TQ's, and R's are temporary matrices of real numbers. The P, Q, matrices are the first and second components of the box variables, and ZT is defined by equation (4.5). Finally the ZLT matrix contains the values of $\lambda_{i,j}$ and CT is a matrix of coefficients obtained from equation (4.11). The acceleration parameter ω is included in CT.

The residuals for all cells are computed in the first block of six DAP Fortran statements. These are stored in R1 and R2. The next set of four statements computes the terms in the correction, see (4.9), to the current values. The box variables are finally updated in the next eight statements.

```
TP1 = P1 − P3
TP2 = P2 − P4
TQ1 = Q1 − Q3
TQ2 = Q2 − Q4
R1 = ZL1*(TP1+TP2)−TQ1+TQ2
R2 = TP1 − TP2+ZLT*(TQ1+TQ2)−ZT

TP1 = CT*R1
TQ1 = ZLT*TP1
TP2 = CT*R2
TQ2 = ZLT*TP2

P1 = P1−TQ1−TP2
Q1 = Q1+TP1−TQ2
P2 = P2−TQ1+TP2
Q2 = Q2−TP1−TQ2
P3 = P3+TQ1+TP2
Q3 = Q3−TP1+TQ2
P4 = P4+TQ1−TP2
Q4 = Q4+TP1+TQ2
```

FIG. 6. *Kernel of the relaxation subroutine in DAP Fortran.*

Figure 7 shows the DAP Fortran code used to compute the maximum residual. The residual matrices are zeroed, and the absolute values of the components of the residual vector are computed, as above. The matrix MR masks off the meaningless values generated at the bottom and right-hand sides of the array. The R1 and R2 matrices are merged to form a matrix of maximum values. The MAXV function is then used to extract the maximum residual.

```
R1 = 0.0
R2 = 0.0
TP1 = P(+,+)−P
TP2 = P(,+)−P(+,)
TQ1 = Q(+,+)−Q
TQ2 = Q(,+)−Q(+,)
R1(MR) = ABS(ZL*(TP1+TP2)−TQ1+TQ2)
R2(MR) = ABS(TP1−TP2+ZL*(TQ1+TQ2)−Z)
ERR = MAXV(MERGE(R1,R2,R1.GT.R2))
```

FIG. 7. DAP *Fortran code to compute the maximum value of the residuals.*

Apart from the branch instructions in the DO loops and GO TO, there are only three scalar operations in this subroutine. The first of these sets an error flag to zero, the next is used to test the maximum residual against the convergence tolerance. If the iteration does not converge in a specified number of iterations, the last of the scalar operations sets the error flag to unity.

The calculation of the velocity field is the first major piece of the algorithm; the time stepping of the vorticity is the other. The first step in the vorticity calculation is to set the vorticity boundary conditions, as defined in § 2. This is relatively expensive because it involves only vector operations to generate the vectors of boundary values. A typical segment of the code is shown in Fig. 8.

```
U2 = P(63,)
U3 = P(62,)
U2 = U2+U2(+)
U3=0.25*(U3+U3(+))
ZBOT = (U3−U2)/VEC(DY(63))
```

FIG. 8. DAP *Fortran code to calculate the boundary values of the vorticity at a solid wall.*

Here (2.6) is used to calculate the vorticity at a solid boundary at $y=0$. It has been assumed that the heights, Δy, of the first two cells bordering the boundary are equal. This gives

$$(4.12) \qquad \zeta(\text{Boundary}) = (\tfrac{1}{2}u(x, 2\Delta y) - 2u(x, \Delta y))/\Delta y.$$

The fact that the velocity is the average of two adjacent box variables has also been used to simplify the coefficients in this piece of code. In this figure U2, U3, and ZBOT are 64 element vectors. ZBOT is the vector of boundary values of the vorticity. Note that U2 and U3 are formed by the reduction operation of extracting a row from a matrix. In contrast, VEC(DY(63)) forms a vector by expanding the scalar DY(63). Similar code segments involving vectors are used to calculate the boundary values of the vorticity on the other three boundaries.

Once the boundary values of the vorticity have been calculated, one can proceed to the solution of the advection diffusion equation for the vorticity, equations (2.9) to (2.15). As was discussed by Gatski, Grosch and Rose [3] and Gatski and Grosch [4], [5], $\zeta^{n+1/2}$ is eliminated between (2.9) and (2.12). This gives an implicit system for ζ^n, which is then solved by an ADI method involving two complete sweeps. In the first sweep one solves for the set $\{\zeta^n_{i+1/2,j}, \phi^n_{i+1/2,j}\}$, $i = 0, 1, \cdots$ for all j, using the values of $\zeta^{n-1/2}_{i,j}$. Next the set $\{\zeta^n_{i,j+1/2}, \psi^n_{i,j+1/2}\}$, $j = 0, 1, \cdots$ for all i, is solved for. Using these values and $\zeta^{n-1/2}_{i,j}$, we solve for the next, and last, approximation to $\{\zeta^n_{i+1/2,j}, \phi^n_{i+1/2,j}\}$.

In the first pass the set $\{\zeta^n_{i+1/2,j}\}$ is the solution of a tridiagonal system, i.e.,

$$(4.13) \qquad a_{i,j}\zeta^n_{i-1/2,j} + b_{i,j}\zeta^n_{i+1/2,j} + c_{i,j}\zeta^n_{i+3/2,j} = q_{i,j}$$

for $i = 1, 2 \cdots$, and fixed j. Taking $j = 1, 2 \cdots$ gives a set of N tridiagonal equations, each for N variables. Next we solve for the set $\{\phi_{i+1/2,j}\}$. It can be seen that the coefficients $\{a_{ij}, b_{ij}, c_{ij}\}$, for both passes are functions of the velocity and the parameters $(\Delta t/\Delta x)$, $(\Delta t/\text{Re}\,\Delta x^2)$, and the cell Reynolds numbers. The forcing terms, the $\{q_{ij}\}$, must be recomputed after each pass. For example, when solving for the $\{\zeta^n_{i+1/2,j}\}$, the q's are functions of the $\{\zeta^n_{i,j+1/2}, \psi^n_{i,j+1/2}\}$. Once the vorticity at time level Δt is computed using this ADI scheme, the time advance of the vorticity can be completed by using the fact that the time average equals the space average, see (2.12).

Each pass of the implicit ADI step requires that the coefficients and forcing terms of the tridiagonal systems be computed. This can be done concurrently for all N systems, i.e., all systems in rows or all systems in columns. A portion of the DAP Fortran code to accomplish this is shown in Fig. 9. The average velocity in the cells is computed in the first four statements. The next seven statements calculate various terms needed to compute the a's, b's, and c's. They are combined in the next block of four statements to form α^-, β^-, α^+, and β^+. The next three statements compute the remaining temporaries required to set the forcing terms, the q_{ij} of (4.13), for all of the equations. Note that two of these statements evaluate the advective and diffusive terms for the orthogonal direction. These terms are then combined to form the q_{ij} matrix. But note that two additional vector operations are required to set the boundary conditions. Finally, the α's and β's are combined to give the coefficient matrices for the tridiagonal systems.

The block of code given in Fig. 9 constitutes one pass in one direction and, as such, is about one quarter of the total amount of code to implement the ADI scheme for (2.9)–(2.15). This segment of DAP Fortran, to compute the vorticity at the tops and bottoms of cells at time level n, is not completely optimized. There are several uses of the MATC and MATR functions to expand vectors to matrices. These matrices could have been precomputed and stored, but it was decided to minimize the storage used at the cost of a few expansions and matrix arithmetic operations. It is also possible, by judicious redefining of some of the temporary matrices, to save two or three matrix additions in this code segment. However it was decided to forego this in the interest of clarity of presentation.

There are two matrix functions in the DAP Fortran code shown in Fig. 10. The first of these is QTHETD. The function implements the $q(\theta)$ function as defined in (2.16a, b). It is programmed using the MERGE for evaluating a two branch function as described in § 3. The second matrix function is TRIIED, the tridiagonal solver.

The DAP Fortran routine TRIIED is given in Fig. 9. There are 64 sets of 64 equations for the vorticity values on the tops of the cells. These equations are solved by the cyclic elimination algorithm, which is the cyclic reduction algorithm (see

```
U = P+P(+,)
U = 0.25*(U+U(,+))
V = Q+Q(+,)
V = 0.25*(V+V(,+))

T1 = 0.5/MATC(RLY)
T2 = MATC(RKY)
QT = QTHETD(0.5*RE*V*MATC(DY))
CC = QT−1.0
QQ = QT+1.0
AA = 1.0+V*MATC(RLY)
BB = 1.0−V*MATC(RLY)

ALFAM = T1(−,)*(CC(−,)*AA(−,)+T2(−,))
BETAM = T1(−,)*(CC(−,)*BB(−,)−T2(−,))
ALFAP = T1*(QQ*AA+T2)
BETAP = T1*(QQ*BB−T2)

CC = 0.5/MATR(DX)
AA = ZETA−DT*CC*(U*(ZX(,+)−ZX)−(PHI(,+)−PHI)/RE)
BB = ZETA(−,)−DT*CC(−,)*(U(−,)*(ZX(−,+)−ZX(−,))−(PHI(−,+)−PHI(−,))/RE)

QQ = 2.0*((1.0−QT(−,))*T1(−,)*BB+(1.0+QT)*T1*AA)
QQ(1,) = ZTOP
QQ(64,) = ZBOT

AA = BETAP
AA(1,) = 0.0
AA(64,) = 0.0
BB = ALFAP−BETAM
BB(1,) = 1.0
BB(64,) = 1.0
CC = −ALFAM
CC(1,) = 0.0
CC(64,) = 0.0

ZY = TRIIED(AA,BB,CC,QQ)
```

FIG. 9. *A portion of the* DAP *Fortran code to carry out the* ADI *calculation.*

```
MATRIX FUNCTION TRIIED(A,B,C,Q)

REAL A(,), B(,), C(,), Q(,)

K = 1

DO 100 L=1,6
A = A/B
C = C/B
Q = Q/B
Q = Q−A*SHNP(Q,K)−C*SHSP(Q,K)
B = 1.0−A*SHNP(C,K)−C*SHSP(A,K)
A = −A*SHNP(A,K)
C = −C*SHSP(C,K)
100  K = K+K

TRIIED = Q/B

RETURN
END
```

FIG. 10. *Tridiagonal equation systems solver in* DAP *Fortran.*

Hockney and Jesshope [7]) applied to all of the equations. This eliminates the back substitution phase of the algorithm.

This subroutine is reasonably efficient but does contain some hidden defects which are inherent in the algorithm. The shift parameter, K, takes on the successive values 2^k for $k = 0, 1, \cdots, 5$, so that in each pass 2^k rows of data are shifted off the array and, more importantly, 2^k rows of zeros are shifted onto the array. Thus, although all of the processors are active all of the time, some of these processors are not doing useful work because they are multiplying by zero or adding a zero. This must be taken into account in any fair calculation of processing rate.

The final calculation in a time step is the computation of the total energy, vorticity and enstrophy (the squared vorticity), as diagnostic measures. This is a simple, straightforward computation using the SUM function. Details will not be given.

5. Results. The numerical algorithm, the DAP architecture and DAP Fortran, and the adaptation of the algorithm to this architecture were presented in previous sections. Timing and performance results are given in this section.

The host program is a standard Fortran program in which COMMON blocks containing box variables, P and Q, the vorticity, the grid sizes, etc. are defined. The host program also handles the input and output, initialization of variables and the calling of the DAP Entry routine. There is only a small amount of computation in the host program and therefore the amount of time spent in this section is insignificant. This is evident once it is realized that the DAP Fortran section is run for a hundred, perhaps several hundred, time steps in a typical case.

In the DAP Entry routine all of the variables which were passed through COMMON are converted from Fortran to DAP format. This is a fairly costly operation: a matrix conversion takes 2252 μs, and a vector or scalar conversion about 50 μs. In total, 7 matrices, 28 vectors, and 23 scalars are converted on entry to the DAP program. This takes 18.3 ms which is a little over 100 addition times. This is a significant overhead only if it is repeated every time step. Because tens, or hundreds, of time steps are taken for each call to the DAP Entry routine, this overhead, and that of conversion upon leaving, is quite unimportant. The only other initialization task in this entry routine is to generate the one bit logical masks. The total time for this is only about 150 μs; less than one addition time. Again this is negligible.

From this discussion it should be clear that the only substantial costs are those associated with the application of the numerical algorithm for each time step. The total overhead in the host Fortran program and in the data conversions in the DAP Entry routine can be shown to be less than the cost of three iterations in the relaxation routine. In the calling sequence in the Entry routine there are only four tests on flag variables and seven scalar arithmetic operations per time step and the time to do this is less than one fifth of that to carry out one relaxation iteration; a typical time step would require about fifty iterations.

The required sequence of calls to the various DAP Fortran routines in order to advance the Navier–Stokes algorithm one time step is: RELAXD (solves for the velocity field by relaxation), FIXZBD (calculates boundary values of the vorticity), ZCALCD (advances the vorticity in time); and FNORMD (calculates the total energy, vorticity, and enstrophy of the field). In ZCALCD there are calls to the matrix functions discussed previously, QTHETD and TRIIED. The function TRIIED solves tridiagonal equations distributed over columns. There are also calls in ZCALCD to the matrix function TRIJED which solves tridiagonal equations distributed over rows.

TABLE 2
Summary of results.

Subprogram	Execution time (msec)	Proportion of transfer time (%)	Processing rate (MFLOPS)
RELAXD	30.2*	6.9	20.2
FIXZBD	1.4	5.9	0.3
ZCALCD	222.4	3.0	10.1
FNORMD	5.4	2.8	15.1
QTHETD	1.6	2.1	5.0
TRIIED	32.0	27.2	10.1
TRIJED	32.0	27.2	10.1

* Per iteration.

Table 2 contains a list of these subprograms; the execution time for each, that for one iteration in the case of RELAXD; and the processing rate. The processing rate is determined by taking the ratio of the number of effective arithmetic operations to the total execution time for the subprogram. In counting the number of effective arithmetic operations only those operations which truly contribute to the solution are counted. In those cases for which some of the processors are not performing useful work, as in TRIIED as described previously, those processors are not counted. Data transfer operations, vital as they are, were not counted as floating point operations. However, the time required to do these transfers was included in the total execution time.

One can see that there is a wide range in both execution time, from 1 to over 200 msec, and processing rates, 0.3 to 20 mflops, for these subprograms. The amount of time spent on data transfers is quite modest for most of the subprograms; in general 2% to 7% except for TRIIED and TRIJED.

There are two reasons why the data transfer overhead is generally so unimportant. The first is that the basic algorithm does not contain many data transfers and these transfers are only between nearest neighbors. The local nature of the data transfers is due to the fact that the differencing scheme is a compact one. The second reason is that the DAP has very efficient data transfer hardware, yielding rates in the neighborhood of 200×10^6 words per second. In contrast to most of the subroutines, 27% of the execution time is used by data transfers in the tridiagonal solvers. These subroutines are mostly data transfer operations; in fact only 18% of the operations are arithmetic operations, but these transfer operations take up only about one fourth of the time because of the efficient implementation of data movements on the DAP.

The subroutine FIXZBD, used to calculate the boundary values of the vorticity, is very inefficient with a processing rate of only 0.3 mflops. This is because there are only vector operations in this subroutine and the vector processing rate is 1/64 of that for matrix operations. Fortunately, the execution time of FIXZBD is a small fraction, approximately 0.5%, of the total execution time if a time step requires only one iteration and about 0.04% of the total excution time if there are 100 iterations per time step. It is obvious that: FIXZBD uses only vector operations; has a very low efficiency; and has a negligible effect on the overall efficiency of the code. It would seem that this conclusion concerning the setting of boundary conditions is independent of the structure of the algorithm.

Subroutine ZCALCD, within which the vorticity is advanced in time, consists of two principal operational parts: the generation of the coefficients for the tridiagonal systems and the solution of these tridiagonal systems. Within this subroutine there are a number of vector and scalar operations, but the time required to evaluate them is only about 14% of the total. Generation of the coefficients for the tridiagonal systems takes about 42% of the execution time so that even if the tridiagonal solvers ran in zero time the execution time would only decrease by a factor of two and the processing rate double. The effective processing rate of 10 megaflops for this routine is due to, first the vector and scalar operations required to generate the coefficients of the tridiagonal systems and, second, the large number of data transfers required in the tridiagonal solvers. The average processing rate is approximately half the maximum possible rate. Given the necessity of treating boundaries and solving the tridiagonal systems, there does not seem to be any more efficient way to handle these problems than that adopted here.

6. Concluding remarks. The adaptation of this Navier–Stokes algorithm to the DAP architecture was quite straightforward and fairly successful. This particular algorithm was chosen because it has been found, when implemented on serial and vector computers, to be flexible, accurate and to have certain advantages with respect to the use of nonuniform grids and the implementation of boundary conditions. It is now being used in a number of application studies and a three-dimensional version is being tested. Although the algorithm is not a standard one, velocity-vorticity variables are used with compact difference schemes, its complexity is comparable to that of more standard algorithms. The very nature of the problem, the numerical solution of the Navier–Stokes equations—a set of nonlinear partial differential equations—dictates that any algorithm must have some high degree of complexity.

This class of applications, as mentioned in the introduction, require millions, perhaps tens of millions of words of memory and, in many applications, in excess of 10^{11} floating point operations per case. The "traditional" bottlenecks of computational fluid dynamics are the lack of sufficient fast memory and a relatively low floating point processing rate. The invention of fast algorithms does not eliminate the need for fast hardware. This experiment was intended to explore the implementation of an algorithm for computational fluid dynamics on one member of the class of SIMD architectures.

Overall this adaptation was quite successful. Within the constraint of fitting the computational mesh to the array size, there are, essentially, no bottlenecks in the relaxation portion of the algorithm. With the exception of some of the boundary processors which are masked off because of the boundary conditions, it was possible to keep all of the processors doing useful work by using a four color relaxation scheme. There are no vector operations in the relaxation subroutine and only one scalar operation per iteration; the comparison of the maximum residual to the error tolerance. It might have been assumed that the determination of the maximum residual would be a major bottleneck. Such is not the case, as the maximum residual is found using only a MERGE and a MAXV function. The total execution time is 107 μsecs which is little more than half of an addition time.

The absence of bottlenecks in the adaptation of the relaxation scheme is strikingly illustrated by the processing rate of subroutine RELAXD. The maximum possible arithmetic processing rate of the DAP is 23 megaflops and RELAXD has a processing rate of a little over 20 megaflops, about 88% of the maximum. This good performance is due to the fact that the relaxation algorithm is an excellent fit to the architecture and that the DAP has very efficient software for the reduction functions, in this case the MAXV function.

The other principal subroutine, ZCALCD, embodies the ADI solver for the implicit formulation of the vorticity transport equation. It is not nearly as efficient as the relaxation routine; with a processing rate of 10 megaflops it is only 43% of the maximum. This routine, and in particular the tridiagonal solver routines at its core, is the nearest thing to a bottleneck in the entire code. The major difficulty is that the cyclic elimination algorithm requires many data transfers and, in the latter stages of the algorithm, many operations on zero data. There does not seem to be any more efficient parallel tridiagonal₁ algorithm than the one used here. It is fortunate that although the processing rate of ZCALCD is somewhat low, the execution time of 220 msec is only about that of seven iterations of the relaxation scheme. Thus this part of the algorithm is only a minor bottleneck.

The overall processing rate depends on the number of iterations per time step. It is clear that if the physics of the flow is such that the field is evolving rapidly then, with a modest size time step, there will be a large change in the velocity per time step. This will require a substantial number of iterations in RELAXD per time step. The alternative is, of course, to choose a small enough Δt so that the number of iterations is small. Considering that the relaxation routine in the most efficient of all of the routines, extra iterations for a larger time step would appear to be a reasonable tradeoff.

This is apparent when one considers some reasonable scenarios. If there is one iteration per time step, the execution time per step is 0.26 seconds and the processing rate is 11.3 mflops. If Δt were increased and there were 100 iterations per time step then the execution time would increase to 3.25 seconds per time step, but the processing rate would also increase to 19.5 mflops.

A good deal of the success in adapting this algorithm to the DAP is due to the fact that it is for a two-dimensional problem and the computational array size was chosen to fit the size of the DAP array. The DAP memory is quite small, a maximum of 128 words, each of 32 bits, per processor. Because the instructions are also stored in the DAP store, the maximum is never available for data storage. Generally only about 3000 bit planes can be used as data memory.

Based on the amount of storage available, two-dimensional problems with up to four times the number of grid points could have been run. The DAP software package includes routines for manipulating array sized segments of data from "big" matrices, i.e., those larger than 64 by 64. In principle there is no barrier to applying this algorithm to these larger two-dimensional problems. Certainly the spectral radius would increase as the grid size was reduced; thus the number of iterations per time step would also increase but the processing rate ought to remain nearly the same. The effective processing rate of the tridiagonal solver would also decrease somewhat as the problem size increased because there would be more data transfers and operations on zero data. However, based on the results reported here and the known efficiency of the "big" matrix manipulation software, one could expect the overall performance on moderately larger two-dimensional problems to be quite similar to that reported in this paper.

This is certainly not true for very large two-dimensional and three-dimensional flow problems. In order to handle these problems, the external memory would have to be used. This would require more complex data structures and very many data transfers from the DAP memory to external memory, each requiring a conversion. This data movement overhead would reduce the efficiency and processing rate by a substantial amount.

The DAP is currently embodied in mid-1970s technology. There are three basic ways in which its hardware could be updated. First the cycle time could be reduced, second the array size could be increased (the MPP has 16K processors and the Connection Machine has 64K), and third, the memory per processor could be increased.

Based on the experiences reported here and analysis of, in particular, three-dimensional flow problems, it is suggested that: the first priority should be a much larger, at least an order of magnitude, memory per processor; next more processors; and finally a smaller cycle time.

There is one further observation of interest. The DAP Fortran code reveals blocks of DAP instructions whose structure suggests a way in which this algorithm might be adapted to an MIMD machine. On an MIMD machine, there would appear to be a basic requirement for a "good" program: that there be reasonably large blocks of code which do not require synchronization or have likely memory conflicts. The size of the code blocks is to be interpreted to mean the product of, say, the numbers of arithmetic operations per grid point and the number of grid points in the field.

Consider, first, the relaxation routine. This can be partitioned in at least three ways; geometrically, by color, and in combination. One could split the array of cells into subarrays and relax these without synchronization. This would be a form of chaotic block relaxation. This would probably converge under some conditions, and deserves some study. Color partitioning among four processors would be a simple extension of the algorithm which was implemented on the DAP, but would require synchronization. A combined scheme might be quite effective.

If we consider the DAP Fortran code for the ADI scheme, Figs. 9 and 10, we can see that there are blocks of code which contain independent instructions. For example in Fig. 9, the calculation of U and V are independent. If the next block of code is rearranged so that QT is computed first, then the other six statements are all independent of each other. The next block of four statements are also independent, and so on. Finally the tridiagonal systems are all independent.

One can thus see that there are, on the average, blocks of 4 or 5 independent statements in the code. Each of these performs the same calculation in all processors. These calculations can thus be split up among the independent processors of an MIMD computer. Without considering the details of the MIMD machine it is difficult to say more, but it appears that this algorithm might be a good candidate for MIMD architectures. However, there clearly could be major problems because of the requirements of large data transfers and synchronization and convergence testing for the relaxation routine. These potential problems require analysis and experimentation on one or more MIMD architectures.

REFERENCES

[1] DAP: *Fortran Language*, Technical Publication 6918, International Computers Limited, 1981.
[2] J. J. DONGARRA, *Performance of various computers using standard linear equations software in Fortran environment*, Argonne National Laboratory Technical Memo, 23, 1984.
[3] T. B. GATSKI, C. E. GROSCH AND M. E. ROSE, *A numerical study of the two-dimensional Navier–Stokes equations in vorticity-velocity variables*, J. Comput. Phys., 48 (1982), pp. 1–22.
[4] T. B. GATSKI AND C. E. GROSCH, *A numerical study of the two- and three-dimensional unsteady Navier–Stokes equations in velocity-vorticity variables using compact schemes*, Proc. Ninth International Conference on Numerical Methods in Fluid Dynamics, Springer-Verlag, New York–Heidelberg–Berlin–Tokyo, 1985, pp. 235–239.
[5] ———, *Embedded cavity drag in steady laminar flow*, AIAA J., 23 (July 1985), pp. 1028–1037.
[6] C. E. GROSCH, *Performance analysis of Poisson solvers on array computers*, in Infotech State of the Art Report: Supercomputers, C. Jesshope and R. W. Hockney, eds., 2, 1979, Infotech International, pp. 147–181.
[7] R. W. HOCKNEY AND C. JESSHOPE, *Parallel Computers: Architecture, Programming and Algorithms*, Adam Hilger, Ltd., Bristol, 1981.
[8] R. W. HOCKNEY, $(r_\infty, h_{1/2}, s_{1/2})$ *measurements on the 2-CPU Cray X-MP*, Univ. Reading, Dept. Comput. Sci., Report RCS 185, 1985.

[9] S. KACZMARZ, *Angenaherte auflosung von systemen linearer gleichungen*, Bull. Acad. Polon, Sci. Lett., A (1937), pp. 355-357.

[10] R. M. MCINVILLE, T. B. GATSKI AND H. A. HASSAN, *Analysis of large vortical structures in shear layers*, AIAA J., 23 (1985), pp. 1165-1171.

[11] J. M. ORTEGA AND R. G. VOIGT, *Solution of partial differential equations on vector and parallel computers*, SIAM Rev., 27 (1985), pp. 149-240.

[12] R. B. PHILIPS AND M. E. ROSE, *Compact finite difference schemes for mixed initial-boundary value problems*, SIAM J. Numer. Anal., 19 (1982), pp. 698-719.

[13] M. E. ROSE, *A "unified" numerical treatment of the wave equation and the Cauchy-Riemann equations*, SIAM J. Numer. Anal., 18 (1981), pp. 372-376.

[14] K. TANABE, *Projection method for solving a singular system of linear equations and its applications*, Numer. Math., 17 (1971), pp. 203-214.

SIAM J. SCI. STAT. COMPUT.
Vol. 8, No. 1, January 1987

REDUCTION OF THE EFFECTS OF THE COMMUNICATION DELAYS IN SCIENTIFIC ALGORITHMS ON MESSAGE PASSING MIMD ARCHITECTURES*

JOEL H. SALTZ†, VIJAY K. NAIK† AND DAVID M. NICOL†

Abstract. The efficient implementation of algorithms on multiprocessor machines requires that the effects of communication delays be minimized. The effects of these delays on the performance of a model problem on a hypercube multiprocessor architecture is investigated, and methods are developed for increasing algorithm efficiency. The model problem under investigation is the solution by red–black Successive Over Relaxation of the heat equation; most of the techniques to be described here also apply equally well to the solution of elliptic partial differential equations by red–black or multicolor SOR methods.

This paper identifies methods for reducing communication traffic and overhead on a multiprocessor and reports the results of testing these methods on the Intel iPSC Hypercube. We examine methods for partitioning a problem's domain across processors, for reducing communication traffic during a global convergence check, for reducing the number of global convergence checks employed during an iteration, and for concurrently iterating on multiple time-steps in a time dependent problem. Our empirical results show that use of these methods can markedly reduce a numerical problem's execution time.

Key words. parallel processing, scientific computation, communication delay, hypercube architecture, convergence checking

AMS(MOS) subject classifications. 34A50, 35-04, 68B20

1. Introduction. The efficient implementation of algorithms on multiprocessor machines requires that the effects of communication delays be minimized. Reduction of communication delay effects in message passing machines may be brought about by restructuring algorithms. Ways in which the effect of communication delays can be reduced by such restructurings include: (1) reducing the quantity of information that must be communicated, (2) reducing the frequency with which messages must be sent, (3) overlapping communication with computation. The above goals may not in practice be mutually compatible. The relative importance of the three aspects of communication delay reduction will depend on the architecture under consideration [9], [10], [13].

The effects of these delays on the performance of a model problem on a hypercube multiprocessor architecture are investigated, and methods are developed for increasing algorithm efficiency. A hypercube multiprocessor [12], [7] is a collection of processors or nodes connected by a communication network with a hypercube topology. A hypercube has 2^m identical nodes where m represents the dimension of the hypercube. Each node in a hypercube is connected to m other neighbors. Nodes are assigned addresses from 0 to $2^m - 1$. Two nodes of a hypercube are connected when the binary expansion of the nodes' addresses differs in one bit position.

The model problem under investigation is the solution by red–black Successive Over Relaxation [14] of the heat equation; most of the techniques to be described here also apply equally well to the solution of elliptic partial differential equations by red–black or multicolor SOR methods. The model problem is solved on an N-dimensional hypercube by decomposing the domain into 2^N regions and assigning

---

* Received by the editors December 9, 1985; accepted for publication (in revised form) April 23, 1986. This research was supported by the National Aeronautics and Space Administration under NASA contract NAS1-17070 and NAS1-18107 while the authors were in residence at ICASE, NASA, Langley Research Center, Hampton, Virginia 23665.

† Institute for Computer Applications in Science and Engineering, NASA, Langley Research Center, Hampton, Virginia 23665.

one region to each processor. The regions are chosen either as strips or as rectangles and are mapped onto the architecture using a Gray code [3], [8]. Due to the grey code mapping, processors assigned adjacent regions of the domain are directly connected.

The two sources of communication delays in a simple iterative method such as SOR are the need to exchange information between the boundaries of the subdomain assigned to each processor and the need to check convergence. We examine a variety of factors which help determine the interprocessor communcation costs. In this paper methods of reducing both of these sources of communication delays are proposed.

The time required to transmit a packet of information from one processor to another to which it is directly linked may be approximately expressed as

$$\frac{b}{\alpha} + \beta$$

where b is the number of bytes contained in the message, α is bandwidth of the communication channel, and β is the overhead for sending a message. When $1/\alpha$ is considerably smaller than β, the time required to send a small message is only weakly dependent on the message size. In this case, there may be significant performance advantages in arranging an algorithm so that information that must be transmitted is sent in large quantities.

In the Intel hypercube used in the experiments described in this paper, $\beta \gg 1/\alpha$. In architectures in which it is possible to mask communication with computations, algorithms can be designed to allow computations to proceed despite high communication latencies [10]. In the Intel hypercube, this type of reorganization is not helpful, as communication may not be overlapped with computation to any appreciable extent. Given a multiprocessor with these characteristics, reducing the number of messages that must be sent by processors is consequently the main goal of the work to be described. In §§ 3, 4 and 5 methods are described that may be used to reduce the number of messages that must be sent by each processor and to consequently reduce the effect of the communication overhead β. Section 3 explores the consequences on the hypercube performance of the simple observation that the number of messages that must be sent by a processor when a domain is partitioned into strips is at most two, while a processor may have to send four messages when a domain is partitioned into square regions. Allowing iterations to sweep over more than one timestep is a method used in § 5 to decrease the number of messages that must be sent.

In a hypercube, it is possible to perform communications that combine results from all processors and to disseminate the results thus obtained in a time that grows logarithmically in the number of processors involved. When communication overheads are large, convergence testing may be quite costly despite this logarithmic growth. In § 4.1 two logarithmic methods for combining the results obtained from local convergence checks are compared. In both methods, for all but very small hypercubes, the communication delays resulting from convergence checking are comparable with or greater in size than the delays arising from the communication of the boundary variable values.

In both of the above schemes, communications for global convergence checking occur after each iteration. Two methods are proposed and tested for reducing the frequency with which communication is required for global convergence checking. The first method, discussed in § 4.2, checks for global convergence only when certain necessary conditions are fulfilled. One necessary condition is that all subdomains have detected convergence at some point in their computations. Other necessary conditions result from the fact that global convergence requires all processors to detect local convergence at a given iteration. In § 4.3 a method is proposed that utilizes a logarithmic method for checking for convergence but employs a statistical methodology to schedule convergence checks only at critical iterations.

In the following sections experimental results will be presented that pertain to the solution of a model problem. The partial differential equation being solved is the heat equation on the unit square with Dirichlet boundary conditions and with the first two modes used as the initial condition. The heat equation is solved using optimally over-relaxed red–black SOR on 64 by 64, 128 by 128, 256 by 256 point meshes with timesteps of 0.004, 0.002 and 0.001, respectively. All experimental results were obtained using a 64 processor Intel iPSC hypercube.

2. Effect of problem size on performance. As has been widely reported [2], [6], in order to obtain better performance from the multiprocessors, one should have a balance between computation and communication costs. If the communication costs are too high compared with the costs of computations, then the performance is bound to deteriorate. The obvious way to improve the performance is to increase the size of the subdomain assigned to each processor, which increases computation time without increasing the communication costs proportionately. In Fig. 1, we depict the performance of the system in terms of efficiency, as the domain size is varied from 64 by 64 through 256 by 256 grid sizes. Here the *efficiency* of an N-processor system is defined as the ratio of the time taken to solve the problem on one processor to the time taken to solve the problem on N processors multiplied by N. As expected, the efficiency drops as the number of processors is increased, but the rate at which it drops becomes more gradual as the grid size is increased. In all the experiments performed here the domain was subdivided into strips, and convergence checking was performed after

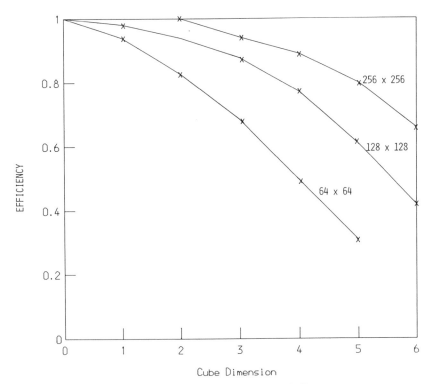

FIG. 1. *Effect of domain size on parallel efficiency.*

each iteration. The model problem was solved for five timesteps, and the efficiencies were computed by measuring the elapsed time to find the solutions of the first five timesteps.

3. The effect of domain partitioning on performance. The cost of communicating information from one processor to another in a hypercube multiprocessor is a function of the amount of data that must be sent, the number of packets of data into which the data is placed, and the logical distance of the processors from one another in the hypercube. The domain of a PDE may be decomposed into regions with a variety of shapes, with certain shapes provably optimal with respect to minimizing the number of variable values that must be communicated across boundaries.[1] The regions may then be mapped onto a hypercube in a way that attempts to minimize the number of intermediate nodes that messages must traverse in going from the boundary of one region to another [8].

We considered domain decompositions consisting of strips and rectangles; such shapes are easier to program and can be mapped onto a hypercube so all processors that need to send messages to one another are directly linked. It is easily demonstrated that in a domain divided into rectangles, less information must be transmitted across boundaries during each iteration than would be the case with a domain divided into strips. On the other hand, in a domain divided into rectangles, regions may have four neighbors, while when the domain is divided into strips, each region may have no more than two neighbors.

We examine the trade-off in costs between the division of a domain into rectangles and the division of a domain into strips in C color SOR [1]. Assume a 2^n by 2^n point domain and 2^m processors. The domain may be divided into 2^m $2^{n-\lfloor m/2 \rfloor}$ by $2^{n-\lceil m/2 \rceil}$ rectangles, or alternatively into 2^n by 2^{n-m} strips. In C color SOR the values of points are adjusted one color at a time. Each time a color is adjusted, all rectangles in the interior of the domain must send four packets. If the number of colors used in the SOR sweeps does not evenly divide the number of points on a side of a rectangle or strip, the number of values to be communicated may differ by one between sweeps over different colors.

Rectangles in the interior of a domain, i.e., those with four neighbors during the course of each iteration, must send $2C$ packets of average size $2^{n-\lfloor m/2 \rfloor}/C$ and must send $2C$ packets of average size $2^{n-\lceil m/2 \rceil}/C$. Strips in the interior of a domain, i.e. those with two neighbors, must send $2C$ packets of average size $2^n/C$.

The comparison of costs between strips and rectangles depends on the overhead for sending each message, on the per-byte cost of transmitting information, on the number of processors, and on the size of the domain. Figure 2 depicts a comparison between local communication costs when the model problem is solved with domains of varying size using 64 processors. For domains of size 256 by 256 or smaller, the use of strips led to smaller communication delays than the use of rectangles, while for a domain with 512 by 512 mesh points the use of rectangles led to the smaller delays. Figure 3 depicts the local communication costs for rectangles compared to the local communication cost for strips for varying numbers of processors in a 64 by 64 point domain. Note that the communication cost for rectangles exceeds that for strips when at least eight processors are utilized. When fewer than eight processors are used, the number of packets that must be sent by each processor in a domain divided into rectangles is equal to the number of packets that must be sent in a strip divided domain.

---

[1] D. Reed, M. Patrick and L. Adams, to be submitted to IEEE Transactions on Computers.

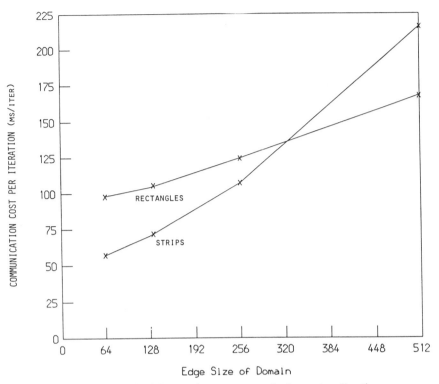

FIG. 2. *Effect of subdomain shape on communication cost per iteration.*

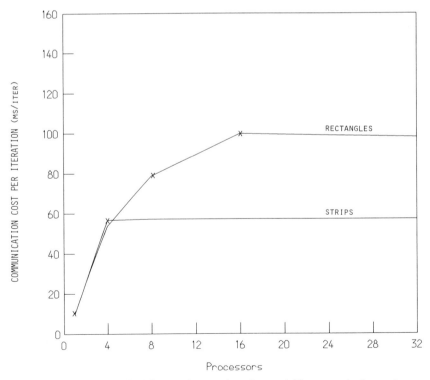

FIG. 3. *Effect of subdomain shape on boundary variable communication cost.*

Moreover, in this case, the amount of information that must be sent by each processor is smaller or equal when the domain is partitioned into rectangles instead of strips. The above local communication costs were measured in the following way. The model problem was solved for a given domain size for 50 iterations over 3 timesteps, and then for the same domain size the program was run without sending any messages. The difference in the execution times between the program runs that sent messages and those that did not was used to give an estimate of time spent in communicating boundary information. Note that neither of the program runs performed any communication for convergence checking.

4. Convergence checking schemes. In this section it will be shown that the communication required in testing for global convergence at the end of an iteration may be quite costly. Several methods for reducing this delay are then experimentally examined.

Our experiments presumed that convergences had been achieved when

$$\|X_i - X_{i-1}\|_\infty \leq \varepsilon$$

where X_i is the vector valued solution approximation after the ith iteration, and ε is our tolerance. The $\|\cdot\|_\infty$ norm above yields the maximal absolute difference between components of X_i and X_{i-1}. Convergence checking in a multiprocessor involves two distinct costs. The first is simply the time required to compute the component differences. The second cost is the time required for the processors to communicate and combine their respective local convergence results to determine whether global convergence is achieved at the end of an iteration. This latter cost is a function of the multiprocessor communication delay and the scheme used to combine the component differences. We will first look at ways to combine differences during a global convergence check on the hypercube. We will then discuss two different ways of reducing the *number* of convergence checks used during an iterative solution.

4.1. Combination methods. We compared two different ways of combining component differences during a convergence check. Both of these methods first require each processor to find the maximal component difference over its own piece of the domain. Each processor then sets its *convergence flag* equal to 1 if this maximal difference over the processor's domain is less than ε; the flag is otherwise 0. Clearly convergence is achieved if and only if every processor's convergence flag is 1. The two methods differ in how they cause processors to exchange and combine these flags. Both schemes have time complexity $O(m)$, m being the dimension of the hypercube.

The first scheme, to be called the tree method, requires $2m$ stages. In m stages, a logical AND is taken of all convergence flags and the resulting flag ends up in node 0. If the value of this logical AND is 1, global convergence has occurred; otherwise global convergence has still not been detected. During each state k, $0 \leq k < m$ of communication, each of $2^m/(k+2)$ processors sends to another processor a flag that indicates its current knowledge of whether global convergence has occurred. Let $\langle d_{m-1}, \cdots, d_0 \rangle$ be the binary expansion of the address of a node, and let $\bar{d}_k$ represent the complement of binary digit d_k. Let $\text{Flag}^k_{\langle d_{m-1}, d_k, \cdots, d_0 \rangle}$ represent the current knowledge of global convergence in the node with address $\langle d_{m-1}, d_k, \cdots, d_0 \rangle$ at the beginning of communication stage k. In stage k, processor $\langle d_{m-1}, d_k, \cdots, d_0 \rangle$ will send $\text{Flag}^k_{\langle d_{m-1}, d_k, \cdots, d_0 \rangle}$ to processor $\langle d_{m-1}, \cdots, \bar{d}_k, \cdots, d_0 \rangle$ if $d_0 = \cdots = d_{k-1} = 0$ and $d_k = 1$. Upon the receipt of the flag, processor $\langle d_{m-1}, \cdots, \bar{d}_k, \cdots, d_0 \rangle$ will set $\text{Flag}^{k+1}_{\langle d_{m-1}, \bar{d}_k, \cdots, d_0 \rangle} = \text{Flag}^k_{\langle d_{m-1}, \cdots, \bar{d}_k, \cdots, d_0 \rangle}$ AND $\text{Flag}^k_{\langle d_{m-1}, d_k, \cdots, d_0 \rangle}$. This process terminates at Node 0. Node 0 at this point distributes the information on whether global convergence has occurred. Distributing the convergence results also require m stages of communication.

Another method of checking for convergence can be accomplished in m stages of communication. This procedure is similar in principle to the cascade method for computing sums [5] and will be called the cascade method for checking convergence. In this method, during each stage of communication each processor P sends a flag Flag_P^k indicating its current knowledge of whether global convergence has occurred to another processor. At the end of the m stages, the resulting flag obtained in all processors is the logical AND of all convergence flags.

The cascade process functions as follows: Let $\langle d_{m-1}, \cdots, d_0 \rangle$ be the binary expansion of the address of a node. In stage k, $0 \le k < m$, processor $\langle d_{m-1}, d_k, \cdots, d_0 \rangle$ will send $\text{Flag}_{\langle d_{m-1}, d_k, \cdots, d_0 \rangle}^k$ to processor $\langle d_{m-1}, \cdots, \bar{d}_k, \cdots, d_0 \rangle$. Upon receipt, processor $\langle d_{m-1}, \cdots, \bar{d}_k, \cdots, d_0 \rangle$ will set $\text{Flag}_{\langle d_{m-1}, \bar{d}_k, \cdots, d_0 \rangle}^{k+1}$ equal to the logical AND of flags $\text{Flag}_{\langle d_{m-1}, \cdots, \bar{d}_k, \cdots, d_0 \rangle}^k$ and $\text{Flag}_{\langle d_{m-1}, \cdots, d_k, \cdots, d_0 \rangle}^k$. This process terminates after m stages, and at this point the flag $\text{Flag}_{\langle d_{m-1}, d_k, \cdots, d_0 \rangle}^m$ in each processor is the logical AND of all convergence flags. The flow of data corresponding to the two convergence checking processes is depicted in Fig. 4. This figure illustrates that the tree method has a single process detect and then report global convergence; the cascade method requires all processors to calculate the global convergence state.

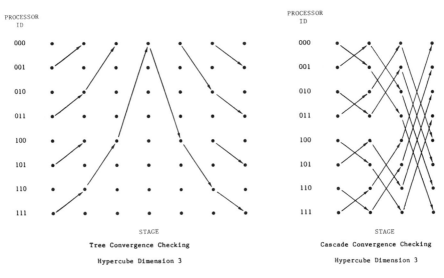

FIG. 4

The cost per iteration of the tree and cascade convergence checking methods is depicted in Fig. 5, along with the cost per iteration of local communication between strips and the per-iteration computation cost for a 64 by 64 mesh point model problem. The cost of convergence checking is estimated by running the model problem for three timesteps, 50 iterations per timestep both with and without the convergence checking methods and comparing the run times. When the convergence checking methods were utilized, a minor modification in the program caused the convergence results thus obtained to be ignored. The additional time required for convergence checking information could hence be ascertained by comparing the timings of programs that otherwise performed identical computations.

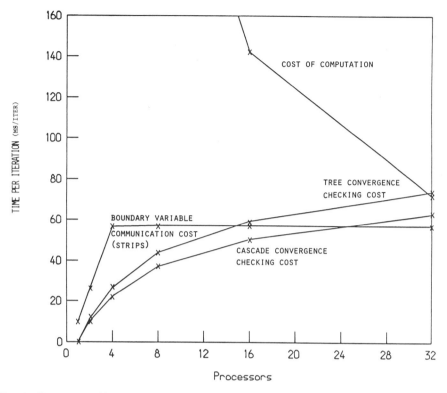

FIG. 5. *Comparison of boundary variable communication cost, convergence checking cost and computation cost.*

The cascade convergence checking method requires each processor to send and to receive four messages per iteration when a cube with 16 processors is used. During each iteration, nodes assigned strips that are on the interior of the domain must send and receive four messages containing boundary variables values, two for the sweep over red points and two for the sweep over black points. When a cube with 16 processors is utilized, the communication cost of sending boundary variable values and of sending convergence flag information is indeed comparable. The cost of sending the boundary variable values is slightly greater, presumably due to larger amounts of data per message.

The cost of the tree method of convergence checking is only slightly greater than the cost of the cascade method despite the fact that it requires twice as many stages. In the tree method, during each stage of the computation a processor is called upon either to send *or* receive a message, while in the cascade method each processor must both send and receive a message during each stage. Further experimentation has indicated that, in a number of contexts, there appears to be a substantial time penalty associated with requiring a processor to both send and receive a message during a given stage of communication.

4.2. Asynchronous convergence checking. This section discusses one means of reducing the number of convergence checks required during an iterative solution. This scheme is called *asynchronous convergence checking,* or the ACC scheme. The ACC's basic idea is to check for global convergence only when certain necessary conditions are fulfilled. One necessary condition is that all subdomains have detected convergence at some point in their computations. Other necessary conditions, to be expanded upon later, result from the fact that global convergence requires that all processors detect local convergence at a given iteration.

Discussion of the ACC is facilitated by a few definitions. At the end of an iteration, a processor's subdomain is in one of two states: *nonconverged*, or *presumptively converged*. This nomenclature emphasizes that convergence over a processor's subdomain does not guarantee global convergence at that iteration, nor does it prohibit a subdomain from oscillating between nonconvergence and presumptive convergence. Global convergence is achieved if and only if all the subdomains achieve presumptive convergence at the end of the same number of iterations. If the computations were to continue, all subdomains would be expected to remain in this state indefinitely. A *convergence sequence* for a subdomain is a maximal sequence of iterations during which the subdomain is presumptively converged; the first iteration of the sequence is the *convergence sequence header*. Thus a convergence sequence header identifies an iteration where a subdomain passes from nonconvergence to presumptive convergence (startup anomalies are accounted for by *defining* each subdomain to be nonconverged before the first iteration). No further convergence headers are produced by that subdomain until it passes out of and then back into presumptive convergence. A subdomain's oscillation between nonconvergence and presumptive convergence gives rise to a series of convergence sequences, each with a distinct header. It is important to note that if global convergence is achieved at iteration j, then j is a convergence sequence header for at least one subdomain. The ACC method looks for global convergence only at certain iterations which serve as convergence sequence headers of one or more subdomains, but not at all the convergence sequence headers found in the system. The global convergence test is made centrally, in a processor known as the *c-host*. The high cost of communication between Intel hypercube nodes and their *system host* led us to designate a hypercube node as *c*-host for global convergence checks.

Under the ACC method, the *c*-host makes an informed guess at when the global convergence might have been achieved; after communicating with the other processors, the *c*-host either confirms or rejects the guess. A rejection is followed by another guess. This process is continued until the confirmation takes place. Implementation of ACC requires each processor to always maintain its subdomain's current convergence state, and the convergence sequence header if the subdomain is presumptively converged. We now separately describe the three component parts of the method, the *initial guess*, the *processor guess response*, and the *guess confirmation/generation*.

Initial guess. As soon as a subdomain is presumptively converged for the first time, its processor reports the corresponding convergence sequence header to the *c*-host. The processor then continues with the computation without waiting for convergence information from other processors. The *c*-host makes the first guess after receiving such a message from each processor; let $\{j_1, \cdots, j_k\}$ be the received header values. The *c*-host optimistically guesses that global convergence is achieved as early as is possible, at iteration $j_{\max} = \max\{j_1, \cdots, j_k\}$. The *c*-host then tells each processor that $j_{\max}$ is a potential point of global convergence.

Processor guess response. Suppose a processor receives a guess (not necessarily the first guess) j_G from the *c*-host. At iteration j_p, $j_p \geqq j_G$, the processor sends back the *current* convergence sequence header if j_p is part of a convergence sequence (an outdated convergence sequence header is thus effectively overwritten in the processor's memory). A message is sent immediately after such a j_p is found.

Guess confirmation/generation. As described above, each processor responds to a guess j_G by returning a convergence sequence header to the *c*-host. The *c*-host either confirms or rejects the guess as soon as every processors' response is received. Letting

j_{max} be the maximal value among these responses, the guess j_G is confirmed if $j_G = j_{max}$; in this case global convergence is achieved at iteration j_G, and the c-host instructs all processors to stop iterating. If $j_G < j_{max}$, then j_G is rejected, and the value j_{max} is sent to all processors as the next guess.

We can show that the ACC identifies an iteration achieving global convergence; furthermore, if the solution cannot drift out of global convergence (even temporarily), then the ACC is guaranteed to identify the first iteration achieving global convergence. The first claim is proven by contradiction. Suppose that ACC confirms iteration j_A as a point of global convergence, but that some processor P has a nonconverged subdomain at iteration j_A. By the confirmation process described above, j_A is the maximum header value in response to a guess j_G, and $j_A = j_G$. Consider P's response to this guess, at (say) iteration j_p. Clearly $j_p \geq j_G$, since P does not respond until it has iterated at least to j_G and is presumptively converged. Furthermore, $j_p > j_G$ since P's subdomain is nonconverged at iteration $j_A = j_G$. But j_A is the maximum among all responses to j_G, so $j_p \leq j_G$, a contradiction. We also show that ACC finds the first globally converged iteration if the solution never diverges from global convergence. Suppose that global convergence is achieved first at iteration j_f, and that the ACC first detects global convergence at j_A. For the sake of contradiction, suppose that $j_A \neq j_f$. Since ACC does detect global convergence, we must have $j_A \geq j_f$; for the sake of contradiction, suppose that $j_A > j_f$. j_A is a convergence sequence header from some processor P; thus P's subdomain was *not* converged at iteration $j_A - 1 \geq j_f$. This is a contradiction, since we have assumed that global convergence at j_f implies convergence in P for all iterations $j \geq j_f$. Thus $j_A = j_f$, showing that ACC finds the first globally converged iteration.

The ACC scheme is asynchronous in that the processors never synchronize waiting for convergence information and in that the processors do not necessarily send the messages to the c-host at the end of the same iteration. Unlike asynchronous chaotic methods, we still presume that the processors synchronize with their neighbors at each iteration. The communication costs required by the ACC method are quite small. The ACC requires substantially fewer messages than standard convergence checking; furthermore, on appropriate architectures the communication may be overlapped with computation. From this aspect, the ACC is clearly superior to standard convergence checking. However, the ACC does incur two additional computational costs. The first (and minimal) cost is execution of the ACC logic; the second cost occurs because each processor continues to iterate until it is told to stop. Thus each processor "overshoots," doing slightly more computation even after global convergence is achieved. In practice, neither of these costs proved to be significant; the improvement over standard convergence checking is substantial, as discussed in § 5.

Further improvements in the ACC scheme are possible. With a cube of large dimension, we can distribute the c-host function by forming clusters of smaller cubes; ACC is then applied locally at a cluster. A cluster reaching "global" convergence is logically equivalent to presumptive convergence in a subdomain; a central c-host would determine global convergence using ACC at a global level. Another improvement is achieved by checking a subdomain's convergence only at selected iterations. The computational cost of checking convergence is saved, at the risk of doing more iterations than are required. In a similar vein, the scheme discussed in the next section formally schedules convergence checks and balances the benefits of skipping checks with its risks.

4.3. Maximized expected useful work. A second method of reducing convergence checking costs *schedules* convergence tests at critical iterations. The scheduling methodology is that of decision making under uncertainty. It is intended for use when only inexact information about convergence behavior can be presumed. This gives it a particular advantage for use by a multiprocessor operating system on general numerical problems. Thus, the "uncertainty" considered within the scheduling mechanism is due to the generality of problem treated by the mechanism, and to the lack of knowledge about the solution's behavior.

Upon the completion of a scheduled test, the next convergence test is scheduled on the basis of the cost of testing convergence and the costs of scheduling the next test "too far" in the future after convergence has been achieved. The iteration chosen is the one maximizing the "expected useful work" per unit time and is thus dubbed the MEW method.

The MEW method entails a certain amount of mathematical formalism. First, we define the ith iteration error estimate E_i:

$$E_i = \| X_i - X_{i-1} \|_\infty.$$

We model the convergence behavior of an iterative method by assuming that

(1) $$E_n \leqq E_1 \cdot e^{-\lambda \cdot (n-1)}.$$

We say that the solution has converged at iteration n if $E_n \leqq \varepsilon$ for our tolerance ε. The key issue in this formulation is the estimation of λ. If the exact value of λ were known, then the first converged iteration is found by solving for n in the equation $\varepsilon = E_1 \cdot e^{-\lambda \cdot n}$. Since the exact value of λ is not known, it must be estimated.

Our treatment of λ is Bayesian (the reader unfamiliar with Bayesian estimation can consult [11] or any standard statistical text). We view a convergence test as a statistical observation of λ. The *observation* of λ created by calculating E_j is derived from relation (1):

(2) $$\hat{\lambda} = \frac{1}{(j-1)} \cdot (\ln (E_j) - \ln (E_1)).$$

Our uncertainity about future convergence convergence behavior is modeled by assuming that $\hat{\lambda}$ is a normal random variable $N(\lambda, \sigma_s^2)$. λ here is the true unknown convergence rate, and σ_s^2 is a sampling variance which we will also estimate. We again emphasize that the normality assumption models our uncertainty about the problem itself, as well as the problem and solution method behavior. This assumption describes what we are willing to believe about the true value of λ, in the absence of any further information.

We furthermore suppose that we have some prior knowledge of what λ might be. This prior knowledge is encoded with a normal (prior) probability distribution $N(\lambda_{pr}, \sigma_{pr}^2)$ describing the likelihood of λ taking any particular value. Given the parameters $\lambda_{pr}, \sigma_{pr}^2$ and an observation $\hat{\lambda}$, Bayes' theorem says that the posterior distribution of λ is normal $N(\lambda_{pt}, \sigma_{pt}^2)$ where

$$\lambda_{pt} = \left(\frac{\sigma_{pr}^2}{\sigma_{pr}^2 + \sigma_s^2} \right) \cdot \hat{\lambda} + \left(\frac{\sigma_s^2}{\sigma_{pr}^2 + \sigma_s^2} \right) \cdot \lambda_{pr}$$

and

$$\sigma_{pt}^2 = \sigma_{pr}^2 \cdot \frac{\sigma_s^2}{\sigma_{pr}^2 + \sigma_s^2}.$$

The posterior distribution incorporates our prior knowledge of λ with the additional information afforded by $\hat{\lambda}$. The scheduling of our next convergence test (presuming $E_j > \varepsilon$) depends in part on this distribution.

We next examine the mechanics of our convergence test scheduling, temporarily deferring discussion of prior determination and the estimation of σ_s^2. Suppose we have a prior distribution of λ, and we make a convergence test at iteration j. We then calculate λ_{pt} and σ_{pt}^2 as described. From iteration j, we view the probable future behavior of convergence at iteration $j + d$ *as though* we are at the first iteration. That is, we presume that the convergence model for iterations $j + d$, $d > 0$, is

$$E_{j+d} \lesseqgtr E_j \cdot e^{-\lambda \cdot d}.$$

It can be shown that sensitivity to measurement errors in λ is reduced by using this modification. The probability of not observing convergence at iteration $j + d$ is easily seen to be identical to the probability that λ is less than the threshold $T_j(d)$, where

$$T_j(d) = \frac{1}{d} \cdot \ln \left(\frac{E_j}{\varepsilon} \right).$$

Appealing to the normal structure of the posterior distribution, we thus have

$$\text{Prob}\,\{\lambda < T_j(d)\} = \Phi \left(\frac{T_j(d) - \lambda_{pt}}{\sigma_{pt}} \right)$$

where Φ is the standard normal cumulative distribution function. We use the probability above as an estimate of the probability that we will not have converged by iteration $j + d$.

We can now detail the scheduling decision. Let I be the delay cost of performing a convergence test, and let D be the time required to perform one iteration without a convergence test. If we schedule the next convergence test at iteration $j + d$, the total time required to do d iterations and perform the test is $d \cdot D + I$. Then the average *required* number of iterations per unit time achieved by this decision is

(3) $$\sum_{i=1}^{d} \Phi \left(\frac{T_j(i) - \lambda_{pt}}{\sigma_{pt}} \right) \Big/ d \cdot D + I.$$

We find the $d = d_{max}$ which maximizes the expression above and schedule the next convergence test at iteration $j + d_{max}$. Maximization of expression (3) balances the cost of testing convergence with the cost and uncertainty of doing more iterations than are required. As a function of d, expression (3) has at most one local maximum which is easily found. The convergence test scheduling decision at iteration $j + d_{max}$ uses the $N(\lambda_{pt}, \sigma_{pt}^2)$ distribution as its prior.

The mechanics of our scheduling policy illustrate how we deal with uncertainty about λ. This policy is also dependent on quantities we now discuss: the sampling variance σ_s^2 and the initial prior distribution of λ. There are situations where significant prior knowledge of convergence behavior is known. The model problem is time-dependent, so we need to solve the equations at each of a number of time steps. If the same iterative method is used each time iteration, the *asymptotic* convergence rates will be the same for all the time iterations. However, the effective convergence rate may vary since initial errors will be different. The convergence behavior of the method at time steps in the near past is a good predictor of the convergence behavior in the near future. In fact, after the first three time steps, we were able to construct very reasonable priors *before* beginning a time step's iterations. We simply used the last timestep's effective λ as the prior mean (found by solving $\varepsilon = E_1 \cdot e^{-\lambda \cdot (N-1)}$ for λ, knowing that exactly N iterations were required); we used the sample variance of the last three timesteps' effective λ's for our prior variance. The Bayesian formulation can also exploit user experience with the solution method's convergence; this experience could be summarized as a prior distribution.

At the beginning of the computation we might well presume no prior knowledge of the convergence behavior. We gain some insight into this behavior by testing for convergence after each of the first few iterations. As before, a convergence test is viewed as an observation of λ. If we could assume that each observation is independent of any other, we could then use the sample mean as the initial prior mean λ_{pr}, and the sample variance as both the sample variance σ_s^2 and the prior variance σ_{pr}^2. However, successive errors E_i and E_{i+1} are not independent. Their correlation leads to a biased estimation of λ_{pr} and the underestimation of σ_{pr}^2. To compensate for this conflict of mathematical assumption and practical reality, we devised the *constrained projection rule*. This rule states that if convergence is tested at iteration j, the next convergence test must be scheduled before iteration $2 \cdot j + 1$. This rule forces additional convergence tests at the beginning of the computation, and affords protection from wildly optimistic scheduling decisions. We thus used the sample statistics to construct our prior information, but then protected ourselves from a bad prior with the constrained projection rule. In our experience, this rule was effectively invoked only at the beginning of the computation. After this startup period, our underlying assumption of independence between observations of λ is better satisfied, and the statistics are more accurate. The variance σ_s^2 is then reasonably taken to be the sample variance of the observed λ's to date.

The MEW method is an excellent vehicle for encapsulating both our prior knowledge, and the knowledge gained about convergence as the solution progresses. Furthermore, it is simple to program, and its sensitivity to changes in the problem or problem distribution across processors lies only in the parameters I and D. Yet the sensitivity to these key parameters and measured behavior variation makes the MEW method more attractive than a simple "test every q iterations" approach, an approach left with the difficult problem of determining q. Most importantly, the empirical study described in the next section shows that MEW is quite effective in reducing convergence checking delay.

5. Convergence checking performance. The effects of employing the three different convergence schemes on the algorithm performance (on a 128 by 128 grid) is depicted in Fig. 6. The model problem was solved on a cube with 1, 2, 4, 8, 16, 32, and 64 processors; our implementation of ACC dedicated one node to the c-host function, so that we did not test this method with 64 processors (the maximum cube size on our system). In each test the domain was subdivided into strips of equal size, assigned one to each processor so that adjacent strips were mapped onto adjacent processors. In Fig. 6, the measured performance in terms of time-steps advanced per second is plotted as a function of the number of processors. Figure 6 illustrates that the performance of all three convergence schemes degrades with an increasing number of processors. The standard convergence scheme checking scheme depicted here involves the use of the tree method of global convergence checking used each iteration. The tree method of convergence checking was utilized as scheduled in the MEW scheme. Results obtained for the cascade method of convergence checking are quite similar to those depicted here. The standard convergence scheme's deterioration is rapid, while the other two schemes degrade gradually. The difference between the MEW and ACC schemes is not significant. Both have essentially the same communication costs, as very few ACC guesses and MEW checks were required on each timestep. The ACC overshot after global convergence was between three and five percent. The MEW scheme has a lower computation cost than ACC because it skips local convergence checking on some iterations altogether. The ACC scheme checks the state of each

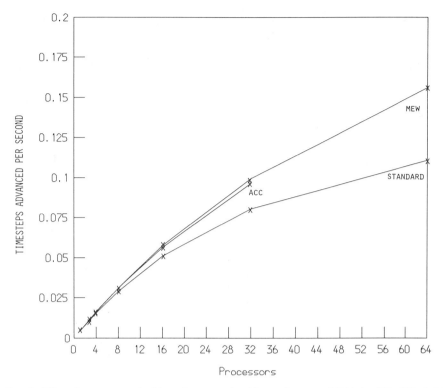

FIG. 6 *Effect of convergence checking schemes on algorithm performance.* (*Grid size* 128 × 128, *Subdomain Shape: Strips.*)

subdomain every iteration, although we observed a 10% improvement by checking every other iteration. The difference in local convergence checking accounts for the slight difference in the two schemes' performance. All three methods showed similar effects on the algorithm performance when the grid size was changed to 64 by 64 or 256 by 256.

6. Reduction of communication delays resulting from windows. Reduction of communication delays in the iterative solution of the linear equations produced by a discretization of a time dependent problem can be effected by iteratively solving more than one timestep during a given stage of the computations. The boundary variable values from more than one timestep can be sent in a packet, thus reducing the effect of the message transmission overhead.

In an iterative solution of a time dependent problem, one generally iterates over each timestep individually until convergence at that timestep is detected. One may instead iterate over more than one timestep during each stage of a computation. Assume that we are iterating over variables at timesteps $t_1, \cdots, t_n$. During each iterative sweep, all variables are updated in each of the timesteps included in the window. Following the sweep, the right-hand sides of equations at timesteps $t_2, \cdots, t_n$ are updated to account for changes in the variable values at the earlier timesteps. Convergence is checked at t_1, and when global convergence is detected at this time the window shifts up one timestep to encompass $t_2, \cdots, t_{n+1}$. It has been shown [9] that the asymptotic rate of convergence of SOR implemented with windows is equivalent to that of SOR applied to each timestep individually. In other words the total number of sweeps over each timestep required for a given degree of error reduction does not, in any asymptotic sense, change with the window size. For finite difference equations in which time discretization is by Crank–Nicholson or backwards Euler methods, the operation count for each sweep over a timestep is minimally effected by the use of windows. In practice, the computational work required to solve a problem increases quite gradually with window size.

Communication costs are reduced in two ways when one iterates over windows of timesteps in a time-dependent problem. The first is the previously stated fact that fewer but larger packets need be sent for the transmission of boundary variable data. Because convergence need be checked only at the lowest timestep in a window, the number of global communications required to check for convergence is reduced by a factor of 1/window-size as long as the total number of sweeps over each timestep does not change with window size, as is approximately the case for small windows. Thus if the total number of sweeps over each timestep were independent of window size and the cost per packet were independent of the size of the packet, the overall cost of communication would be reduced by a factor of 1/window-size. Finally, some computation time is saved because the computations required for local convergence checking need only be carried out at the lowest timestep in a window.

Algorithm performance is improved by the use of windows of a relatively small size. A number of experiments were carried out to demonstrate this; the results of one set are shown in Fig. 7. The model problem was solved on a 64 by 64 point domain, and the rate of computation resulting from the use of windows of sizes 1, 2 and 3 is shown. A notable improvement in performance is seen in comparing windows of sizes 1 and 2; a less marked improvement in performance is seen when a window of size 3 was utilized. This result is expected as the computational cost increases as window

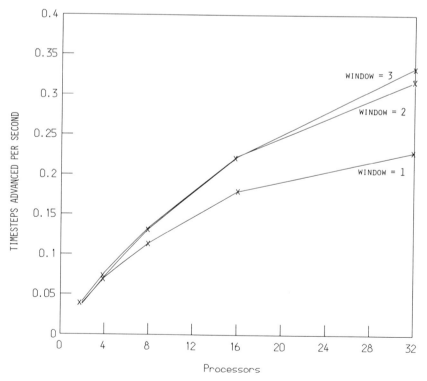

FIG. 7. *Effect of windows on performance.* (*Grid:* 64×64, *Shape: Strips, Standard Conv. Checking.*)

size is increased, and communication delays can be reduced by no more than a factor of 1/window size.

The use of windows decreases the cost of communicating boundary variables and communication flags at the cost of increased storage requirements and an increase in the computation required for each timestep. The methods for reducing the costs of global convergence checking described here have minimal costs and storage requirements. It is hence natural that the methods should be used together. In Fig. 8 are depicted results for the model problem solved on a 128 by 128 point domain using windows of sizes 1 and 2 with Bayesian MEW convergence test scheduling and using windows of sizes 1 and 2 with standard convergence testing. The use of both windowing and Bayesian convergence test scheduling together led to additional improvements in performance over that obtained through the use of either separately.

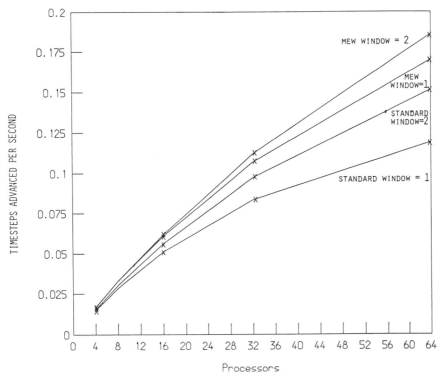

FIG. 8. *Effect of windows and of convergence checking schemes on performance.* (*Grid*: 128 × 128, *Shape*: *Strips.*)

7. Conclusion. The sources of communication delays in the solution of a model problem by red–black SOR have been identified and their relative contribution quantified under a number of circumstances. A number of methods have been proposed and tested to reduce the effects of each of these sources of communication delay.

In a message passing multiprocessor whose overhead for communication β is substantially larger than $1/\alpha$, the time required to send a byte, there is considerable motivation to reduce the number of messages that must be sent. In § 3 the discussion and experimental tests on domain partitioning indicate that improvements in performance may in many circumstances be obtained by reducing the number of messages that must be sent even when the total number of bytes to be sent must increase. In § 5 it is seen that through the use of windows the number of messages that must be sent is decreased. In this case the trade-off is a small increase in the cost of computation, and again an overall performance improvement is noted.

Checking global convergence when message overhead is high is quite costly, and methods were described in § 3 to perform tests efficiently and to reduce the number of such tests required. It is demonstrated in § 5 that the effects of using windows and of using methods that reduce the effects of convergence costs can have a complementary effect of performance.

It should be noted that convergence testing is the only nonlocal communication in red–black SOR. Both the ACC and the MEW method greatly reduce global communication and are consequently expected to be quite useful in architectures where the interprocessor connectivity is more restricted, such as a ring or a mesh multiprocessor. In these architectures, combining results from all processors may be quite expensive for large machines.

Acknowledgments. We would like to thank the Mathematics and Statistics Research Section at Oak Ridge National Laboratory for generously granting us use of their Intel Personal Super-Computer. We are particularly indebted to Mike Heath and Tom Dunigan for assistance during the course of this work. We are grateful to Bob Voigt for constant support and encouragement.

REFERENCES

[1] L. M. ADAMS AND J. M. ORTEGA, *A multi-color SOR method for parallel computation,* Proc. of the International Conference on Parallel Processing, K. E. Batcher, W. C. Meilander and J. L. Potter, eds., August 24–27, 1982, pp. 53–56.

[2] G. C. FOX, *Concurrent processing for scientific calculations,* COMPCON84, 28th IEEE Computer Society International Conference, 1984, pp. 70–73.

[3] E. M. REINGOLD, J. NIEVERGELT AND N. DEO, *Combinatorial Algorithms,* Prentice-Hall, Englewood Cliffs, NJ, 1977, pp. 173–189.

[4] C. L. SEITZ, *The cosmic cube,* Comm. ACM, 28 (1985), pp. 22–33.

[5] R. HOCKNEY AND C. JESSHOPE, *Parallel computers: Architecture Programming, and Algorithms,* Adam Hilger Ltd., Bristol, UK, 1981.

[6] J. ORTEGA AND R. VOIGT, *Solution of partial differential equations on vectors and parallel computers,* SIAM Rev., 27 (June 1985), pp. 149–240.

[7] J. RATTNER, *Concurrent processing: A new direction in scientific computing,* AFIPS Conference Proceedings 1985 National Computer Conference, Vol. 54, pp. 157–166.

[8] Y. SAAD AND M. H. SCHULTZ, *Topological properties of hypercubes,* Research Report YALEU/DCS/RR-389, Yale University, New Haven, CT, 1985.

[9] J. H. SALTZ, *Parallel and adaptive algorithms in scientific and medical computing: robust method for the solution of partial differential equations on multiprocessor machines,* Ph.D. thesis, Duke University, 1985.

[10] J. H. SALTZ AND V. K. NAIK, *Towards developing robust algorithms for solving partial differential equations on MIMD machines,* ICASE Report No. 85-39, NASA Contractor Report No. 177979, 1985.

[11] S. A. SCHMITT, *An Elementary Introduction to Bayesian Statistics,* Addison-Wesley, Reading, MA, 1969.

[12] C. L. SEITZ, *The cosmic cube,* Comm. ACM, 28 (1985), pp. 22–33.

[13] R. G. VOIGT, *Where are the parallel algorithms,* 1985 National Computer Conference Proceedings, AFIPS Press, Reston, Virginia, 1985, pp. 329–334.

[14] D. M. YOUNG, *Iterative Solutions of Large Linear Systems,* Academic Press, New York, 1971.

Part II

Reprinted from the SIAM Journal on Scientific and Statistical Computing
Volume 8, Number 2, March 1987.

SIAM J. SCI. STAT. COMPUT.
Vol. 8, No. 2, March 1987

A FULLY PARALLEL ALGORITHM FOR THE SYMMETRIC EIGENVALUE PROBLEM*

J. J. DONGARRA† AND D. C. SORENSEN†

Abstract. In this paper we present a parallel algorithm for the symmetric algebraic eigenvalue problem. The algorithm is based upon a divide and conquer scheme suggested by Cuppen for computing the eigensystem of a symmetric tridiagonal matrix. We extend this idea to obtain a parallel algorithm that retains a number of active parallel processes that is greater than or equal to the initial number throughout the course of the computation. We give a new deflation technique which together with a robust root finding technique will assure computation of an eigensystem to full accuracy in the residuals and in the orthogonality of eigenvectors. A brief analysis of the numerical properties and sensitivity to round off error is presented to indicate where numerical difficulties may occur. The algorithm is able to exploit parallelism at all levels of the computation and is well suited to a variety of architectures.

Computational results are presented for several machines. These results are very encouraging with respect to both accuracy and speedup. A surprising result is that the parallel algorithm, even when run in serial mode, can be significantly faster than the previously best sequential algorithm on large problems, and is effective on moderate size problems when run in serial mode.

Key words. parallel algorithm, symmetric eigenvalue problem, divide and conquer, tridiagonal

AMS (MOS) subject classification. 65F15

1. Introduction. The symmetric eigenvalue problem is one of the most fundamental problems of computational mathematics. It arises in many applications and therefore represents an important area for algorithmic research. The problem has received considerable attention in the literature and was probably the first algebraic eigenvalue problem for which reliable methods were obtained. It would be surprising, therefore, if a new method were to be found that would offer a significant improvement in execution time over the fundamental algorithms available in standard software packages such as EISPACK [12]. However, it is reasonable to expect that eigenvalue calculations might be accelerated through the use of parallel algorithms for parallel computers that are becoming available. We shall present such an algorithm in this paper. The algorithm is able to exploit parallelism at all levels of the computation and is well suited to a variety of architectures. However, the surprising result is that the parallel algorithm, even when run in serial mode, is significantly faster than the previously best sequential algorithm on large problems, and is effective on moderate size (order $\geqq 30$) problems when run in serial mode.

The problem we consider is the following: Given a real $n \times n$ symmetric matrix A, find all of the eigenvalues and corresponding eigenvectors of A. It is well known [14] that under these assumptions

$$(1.1) \qquad A = QDQ^T \quad \text{with } Q^TQ = I,$$

so that the columns of the matrix Q are the orthonormal eigenvectors of A and $D = \text{diag}(\delta_1, \delta_2, \cdots, \delta_n)$ is the diagonal matrix of eigenvalues. The standard algorithm

---

* Received by the editors December 23, 1985; accepted for publication (in revised form) May 27, 1986. This article was presented at the Second SIAM Conference on Parallel Processing for Scientific Computing, Norfolk, Virginia, November 20, 1985. This work was supported in part by the Applied Mathematical Sciences subprogram of the Office of Energy Research, U.S. Department of Energy under contracts W-31-109-Eng-38, DE-AC05-840R21400 and DE-FG02-85ER25001.

† Mathematics and Computer Science Division, Argonne National Laboratory, 9700 South Cass Avenue, Argonne, Illinois 60439.

for computing this decomposition is first to use a finite algorithm to reduce A to tridiagonal form using a sequence of Householder transformations, and then to apply a version of the QR-algorithm to obtain all the eigenvalues and eigenvectors of the tridiagonal matrix [14]. The primary purpose of this paper is to describe a method for parallelizing the computation of the eigensystem of the tridiagonal matrix. However, the method we present is intended to be used in conjunction with the initial reduction to tridiagonal form to compute the complete eigensystem of the original matrix A. We, therefore, briefly touch upon the issues involved in parallelizing this initial reduction and suggest a way to combine the parallel initial reduction with the tridiagonal algorithm to obtain a fully parallel algorithm for the symmetric eigenvalue problem.

The method is based upon a divide and conquer algorithm suggested by Cuppen [3]. A fundamental tool used to implement this algorithm is a method that was developed by Bunch, Nielsen and Sorensen [2] for updating the eigensystem of a symmetric matrix after modification by a rank-one change. This rank-one updating method was inspired by some earlier work of Golub [4] on modified eigenvalue problems. The basic idea of the new method is to use rank-one modifications to tear out selected off-diagonal elements of the tridiagonal problem in order to introduce a number of independent subproblems of smaller size. The subproblems are solved at the lowest level using the subroutine TQL2 from EISPACK and then results of these problems are successively glued together using the rank-one modification routine SESUPD that we have developed based upon the ideas presented in [2].

In the following discussion we describe the partitioning of the tridiagonal problem into smaller problems by rank-one tearing. Then we describe the numerical algorithm for gluing the results back together. The organization of the parallel algorithm is laid out, and finally some computational results are presented. Throughout this paper we adhere to the convention that capital Roman letters represent matrices, lower case Roman letters represent column vectors, and lower case Greek letters represent scalars. A superscript T denotes transpose. All matrices and vectors are real, but the results are easily extended to matrices over the complex field.

2. Partitioning by rank-one tearing. The crux of the algorithm is to divide a given problem into two smaller subproblems. To do this, we consider the symmetric tridiagonal matrix

$$(2.1) \qquad T = \begin{pmatrix} T_1 & \beta e_k e_1^T \\ \beta e_1 e_k^T & T_2 \end{pmatrix} = \begin{pmatrix} \hat{T}_1 & 0 \\ 0 & \hat{T}_2 \end{pmatrix} + \theta\beta \begin{pmatrix} e_k \\ \theta^{-1} e_1 \end{pmatrix} (e_k^T, \theta^{-1} e_1^T)$$

where $1 \leq k \leq n$ and e_j represents the jth unit vector of appropriate dimension. The kth diagonal element of T_1 has been modified to give $\hat{T}_1$ and the first diagonal element of T_2 has been modified to give $\hat{T}_2$. Potential numerical difficulties associated with cancellation may be avoided through the appropriate choice of θ. If the diagonal entries to be modified are of the same sign, then $\theta = \pm 1$ is chosen so that $-\theta\beta$ has this sign and cancellation is avoided. If the two diagonal entries are of opposite sign, then the sign of θ is chosen so that $-\theta\beta$ has the same sign as one of the elements and the magnitude of θ is chosen to avoid severe loss of significant digits when $\theta^{-1}\beta$ is subtracted from the other. This is perhaps a minor detail, but it does allow the partitioning to be selected solely on the basis of position and without regard to numerical considerations.

Now we have two smaller tridiagonal eigenvalue problems to solve. According to (1.1) we compute the two eigensystems

$$\hat{T}_1 = Q_1 D_1 Q_1^T, \qquad \hat{T}_2 = Q_2 D_2 Q_2^T.$$

This gives

$$T = \begin{pmatrix} Q_1 D_1 Q_1^T & 0 \\ 0 & Q_2 D_2 Q_2^T \end{pmatrix} + \theta\beta \begin{pmatrix} e_k \\ \theta^{-1} e_1 \end{pmatrix} (e_k^T, \theta^{-1} e_1^T)$$

(2.2)

$$= \begin{pmatrix} Q_1 & 0 \\ 0 & Q_2 \end{pmatrix} \left(\begin{pmatrix} D_1 & 0 \\ 0 & D_2 \end{pmatrix} + \theta\beta \begin{pmatrix} q_1 \\ \theta^{-1} q_2 \end{pmatrix} (q_1^T, \theta^{-1} q_2^T) \right) \begin{pmatrix} Q_1^T & 0 \\ 0 & Q_2^T \end{pmatrix}$$

where $q_1 = Q_1^T e_k$ and $q_2 = Q_2^T e_1$. The problem at hand now is to compute the eigensystem of the interior matrix in (2.2). A numerical method for solving this problem has been provided in [2] and we shall discuss this method in the next section.

It should be fairly obvious how to proceed from here to exploit parallelism. One simply repeats the tearing on each of the two halves recursively until the original problem has been divided into the desired number of subproblems and then the rank-one modification routine may be applied from bottom up to glue the results together again.

3. The updating problem. The general problem we are required to solve is that of computing the eigensystem of a matrix of the form

(3.1) $$\hat{Q}\hat{D}\hat{Q}^T = D + \rho zz^T$$

where D is a real $n \times n$ diagonal matrix, ρ is a nonzero scalar, and z is a real vector of order n. It is assumed without loss of generality that z has Euclidean norm 1.

We seek a formula or an eigenpair for the matrix on the right-hand side of (3.1). Let us assume for the moment that $D = \text{diag}(\delta_1, \delta_2, \cdots, \delta_n)$ with $\delta_1 < \delta_2 < \cdots < \delta_n$ and that no component ζ_i of the vector z is zero. In § 4 we discuss how this may always be arranged. If q, λ is such an eigenpair, then

$$(D + \rho zz^T)q = \lambda q,$$

and a simple rearrangement of terms gives

$$(D - \lambda I)q = -\rho(z^T q)z.$$

If $\lambda = \delta_i$ for some i then our assumption that the ith component of z is nonzero implies $z^T q = 0$. This together with the assumption of distinct eigenvalues implies that q is the eigenvector e_i of D, but then $0 = z^T e_i$ would contradict the original assumption. Thus, multiplying on the left by $z^T (D - \lambda I)^{-1}$ is valid and gives

$$z^T q = -\rho(z^T q)z^T(D - \lambda I)^{-1}z.$$

Our assumptions again imply that $z^T q \neq 0$; hence

$$1 + \rho z^T (D - \lambda I)^{-1} z = 0$$

must be satisfied by λ. Starting with a λ that is a root to this last equation and putting

$$q = \theta(D - \lambda I)^{-1} z$$

for some scalar θ, one may easily verify that q, λ is an eigenpair for $D + \rho zz^T$.

If we write this equation in terms of the components ζ_i of z, then λ must be a root of the equation

(3.2) $$f(\lambda) \equiv 1 + \rho \sum_{j=1}^{n} \frac{\zeta_j^2}{\delta_j - \lambda} = 0.$$

Golub [4] refers to this as the secular equation and the behavior of its roots is pictorially described by the graph in Fig. 1.

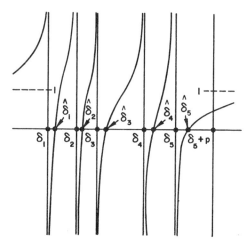

FIG. 1. *The secular equation.*

Moreover, as shown in [2] the eigenvectors (i.e., the columns of $\hat{Q}$ in (3.1)) are given by the formula

(3.3) $$\hat{q}_i = \gamma_i \Delta_i^{-1} z$$

with γ_i chosen to make $\|\hat{q}_i\| = 1$, and with $\Delta_i = \text{diag}\,(\delta_1 - \hat{\delta}_i, \delta_2 - \hat{\delta}_i, \cdots, \delta_n - \hat{\delta}_i)$. Due to this structure, an excellent numerical method may be devised to find the roots of the secular equation and as a by-product to compute the eigenvectors to full accuracy. It must be stressed, however, that great care must be exercised in the numerical method used to solve the secular equation and to construct the eigenvectors from formula (3.3).

In the following discussion we assume that $\rho > 0$ in (3.2). A simple change of variables may always be used to achieve this, so there is no loss of generality. The method we shall describe was inspired by the work of Moré [9] and Reinsch [10], [11], and relies on the use of simple rational approximations to construct an iterative method for the solution of equation (3.2). Given that we wish to find the ith root $\hat{\delta}_i$ of the function f in (3.2), we may write this function as

$$f(\lambda) = 1 + \phi(\lambda) + \psi(\lambda)$$

where

$$\psi(\lambda) = \rho \sum_{j=1}^{i} \frac{\zeta_j^2}{\delta_j - \lambda}$$

and

$$\phi(\lambda) \equiv \rho \sum_{j=i+1}^{n} \frac{\zeta_j^2}{\delta_j - \lambda}.$$

From the graph in Fig. 1 it is seen that the root $\hat{\delta}_i$ lies in the open interval (δ_i, δ_{i+1}) and for λ in this interval all of the terms of ψ are negative and all of the terms of ϕ are positive. We may derive an iterative method for solving the equation

$$-\psi(\lambda) = 1 + \phi(\lambda)$$

by starting with an initial guess λ_0 in the appropriate interval and then constructing simple rational interpolants of the form

$$\frac{p}{q - \lambda}, \quad r + \frac{s}{\delta - \lambda}$$

where δ is fixed at the current value of $\hat{\delta}_{i+1}$, and the parameters p, q, r, s are defined by the interpolation conditions

(3.4)
$$\frac{p}{q - \lambda_0} = \psi(\lambda_0), \qquad r + \frac{s}{\delta - \lambda_0} = \phi(\lambda_0),$$

$$\frac{p}{(q - \lambda_0)^2} = \psi'(\lambda_0), \qquad \frac{s}{(\delta - \lambda_0)^2} = \phi'(\lambda_0).$$

The new approximate λ_1 to the root $\hat{\delta}_i$ is then found by solving

(3.5)
$$\frac{-p}{q - \lambda} = 1 + r + \frac{s}{\delta - \lambda}.$$

It is possible to construct an initial guess which lies in the open interval $(\delta_i, \hat{\delta}_i)$. A sequence of iterates $\{\lambda_k\}$ may then be constructed as we have just described with λ_{k+1} being derived from λ_k as λ_1 was derived from λ_0 above. The following theorem, proved in [2] then shows that this iteration converges quadratically from one side of the root and does not need any safeguarding.

THEOREM 3.6. *Let $\rho > 0$ in* (3.2). *If the initial iterate λ_0 lies in the open interval* $(\delta_i, \hat{\delta}_i)$ *then the sequence of iterates $\{\lambda_k\}$ as constructed in* (3.4)–(3.5) *are well defined and satisfy $\lambda_k < \lambda_{k+1} < \hat{\delta}_i$ for all $k \geq 0$. Moreover, the sequence converges quadratically to the root $\hat{\delta}_i$.*

In our implementation of this scheme (3.5) is cast in such a way that we solve for the iterative correction $\tau = \lambda_1 - \lambda_0$. The quantities $\delta_j - \lambda_k$ which are used later in the eigenvector calculations are maintained and these iterative corrections are applied directly to them as well as to the eigenvalue approximation. Cancellation in the computation of these differences is thus avoided because the corrections become smaller and smaller and are eventually applied to the lowest order bits. These values are then used directly in the calculation of the updated eigenvectors to obtain the highest possible accuracy. The rapid convergence of the iterative method allows the specification of very stringent convergence criteria that will ensure a relative residual and orthogonality of eigenvectors to full machine accuracy. The stopping criteria used are

(i) $|f(\lambda)| \leq \eta \max(|\delta_1|, |\delta_n|)$, and

(ii) $|\tau| \leq \eta \min(|\delta_i - \lambda|, |\delta_{i+1} - \lambda|)$,

where λ is the current iterate and τ is the last iterative correction that was computed. The condition on τ is very stringent. The purpose of such stringent stopping criteria will be clarified in the next section when we discuss orthogonality of computed eigenvectors. Let it suffice at this point to say that condition (i) assures a small residual and that (ii) assures orthogonal eigenvectors.

In most problems these criteria are easily satisfied. However, there are pathological situations involving nearly equal eigenvalues that make (ii) very difficult to satisfy. It is here that the basic root finding method described above must be modified. The problem stems from the fact that the iterative corrections cease to modify the value of f due to round off error. When working in single precision, this situation can be rectified through the use of extended precision accumulation of inner products in the evaluation of f and its derivative. However, this becomes less attractive when working in 64-bit arithmetic as is done in most scientific calculations. Whether or not we shall be able to provide a root finder that will satisfy these stringent requirements in 64-bit arithmetic for very pathological cases remains to be seen.

This has been a brief description of the rank-one updating scheme. Full theoretical details are available in [2]. This calculation represents the workhorse of the parallel algorithm. The method seems to be very robust in practice and exhibits high accuracy. It does not seem to suffer the effects of nearly equal roots as Cuppen suggests [3] but instead was able to solve such ill-conditioned problems as the Wilkinson matrices W_{2k+1}^+ [15, p. 308] to full machine precision and with slightly better residual and orthogonality properties than the standard algorithm TQL2 from EISPACK. In the next section we offer some reasons for this behavior.

4. Deflation and orthogonality of eigenvectors. At the outset of this discussion we made the assumption that the diagonal elements of D were distinct and that no component of the vector z was zero. These conditions are not satisfied in general, so deflation techniques must be employed to ensure their satisfaction. A deflation technique was suggested in [2] to provide distinct eigenvalues which amounts to rotating the basis for the eigenspace corresponding to a multiple eigenvalue so that only one component of the vector z corresponding to this space is nonzero when represented in the new basis. Those terms in (3.2) corresponding to zero components of z may simply be dropped. The eigenvalues and eigenvectors corresponding to these zero components remain static. In finite precision arithmetic the situation becomes more interesting. Terms corresponding to small components of z may be dropped. This can have a very dramatic effect upon the amount of work required in our parallel method. As first observed by Cuppen [3], there can be significant deflation in the updating process as the original matrix is rebuilt from the subproblems.

This deflation can occur in two ways in exact arithmetic, either through zero components of z or through multiple eigenvalues. In order to obtain an algorithm suitable for finite precision arithmetic, we must refine these notions to include "nearly zero" components of z and "nearly equal" eigenvalues. Analysis of the first situation is straightforward. The second situation can be quite delicate in certain pathological cases, however, so we shall discuss it here in some detail. It turns out that the case of nearly equal eigenvalues may be reduced to the case of small components of z.

It is straightforward to see that when $z^T e_i = 0$ the ith eigenvalue and corresponding eigenvector of D will be an eigenpair for $D + \rho z z^T$. Let us ask the question "when is an eigenpair of D a good approximation to an eigenpair for the modified matrix?" This question is easily answered. Recall that $\|z\| = 1$, so

$$\|(D + \rho z z^T)e_i - \delta_i e_i\| = |\rho \zeta_i| \|z\| = |\rho \zeta_i|.$$

Thus we may accept this eigenpair as an eigenpair for the modified matrix whenever

$$|\rho \zeta_i| \leq \text{tol}$$

where $\text{tol} > 0$ is our error tolerance. Typically $\text{tol} = \text{macheps}(\eta \|A\|)$, where macheps is machine precision and η is a constant of order unity. However, at each stage of the updating process we may use

$$\text{tol} = \text{macheps } \eta(\max(|\delta_1|, |\delta_n|) + |\rho|)$$

since at every stage this will represent a bound on the spectral radius of a principal submatrix of A. Let us now suppose there are two eigenvalues of D separated by ε so that $\varepsilon = \delta_{i+1} - \delta_i$. Consider the 2×2 submatrix

$$\begin{pmatrix} \delta_i & \\ & \delta_{i+1} \end{pmatrix} + \rho \begin{pmatrix} \zeta_i \\ \zeta_{i+1} \end{pmatrix} (\zeta_i, \zeta_{i+1})$$

of $D + \rho z z^T$ and let us construct a Givens transformation to introduce a zero in one of the two corresponding components in z. Then

$$\begin{pmatrix} \gamma & \sigma \\ -\sigma & \gamma \end{pmatrix} \left(\begin{pmatrix} \delta_i & \\ & \delta_{i+1} \end{pmatrix} + \rho \begin{pmatrix} \zeta_i \\ \zeta_{i+1} \end{pmatrix} (\zeta_i, \zeta_{i+1}) \right) \begin{pmatrix} \gamma & -\sigma \\ \sigma & \gamma \end{pmatrix}$$

$$= \begin{pmatrix} \hat{\delta}_i & \\ & \hat{\delta}_{i+1} \end{pmatrix} + \rho \begin{pmatrix} \tau \\ 0 \end{pmatrix} (\tau, 0) + \varepsilon \sigma \gamma \begin{pmatrix} 0 & 1 \\ 1 & 0 \end{pmatrix}$$

where $\gamma^2 + \sigma^2 = 1$, $\hat{\delta}_i = \delta_i \gamma^2 + \delta_{i+1} \sigma^2$, $\hat{\delta}_{i+1} = \delta_i \sigma^2 + \delta_{i+1} \gamma^2$ and $\tau^2 = \zeta_i^2 + \zeta_{i+1}^2$. Now, if we put G_i equal to the $n \times n$ Givens transformation constructed from the identity by replacing the appropriate diagonal block with the 2×2 rotation just constructed, we have

(4.1) $G_i(D + \rho z z^T) G_i^T = \hat{D} + \rho \hat{z} \hat{z}^T + E_i$

with $e_i^T \hat{z} = \tau$ and $e_{i+1}^T \hat{z} = 0$, $e_i^T \hat{D} e_i = \hat{\delta}_i$, $e_{i+1}^T \hat{D} e_{i+1} = \hat{\delta}_{i+1}$, and

$$\| E_i \| = |\varepsilon \sigma \gamma|.$$

If we choose, instead, to zero out the ith component of z, then we simply apply G_i on the right and its transpose on the left in equation (4.1) to obtain the desired similar result. The only exception to the previous result is that the sign of the matrix E_i is reversed. Of course this deflation is only done when

$$|\varepsilon \gamma \sigma| \leq \text{tol}$$

is satisfied.

The result of applying all of the deflations is to replace the updating problem (3.1) with one of smaller size. When appropriate, this is accomplished by applying similarity transformations consisting of several Givens transformations. If G represents the product of these transformations the result is

$$G(D + \rho z z^T) G^T = \begin{pmatrix} D_1 - \rho z_1 z_1^T & 0 \\ 0 & D_2 \end{pmatrix} + E$$

where

$$\| E \| \leq \text{tol} \, \eta_2$$

with η_2 of order unity. The cumulative effect of such errors is additive, and thus the final computed eigensystem $\hat{Q} \hat{D} \hat{Q}^T$, which satisfies

$$\| A - \hat{Q} \hat{D} \hat{Q}^T \| \leq \eta_3 \text{tol}$$

where η_3 is again of order 1 in magnitude. The reduction in size of $D_1 - \rho z_1 z_1^T$ over the original rank-one modification can be spectacular in certain cases. The effects of such deflation can be dramatic, for the amount of computation required to perform the updating is greatly reduced.

Let us now consider the possible limitations on orthogonality of eigenvectors due to nearly equal roots. Our first result is a perturbation lemma that will indicate the inherent difficulty associated with nearly equal roots.

LEMMA 4.2. *Let*

(4.3) $$q_\lambda^T \equiv \left(\frac{\zeta_1}{\delta_1 - \lambda}, \frac{\zeta_2}{\delta_2 - \lambda}, \cdots, \frac{\zeta_n}{\delta_n - \lambda} \right) \left[\frac{\rho}{f'(\lambda)} \right]^{1/2}$$

where f is defined by formula (3.2). Then for any $\lambda, \mu \notin \{\delta_i : i = 1, \cdots, n\}$

(4.4) $$|q_\lambda^T q_\mu| = \frac{1}{|\lambda - \mu|} \frac{|f(\lambda) - f(\mu)|}{[f'(\lambda) f'(\mu)]^{1/2}}.$$

Proof. Note that

(4.5)
$$q_\lambda^T q_\mu = \left(\sum_{j=1}^n \frac{\zeta_j^2}{(\delta_j - \lambda)(\delta_j - \mu)} \right) \frac{|\rho|}{[f'(\lambda)f'(\mu)]^{1/2}}.$$

But

$$\frac{\lambda - \mu}{(\delta_j - \lambda)(\delta_j - \mu)} = \frac{1}{(\delta_j - \lambda)} - \frac{1}{(\delta_j - \mu)}.$$

Thus

$$(\lambda - \mu)\rho \sum_{j=1}^n \frac{\zeta_j^2}{(\delta_j - \lambda)(\delta_j - \mu)} = \rho \sum_{j=1}^n \frac{\zeta_j^2}{\delta_j - \lambda} - \rho \sum_{j=1}^n \frac{\zeta_j^2}{\delta_j - \mu} = f(\lambda) - f(\mu)$$

and the result follows. $\square$

Note that in (4.3) q_λ is always a vector of unit length, and the set of n vectors selected by setting λ equal to the roots of the secular equation is the set of eigenvectors for $D + \rho z z^T$. Moreover, (4.4) shows that those eigenvectors are mutually orthogonal whenever λ and μ are set to distinct roots of f. Finally, the term $|\lambda - \mu|$ appearing in the denominator of (4.4) sends up a warning that it may be difficult to attain orthogonal eigenvectors when the roots λ and μ are close. We wish to examine this situation now. We will show that, as a result of the deflation process, the $\{\delta_i\}$ are sufficiently separated, and the weights ζ_i are uniformly large enough that the roots of f are bounded away from each other. This statement is made explicit in the following.

LEMMA 4.6. *Let λ be the root of f in the ith subinterval (δ_i, δ_{i+1}). If the deflation test is satisfied then either*

(i) $\quad |\delta_{i+1} - \lambda| \geq \frac{1}{2}|\delta_{i+1} - \delta_i| \quad and \quad |\delta_i - \lambda| \geq \dfrac{\text{tol}^2}{|\rho(\delta_{i+1} - \delta_i)| + 2\rho^2}, \text{ or}$

(ii) $\quad |\delta_i - \lambda| \geq \frac{1}{2}|\delta_{i+1} - \delta_i| \quad and \quad |\delta_{i+1} - \lambda| \geq \dfrac{\text{tol}^2}{2\rho^2}(\delta_{i+1} - \delta_i).$

Proof. In case (i) the fact that $f(\lambda) = 0$ provides

$$\rho \sum_{j=1}^i \frac{\zeta_j^2}{\lambda - \delta_j} = 1 + \rho \sum_{j=i+1}^n \frac{\zeta_j^2}{\delta_j - \lambda}.$$

From this equation we find that

$$|\rho| \frac{\zeta_i^2}{\lambda - \delta_i} \leq 1 + \frac{|\rho|}{\delta_{i+1} - \lambda} \leq 1 + \frac{2|\rho|}{\delta_{i+1} - \delta_i},$$

and it follows readily that

$$|\delta_{i+1} - \delta_i| \left(\frac{|\rho|\zeta_i^2}{|\delta_{i+1} - \delta_i| + 2|\rho|} \right) \leq |\delta_i - \lambda|.$$

The deflation rules assure us that $|\rho|\zeta_i^2 \geq \text{tol}^2/|\rho|$ and the result follows. Case (ii) is similar. $\square$

The form of the result given in Lemma 4.6 will have importance in the following lemma which gives better insight to the quality of numerical orthogonality attainable with this scheme. The bounds obtained are certainly less than one would hope for. Moreover, it is unfortunate that only the magnitude of the weights enter into the estimate. This obviously does not take into account the deflation due to nearly equal eigenvalues. Unfortunately, we have not been able to improve these estimates by other means and are left with this crude bound.

LEMMA 4.7. *Suppose that $\hat{\lambda}$ and $\hat{\mu}$ are numerical approximations to exact roots λ and μ of f. Assume that these roots are distinct and let the relative errors for the quantities $\delta_i - \lambda$ and $\delta_i - \mu$ be denoted by θ_i and η_i, respectively. That is, the computed quantities*

(4.8) $$\delta_i - \hat{\lambda} = (\delta_i - \lambda)(1 + \theta_i) \quad and \quad \delta_i - \hat{\mu} = (\delta_i - \mu)(1 + \eta_i)$$

for $i = 1, 2, \cdots, n$. Let $q_{\hat{\lambda}}$ and $q_{\hat{\mu}}$ be defined according to formula (4.3) using the computed quantities given in (4.8). If $|\theta_i|, |\eta_i| \leq \varepsilon \ll 1$, then

$$|q_{\hat{\lambda}}^T q_{\hat{\mu}}| = |q_\lambda^T E q_\mu| \leq \varepsilon (2 + \varepsilon) \left(\frac{1 + \varepsilon}{1 - \varepsilon}\right)^2$$

with E a diagonal matrix whose ith diagonal element is

$$E_{ii} = \frac{\theta_i + \eta_i + \theta_i \eta_i}{(1 + \theta_i)(1 + \eta_i)} \left[\frac{f'(\lambda)f'(\mu)}{f'(\hat{\lambda})f'(\hat{\mu})}\right]^{1/2}.$$

Proof. From formula (4.3) we have

$$-q_{\hat{\lambda}}^T q_{\hat{\mu}} = -\left(\sum_{j=1}^n \frac{\zeta_j^2}{(\delta_j - \lambda)(\delta_j - \mu)(1 + \theta_j)(1 + \eta_j)}\right) \frac{|\rho|}{[f'(\hat{\lambda})f'(\hat{\mu})]^{1/2}}$$

$$= \left(\sum_{j=1}^n \frac{\zeta_j^2}{(\delta_j - \lambda)(\delta_j - \mu)} - \sum_{j=1}^n \frac{\zeta_j^2}{(\delta_j - \lambda)(\delta_j - \mu)(1 + \theta_j)(1 + \eta_j)}\right) \frac{|\rho|}{[f'(\hat{\lambda})f'(\hat{\mu})]^{1/2}}$$

due to the orthogonality of the exact vectors. Thus,

$$|q_{\hat{\lambda}}^T q_{\hat{\mu}m}| = \left| \sum_{j=1}^n \left(\frac{\zeta_j^2}{(\delta_j - \lambda)(\delta_j - \mu)}\right)\left(1 - \frac{1}{(1 + \theta_i)(1 + \eta_i)}\right) \frac{\rho}{[f'(\hat{\lambda})f'(\hat{\mu})]^{1/2}} \right|.$$

Since the quantity

$$\frac{f'(\lambda)}{f'(\hat{\lambda})} = \frac{\displaystyle\sum_{j=1}^n \frac{\zeta_j^2}{(\delta_j - \lambda)^2}}{\displaystyle\sum_{j=1}^n \frac{\zeta_j^2}{(\delta_j - \lambda)^2 (1 + \theta_j)^2}} \leq (1 + \varepsilon)^2$$

and since

$$\max E_{ii} \leq \frac{\varepsilon + \varepsilon + \varepsilon^2}{(1 - \varepsilon)(1 - \varepsilon)}$$

the result follows.   □

This shows that orthogonality can be assured whenever it is possible to provide small relative errors when computing the differences $\delta_i - \lambda$. Since, as we mentioned in § 3, these quantities are updated with the iterative corrections to λ and since deflation has guaranteed that the quantities in Lemma 4.6 are bounded away from zero, it will be possible in theory to provide small relative errors. Obviously, the analysis given here, simple as it may be, could form the core of a rigorous error analysis of the method. As yet we lack a root finder that could be proven to satisfy numerically the relative error requirements. The one described above will do so in finite precision but may require extended precision accumulation of inner products in pathological cases. However, in practice we have not experienced difficulty with the exception of contrived examples. Cuppen [3] has shown that the computed eigenvectors may be safely reorthogonalized when needed. We hope to avoid this alternative, though.

5. Reduction to tridiagonal form and related issues. This algorithm is designed to work in conjunction with Householder's reduction of a symmetric matrix to tridiagonal form. In this standard technique a sequence of $n-1$ Householder transformations is applied to form

$$A_{k+1} = (I - \alpha_k w_k w_k^T) A_k (I - \alpha_k w_k w_k^T),$$

with

$$A_k = \begin{pmatrix} T_k & 0 \\ 0 & \hat{A}_k \end{pmatrix}$$

where T_k is a tridiagonal matrix of order $k-1$. See [12] for details. We note here that we can form $(I - \alpha ww^T) A (I - \alpha ww^T)$ using the following algorithm.

ALGORITHM 5.1.

    1. $\nu = Aw$
    2. $y^T = \nu^T - \alpha (w^T \nu) w^T$
    3. Replace A by $A - \alpha \nu w^T - \alpha w y^T$.

Steps 1 and 3 may all be parallelized because A may be partitioned into blocks of columns $A = (A_1, A_2, \cdots, A_j)$ and each of the contributions corresponding to these columns may be carried out independently in Steps 1 and 3. For example, in Step 3,

$$A_i \leftarrow A_i - \alpha \nu w_i^T - \alpha w y_i^T$$

where the vectors w and y have been partitioned in a corresponding manner. In Step 2 the partial results will have to be stored in temporary locations until all are completed and then they may be added together to obtain the final result. Note also that when the calculations are arranged this way advantage may be taken of vector operations when they are available.

Algorithm 5.1 has some disadvantages when incorporated into the reduction of a symmetric matrix to tridiagonal form. At the kth stage of the reduction we have

$$\begin{pmatrix} T^{(k)} & \beta e_k e_1^T \\ \beta e_1 e_k^T & A^{(k)} \end{pmatrix}.$$

The reduction is advanced one step through the application of Algorithm 5.1 to the submatrix $A^{(k)}$. First, a fork-join synchronization construct is imposed since the matrix-vector product requires the entire matrix $A^{(k)}$ to be in place before this product can be completed, so that no portion of Step 2 may begin until Step 1 is finished. Second, due to symmetry, only the lower triangle of $A^{(k)}$ need be computed and this implies that vector lengths shorten during the computation.

When used in conjunction with the rank-one tearing scheme, these drawbacks may be overcome. Suppose the final result of this decomposition is T and that this matrix would be partitioned into $(T_1, T_2, \cdots, T_m)$ by the rank-one tearing if it were known. It is not necessary to wait until the entire reduction is completed, for $T^{(k)}$ represents a leading principal submatrix of T. Thus, as soon as the first subtridiagonal matrix T_1 is exposed, the process of computing its eigensystem may be initiated. Similarly, as soon as T_2 is exposed its eigensystem may be computed. Then a rank-one update may occur, and so on. In this way a number of independent processes may be spawned early on, and the number of such processes ready to execute will remain above a reasonable level throughout the course of the computation. An efficient implementation of this scheme is difficult and will be the subject of a subsequent paper. Issues such as proper level of partitioning will have added importance due to the desire to have parallel processes set in motion as soon as possible.

When we do not wish to find eigenvectors there is no reason to store the product Q of these Householder transformations. Nor is it necessary to accumulate the product of the successive eigenvector transformations resulting from the updating problem. That is, we do not need to overwrite Q with

$$Q \leftarrow Q \begin{pmatrix} Q_1 & 0 \\ 0 & Q_2 \end{pmatrix} \hat{Q}$$

where Q_1, Q_2 and $\hat{Q}$ are the matrices appearing in (2.2) and (3.1) above. Instead, we may simply discard Q. Then the vector q_1 may be formed as $\hat{T}_1$ is transformed to D_1 in (2.2) by accumulating the products of the transformations constructed in TQL2 that make up Q_1 against the vector e_k. If there is more than one division, then Q_1 will have been calculated with the updating scheme. In this case we do not calculate all of Q_1, but instead use the component-wise formula for the eigenvectors to pick off the appropriate components needed to form q_1.

This algorithm can be generalized to handle band matrices as well. Instead of performing a rank-one tearing to split the matrix into two independent subproblems, we proceed by making $(m+1)m/2$ rank-one changes designed to split the matrix, (m is the half bandwidth, $m = 1$ for tridiagonal matrices).

$$
\begin{array}{ccccccccc}
 & & & \cdot & \cdot & \cdot & & & \\
 & & \times & \times & \times & \times & \times & & \\
 & & & \times & \times & \times & \times & | & \times \\
\text{ith row} & & & & \times & \times & \times & | & \times & \times \\
\text{$i+1$th row} & & & & & \times & \times & | & \times & \times & \times \\
 & & & & & & \times & | & \times & \times & \times & \times \\
 & & & & & & & \times & \times & \times & \times & \times \\
 & & & & & & & & \cdot & \cdot & \cdot
\end{array}
$$

The three rank-one changes for this band matrix, ($m = 2$), involve the following elements:

$$a_{i-1,i-1}, \qquad a_{i-1,i+1},$$
$$a_{i+1,i-1}, \qquad a_{i+1,i+1},$$
$$a_{i,i}, \qquad a_{i,i+1},$$
$$a_{i+1,i}, \qquad a_{i+1,i+1},$$

and

$$a_{i,i}, \qquad a_{i,i+2},$$
$$a_{i+2,i}, \qquad a_{i+2,i+2}.$$

The order in which they are applied does not matter in exact arithmetic. We have not studied the numerical properties of this scheme, however.

6. The parallel algorithm. Although it is fairly straightforward from § 2 to see how to obtain a parallel algorithm, certain details are worth discussing further. We shall begin by describing the partitioning phase. This phase amounts to constructing a binary tree with each node representing a rank-one tear and hence a partition into two subproblems. A tree of height 3 therefore represents a splitting of the original problem into 8 smaller eigenvalue problems. Thus, there are two standard symmetric tridiagonal eigenvalue problems to be solved at each leaf of the tree. Each of these problems may be spawned independently without fear of data conflicts. The tree is then traversed in reverse order with the eigenvalue updating routine SESUPD applied at each node joining the results from the left son and right son calculations. The leaves each define independent rank-one updating problems and again there are no data conflicts between them. The only data dependency at a node is that the left and right son calculations must have been completed. When this condition is satisfied, the results of two adjacent eigenvalue subproblems are ready to be joined through the rank-one updating process and this node may spawn the updating process immediately. Information required at a node to define the problem consists of the index of the element torn out, together with the dimension of the left and right son problems. For example, if $n = 50$ with a tree of height 3 we have

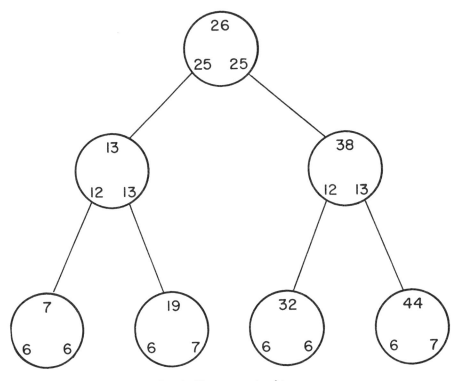

FIG. 2. *The computational tree.*

This tree defines 8 subproblems at the lowest level. There are two calls to TQL2 required at each leaf of the tree in Fig. 2 to solve tridiagonal eigenvalue problems. The beginning indices of these problems are 1, 7, 13, 19, 26, 32, 38, 44 and the dimension of each of them may be read off from left to right at the lowest level as 6, 6, 6, 7, 6, 6, 6, 7 respectively. As soon as the calculation for the problems beginning at indices 1 and 7 have been completed a rank-one update may proceed on the problem beginning at index 1 with dimension 12. The remaining updating problems at this level begin at indices 13, 26, 38. There are then two updating problems at indices 1 and 26 each of dimension 25 and a final updating problem at index 1 of dimension 50.

Evidently, we lose a degree of large grain parallelism as we move up a level on the tree. However, there is more parallelism to be found at the root finding level and the amount of this increases as we travel up the tree so there is ample opportunity for load balancing in this scheme. The parallelism at the root finding level stems from the fact that each of the root calculations is independent and requires only read access to all but one array. That is the array that contains the diagonal entries of the matrix Δ_i described in § 3. For computational efficiency we may decide on an advantageous number of processes to create at the outset. In the example above that number was 8. Then as we travel up the tree the root-finding procedure is split into 2,4, and finally 8 parallel parts in each node at levels 3, 2, 1, respectively. As these computations are roughly equivalent in complexity on a given level it is reasonable to expect to keep all processors devoted to this computation busy throughout.

7. Implementation and library issues. The implementation described here is for computers with a shared memory architecture. The algorithm itself is not limited to this memory model; however, Jessop [5] has an implementation of a similar algorithm for a hypercube that is also based upon Cuppen's divide and conquer scheme.

Obviously, the implementation of this scheme is not so straightforward as simply parallelizing a loop using a fork-join construct. The synchronization mechanism requires more sophistication since it must be able to spawn processes at the root finding level based upon computation that has taken place. This process allocation problem is dynamic rather than static since, due to the possibility of deflation, it will not be known in advance how many roots will have to be calculated at a given level. If there are only a few roots to be found, then the desire for reasonable granularity will dictate fewer processes to be spawned.

In addition to requiring a certain level of sophistication in the synchronization scheme, we would like to adhere as much as possible to the principles of transportability. This algorithm is obviously a candidate for a library subroutine and potentially will find use on a wide variety of machines. When designing library subroutines, one wishes to conceal machine dependencies as much as possible from the user. These important considerations seem to be difficult to accommodate if we are to invoke parallelism at the level described above. It would appear that the user must be conscious of the number of parallel processes required by the library subroutines throughout his program. Should the library routines be called from multiple branches of a user's parallel program, then he could inadvertently attempt to create many more processes than allowed due to physical limitations.

We believe there is hope for implementing this algorithm while adhering to the goals set out in the previous two paragraphs. It may be accomplished by adopting a programming technique that is inspired by the work of Lusk and Overbeek [7], [8] and by Babb [1] on methodologies for implementing transportable parallel codes. We use a package called SCHEDULE [13] that we have been developing while this algorithm was being devised and tested. SCHEDULE is a package of Fortran subroutines designed to aid in programming explicitly parallel algorithms for numerical calculations. The design goal of SCHEDULE is to aid a programmer familiar with a Fortran programming environment to implement a parallel algorithm in a style of Fortran that will lend itself to transporting the resulting program across a wide variety of parallel machines. An important part of this package is the provision of a mechanism for dynamically spawning processes even when such a capability is not present within the parallel language extensions provided for a given machine. The Alliant computer is an example. A detailed discussion of this package is beyond the scope of this paper and will be presented elsewhere. A description of the package and its capabilities is available in [13].

8. Performance. In this section we present and analyze the results of this algorithm on a number of machines. The same algorithm has been run on a VAX 11/785, Denelcor HEP, Alliant FX/8, and a CRAY X-MP-4.

TABLE 8.1

A comparison on the CRAY X-MP for TQL2 vs. the parallel algorithm run sequentially.

n	Ratio of time TQL2/SESUPD	TQL2 $\|Ax - \lambda x\|$	SESUPD $\|Ax - \lambda x\|$	TQL2 $\|X^T X - I\|$	SESUPD $\|X^T X - I\|$
50	.78	1.6×10^{-12}	4.8×10^{-13}	1.9×10^{-12}	1.2×10^{-13}
100	1.26	2.6×10^{-12}	7.6×10^{-13}	3.9×10^{-12}	2.5×10^{-12}
200	1.93	6.1×10^{-12}	1.8×10^{-12}	7.0×10^{-12}	5.8×10^{-11}
300	3.62	1.1×10^{-11}	3.3×10^{-12}	1.1×10^{-11}	2.8×10^{-12}
400	4.70	1.2×10^{-11}	3.8×10^{-12}	1.4×10^{-11}	3.8×10^{-12}

TABLE 8.2

Ratio of execution time TQL2 time/parallel time.
order = 150

	VAX 785/FPA	Denelcor HEP	Alliant FX/8	CRAY X-MP-1	CRAY X-MP-4
random matrix	2.6	12	15.2	1.8	4.5

We have compared our implementation of the algorithm described in this paper to TQL2 from the EISPACK collection. Table 8.1 gives the ratio of execution time for TQL2 from EISPACK run sequentially and the algorithm presented here run in parallel on the same machine. In all cases, the TQL2 code used to test against and the TQL2 code used at lowest level in our algorithm were exactly the same code. Both the parallel algorithm and the serial version of TQL2 were called by a common driver test routine during the same computer run. This assures that both routines were compiled under the same compiler options and ran in the same computing environment to produce this timing data. The timings for TQL2 were obtained by executing it as a single process. By this we mean that the code for TQL2 executed on a single processor of the Alliant and CRAY machines and as the only created process executing on the HEP machine. In all cases the computations were carried out as though the tridiagonal matrix had come from Householder's reduction of a dense symmetric matrix to tridiagonal form. The identity was passed in place of the orthogonal basis that would have been provided by this reduction, but the arithmetic operations performed were the same as those that would have been required to transform that basis into the eigenvectors of the original symmetric matrix.

As can be seen in Table 8.2, the performance of the parallel algorithm as implemented to run on a sequential machine is quite impressive. The surprising result here is the observed speedup even in serial mode of execution. This is unusual in a parallel algorithm. Often more work is associated with synchronization and computational overhead required to split the problem into parallel parts.

These results are remarkable because in all cases speedups greater than the number of physical processors were obtained. The gain is due to the numerical properties of the deflation portion of the parallel algorithm. We do not fully understand why the algorithm performs as much deflation as is apparent by the comparisons. In all cases the word length was 64 bits and the same level of accuracy was achieved by both methods. The measurements of accuracy used was the maximum 2-norm of the residuals $Tq - \lambda q$ and of the columns of $Q^T Q - I$. The results in Table 8.1 are typical of the performance of this algorithm on random problems with speedups becoming more dramatic as the matrix order increases. In problems of order 500 speedups of 15 have

TABLE 8.3

A comparison on the Alliant FX/8 for TQL2 vs. the parallel algorithm on (1, 2, 1) matrix.

n	Ratio TQL2/SESUPD	TQL2 $\|Ax - \lambda x\|$	SESUPD $\|Ax - \lambda x\|$	TQL2 $\|X^T X - I\|$	SESUPD $\|X^T X - I\|$
100	9.4	9.6×10^{-15}	1.9×10^{-15}	7.8×10^{-15}	5.5×10^{-16}
200	15.4	1.7×10^{-14}	2.7×10^{-15}	1.1×10^{-14}	2.2×10^{-15}
300	17.7	1.9×10^{-14}	3.2×10^{-15}	1.7×10^{-14}	2.6×10^{-15}
400	20.0	2.9×10^{-14}	4.0×10^{-15}	2.0×10^{-14}	9.2×10^{-15}

TABLE 8.4

A comparison on the Alliant FX/8 for TQL2 vs. the parallel algorithm on a random matrix.

n	Ratio of time TQL2/SESUPD	TQL2 $\|Ax - \lambda x\|$	SESUPD $\|Ax - \lambda x\|$	TQL2 $\|X^T X - I\|$	SESUPD $\|X^T X - I\|$
100	12.1	1.6×10^{-14}	1.9×10^{-13}	1.6×10^{-14}	2.4×10^{-15}
200	19.5	2.1×10^{-14}	2.2×10^{-13}	2.8×10^{-14}	2.3×10^{-15}
300	38.8	4.2×10^{-14}	8.8×10^{-13}	3.7×10^{-14}	5.2×10^{-15}
400	60.7	3.5×10^{-14}	8.2×10^{-13}	3.7×10^{-14}	4.6×10^{-14}

been observed on the CRAY-XMP-4 and speedups over 50 have been observed on the Alliant FX/8, which are 4 and 8 processor machines respectively. The CRAY results can actually be improved because parallelism at the root finding level was not exploited in the implementation run on the CRAY but was fully exploited on the Alliant.

In Tables 8.3 and 8.4 we show a more complete set of runs on the Alliant/FX8. These test problems show two types of behavior. In the (1, 2, 1) matrix not very much deflation takes place. On the random matrix considerable deflation takes place. The observation of Cuppen that this deflation occurs in many cases was very fortunate. It brought our attention to this algorithm, but we did not really expect the remarkable performance observed here. In the case where many eigenvectors are sought along with the eigenvalues this algorithm seems to be very promising. However, as we mentioned in § 5 it is not necessary to compute the eigenvectors if they are not needed. We cannot recommend this algorithm in the case where only a few eigenvalues and eigenvectors are sought. A multisectioning algorithm such as the one developed by Lo, Philippe and Sameh [6] is to be preferred in this case.

REFERENCES

[1] R. G. BABB II, *Parallel processing with large grain data flow techniques*, IEEE Computer, 17 (1984), pp. 55–61.
[2] J. R. BUNCH, C. P. NIELSEN AND D. C. SORENSEN, *Rank-one modification of the symmetric eigenproblem*, Numer. Math., 31 (1978), pp. 31–48.
[3] J. J. M. CUPPEN, *A divide and conquer method for the symmetric tridiagonal eigenproblem*, Numer. Math., 36 (1981), pp. 177–195.
[4] G. H. GOLUB, *Some modified matrix eigenvalue problems*, SIAM Rev., 15 (1973), pp. 318–334.
[5] L. JESSOP, *Solving the symmetric tridiagonal eigenvalue problem on the hypercube*, Yale Computer Science Research Report, in preparation.
[6] S. LO, B. PHILIPPE AND A. SAMEH, *A parallel algorithm for the real symmetric tridiagonal eigenvalue problem*, Center for Supercomputing Research and Development Report, Univ. Illinois, Urbana, IL, November 1985.

[7] E. LUSK AND R. OVERBEEK, *Implementation of monitors with macros: A programming aid for the* HEP *and other parallel processors*, ANL-83-97, 1983.

[8] ———, *An approach to programming multiprocessing algorithms on the Denelcor* HEP, ANL-83-96, 1983.

[9] J. J. MORÉ, *The Levenberg–Marquardt algorithm: implementation and theory*, Proc. Dundee Conference on Numerical Analysis, G. A. Watson, ed., Springer-Verlag, New York, 1978.

[10] C. H. REINSCH, *Smoothing by spline functions*, Numer. Math., 10 (1967), pp. 177–183.

[11] ———, *Smoothing by spline functions* II, Numer. Math., 16 (1971), pp. 451–454.

[12] B. T. SMITH, J. M. BOYLE, J. J. DONGARRA, B. S. GARBOW, Y. IKEBE, V. C. KLEMA AND C. B. MOLER, *Matrix Eigensystem Routines—EISPACK Guide*, Lecture Notes in Computer Science, 6, 2nd ed., Springer-Verlag, Berlin, 1976.

[13] D. C. SORENSEN, SCHEDULE *Users Guide*, ANL-MCS-TM-76, Argonne National Laboratory, Argonne, IL, May 1986.

[14] G. W. STEWART, *Introduction to Matrix Computations*, Academic Press, New York, 1973.

[15] J. H. WILKINSON, *The Algebraic Eigenvalue Problem*, Clarendon Press, Oxford, 1965.

SIAM J. SCI. STAT. COMPUT.
Vol. 8, No. 2, March 1987

A MULTIPROCESSOR ALGORITHM FOR THE SYMMETRIC TRIDIAGONAL EIGENVALUE PROBLEM*

SY-SHIN LO†, BERNARD PHILIPPE† AND AHMED SAMEH†

Abstract. A multiprocessor algorithm for finding few or all eigenvalues and the corresponding eigenvectors of a symmetric tridiagonal matrix is presented. It is a pipelined variation of EISPACK routines—BISECT and TINVIT which consists of the three steps: isolation, extraction-inverse iteration, and partial orthogonalization. Multisections are performed for isolating the eigenvalues in a given interval, while bisection or the Zeroin method is used to extract these isolated eigenvalues. After the corresponding eigenvectors have been computed by inverse iteration, the modified Gram–Schmidt method is used to orthogonalize certain groups of these vectors. Experiments on the Alliant FX/8 and CRAY X-MP/48 multiprocessors show that this algorithm achieves high speed-up over BISECT and TINVIT; in fact it is much faster than TQL2 when all the eigenvalues and eigenvectors are required.

Key words. eigenvalues, multiprocessors, tridiagonal matrices

AMS(MOS) subject classification. 65F15

1. Introduction. This paper deals with solving the real symmetric tridiagonal eigenvalue problem on a multiprocessor. The main purpose of this study is solving for a few of the eigenvalues and the corresponding eigenvectors of large tridiagonal symmetric matrices such as those resulting from the Lanczos tridiagonalization of a sparse symmetric matrix. In fact, we show that our scheme, the origins of which date back to the Illiac IV [8] and [7], is equally or more effective than other multiprocessor schemes for obtaining either all the eigenvalues, or all the eigenvalues and eigenvectors of a symmetric tridiagonal matrix.

Two kinds of methods are usually used for solving this problem on a uniprocessor. When only a part of the spectrum is desired, the combination of bisection and inverse iteration is the method of choice. For the whole eigenvalue problem, the QR (or QL) method is more effective [2]. These methods are implemented in EISPACK : BISECT and TINVIT for the partial eigenvalue problem, and TQL1 (eigenvalues only) and TQL2 (eigenvalues and eigenvectors) for the whole problem. A multiprocessor version of TQL2 has already been designed [4] using a divide and conquer technique.

In §2 we give a brief description of the method, in §3 we analyze the various steps of the computation with respect to efficient use of the parallelism offered by the multiprocessor. In §4, we compare our scheme with all of the above schemes on the Alliant FX/8 and the CRAY X-MP/48 multiprocessors.

2. Description of the method. Let **T** be a symmetric tridiagonal matrix of order n with d_i and e_i as the diagonal and subdiagonal elements, respectively,

$$\mathbf{T} = [e_i, d_i, e_{i+1}].$$

Let $p_n(\lambda)$ be its characteristic polynomial:

$$p_n(\lambda) = \det(\mathbf{T} - \lambda \mathbf{I}).$$

* Received by the editors December 23, 1985; accepted for publication (in revised form) May 12, 1986. This work was supported in part by the National Science Foundation under Grants US NSF DCR84-10110 and US NSF DCR85-09970, the U.S. Department of Energy under Grant US DOE DE-FG02-85ER25001, the IBM Donation, and the French Ministry of Defense under Grant DRET No. 84-823. This paper was submitted to the Second SIAM Conference on Parallel Processing for Scientific Computing that was held in Norfolk, Virginia during November 18–21, 1985.

† Center for Supercomputing Research and Development, University of Illinois, Urbana, Illinois 61801.

The sequence of the principal minors of the matrix can be built using the following recursion:

$$p_0(\lambda) = 1,$$

(2.1) $$p_1(\lambda) = d_1 - \lambda,$$

$$p_i(\lambda) = (d_i - \lambda)p_{i-1}(\lambda) - e_i^2 p_{i-2}(\lambda), \qquad i = 2, \cdots, n.$$

We assume that no subdiagonal element is zero, since if some e_i is equal to 0, the problem can be partitioned into two smaller problems. The sequence $\{p_i(\lambda)\}$ is called the Sturm sequence of $\mathbf{T}$ in λ. It is well known [11] that the number of eigenvalues smaller than a given λ is equal to the number of sign variations in the Sturm sequence (2.1). Hence one can find the number of eigenvalues lying in a given interval $[a, b]$ by computing the Sturm sequences at a and b. The linear recurrence (2.1), however, suffers from the possibility of over- or underflow. This is remedied by replacing the Sturm sequence $p_i(\lambda)$ by the sequence

$$q_i(\lambda) = \frac{p_i(\lambda)}{p_{i-1}(\lambda)}, \qquad i = 1, n.$$

The second order linear recurrence (2.1) is then replaced by the nonlinear recurrence

(2.2) $$q_1(\lambda) = d_1 - \lambda, \quad q_i(\lambda) = d_i - \lambda - \frac{e_i^2}{q_{i-1}(\lambda)}, \quad i = 2, \cdots, n.$$

Here, the number of eigenvalues that are smaller than λ is equal to the number of negative terms in the sequence $\{q_i(\lambda)\}$.

Therefore, given an initial interval, we can find the eigenvalues lying in it by repeated bisection or multisection of the interval. This partitioning process can be performed until we obtain each eigenvalue to a given accuracy. On the other hand, we can stop the process once we have isolated each eigenvalue. In the latter case the eigenvalues may be extracted using a faster method. Several methods are available for extracting an isolated eigenvalue:

    –Bisection (linear convergence);

    –Newton's method (quadratic convergence);

    –The Zeroin scheme, which is based on the secant and bisection methods (convergence of order $(\sqrt{5}+1)/2$).

Ostrowski [10] defines an efficiency index which links the amount of computation to be done at each step and the order of the convergence. The respective indices of the three methods are 1, 1.414 and 1.618. This index, however, is not the only aspect to be considered here. Both Zeroin and Newton methods require the use of the linear recurrence (2.1) in order to obtain the value of det $(\mathbf{T} - \lambda \mathbf{I})$, or its derivative as well, for a given λ. Hence, if the possibility of over- or underflow is small we select the Zeroin method; otherwise we select the bisection method. After the computation of an eigenvalue, the corresponding eigenvector can be found by inverse iteration [6]. This is a very fast process where one iteration is often sufficient to achieve convergence.

It is possible that some eigenvalues are computationally coincident; hence, the isolation process actually performs "isolation of clusters," where a cluster is defined as a single eigenvalue or a number of computationally coincident eigenvalues. If such a cluster of coincident eigenvalues is isolated the extraction step is skipped, since convergence has been reached. Observing that, there can be loss of orthogonality for those eigenvectors corresponding to close eigenvalues; orthonormalization of such eigenvectors via the Modified Gram–Schmidt method is necessary.

In summary, the whole computation consists of the following five steps:
1) Isolation by partitioning;
2) Extraction of a cluster by bisection or by the Zeroin method;
3) Computation of the eigenvectors of the cluster by inverse iteration;
4) Grouping of close eigenvalues;
5) Orthogonalization of the corresponding groups of vectors by the Modified Gram-Schmidt process.

3. The parallel algorithm.

3.1. The partitioning process. Obviously, the parallelism in this process is achieved by performing simultaneously the computation of several Sturm sequences. However, there are several ways for achieving this; two options are

- Performing bisection on several intervals;
- Performing a partition of one interval into several subintervals.

A multisection of order k splits the interval $I = [a, b]$ into $k+1$ subintervals $I_i = [x_i, x_{i+1}]$, where $x_i = a + i((b-a)/(k+1))$ for $i = 0, \cdots, k+1$. If there exists only one eigenvalue in the interval I and if we wish to compute it with an absolute error ε, then it is necessary to perform

$$n_k = \log_2 \left(\frac{(b-a)}{(2\varepsilon)} \right) \Big/ \log_2 (k+1)$$

multisections of order k. Thus, the efficiency of the multisection of order k compared to bisection (multisection of order 1) is

$$E_f = n_1/(k\, n_k) = (\log_2 (k+1))/k.$$

Hence, for extraction of eigenvalues, we prefer to perform parallel bisections rather than one multisection of high order. On the other hand, during the isolation step, the efficiency of multisectioning is higher because: (i) a multisection creates more tasks than bisection, and (ii) there are several eigenvalues in one interval. The way we propose to use bisections or multisections is almost the same as that stated in [1].

3.2. The computation of the Sturm sequence. The recurrence (2.2) is intrinsically serial, so parallelism is not possible in this computation. The algorithm in [3] may be used, however, to vectorize the linear recurrence (2.1). Here, the computation of the regular Sturm sequence (2.1) is equivalent to solving a lower-triangular system of order $n+1$ consisting of three diagonals,

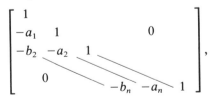

where $a_i = d_i - \lambda$, and $b_i = -e_i^2$. For a vector length $k < n/2$ the total number of arithmetic operations in the parallel algorithm is roughly $10n + 11k$ while it is only $4n$ for the serial algorithm (we do not consider the operation that computes e_i^2, since this quantity can be provided by the user); resulting into an arithmetic redundancy which varies between 2.5 and 4.

This algorithm, therefore, is efficient only when vector operations are at least 4 times faster than sequential operations, which excludes the FX/8. The results on one processor of a CRAY X-MP are displayed in Fig. 1. In this figure, three methods are compared:

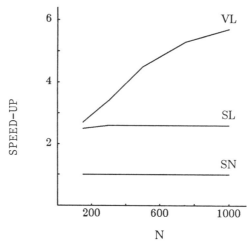

FIG. 1. *Computation of Sturm sequence on* CRAY X-MP, *speed-up over* SN. *N is the order of test matrices of* $[-1, 2, -1]$.

- Sequential computation of the linear recurrence (2.1) (SL);
- Vector computation of the linear recurrence (2.1) (VL);
- Sequential computation of the nonlinear recurrence (2.2) (SN).

Using 64 bit arithmetic on the test matrix $[-1, 2, -1]$, we have evaluated elements of the Sturm sequence (2.1) with no over- or underflow. The (SL) method is always faster than the (SN) method. The method (VL) (coded in FORTRAN) can reach a speed-up of 2.1 over the (SL) method and of 5.7 over the (SN) method.

3.3. Computation of the eigenvectors and orthonormalization. The computation of an eigenvector can be started as soon as the corresponding eigenvalue is computed. So, we consider the extraction of an eigenvalue and the computation of its eigenvector as two parts of the same task, with the order of potential parallelism being dependent on the number of desired eigenvalues.

Orthonormalization is only performed on eigenvectors whose corresponding eigenvalues meet a predefined grouping criterion. The modified Gram–Schmidt method is used to orthonormalize each group. The algorithm is as follows:

> **do** $k = 1, p$
>> normalize (z_k)
>> **do** $j = k+1, p$
>>> $z_j = z_j - (z_j \cdot z_k) z_k$
>> **od**
> **od**

where z_j and z_k are vectors, and $(z_j \cdot z_k)$ denotes their inner product. The statement in the inner loop is a vector instruction which updates the vector z_j with respect to the base vector z_k. Considering the dependency of the variables, we see that the inner loop is a **doall** loop, since all the iterations j are independent of one another for a particular k. On the other hand, the outer loop is a **doacross** loop, since any iteration k cannot start before vector z_k has been updated with respect to vectors $z_1, \cdots, z_{k-1}$ and as soon as it has been updated it is ready to be used as base vector for $z_{k+1}, \cdots, z_p$. These dependency relations are shown in Fig. 2.

Two schemes have been designed to perform the above process. One is a doall-inner-sequential-outer algorithm (called PS); the second, with some synchronization

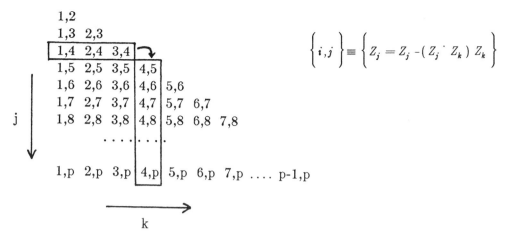

FIG. 2. *Diagram of dependencies.*

mechanisms, is a doall-inner-pipelined-outer algorithm (called PP). Because of the synchronization overhead, the second method is to be preferred only when the order of the matrix and the size of the group are large. Table 1 shows a comparison of the two algorithms on the CRAY X-MP/48. The efficiency of the pipelined method in this case is the consequence of the low overhead of the synchronization mechanisms on the CRAY multiprocessor.

TABLE 1
Two implementations for the modified Gram–Schmidt Method.

	1 processor	2 processors	4 processors
Pipelined outer loop (PP)	26.13	13.61	8.20
Sequential outer loop (PS)	23.18	15.60	11.97
Speed-Up (PS/PP)	.89	1.15	1.46

Test performed on the CRAY X-MP for a matrix of order 1000.

If we consider processing several groups of vectors in parallel, then we have three levels of parallelism:
1) Concurrent processing of the groups;
2) Concurrent updating of vectors;
3) Vectorizing the updating step of each vector.
It is necessary to select the algorithm depending on the levels of parallelism in the architecture. For example, to orthonormalize large groups of eigenvectors, Level 2 and Level 3 can be adopted on multiprocessors like the CRAY X-MP/48 and the Alliant FX/8; whereas all three levels of parallelism can be adopted on a hierarchical structured system such as the Cedar machine [9], which contains several "clusters" of multiprocessors, each processor having vector capability.

4. Implementation and experiments.
4.1. Implementation. In this section, we describe the specific implementations of our algorithm TREPS on the multiprocessors Alliant FX/8 (consisting of 8 processors) and the CRAY X-MP/48 (consisting of 4 processors). The implementation on the Alliant is slightly different from the implementation on the CRAY.

During the orthogonalization process on the CRAY, the groups of eigenvectors to be orthonormalized are split into two classes depending on their sizes: the small groups are processed, one per processor, in parallel; and the large groups are processed one group at a time, using all the processors with the parallel-inner pipelined-outer loop algorithm. With 4 processors, a group of more than 10 eigenvalues is regarded as large.

For both implementations, the repartitioning of the intervals containing an isolated cluster is dynamic. These intervals are stored in a stack. As soon as one processor is ready, it fetches a new task (i.e., a new subinterval) from the stack. The updating of the pointer to the top of the stack is protected as a critical section by locks. It has to be pointed out that multitasking on the Alliant FX/8 is easier and less costly than that on the CRAY X-MP/48, since on the former system the creation of tasks is automatic. Moreover, on the CRAY we have used the usual trick, which consists of declaring as many tasks as there are processors, and making them active or idle depending on the number of processes involved so as to reduce the cost of task creation. This manipulation adds some complexity to the code, but it is the price to be paid if one is to obtain good performance on the CRAY X-MP/48.

4.2. Performance. To analyze the speed of this program, we start by comparing TREPS1, a version of the program which performs the extraction stage via bisection, with the EISPACK subroutines BISECT and TINVIT on the sequential machine VAX 785. For several runs with different tridiagonal matrices, we found that, even on a VAX 785, TREPS1 is no more than 20% slower than BISECT+TINVIT. In Table 2 we show such an experiment for the matrix $[-1, 2, -1]$ (unless otherwise stated, all test matrices are of this form). On the FX/8, with some synchronization directives, TREPS ran in vector-concurrent mode, with high speed-ups when the number of desired eigenvalues exceeds the number of processors. All experiments on the Alliant FX/8 are performed in double precision. In Table 3, we show the performance of TREPS1 when *all* the eigenvalues and vectors are obtained on the FX/8. In Table 4,

TABLE 2
Timings for TREPS *and* BISECT+TINVIT *Subroutines on* VAX 785.

N		TREPS1	BISC+TINV
100	Time (seconds)	4.03	3.6
	Ratio	1.11	1
300	Time (seconds)	34.13	31.58
	Ratio	1.08	1

Computations are in single precision. N is the order of the test matrix.

TABLE 3
Time and speed-up for TREPS1 *on* Alliant FX/8.

CE's	Time (second)	Speed-Up
1	115.59	1.0
2	57.12	2.0
4	28.89	4.0
8	14.78	7.8

Test matrices are of order 500.

TABLE 4

Speed-up for TREPS1 *as function of number of eigenvalues and vectors.*

	Time in seconds		
p	1 CE	8 CEs	Speed-Up
1	.15	.15	1
2	.25	.12	2.1
4	.51	.14	3.6
8	1.03	.14	7.4
10	1.29	.26	5.0
20	2.59	.42	6.2
50	6.67	.97	6.9
100	13.33	1.86	7.2
200	27.09	3.74	7.2
300	40.85	5.46	7.5

Test matrix $[-1, 2, -1]$ is of order 300. p is the number of desired eigenvalues and eigenvectors.

TABLE 5

Time for steps in TREPS1 *and* TREPS2.

N		Total	Isolation	Extr + Inv.	Orthonorm.	
500	TREPS1	14.78	.62	13.78	.38	(sec)
		100	4.2	93.2	2.6	(%)
	TREPS2	3.71	.62	2.71	.38	(sec)
		100	4.9	79.8	15.3	(%)
1000	TREPS1	67.68	3.35	54.0	10.33	(sec)
		100	16.7	73.1	10.2	(%)
	TREPS2	24.47	3.39	11.02	10.06	(sec)
		100	13.9	45.0	41.1	(%)

Computing all the eigenvalues and eigenvectors. Computations are done on Alliant FX/8 in double precision.

we measure the speed-up of TREPS1 on the FX/8 as a function of the desired p smallest eigenvalues for a matrix of order 300. On one processor, the time to compute p eigenvalues is proportional to p (in this situation the multisections become bisections, and our program is essentially equivalent to BISECT+TINVIT). On 8 processors, the speed-up over one processor increases from 1 to 5.0 when the number of desired eigenvalues and vectors varies from 1 to 10. It increases from 6.9 (for 30 eigenvalues) to 7.5 (for all of the 300 eigenvalues). Similar results are obtained with the version TREPS2, in which we use the Zeroin method (see [5]) for extraction of the eigenvalues.

Let us now look at the percentage of the computational time involved in each stage. We consider the time for grouping close eigenvalues as negligible. The step for extracting the eigenvalues and computing the eigenvectors is more time-consuming than the isolation process for TREPS1. The orthonormalization time depends heavily on the problem; in the extreme case when orthogonalization of all n vectors is necessary, the elapsed time can reach up to 50% of the whole time needed to solve the problem. Some examples are given in Table 5.

4.3. Comparison with other subroutines. In this section we compare the performance of our algorithm with BISECT+TINVIT, TQL2, and that in [4] when *all* the eigenvalues and eigenvectors are required. We also compare our algorithm with BISECT and TQL1 when only the eigenvalues are needed. To evaluate the numerical perform-ance, we compare the norm of the residuals, $\max_i \| T z_i - \lambda_i z_i \|_2$, for the computed eigenvalues and eigenvectors for TREPS, BISECT+TINVIT, TQL2, and SESUPD [4]. Orthogonality of the eigenvectors is also checked by computing the $\max_{i,j} |Z^T Z - I|_{i,j}$, where $Z = [z_1, \cdots, z_n]$. Table 6 shows the results on the FX/8, machine precision of 1.11×10^{-16}, for the test matrix $[-1, 2, -1]$ of order 500. We see that for the above test matrix both the residuals and the quality of the eigenvectors and orthogonality of

TABLE 6

Residual and orthonormality of computed eigenvalues and eigenvectors.

	$\max_i \| T z_i - \lambda_i z_i \|_2$	$\max_{i,j} |Z^T Z - I|_{i,j}$
TREPS1	1.00×10^{-12}	1.69×10^{-12}
TREPS2	4.12×10^{-13}	1.31×10^{-12}
TQL2	3.88×10^{-14}	2.66×10^{-14}
BISECT+TINVIT	9.75×10^{-13}	2.77×10^{-12}
SESUPD	5.87×10^{-15}	6.61×10^{-15}

Test matrices are of order 500.

TABLE 7a

Time and speed-up for computing all the eigenvalues and eigenvectors.

		Alliant		CRAY X-MP	
		1 CE	8 CE	1 CPU	4 CPU
TREPS1	time (sec)	115.6	14.8	11.06	3.04
	speed-up	1	7.8	1	3.6
TREPS2	time (sec)	25.7	3.7	1.72	.64
	speed-up	1	6.9	1	2.7
TQL2	time (sec)	486.4	103.1	6.68	—
	speed-up	1	4.7	1	—
BISECT+TINVIT	time (sec)	140.6	136.2	12.98**	—
	speed-up	1	1.0	1	—
SESUPD	time (sec)	—	17.91	—	—
	speed-up	—	—	—	—

Test matrix is of order 500.
** Probably has full orthonormalization due to the different grouping criterion used in the version of TINVIT on the Cray X-MP.

TABLE 7b

Speed-up over TQL2 on the Alliant for computing all the eigenvalues and eigenvectors.

i	Algorithm	$\dfrac{\text{Time (TQL2 on 1 CE)}}{\text{Time (algorithm } i \text{ on 8 CEs)}}$	$\dfrac{\text{Time (TQL2 on 8 CEs)}}{\text{Time (algorithm } i \text{ on 8 CEs)}}$
1	TREPS1	32.9	7
2	TREPS2	131.5	28
3	TQL2	4.7	1
4	BISECT+TINVIT	3.6	.8
5	SESUPD	27.1	5.8

Test matrix is of order 500.

TREPS1 and TREPS2 are close to that of BISECT+TINVIT but not as good as those of TQL2 and SESUPD [4].

In Tables 7a and 7b we give timing results comparing the performance of the above algorithms on both the FX/8 and the CRAY X-MP. Note that the time for TQL2 on one CE is 131 times slower than the time required by TREPS2 on 8 CE's, and that the time for TQL2 on 8 CE's is 28 times slower than that of TREPS2. Furthermore, TREPS2 is 4.8 times faster than SESUPD. In Tables 8a and 8b we compare both versions of our algorithm with TQL1 and BISECT for obtaining all the eigenvalues only. In Table 9 we show timing results for obtaining all the eigenvalues and eigenvectors of a random tridiagonal matrix on the Alliant FX/8.

TABLE 8a

Time and speed-up for computing all the eigenvalues.

		Alliant		CRAY X-MP	
		1 CE	8 CE	1 CPU	4 CPU
TREPS1	time (sec)	105.3	13.2	10.45	2.67
	speed-up	1	8.0	1	3.9
TREPS2	time (sec)	16.6	2.1	1.09	.4
	speed-up	1	7.9	1	2.7
TQL1	time (sec)	10.5	8.8	.87	—
	speed-up	1	1.2	1	—
BISECT	time (sec)	128.1	126.1	9.88	—
	speed-up	1	1.0	1	—

Test matrix is of order 500.

TABLE 8b

Speed-up over TQL1 on the Alliant for computing all the eigenvalues.

i	Algorithm	$\dfrac{\text{Time (TQL1 on 1 CE)}}{\text{Time (algorithm } i \text{ on 8 CEs)}}$	$\dfrac{\text{Time (TQL1 on 8 CEs)}}{\text{Time (algorithm } i \text{ on 8 CEs)}}$
1	TREPS1	.8	.7
2	TREPS2	5	4.2
3	TQL1	1.2	1
4	BISECT	.08	.07

Test matrix is of order 500.

TABLE 9

Computing all the eigenvalues and vectors of a random tridiagonal matrix on the Alliant FX/8.

	Time (second)	$\max_{i} \| Tz_i - \lambda_i z_i \|_2$	$\max_{i,j} \| Z^T Z - I \|_{i,j}$	Speed-up over TQL2
TREPS1	15.04	5.6×10^{-13}	5.1×10^{-12}	8
TREPS2	4.14	4.6×10^{-13}	1.3×10^{-11}	29
TQL2	120.54	2.8×10^{-14}	1.6×10^{-14}	1
BISECT+TINVIT	134.89	5.2×10^{-13}	6.4×10^{-12}	.9
SESUPD	6.65	2.5×10^{-14}	3.0×10^{-14}	18

Test matrices are of order 500.

TABLE 10

Results for full symmetric matrices on the Alliant FX/8.

Test matrix		Time (second)	$\max_{i,j} \lvert Z^T Z - I \rvert_{i,j}$
R	TREPS1	24.59	3.1×10^{-13}
	TREPS2	38.64	3.1×10^{-13}
A	TREPS1	23.96	1.1×10^{-12}
	TREPS2	12.64	5.7×10^{-13}

Test matrices are of order 500. **R** is full random symmetric matrix. $\mathbf{A} = (\mathbf{I} - 2uu^T)\mathbf{T}(\mathbf{I} - 2uu^T)$, where $\mathbf{T} = [-1, 2, -1]$.

Table 10 compares the times consumed by both versions of our algorithm on full symmetric matrices. The times indicated do not take into account the reduction to the tridiagonal form. For the matrix $\mathbf{A} = (\mathbf{I} - 2uu^T)\mathbf{T}(\mathbf{I} - 2uu^T)$, where $\mathbf{T} = [-1, 2, -1]$ and $u^T u = 1$, TREPS2 is very fast; but for a full symmetric random matrix **R**, TREPS2 is slower than TREPS1. This leads us to recall the implementation of the extraction algorithm. As mentioned earlier, although the Zeroin method is much faster than bisection, it may suffer from under- or overflow. Such problems are heralded by lack of convergence in the computation of some of the eigenvectors. To remedy this problem in TREPS2, we switch to bisection whenever the inverse iteration does not converge. The matrix **R** used in this experiment is an extreme case, where every single eigenvalue has first been computed by the Zeroin method, then recomputed by bisection; this explains the poor performance of TREPS2.

5. Conclusion. The algorithms TREPS1 and TREPS2 which have been presented in this paper are well suited for multiprocessors. A speed-up which is almost equal to the number of processors can be obtained as long as the number of desired eigenvalues is several times larger than the number of processors. They also achieve high efficiency because the amount of arithmetic operations for each element of data (a total of $O(n)$ elements) is high, thus avoiding the traditional bottleneck of memory bandwidth.

TREPS2, which extracts the eigenvalues using the Zeroin method, is much faster than the combination of EISPACK's BISECT and TINVIT, as well as TQL2. It can also be faster than SESUPD [4], on a multiprocessor such as the FX/8, especially when the linear recurrence (2.1) is well behaved. In fact we consider TREPS2 to be the algorithm of choice for obtaining either all the eigenvalues (it is faster than TQL1), or few of the eigenvalues and the corresponding eigenvectors of a tridiagonal matrix. Furthermore, comparisons with [4] indicate that TREPS2 is equally competitive with other multiprocessor algorithms that seek all the eigenvalues and vectors of full symmetric matrices. This is especially true since the back-transformation involved, in the full case, can be performed by matrix multiplication routines which are very efficient on both the FX/8 and the CRAY X-MP/48.

Acknowledgment. The authors would like to thank John Larson at CRAY Research for his valuable help in performing the experiments on the CRAY X-MP.

REFERENCES

[1] H. J. BERNSTEIN AND M. GOLDSTEIN, *Parallel implementation of bisection for the calculation of eigenvalues of tridiagonal symmetric matrices*, Courant Institute of Mathematical Sciences Report, New York University, New York, 1985.

[2] H. BOWDLER, R. MARTIN, C. REINSCH AND J. H. WILKINSON, *The* QR *and* QL *algorithms for symmetric matrices, Contribution* II/3, in Handbook for automatic computation, Vol. II, Linear Algebra, Springer-Verlag, Berlin, New York, 1971, pp. 227–240.

[3] S. C. CHEN, D. J. KUCK AND A. H. SAMEH, *Practical parallel band triangular system solvers*, ACM Trans. Math. Software, 4 (1978), pp. 270–277.

[4] J. J. DONGARRA AND D. C. SORENSEN, *A fast algorithm for the symmetric eigenvalue problem*, IEEE Proc. 7th Symposium on Computer Arithmetic, Urbana, IL, 1985, pp. 338–342, this Journal, 8 (1987), to appear.

[5] G. E. FORSYTHE, M. A. MALCOM AND C. B. MOLER, *Computer Methods for Mathematical Computations*, Prentice-Hall, Englewood Cliffs, NJ, 1977.

[6] G. H. GOLUB AND C. F. VAN LOAN, *Matrix Computations*, The Johns Hopkins University Press, Baltimore, 1983.

[7] H.-M. HUANG, *A Parallel Algorithm for Symmetric Tridiagonal Eigenvalue Problems*, CAC Document No. 109, Center for Advanced Computation, Univ. Illinois at Urbana-Champaign, February 1974.

[8] D. KUCK AND A. SAMEH, *Parallel computation of eigenvalues of real matrices*, IFIP Congress 1971, 2 (1972), pp. 1266–1272.

[9] D. KUCK, D. LAWRIE, A. SAMEH AND E. DAVIDSON, *Construction of a large-scale multiprocessor*, Cedar Document No. 45, Univ. Illinois at Urbana-Champaign, 1984.

[10] A. OSTROWSKI, *Solution of Equations and Systems of Equations*, Academic Press, New York, 1966.

[11] J. H. WILKINSON, *The Algebraic Eigenvalue Problem*, Oxford Univ. Press, Oxford, 1965.

SIAM J. SCI. STAT. COMPUT.
Vol. 8, No. 2, March 1987

A COMPARISON OF DOMAIN DECOMPOSITION TECHNIQUES FOR ELLIPTIC PARTIAL DIFFERENTIAL EQUATIONS AND THEIR PARALLEL IMPLEMENTATION*

DAVID E. KEYES† AND WILLIAM D. GROPP‡

Abstract. Several preconditioned conjugate gradient (PCG)-based domain decomposition techniques for self-adjoint elliptic partial differential equations in two dimensions are compared against each other and against conventional PCG iterative techniques in serial and parallel contexts. We consider preconditioners that make use of fast Poisson solvers on the subdomain interiors. Several preconditioners for the interfacial equations are tested on a set of model problems involving two or four subdomains, which are prototypes of the stripwise and boxwise decompositions of a two-dimensional region. Selected methods have been implemented on the Intel Hypercube by assigning one processor to each subdomain, making use of up to 64 processors. The choice of a "best" method for a given problem depends in general upon: (a) the domain geometry, (b) the variability of the operator, and (c) machine characteristics such as the number of processors available and their interconnection scheme, the memory available per processor, and communication and computation rates. Illustrations from the first two categories are provided herein. A comparison paper [23] emphasizes the importance of the third category.

Key words. domain decomposition, substructuring, elliptic problems, Schur complement, preconditioning, parallel algorithms

AMS(MOS) subject classifications. 65N20, 65F10, 68A20

1. Introduction. A number of methods based on domain decomposition have been proposed in recent years for the numerical solution of elliptic partial differential equations. Such methods are based upon the observation that the domain of problem definition may be regarded as the union of two or more subdomains, on each of which the restriction of the original problem may take on a particularly convenient form. Decomposition by domain also provides a natural route to parallelism. For some problems, these methods can be interesting even as serial algorithms, when the advantages that arise from isolating the subproblems can be made to outweigh the extra work involved in enforcing the proper conditions at the interfaces of the subdomains. A fortiori, they are interesting as parallel methods since reasonably large independent subtasks can readily be identified. We compare the performance of several domain decomposition methods and a class of undecomposed domain methods on a common set of two-dimensional, linear, scalar problems, and examine the parallelizability of each. Our aims are to point out the unity under certain conditions of methods which have been presented independently, and also to identify some problem characteristics which tend to favor certain methods over others in the context of parallelism.

Apart from the advantage of reformulating a large discrete problem as a collection of smaller problems which can be solved independently, there are at least two other

---
* Received by the editors January 6, 1986; accepted for publication (in revised form) March 31, 1986. This article was presented at the Second SIAM Conference on Parallel Processing for Scientific Computing that was held in Norfolk, Virginia on November 18–21, 1985.

† Research Center for Scientific Computation, and Department of Mechanical Engineering, Yale University, Box 2157, Yale Station, New Haven, Connecticut 06520. The research of this author was supported by the Office of Naval Research under contract N00014-82-K-0184.

‡ Research Center for Scientific Computation, Yale University, Box 2158, Yale Station, New Haven, Connecticut 06520. The research of this author was supported in part by the Office of Naval Research under contract N00014-82-K-0184, the National Science Foundation under grant MCS-8106181, and the Air Force Office of Scientific Research under contract AFOSR-84-0360.

motivations for considering domain decomposition methods, which may be present individually or in combination with the first in any given problem. All are of the "divide-and-conquer" type. Domains of irregular shape can be decomposed into subdomains of regular shape on which tensor-product-based discretization schemes can be employed, leading to discrete operators of regular structure. Also, regions of relative nonuniformity of the differential operator, whether due to coefficient variability or even substantially different physics, can be isolated into different subdomains, again resulting in exploitable locally regular structure. An example of each of these motivations is given.

The decomposition topologies considered involve both simple interfaces (with and without overlap regions) and cross-points. We compare Schur complement matrix methods (e.g., [2], [14], [20]), full partitioned matrix methods based on block Gaussian elimination not making explicit use of the reduced Schur complement system (e.g., [5]), and other methods of variational type (e.g., [19]). These classes of methods are similar at the discrete level, employing preconditioned conjugate gradient (PCG) iterations as the outer loop, and an exact equivalence between the iterates of the first two can be established under certain conditions. In all of these methods the largest implicit problems are Dirichlet or Neumann solves over the subdomains; therefore an easy handle on parallelism can be provided from an a priori dissection of the grid. However, global communication is required in forming the inner products of the PCG iterations (and also in one class of preconditioning methods), so the optimum parallel implementation is not completely straightforward. The optimum number of subdomains is generally both architecture- and problem-dependent, since the communication cost per iteration and the overall number of iterations tend to increase with the number of subdomains.

A variety of preconditioners have been proposed, for some of which there exist theoretical results showing the convergence rate of the iterations to be asymptotically independent of the spatial resolution, or only weakly dependent thereon. Some of these optimal preconditioners are exact for uniform operators, and in practice work best when the operator coefficients do not vary too much *along* the interfaces. For problems in which there is variation along the interfaces, the condition number of the system, though asymptotically independent of resolution, is larger and it is interesting to consider alternative low-bandwidth approximations to the Schur complement matrix, at least for sufficiently low resolution. We designate this type of preconditioning Modified Schur Complement (MSC), and include some examples in our comparisons.

The outline of this article is as follows. In § 2 we review some recent contributions to the domain decomposition literature, summarizing methods and key theoretical results, and introducing MSC preconditioning. Section 3 contains an experimental comparison of various methods on the same small-scale model problems, all implemented serially. Parallel implementation issues for domain decomposition methods are discussed in § 4. We present some machine timings and iteration counts obtained on the Intel Hypercube for three leading methods applied to the model problem of Laplace's equation in the unit square, and draw some conclusions in § 5. Practical limitations confine the examples to a relatively small region of the parameter space of problem size and number of subdomains. In a companion paper [23], we consider theoretically a larger region of this space for three communication topologies: ring, a two-dimensional mesh, and an *n*-cube. Onto these we consider the natural decomposition mappings: a decomposition into strips onto the ring, a decomposition into boxes onto the mesh, and decompositions of both types onto the *n*-cube. Serial complexity comparisons and parallel efficiency comparisons of the methods are presented.

2. A review of recent PCG-based domain decomposition methods. The substructuring of elliptic partial differential equations by domain has served as a practical computational technique for over twenty years (e.g., [32]), and its theoretical origins (as a method of proving the solvability of the Dirichlet problem on irregular regions) extend back to the last century [36]. A briefly annotated bibliography of various direct and iterative approaches is contained in the introduction of [2]. Here we summarize only recent domain decomposition algorithms which make use of preconditioned conjugate gradient iteration in the outer loop, which appear to have originated with [12]. There are other types of domain decomposition-related methods such as Schwarz–Jacobi [35] and Schwarz-multigrid [29] which are not considered in this article.

2.1. Problem definition. The methods will be illustrated on a model second-order, positive definite, self-adjoint elliptic Dirichlet problem on a bounded domain in R^2 with a piecewise smooth boundary:

(2.1a) $$Lu = f \quad \text{in } \Omega, \qquad a = 0 \quad \text{on } \partial\Omega,$$

in the weak formulation, in which we seek $u \in H_0^1(\Omega)$ such that for all $v \in H_0^1(\Omega)$

(2.1b) $$A_\Omega(u, v) = (f, v),$$

where

$$A_\Omega(u, v) \equiv \sum_{p,q=1}^{2} \int_\Omega a_{pq}(\mathbf{x}) \frac{\partial u}{\partial x_p} \frac{\partial v}{\partial x_q} \, d\mathbf{x}$$

and

$$(f, v) \equiv \int_\Omega fv \, d\mathbf{x}.$$

Given a triangulation of Ω, we define the discrete subspace of H_0^1 consisting of piecewise linear functions vanishing on $\partial\Omega$, H_{0h}^1. Note that the dimension of H_{0h}^1 is the number of vertices in the interior of Ω, defined as n. For all of the algorithms to be described but one, it is sufficient to consider the usual cardinal basis for H_{0h}^1, consisting of C^0 piecewise linear functions of the smallest possible support, denoted $\{\psi_j\}_{j\in N}$, $N = \{1, 2, \cdots, n\}$. The discrete approximation to u in H_{0h}^1 is then represented by a vector of nodal coefficients, u_h.

The Galerkin formulation of (2.1b) leads to the matrix equation

(2.2) $$Au_h = f_h$$

where

$$[A]_{ij} = \sum_{p,q=1}^{2} \int_\Omega a_{pq} \frac{\partial \psi_j}{\partial x_p} \frac{\partial \psi_i}{\partial x_q} \, d\mathbf{x}, \qquad i, j \in N,$$

and

$$[f_h]_i = \int_\Omega f\psi_i \, d\mathbf{x}, \qquad i \in N.$$

The simplest decomposition on which all of the methods can be compared is that involving two simply connected subdomains. Though it is somewhat academic from the point of view of parallel processing, we consider this case first because it generalizes straightforwardly to multiple-strip decompositions and allows presentation of the basic ideas without cumbersome notation. For all of the algorithms to be described but one, the intersections of the subdomains are restricted to be interfaces of lower dimension. Referring to Fig. 1(a), we define $\gamma_{12} = \partial\Omega_1 \cap \partial\Omega_2$.

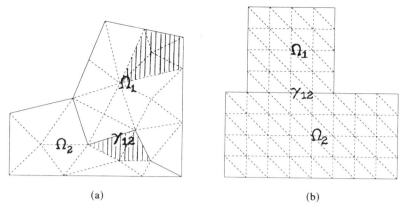

(a)   (b)

FIG. 1. *Sample domains illustrating the triangulation and substructuring described in § 2.1. (a) A general domain showing partitioning into two subdomains with a common interface (or separator set) lying along segments of the triangulation. Support of typical nodal basis functions ψ_{1j}, $j \in N_1$ and ψ_{2j}, $j \in N_0$ are shaded. (b) A model geometry for the use of fast Poisson solvers on the subdomains: a union of uniformly triangulated rectangles.*

The triangulation must be such that the segments of γ_{12} coincide with sides of the triangular elements. Let f_k denote the restriction of f to Ω_k. With a slight abuse of the usual notation, we define the discrete subspaces of functions over each subdomain which vanish on the outer boundary, but may be nonvanishing on the interface boundary, H_{kh}^1, $(k = 1, 2)$, and their subsets, H_{0kh}^1, of functions which vanish also on γ_{12}. The H_{0kh}^1 have cardinal bases $\{\psi_{kj}\}_{j \in N_k}$, where N_k is an index set for the nodes interior to Ω_k, of dimension n_k. Denote by $\{\psi_{kj}\}_{j \in N_0}$, where N_0 is an index set of dimension n_0 for the nodes on the interface, the bases for the functions in H_{kh}^1 which vanish at the interior nodes of Ω_k, but have nonvanishing trace on γ_{12}.

Equation (2.2) can be symmetrically permuted into the form

$$(2.3) \qquad \begin{bmatrix} A_{00} & A_{01} \\ A_{10} & A_{11} \end{bmatrix} \begin{pmatrix} u_0 \\ u_1 \end{pmatrix} = \begin{pmatrix} f_0 \\ f_1 \end{pmatrix}$$

where the first block row corresponds to the unknowns defined at the nodes of the separator set γ_{12}, and where A_{11} is itself a 2×2 block diagonal matrix, one block corresponding to the nodal values in each subdomain. In (2.3) and hereafter the subscript h is dropped where there is no ambiguity between the continuous and discrete formulations. The matrix A is symmetric and positive definite, as are its diagonal blocks, by the hypotheses preceding (2.1). Consequently, the interior unknowns may be formally eliminated in forming the Schur complement system (sometimes denoted the *capacitance*[1] system)

$$(2.4) \qquad\qquad\qquad Cu_0 = g$$

where $C = A_{00} - A_{01}A_{11}^{-1}A_{10}$ and $g = f_0 - A_{01}A_{11}^{-1}f_1$.

---

[1] A capacitance matrix formulation has been extensively used in the context of *imbedding* an irregular region in a regular one since Hockney's description of its application to electrostatics in 1970 (whence the name) [24]. In the imbedding variant, the reduced system unknowns correspond to the values on the irregularly shaped boundary. Imbedding and decomposition examples are considered together in [7]. Conjugate gradient iterations with a symmetrizer-preconditioner were applied to the imbedding variant in [31].

As the Schur complement of A_{00} in A, C is also symmetric and positive definite. Construction of the right-hand side of (2.4) requires one solve on each subdomain with homogeneous Dirichlet conditions on the interface. Having solved (2.4) for u_0, the interior unknowns can be recovered from the lower block row of (2.3), again at the cost of one solve on each subdomain with u_0 as inhomogeneous Dirichlet data.

In the two-subdomain case it is helpful for illustrative purposes to rewrite (2.3) in the expanded form

$$
(2.5) \qquad
\begin{bmatrix}
A_{00} & A_{01}^{(1)} & A_{01}^{(2)} \\
A_{10}^{(1)} & A_{11}^{(1)} & 0 \\
A_{10}^{(2)} & 0 & A_{11}^{(2)}
\end{bmatrix}
\begin{pmatrix}
u_0 \\
u_1^{(1)} \\
u_1^{(2)}
\end{pmatrix}
=
\begin{pmatrix}
f_0 \\
f_1^{(1)} \\
f_1^{(2)}
\end{pmatrix}
$$

where $u_1^{(1)}$ and $u_1^{(2)}$ are the unknowns in subdomains 1 and 2, respectively, and to decompose the interface diagonal block as

$$
A_{00} = A_{00}^{(1)} + A_{00}^{(2)}
$$

where

$$
[A_{00}^{(k)}]_{ij} = \sum_{p,q=1}^{2} \int_{\Omega_k} a_{pq} \frac{\partial \psi_j}{\partial x_p} \frac{\partial \psi_i}{\partial x_q} \, d\mathbf{x}, \qquad i,j \in N_0.
$$

The dimensions of $A_{11}^{(1)}$ and $A_{11}^{(2)}$ are n_1 and n_2, respectively, with $n = n_0 + n_1 + n_2$.

The case of Poisson's equation on a union of rectangles, uniformly triangulated as in Fig. 1(b), will be frequently considered in the sequel. For this so-called Courant triangulation, fast Poisson solvers [37] may be used to invert the $A_{11}^{(k)}$.

Since it explicitly involves the inverses of the $A_{11}^{(k)}$, the matrix operator C can be expensive to construct, generally requiring n_0 solves on each subdomain. Historically, domain decomposition was first approached in this way [32], and it remains a useful procedure when the formation of the factors of C can be amortized over a large number of right-hand sides, for instance when the same discrete linear system arises at successive steps in a time-dependent problem (e.g., [30]).

For cases in which the construction of C cannot be so amortized, for instance when a new system like (2.2) arises at each step in a nonlinear problem, more efficient methods have been developed by means of preconditioned conjugate gradient iteration, which at each step require a matrix-vector multiply involving C, without its explicit construction. Each PCG iteration still requires one solve on each subdomain, so the effectiveness of the PCG-based techniques depends on keeping the number of steps small through a preconditioning which is considerably less expensive to construct and apply than C^{-1} itself.

Of course, PCG iterations can also be used to solve the full systems in the form of (2.2) and (2.3), the type of preconditioning which is natural and efficient being different in each case. In subsequent sections we make some comparisons as to the effectiveness and generality of techniques which take each of these three formulations as their starting points. We refer to methods which depart directly from (2.2) as global matrix methods (GMM), from (2.3) as partitioned matrix methods (PMM), and from (2.4) as Schur complement matrix methods (SCM). For subsequent reference to individual steps, we present below the form of the PCG algorithm used in applications for solving the symmetric $n \times n$ linear system $\mathscr{A}x = b$ with (symmetric) preconditioner $\mathscr{B}$:

ALGORITHM PCG

Choose initial iterate:

(PCG.1) $\qquad x^0,\ \text{arbitrary}$

Compute initial residual:

(PCG.2) $\qquad r^0 \leftarrow b - \mathcal{A}x^0$

Compute preconditioned residual:

(PCG.3) $\qquad s^0 \leftarrow \mathcal{B}^{-1} r^0$

Initialize direction:

(PCG.4) $\qquad p^0 \leftarrow s^0$

Compute $\mathcal{B}$-inner-product:

(PCG.5) $\qquad \gamma^0 \leftarrow (r^0, s^0)$

For $k = 0$ Step 1 Until *Convergence,* **Do**

    Compute matrix-vector product:

(PCG.6) $\qquad q^k \leftarrow \mathcal{A}p^k$

    Compute $\mathcal{A}$-inner-product:

(PCG.7) $\qquad \tau^k \leftarrow (p^k, q^k)$

    Compute step length:

(PCG.8) $\qquad \alpha^k \leftarrow \gamma^k / \tau^k$

    Update solution:

(PCG.9) $\qquad x^{k+1} \leftarrow x^k + \alpha^k p^k$

    Compute new residual:

(PCG.10) $\qquad r^{k+1} \leftarrow r^k - \alpha^k q^k$

    Compute new preconditioned residual:

(PCG.11) $\qquad s^{k+1} \leftarrow \mathcal{B}^{-1} r^{k+1}$

    Compute $\mathcal{B}$-inner-product:

(PCG.12) $\qquad \gamma^{k+1} \leftarrow (r^{k+1}, s^{k+1})$

    Compute orthogonalization coefficient:

(PCG.13) $\qquad \beta^k \leftarrow \gamma^{k+1} / \gamma^k$

    Update direction:

(PCG.14) $\qquad p^{k+1} \leftarrow s^{k+1} + \beta^k p^k$

End For

In addition to the storage and workspace requirements for the application of $\mathcal{A}$ and $\mathcal{B}^{-1}$, the algorithm requires storage for four vectors of length n. As is well known (e.g., [12]), the $\mathcal{A}$-norm of the error at the kth iteration of PCG is bounded according to

$$\frac{\|x^k - x\|_{\mathcal{A}}}{\|x^0 - x\|_{\mathcal{A}}} \leq 2 \left(\frac{\sqrt{\kappa} - 1}{\sqrt{\kappa} + 1} \right)^k$$

where κ is the condition number of $\mathcal{B}^{-1}\mathcal{A}$, and the algorithm produces exact convergence in a number of iterations which is at most the number of distinct eigenvalues of $\mathcal{B}^{-1}\mathcal{A}$. The operators $\mathcal{A}$ and $\mathcal{B}$ are said to be *spectrally equivalent* if there exist positive constants γ_0 and γ_1 independent of the discretization such that for all x, $\gamma_0(x, \mathcal{B}x) \leq (x, \mathcal{A}x) \leq \gamma_1(x, \mathcal{B}x)$.

2.2. Schur complement methods (SCM). The Schur complement methods are realized by taking $\mathcal{A}$ in Algorithm PCG to be C and selecting appropriate $\mathcal{B}$. The iterations occur on vectors of length n_0. Note that by construction the product Cp^k consists of the residuals at the nodes along γ_{12} of the original discrete operator applied to the vector which satisfies the discrete equations with homogeneous boundary conditions on $\partial\Omega$ in each of the subdomains and equals p^k on γ_{12}. Four related choices of $\mathcal{B}$ are reviewed in this subsection.

Dryja [14], [15] showed that C of (2.4) is spectrally equivalent to the matrix $K^{1/2}$, where K is the tridiagonal matrix of order n_0 with diagonal elements 2 and off-diagonal elements -1, the discrete Laplacian operator over a uniform grid in one dimension. For notational convenience, we define the average nodal spacing along the interface, $h = (n_0 + 1)^{-1}$. Inserting a factor of 2 for consistent scaling across the methods to follow, Dryja's preconditioner has the eigendecomposition

$$M_D \equiv 2K^{1/2} = W\Lambda_D W^T$$

where

$$[W]_{ij} = \sqrt{2h} \sin ij\pi h,$$

and

$$\Lambda_D = \text{diag}(\lambda_j^D)$$

where

$$\lambda_j^D = 2\sqrt{\sigma_j},$$

with

$$\sigma_j = 4 \sin^2 \frac{j\pi h}{2}.$$

The condition number of $K^{1/2}$, which is equal to λ_{n_0}/λ_1, grows in proportion to the number of interfacial unknowns n_0 as this number becomes large. Through their spectral equivalence, the same is true of C, which implies that the convergence of the unpreconditioned Schur complement system iteration will deteriorate as the mesh is refined. The action of M_D^{-1} on a vector can be computed with a pair of sine transforms in $O(n_0 \log n_0)$ operations; hence the cost of the preconditioning is inexpensive in comparison with the cost of forming a matrix multiplication with a general C, which involves two-dimensional subdomain solves.

By means of FFT's in one dimension, Dryja also gave an $O(n_0 \log n_0)$ method for performing the subdomain solves for the case $L = -\Delta$ and Ω a union of two rectangular subregions, by exploiting the regular sparsity pattern of the right-hand sides arising during the PCG iterations. In this case the overall operation count for solving (2.2) is dominated by the pre- and post-processing involved in forming g of (2.4) and backsolving, instead of by solving the Schur complement system. For more general operators and domain geometries, the cost of one PCG iteration is comparable to the pre- and post-processing, namely $O(n_0^2 \log n_0)$.

Golub and Mayers [20] arrived heuristically at a preconditioner for C by starting from the observation that the elements $[C]_{ij}$ may often be well approximated as constant along a diagonal. In other words, the influence of the data at interfacial node j on the residual at interfacial node i depends (approximately) only on the discrete distance along the interface, $|i-j|$. This led Golub and Mayers to solve a discrete infinite domain Laplace problem with an infinite interface dividing two half-planes, the data on the interface and at infinity prescribed to be zero everywhere except at the origin, where it was taken as one. The ijth element of their preconditioner of Toeplitz form was then defined as the residual of the discrete Laplacian at the point on the interface at a distance $|i-j|$ from the origin. This preconditioner was tested and found superior to Dryja's on the problem considered in [20]. Though computationally complicated to construct, they noticed that a second, FFT-implementable preconditioner could be derived by replacing a term in their generating function expression for the interface residual by Dryja's preconditioner. Their result,

$$M_G = W \Lambda_G W^T$$

where

$$\Lambda_G = \mathrm{diag}\,(\lambda_j^G)$$

where

$$\lambda_j^G = 2\sqrt{\sigma_j + \frac{\sigma_j^2}{4}},$$

or

$$M_G = 2(K + \tfrac{1}{4}K^2)^{1/2},$$

has been also employed as an effective refinement of M_D in other investigations [2], [16].

Bjorstad and Widlund [2] showed that C, $C^{(1)} \equiv A_{00}^{(1)} - A_{01}^{(1)}(A_{11}^{(1)})^{-1}A_{10}^{(1)}$, and $C^{(2)} \equiv A_{00}^{(2)} - A_{01}^{(2)}(A_{11}^{(2)})^{-1}A_{10}^{(2)}$, are all spectrally equivalent. (Note that $C = C^{(1)} + C^{(2)}$.) Assuming that Ω is decomposed in such a way that it is computationally convenient to solve Neumann problems on one of the subdomains, say Ω_1, with zero Dirichlet data on $\partial\Omega_1 \cap \partial\Omega$ and natural boundary conditions on γ_{12}, they proposed $C^{(1)}$ as a preconditioner for C, acting on a suggestion of Dryja's. Applying $(C^{(1)})^{-1}$ to a vector p_0 of dimension n_0 requires solving the Ω_1 Neumann problem

$$\begin{bmatrix} A_{00}^{(1)} & A_{01}^{(1)} \\ A_{00}^{(1)} & A_{11}^{(1)} \end{bmatrix} \begin{pmatrix} q_0 \\ q_1^{(1)} \end{pmatrix} = \begin{pmatrix} p_0 \\ 0 \end{pmatrix},$$

whence $q_0 = (C^{(1)})^{-1}p_0$. In the case of Poisson's equation on the union of two rectangular uniformly gridded regions, as pictured in Fig. 1(b), an explicit FFT-implementable expression for $C^{(1)}$ was derived in [2]. We shall define M_B as twice $C^{(1)}$ in what follows for purposes of comparison. Let m_1 be the number of internal grid points in the vertical direction in Ω_1. Then

$$M_B = W\Lambda_B W^T$$

where

$$\Lambda_B = \operatorname{diag}(\lambda_j^B)$$

where

$$\lambda_j^B = 2\left(\frac{1+\rho_j^{m_1+1}}{1-\rho_j^{m_1+1}}\right)\sqrt{\sigma_j + \frac{\sigma_j^2}{4}},$$

where

$$\rho_j = \frac{r_{j-}}{r_{j+}}$$

and

$$r_{j\pm} = 1 + \frac{\sigma_j}{2} \pm \sqrt{\sigma_j + \frac{\sigma_j^2}{4}}.$$

This is a diagonal rescaling of M_G which takes account of the aspect ratio, m_1/n_0, of one of the subdomains. In the case where Ω is a rectangle and Ω_1 and Ω_2 are symmetrically disposed about the interface, $C^{(1)} = C^{(2)}$, $M_B = C$, and the Bjorstad-Widlund method converges in one step.

Chan has carried this circle of ideas further for the special case where Ω is a rectangle and L is the Laplacian by finding the Fourier decomposition of C itself [8]. Referring to Fig. 2(a), let m_2 be the number of internal grid points in the vertical direction in Ω_2.

Then in the previous notation,

$$M_C = W\Lambda_C W^T$$

where

$$\Lambda_C = \operatorname{diag}(\lambda_j^C)$$

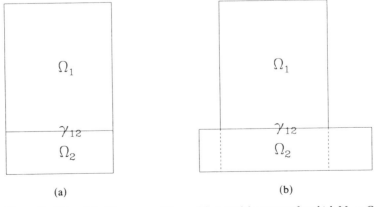

(a)   (b)

FIG. 2. *The applicability of the Chan preconditioner.* (a) *A model geometry for which $M_C = C$.* (b) *A model geometry for which M_C is not exact but furnishes a useful aspect ratio-sensitive preconditioner.*

where

$$\lambda_j^C = \left(\frac{1+\rho_j^{m_1+1}}{1-\rho_j^{m_1+1}} + \frac{1+\rho_j^{m_2+1}}{1-\rho_j^{m_2+1}}\right)\sqrt{\sigma_j + \frac{\sigma_j^2}{4}}.$$

By taking account of the aspect ratio of both of the subdomains, Chan's method converges in one step even in the unsymmetric case, and thus may be regarded as a direct fast Poisson solver. Of course, fast Poisson solvers not making use of domain decomposition can already be applied when Ω is a rectangle, and the serial computational complexity of Chan's approach can be made nearly equal to that of these algorithms by solving the Schur complement system in Fourier transform space [33]. However, Chan's preconditioner may also be applied in the iterative manner of the other preconditioners in a more general geometry like that of Fig. 2(b), for which a fast Poisson solver is not available, although exact only for the inscribed $n_0 \times (m_1 + m_2)$ rectangle.

In aid of visualizing C and these approximations thereto, surface plots of their elements as a function of their indices are given in Fig. 3 for the case of Poisson's equation in the unit square with $n_0 = 15$, $m_1 = m_2 = 7$. For clarity, Fig. 3(a) shows $C(= M_C = M_B)$ and the remaining plots show differences of C and various other preconditioners. Corresponding estimates of the condition numbers $\kappa(M^{-1}C)$ are listed along with convergence data in the first row of Table 1 in § 3.

The Chan and Bjorstad–Widlund methods are both exact for the Laplacian in a symmetrically decomposed rectangular domain. For a given h, the Golub–Mayers method coincides with these two methods in the infinite aspect ratio limit of the domain geometry:

$$\lim_{\substack{m_1\to\infty \\ m_2\to\infty}} \lambda_j^C = 2\sqrt{\sigma_j + \frac{\sigma_j^2}{4}} = \lambda_j^G.$$

The Dryja preconditioner is not exact for any domain geometry limit. All four of the preconditioners discussed above are *optimal* for the two-subdomain case in the sense that the condition number of the Schur complement system approaches a constant independent of h as the mesh is refined with fixed geometry. References [8], [1], [2] may be consulted for further comparisons between C, $C^{(1)}$, $C^{(2)}$, M_G, and M_D in various limits for h, m_1, and m_2, all within the context of the two-subdomain case.

References [1] and [2] are of additional interest in providing motivation from the underlying continuous problem for the $K^{1/2}$-family of preconditioners. It is shown therein that the capacitance system (2.4) is the discrete analogue of a zero jump condition along the interface for the normal derivatives of the functions which solve the continuous Dirichlet problems in each subdomain with data u_0 on the interface. For the case of two half-planes, the continuous operator acting on u_0 is shown in [1] to be equal (in Fourier space) to twice the square root of the continuous one-dimensional Laplacian. Hence, to the extent that the subdomain boundaries are "far" from the interface, one expects a multiple of the square root of the one-dimensional Laplacian to serve as an effective preconditioner for the finite domain problem. In the discrete case, this is precisely $M_D = 2K^{1/2}$. Problems with subdomains of small aspect ratio benefit from the refinements to M_D described in this section, since the boundaries are not far removed in such cases.

A disadvantage of working with the Schur complement system, independent of preconditioner, is that the subdomain solves are presumed to be carried out exactly. In the general nonseparable case of interest, fast Poisson solvers are not available, and

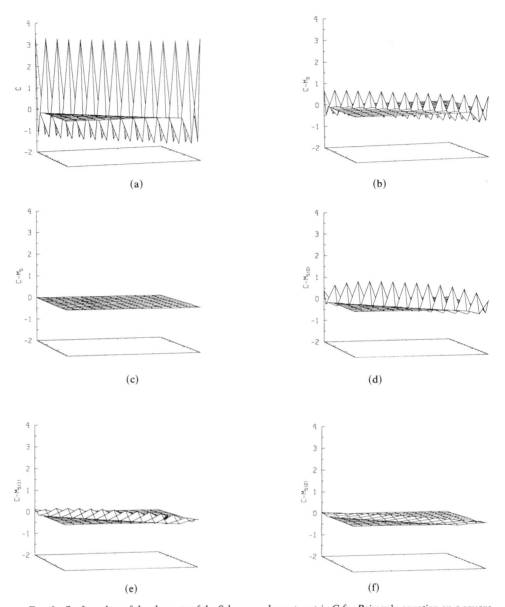

FIG. 3. *Surface plots of the elements of the Schur complement matrix C for Poisson's equation on a square uniformly discretized with 16 subintervals on a side, and differences of C and various preconditioners described in §§ 2.2 and 2.4.* (a) *C itself;* (b) $C - M_D$; (c) $C - M_G$; (d) $C - M_{S(0)}$; (e) $C - M_{S(1)}$; (f) $C - M_{S(2)}$.

one is faced with the necessity of direct sparse solvers in the computation of Cp^k, or of nested iterations. In the latter case, the convergence criterion for the inner iterations could conceivably be tuned to the rate of progress of the outer iteration to save computational work, but a more fully coupled framework of simultaneous iteration is possible, which we review in the next subsection.

2.3. Partitioned matrix methods (PMM). The partitioned matrix methods are realized by taking $\mathscr{A}$ to be A of (2.3) and selecting appropriate $\mathscr{B}$. The iterations occur on vectors of length n, rather than n_0. We begin with the following theorem, due to Eisenstat [18].

THEOREM 2.1. *Let the* $n \times n$ *partitioned matrix* A *and the* $n_0 \times n_0$ *Schur complement matrix* C *be defined as in* (2.3) *and* (2.4), *respectively, with corresponding right-hand sides* f *and* g.

(i) *Algorithm* PCG *applied to* $Cv = g$ *with initial iterate* v^0 *and preconditioner* M *is equivalent to algorithm* PCG *applied to* $Au = f$ *with initial iterate*

$$u^0 = \begin{pmatrix} v^0 \\ A_{11}^{-1}(f_1 - A_{10}v^0) \end{pmatrix}$$

and preconditioner

(2.6)
$$B = \begin{bmatrix} M + A_{01}A_{11}^{-1}A_{10} & A_{01} \\ A_{10} & A_{11} \end{bmatrix},$$

in the sense that, for all $k \geq 0$,

$$u^k = \begin{pmatrix} v^k \\ A_{11}^{-1}(f_1 - A_{10}v^k) \end{pmatrix}.$$

(ii) *There is no advantage to choosing an initial iterate more general than* u^0 *as above, in the sense that* $\|u^k - u\|_A \leq \|w^k - u\|_A$, *where* w^k *is the* kth *iterate generated by* PCG *from the initial iterate*

$$w^0 = u^0 + \begin{pmatrix} 0 \\ \xi^0 \end{pmatrix}.$$

Proof. (i) Since A_{11}, M, and B are symmetric positive definite matrices, we may write $M = Q^T Q$ and $B = P^T P$, where

$$P = \begin{bmatrix} Q & 0 \\ A_{11}^{-1/2}A_{10} & A_{11}^{1/2} \end{bmatrix}.$$

The Schur complement system PCG iteration is equivalent to conjugate gradient (CG) iteration on $\hat{C}\hat{v} = \hat{g}$ with initial iterate $\hat{v}^{(0)} = 0$, where $\hat{C} \equiv Q^{-T}CQ^{-1}$, $\hat{v} \equiv Q(v - v^{(0)})$ and $\hat{g} \equiv Q^{-T}(g - Cv^{(0)})$; and similarly the partitioned system PCG iteration is equivalent to CG iteration on $\hat{A}\hat{u} = \hat{f}$ with initial iterate $\hat{u}^{(0)} = 0$, where $\hat{A} \equiv P^{-T}AP^{-1}$, $\hat{u} \equiv P(u - u^{(0)})$ and $\hat{f} \equiv P^{-T}(f - Au^{(0)})$. But note that

$$\hat{A} = \begin{bmatrix} Q^T & A_{10}^T A_{11}^{-1/2} \\ 0 & A_{11}^{1/2} \end{bmatrix}^{-1} \begin{bmatrix} A_{00} & A_{01} \\ A_{10} & A_{11} \end{bmatrix} \begin{bmatrix} Q & 0 \\ A_{11}^{-1/2}A_{10} & A_{11}^{1/2} \end{bmatrix}^{-1}$$

$$= \begin{bmatrix} Q^{-T} & -Q^{-T}A_{10}^T A_{11}^{-1} \\ 0 & A_{11}^{-1/2} \end{bmatrix} \begin{bmatrix} A_{00} & A_{01} \\ A_{10} & A_{11} \end{bmatrix} \begin{bmatrix} Q^{-1} & 0 \\ -A_{11}^{-1}A_{10}Q^{-1} & A_{11}^{-1/2} \end{bmatrix}$$

$$= \begin{bmatrix} Q^{-T}(A_{00} - A_{01}A_{11}^{-1}A_{10}) & 0 \\ A_{11}^{-1/2}A_{10} & A_{11}^{1/2} \end{bmatrix} \begin{bmatrix} Q^{-1} & 0 \\ -A_{11}^{-1}A_{10}Q^{-1} & A_{11}^{-1/2} \end{bmatrix}$$

$$= \begin{bmatrix} Q^{-T}CQ^{-1} & 0 \\ 0 & I \end{bmatrix} = \begin{bmatrix} \hat{C} & 0 \\ 0 & I \end{bmatrix}.$$

Similarly,

$$\hat{f} = \begin{bmatrix} Q^T & A_{10}^T A_{11}^{-1/2} \\ 0 & A_{11}^{1/2} \end{bmatrix}^{-1} \begin{pmatrix} f_0 - A_{01}A_{11}^{-1}(f_1 - A_{10}v^0) - A_{00}v^0 \\ 0 \end{pmatrix}$$

$$= \begin{bmatrix} Q^{-T} & -Q^{-T}A_{10}^T A_{11}^{-1} \\ 0 & A_{11}^{-1/2} \end{bmatrix} \begin{pmatrix} g - Cv^0 \\ 0 \end{pmatrix} = \begin{pmatrix} \hat{g} \\ 0 \end{pmatrix}.$$

Thus the partitioned matrix PCG iteration is equivalent to CG iteration on

$$\begin{bmatrix} \hat{C} & 0 \\ 0 & I \end{bmatrix}\begin{pmatrix} \hat{v} \\ \hat{\xi} \end{pmatrix} = \begin{pmatrix} \hat{g} \\ 0 \end{pmatrix}$$

with initial iterate $\xi^{(0)} = 0$, $\hat{v}^{(0)} = 0$ and the equivalence is established.

(ii) To prove optimality, we first define $\hat{w}^k \equiv P(w^k - u^0)$, and note that

$$\hat{w}^0 = \begin{pmatrix} 0 \\ A_{11}^{1/2}\xi^0 \end{pmatrix} \quad \text{and} \quad \hat{u} = \begin{pmatrix} \hat{v} \\ 0 \end{pmatrix}.$$

Then

$$\begin{aligned}
\| w^k - u \|_A^2 &= \| \hat{w}^k - \hat{u} \|_{\hat{A}}^2 \\
&= \min_{P_k} \| (I - \hat{A}P_k(\hat{A}))(\hat{w}^0 - \hat{u}) \|_{\hat{A}}^2 \\
&= \min_{P_k} \left\| \begin{pmatrix} -(I - \hat{C}P_k(\hat{C}))\hat{v} \\ (I - P_k(I))A_{11}^{1/2}\xi^0 \end{pmatrix} \right\|_{\hat{A}}^2 \\
&= \min_{P_k} \{ \| (I - \hat{C}P_k(\hat{C}))\hat{v} \|_{\hat{C}}^2 + \| (1 - P_k(1))A_{11}^{1/2}\xi^0 \|_2^2 \} \\
&\geqq \min_{P_k} \{ \| (I - \hat{C}P_k(\hat{C}))\hat{v} \|_{\hat{C}}^2 \} \\
&= \min_{P_k} \| (I - \hat{A}P_k(\hat{A}))(\hat{u}^0 - \hat{u}) \|_{\hat{A}}^2 \\
&= \| \hat{u}^k - \hat{u} \|_{\hat{A}}^2 \\
&= \| u^k - u \|_A^2,
\end{aligned}$$

where P_k is the set of polynomials of order k, and the second and penultimate steps rely on the optimality property of CG iteration (see [11, Chap. 3], for instance). □

By this theorem, any Schur complement system preconditioner M can be applied to the interfacial equations of the partitioned matrix by its incorporation into the matrix B as shown in (2.6). Moreover, the theorem suggests a form for the preconditioner for a more general algorithm in which is it not required that the subdomain solves corresponding to A_{11}^{-1} be carried out exactly. For instance, if A derives from a nonseparable operator L, fast Poisson solvers may be used to precondition the subdomain solves. More costly exact subdomain solves are thereby avoided. To allow for this type of generality, we take $\mathcal{B}$ to be $\tilde{B}$, where

$$(2.7) \qquad \tilde{B} = \begin{bmatrix} \tilde{B}_{00} & \tilde{B}_{01} \\ \tilde{B}_{10} & \tilde{B}_{11} \end{bmatrix} \equiv \begin{bmatrix} M + \tilde{A}_{01}\tilde{A}_{11}^{-1}\tilde{A}_{10} & \tilde{A}_{01} \\ \tilde{A}_{10} & \tilde{A}_{11} \end{bmatrix},$$

and where the $\tilde{A}_{ij}$ are determined on a problem-specific basis. A convenient form for the $\tilde{A}_{ij}$ may be derived from a permutation conformal to that of (2.3) of the discrete Galerkin equations for

$$(2.8) \qquad \tilde{A}_\Omega(u, v) = (f, v)$$

where

$$\tilde{A}_\Omega(u, v) \equiv \sum_{k=1}^{2} \tilde{A}_{\Omega_k}(u, v)$$

where for each subdomain

$$\tilde{A}_{\Omega_k}(u, v) \equiv \sum_{p,q=1}^{2} \int_{\Omega_k} \tilde{a}_{pq}^k \frac{\partial u}{\partial x_p} \frac{\partial v}{\partial x_q} \, d\mathbf{x},$$

and where the constants $\tilde{a}_{pq}^k$ are chosen for each subdomain k in such a way that the resulting matrix $\tilde{A}$ is spectrally equivalent to A. This iteration is, of course, no longer equivalent to any reduced system iteration in the manner described above, and the scaling of M relative to the $\tilde{A}_{ij}$ becomes an issue, where it was not previously.

An efficient implementation of partitioned matrix preconditioners of the form (2.7) has been presented by Bramble, Pasciak and Schatz [5], wherein it is described how the operation $\mathscr{B}^{-1}r$ can be carried out at the cost of *two* subdomain solves per subdomain per iteration, plus the cost of applying M^{-1}. In the language of function-space decompositions, the solution u is written as the sum of a harmonic component, u^H, and a perpendicular component, u^P, such that in each subdomain k, $u^P|_k \in H^1_{0kh}$ satisfies

$$\tilde{A}_{\Omega_k}(u^P, v) = \tilde{A}_{\Omega_k}(u, v)$$

for all $v \in H^1_{0kh}$; and $u^H|_k \in H^1_{kh}$ satisfies $u^H = u$ on γ_{12} and

$$\tilde{A}_{\Omega_k}(u^H, v) = 0$$

for all $v \in H^1_{0kh}$.

In matrix terms, to solve

$$\tilde{B}\begin{pmatrix} u_0 \\ u_1 \end{pmatrix} = \begin{pmatrix} f_0 \\ f_1 \end{pmatrix}$$

for u, one first solves

$$\tilde{A}_{11} u_1^P = f_1$$

for u_1^P, then

$$M u_0 = f_0 - \tilde{A}_{01} u_1^P$$

for u_0, then

$$\tilde{A}_{11} u_1^H = -\tilde{A}_{10} u_0$$

for u_1^H and sets $u_1 = u_1^H + u_1^P$.

It is tempting to consider as a more economical alternative for $\mathscr{B}$ the matrix

$$\begin{bmatrix} M & 0 \\ \tilde{A}_{10} & \tilde{A}_{11} \end{bmatrix},$$

whose inversion allows skipping the first of the three steps above (and thus leads to an algorithm with no more subdomain solves per iteration than SCM), but this is not a symmetric preconditioner. The penalty for preserving a nest-free iterative structure in the case where the subdomain solves with A_{11} are too expensive to be done directly is thus an extra solve per subdomain with $\tilde{A}_{11}$ in the preconditioning step, and also the extra work in the multiplication and dot product steps due to the vector length of n instead of n_0.

In [6] the same authors consider a generalization of the Bjorstad-Widlund preconditioning in which the M of (2.7) is given by

$$\tilde{C}^{(1)} = \tilde{A}_{00}^{(1)} - \tilde{A}_{01}^{(1)}(\tilde{A}_{11}^{(1)})^{-1}\tilde{A}_{10}^{(1)}.$$

In matrix terms, to solve

$$\tilde{B}\begin{pmatrix} u_0 \\ u_1 \end{pmatrix} = \begin{pmatrix} f_0 \\ f_1 \end{pmatrix}$$

for u, one first solves the Dirichlet problem in Ω_2:

$$\tilde{A}_{11}^{(2)}v = f_1^{(2)},$$

then the Neumann problem on Ω_1:

$$\begin{bmatrix} \tilde{A}_{00}^{(1)} & \tilde{A}_{01}^{(1)} \\ \tilde{A}_{10}^{(1)} & \tilde{A}_{11}^{(1)} \end{bmatrix} \begin{pmatrix} u_0 \\ u_1^{(1)} \end{pmatrix} = \begin{pmatrix} f_0 - \tilde{A}_{01}^{(2)}v \\ f_1^{(1)} \end{pmatrix},$$

then the Dirichlet problem in Ω_2:

$$\tilde{A}_{11}^{(2)}u_1^{(2)} = f_1^{(2)} - \tilde{A}_{10}^{(2)}u_0.$$

Since one of the subdomains solves is eliminated, the serial complexity of this method is less than that of the function-space decomposition technique just described, but the remaining subdomain solves are inherently sequential, and generalization to the many-subdomain case can only be carried out for decompositions (such as stripwise) in which the boundaries of the subdomains on which the natural boundary conditions are posed do not intersect.

2.4. Modified Schur Complement (MSC) preconditioners. Because the Schur complement matrix C is close to being tridiagonal, as illustrated for the Laplacian operator in Fig. 3, it is natural to consider the use of tridiagonal or other low-bandwidth preconditioners for it. Such an approximation of one matrix by another constrained to satisfy various sparsity requirements has often proved useful in connection with iterative methods. In this context, it was proposed independently by Chan and Resasco [9] and Eisenstat [18]. We can generate a class of interfacial preconditioners of the form

$$(2.9a) \qquad\qquad M_{S(k)} = \tilde{A}_{00} - E_k$$

where E_k is a symmetric matrix with semi-bandwidth k which satisfies

$$(2.9b) \qquad\qquad E_k v_i = (\tilde{A}_{01}\tilde{A}_{11}^{-1}\tilde{A}_{10})v_i$$

for some $k+1$ vectors v_i, $i = 0, \cdots, k$. We have used $\tilde{A}_{11}$ rather than A_{11} in (2.9b) because this technique is motivated by variable coefficient problems for which exact subdomain solvers are too expensive to consider.

Note that the construction of E_k requires $k+1$ solves on each subdomain, which is in general $(k+1)/2$ times the cost of one preconditioning step with $\mathcal{B}$ of the form (2.7). For $k=0$, we consider the vector $v_0 = (1, 1, \cdots)^T$; for $k=1$, the vectors $v_0 = (1, 0, 1, 0, \cdots)^T$ and $v_1 = (0, 1, 0, 1, \cdots)^T$; and so forth. Equation (2.9b) gives $(k+1)n_0$ scalar equations for the $(k+1)(n_0 - k/2)$ distinct elements of E_k, but the overdetermination is consistent due to the symmetry of the product of matrices on the right-hand side. For the set of v_i recommended above, the diagonal elements of E_k can be read off from (2.9b) and the remaining elements can be obtained in $O(kn_0)$ operations. Note that $M_{S(k)}^{-1}$ can also be applied at the cost of only $O(kn_0)$ operations once its factorization is stored.

Surface plots of the differences between C (for the Laplacian) and $M_{S(0)}$, $M_{S(1)}$, and $M_{S(2)}$ are shown in Fig. 3 and their associated estimated condition numbers appear in Table 1.

For small k, which is the only practical limit, this class of preconditioners turns out to be markedly inferior to the optimal class described earlier for constant coefficient operators on uniform grids. However, it can be competitive when the interfaces are not placed along level curves of the coefficients. Figure 4 shows surface plots of the Schur complement matrix C and differences of C and various preconditioners for a problem with the same model geometry, but with the nonseparable operator equation

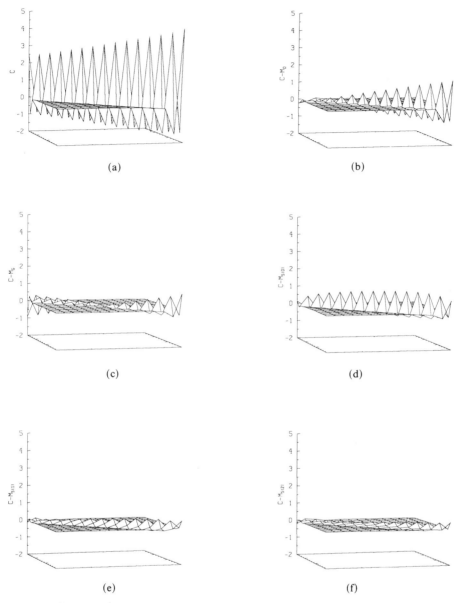

FIG. 4. *Surface plots of the elements of the Schur complement matrix C for a nonseparable operator on a square uniformly discretized with 16 subintervals on a side, and differences of C and various preconditioners described in §§ 2.2 and 2.4. (a) C itself; (b) $C - M_D$; (c) $C - M_G$; (d) $C - M_{S(0)}$; (e) $C - M_{S(1)}$; (f) $C - M_{S(2)}$. (The plot for $C - M_C = C - M_B$ is indistinguishable from $C - M_G$ on this scale.)*

$\nabla \cdot (a \nabla u) = f$, where $a = 1 + b \tan^{-1}(x - \frac{1}{2}) + c \tan^{-1}(d(y - \frac{1}{2}))$, and with all of the tilde-quantities in (2.9) obtained from the subdomain averaging of the x- and y-direction diffusion coefficients in the opposite direction to achieve separability within subdomains. Estimated condition numbers for this problem, using PMM with interfacial preconditioners from both the optimal and MSC classes appear in Table 7 of § 3.2. Observe the sensitivity of the higher-order MSC preconditioners to the variation of a along the interface, which is lacking in the optimal preconditioners. The plots are for $b = 0.65$, $c = 0.35$, $d = 10.0$.

The MSC preconditioners have the advantage of being self-scaling, relative to the $\tilde{A}_{ij}$, and can enjoy a decisive advantage over a poorly scaled optimal interface preconditioner in the PMM context. However, it is not difficult to choose a good scaling for the optimal preconditioners (see [5]).

2.5. Methods of variational type. Glowinski and several coauthors have contributed extensively to the literature of domain decomposition techniques in the course of their work on the numerical modeling of steady, compressible inviscid flow and of unsteady, incompressible viscous flow (see [19] and the references therein). Both of these subrealms of the Navier–Stokes equations may be operator-split and discretized in such a way that the subtasks of greatest computational complexity are scalar problems of Poisson type with a large number of degrees of freedom and wide variability in the coefficients in irregular geometry. We briefly describe here three algorithms of conjugate gradient type presented in [13], [19] which enter into the comparisons in § 3. Like the Schur complement methods, all of these methods iterate on degrees of freedom at the boundaries of the subdomains only, with each iteration requiring one or two exact interior solves per subdomain. Two of the methods use a partitioning of the domain into subdomains with nonintersecting interiors, as in Figs. 1 and 2. The remaining method is related to the Schwartz alternating procedure in that the subdomains overlap in regions of nonzero measure.

The algorithms are summarized below in matrix operator form, without derivation, for the model Poisson problem (2.1b). It suffices to identify the vectors in Algorithm PCG in terms of the physical variables and to specify the operators $\mathscr{A}$ and $\mathscr{B}^{-1}$.

The first two algorithms are based on the equivalence of

$$-\Delta y = f \quad \text{in } \Omega, \qquad y = 0 \quad \text{on } \partial\Omega,$$

and the problem

$$y = \arg \min_{z \in H_0^1(\Omega)} \left\{ \frac{1}{2} \int_\Omega |\nabla z|^2 \, d\mathbf{x} - \int_\Omega fz \, d\mathbf{x} \right\}.$$

Upon partitioning the domain and carrying out the minimization on each of the subdomains separately, either the normal derivative or the trace of the solution along the interface can be regarded as the principal unknown, and its value iteratively updated until continuity of the other is satisfied. Through intermediate saddle-point formulations dual conjugate gradient algorithms are derived.

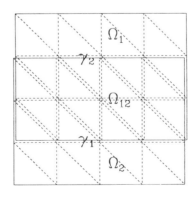

Fig. 5. *Sample domain illustrating the overlap decomposition (subdomains staggered for clarity).*

In the first algorithm ([13, § 4.1] or [19, § 2.2.2]), the unknown vector represents the discrete normal derivative of the solution along the interface adjusted for sign, $x = (-1)^{k-1} \partial u_k / \partial n_k$, $\mathscr{A}$ is the matrix $(C^{(1)})^{-1} + (C^{(2)})^{-1}$, and $\mathscr{B}$ is the matrix defined by (for $k = 1$ or $k = 2$)

$$[\mathscr{B}]_{ij} = h^{-1} \int_{\gamma_{12}} \psi_{kj} \psi_{ki} \, ds, \qquad i, j \in N_0.$$

In the uniform mesh case, $\mathscr{B} = I - (1/6)K$. This method we denote by Saddle-1.

In the second algorithm ([13, § 4.2]), denoted Saddle-2, the unknown vector represents the solution itself at the interface nodes, $\mathscr{A}$ is precisely the Schur complement C, and $\mathscr{B}$ is the matrix defined by

$$[\mathscr{B}]_{ij} = \sum_{k=1}^{2} \int_{\Omega_k} \nabla \psi_{kj} \cdot \nabla \psi_{ki} \, dx, \qquad i, j \in N_0.$$

In the uniform mesh case $\mathscr{B} = 2(I + \frac{1}{2}K)$. These preconditioners commute with their respective $\mathscr{A}$-matrices, the spectra of which can be constructed from the eigen-decompositions given in § 2.2. It is readily verified that in both cases $\kappa(\mathscr{B}^{-1}\mathscr{A})$ grows asymptotically in proportion to $1/h$.

The other method ([19, § 2.3.5 and § 2.3.7]) uses a decomposition with overlapping subdomains, as illustrated for a two subdomain case in Fig. 5. The overlap region is denoted by Ω_{12} and distinct internal subdomain boundaries γ_1 and γ_2 are defined as shown. We denote this method by CG-Schwarz (or CGS).

The unknown vector represents the trace of the solution along $\gamma_1 \cup \gamma_2$, and is partitioned accordingly, $u \equiv (u_1, u_2)^T$. For the case of the Laplacian, the algorithm is based on the equivalence of

$$-\Delta y = f \quad \text{in } \Omega, \qquad y = 0 \quad \text{on } \partial \Omega,$$

and the problem

$$u \equiv (u_1, u_2) = \arg \min_{v \in V_1 \times V_2} \left\{ \frac{1}{2} \int_{\Omega_{12}} [|\nabla(y_2 - y_1)|^2 + |y_2 - y_1|^2] \, dx \right\}$$

where the $y_k \in H^1(\Omega_k)$ are the solutions of

$$-\Delta y_k = f_k \quad \text{in } \Omega_k,$$

$$y_k = 0 \quad \text{on } \partial \Omega_k \cap \partial \Omega,$$

$$y_k = v_k \quad \text{on } \gamma_k,$$

and where V_k is the space consisting of the traces on γ_k of functions in $H^1(\Omega_k)$ which vanish on $\partial \Omega_{12} \cap \partial \Omega$, for $k = 1, 2$.

We introduce H^1_{12h}, the discrete subspace of $H^1(\Omega_{12})$ consisting of piecewise linear functions vanishing on $\partial \Omega_{12} \cap \partial \Omega$, but not necessarily on γ_1 or γ_2, and we denote a basis for it by $\{\chi_j\}$, $j \in N_{12}$. Let N_{01} and N_{02} be index sets for the nodes along γ_1 and γ_2, respectively.

The action of $\mathscr{A}$ on a vector $x \equiv (x_1, x_2)^T$ is implicitly defined as follows. First, the pair of subdomain Dirichlet problems with boundary data x_k on the γ_k,

$$A_k y_k = -C_k x_k,$$

is solved for the y_k, where

$$[A_k]_{ij} = \int_{\Omega_k} \nabla \psi_{kj} \cdot \nabla \psi_{ki} \, dx, \qquad i, j \in N_k$$

and

$$[C_k]_{ij} = \int_{\Omega_k} \nabla \psi_{kj} \cdot \nabla \psi_{ki}\, d\mathbf{x}, \qquad i \in N_k, j \in N_{0k}.$$

Then the difference of the y_k over the region of common definition,

$$\delta y_k = y_k|_{\Omega_{12}} - y_l|_{\Omega_{12}},$$

is computed, where l is the complement of k in $\{1, 2\}$. Then another pair of subdomain Dirichlet problems with forcing due to the difference in the y_k over the overlap region,

$$A_k z_k = F_k \delta y_k,$$

is solved for the z_k, where

$$[F_k]_{ij} = \int_{\Omega_{12}} [\nabla \chi_j \cdot \nabla \psi_{ki} + \chi_j \psi_{ki}]\, d\mathbf{x}, \qquad i \in N_k, \quad j \in N_{12}.$$

Finally,

$$\mathscr{A}x = \begin{pmatrix} D_1 \delta y_1 - E_1 z_1 \\ D_2 \delta y_2 - E_2 z_2 \end{pmatrix},$$

where

$$[D_k]_{ij} = \int_{\Omega_{12}} [\nabla \chi_j \cdot \nabla \psi_{ki} + \chi_j \psi_{ki}]\, d\mathbf{x}, \qquad i \in N_{0k}, \quad j \in N_{12},$$

and

$$[E_k]_{ij} = \int_{\Omega_k} \nabla \psi_{kj} \cdot \nabla \psi_{ki}\, d\mathbf{x}, \qquad i \in N_{0k}, \quad j \in N_k.$$

We may consider different preconditioners, which are of the form $\mathscr{B} = \operatorname{diag}(\mathscr{B}_1, \mathscr{B}_2)$. In § 2.3.5 of [19], an essentially unpreconditioned form of the algorithm is proposed in which $\mathscr{B}_k$ has the interfacial line integral form of $\mathscr{B}$ in the Saddle-1 method. In the experiments in § 3 we in fact report on $\mathscr{B}_k = I$. In § 2.3.7 the preconditioner

$$[B_k]_{ij} = \int_{\Omega_k} \nabla \psi_{kj} \cdot \nabla \psi_{ki}\, d\mathbf{x}, \qquad i, j \in N_{0k}$$

is used. Though not mentioned in [19], we also consider $\mathscr{B}_k = K^{1/2}$ in the numerical experiments. Note that, like the PMM, the overlap decomposition-based method requires two Dirichlet problems to be solved in each subdomain per iteration.

2.6. Generalization to multiple nonintersecting interfaces.
The two-subdomain case may possess genuine interest for many problems of physical origin, but it is of limited interest when implementation of domain decomposition algorithms on ensemble architectures with a large number of processors is considered. The multiple subdomain case has been studied by Dryja and Proskurowski in [16] and [17], in which serial implementations making use of up to 32 subdomains have been tested, and by Chan and Resasco in [10]. The multiple strip case can be accommodated by our notation of (2.3) and (2.4) by letting u_0 represent all of the separator set unknowns, ordered by interface, and letting u_1 represent all of the interior unknowns, ordered by subdomain. If Ω is uniformly triangulated, and if there are p subdomains of equal size with n_0 interior gridpoints along each interface and m gridpoints across, then A_{00} is

a block matrix with $p-1$ diagonal blocks of size n_0, and A_{11} is a block matrix with p diagonal blocks of size $n_0 m$. Under our assumptions on L, the Schur complement (which is block tridiagonal with blocks of size n_0) is symmetric and positive definite, and the following is proved in [16]:

THEOREM 2.2. *Let the Schur complement C be defined as following* (2.4) *and above, and let $\tilde{M}_D$ be defined as the* $(p-1) \times (p-1)$ *block diagonal matrix with $n_0 \times n_0$ diagonal blocks M_D. Then, for all x,*

$$(2.10) \qquad w\gamma_0(x, \tilde{M}_D x) \leq (x, Cx) \leq w^{-1}\gamma_1(x, \tilde{M}_D x)$$

where γ_0 and γ_1 are positive constants independent of h, and w is the minimum of the strip widths.

This makes $\tilde{M}_D$ an optimal preconditioner for C for a given decomposition, and similar block-diagonal extensions can be made for the other single-interface preconditioners. The analogous block preconditioner $\tilde{M}_G$ is also tested in [16]. The reference [17] considers a multiple subdomain generalization of the alternating Neumann-Dirichlet method, first presented for the two-strip case in [3]. Finally, [10] presents an exact eigendecomposition of the multiple-strip Schur complement matrix which generalizes Chan's method [8] to a multiple-strip domain-decomposed fast Poisson solver.

Note from (2.10) that the block preconditioning of C by $\tilde{M}_D$ suffers as the strips become thin, that is as the number of subdomains is increased for fixed domain geometry. In [10] this is traced to ignoring the off-diagonal blocks of C. By means of the exact eigendecomposition, these blocks may be shown to be insignificant in the limit of large aspect ratio subdomains ("thick" strips), but more and more significant in the limit of small aspect ratio subdomains. Since $w \propto p^{-1}$, the bound on the condition number from (2.10), $\gamma_1/(\gamma_0 w^2)$, increases like p^2. The inability of stripwise decompositions to accommodate large numbers of subdomains without a deterioration of convergence is a major weakness when it comes to large-scale parallel implementations. A more implicit means of handling the interfaces is required.

2.7. Generalization to intersecting interfaces. An extension to decompositions in which interfaces intersect in *vertices* or *crosspoints*, resulting in the formation of boxes instead of strips, is given by Bramble et al. in [5]; this development is in fact the focus of their paper. (The single interface version of the PMM presented in § 2.3 is a special case.) Constraints of space and focus prohibit the full development of their technique here, but a brief account of its implications for the discrete version of the problem is furnished below.

The key step is the further decomposition in function space of the discrete harmonic component of u, u^H. Recall from § 2.3 that $u = u^P + u^H$, where in each subdomain k, $u^P|_k$ vanishes on $\partial\Omega_k$ and satisfies

$$\tilde{A}_{\Omega_k}(u^P, v) = \tilde{A}_{\Omega_k}(u, v)$$

for all $v \in H^1_{0kh}$; and $u^H|_k$ satisfies $u^H = u$ on $\partial\Omega_k$ and

$$\tilde{A}_{\Omega_k}(u^H, v) = 0$$

for all $v \in H^1_{0kh}$. We now set $u^H = u^E + u^V$, where in each subdomain k, $u^V|_k$ and $u^E|_k$ each satisfy

$$\tilde{A}_{\Omega_k}(u^V, v) = \tilde{A}_{\Omega_k}(u^E, v) = 0$$

for all $v \in H^1_{0kh}$, and u^V is linear along the edges of $\partial\Omega_k$ and agrees with u at the vertices, and u^E vanishes at the vertices. A finite element basis for u is then constructed which consists of the usual C^0 piecewise linear basis functions of smallest possible support defined at the nodes interior to each Ω_k and at the nodes along each edge (except at the intersections of the edges), and a special set of basis functions defined at the crosspoints with support extending out along the edges which connect the crosspoints. These special basis functions each vanish at all crosspoints but one and at all interior nodes, and are linear along the edges. The Galerkin equations involving the crosspoint degrees of freedom thus possess a nonlocal connectedness. If the nodal values of u are permuted as before so that u_0 represents the separator nodes (edges *and* crosspoints), and u_1 the interior nodes, then the computation of u_1^P and u_1^H proceed as before, as independent Dirichlet solves over each subdomain. However, the calculation of u_0 from

$$Mu_0 = f_0 - \tilde{A}_{01}u_1^P$$

proceeds in another series of independent solves as follows. M is a block diagonal matrix with a diagonal block corresponding to the nodes along each edge. These blocks are each essentially matrices of the form M_D, leaving scaling considerations aside. The final block corresponds to a diagonally dominant difference equation for the internal crosspoint nodes and has a sparsity structure identical to a graph of the decomposition: each edge connecting one vertex i to another vertex j contributes a nonzero to the ith row in column j. For a decomposition of the unit square into uniform square subdomains, this matrix is simply the discrete Laplacian, to within a scaling factor. The right-hand side involves inner products between the interfacial nodal coefficient vectors. The reader is referred to [5] for the complete details. We conclude by paraphrasing Theorem 1 and Remark 2.6 therein as follows, in which it is assumed that the underlying triangulation and decomposition into subdomains are quasi-uniform of sizes h and d, respectively.

THEOREM 2.3. *Let the matrix A be defined as in (2.3) and above, and let $\tilde{B}$ be defined as in (2.7), where M is the separator set preconditioner of [5]. Then, for all x,*

(2.11) $$\gamma_0(x, \tilde{B}x) \leq (x, Ax) \leq \gamma_1(x, \tilde{B}x)$$

where γ_0 and γ_1 are positive constants such that for some positive constant c_1,

$$\frac{\gamma_1}{\gamma_0} \leq c_1\left(1 + \ln\left(\frac{d}{h}\right)^2\right).$$

If, instead, the vertex difference equation block of M is replaced by a weighted identity operator then for some positive constant c_2,

$$\frac{\gamma_1}{\gamma_0} \leq c_2 d^{-2}\left(1 + \ln\left(\frac{d}{h}\right)^2\right).$$

The implications of this theorem for the many subdomain decomposition are illustrated by the following special case. Consider a square domain uniformly discretized with n subintervals on a side and uniformly decomposed into p square subdomains of $n/\sqrt{p}$ subintervals on a side. Then $d \propto \sqrt{p}$ and $d/h = n/\sqrt{p}$. Therefore, by Theorem 2.3, when the crosspoints are treated implicitly the condition number is bounded by $c_1(1 + \ln(n/\sqrt{p})^2)$; and when they are decoupled the condition number is bounded by a $c_2 p(1 + \ln(n/\sqrt{p})^2)$. In the former case the condition number is bounded by a constant if subdomains are introduced as required with increasing resolution to keep the number of subintervals on a subdomain side fixed. In the latter case, the condition number grows in proportion to the number of subdomains.

A simpler alternative for handling the crosspoints in the decoupled case is to employ the usual cardinal finite element basis for all of the interior degrees of freedom, including the crosspoints, along with a weighted identity operator for the corresponding block of M. This method requires no special computations to form the right-hand side of the crosspoint system. The examples of § 3 labeled "PMM without vertex coupling" employ this simpler alternative.

3. Experimental comparisons of domain decomposition techniques. The methods described in § 2 were tested on a variety of model problems chosen to reveal their relative strengths and weaknesses. Four of the problems we consider are posed on the unit square, symmetrically divided into two strips or four boxes by straight segments bisecting opposite sides. The operators include the cases of uniform, discontinuous, and smoothly varying nonseparable coefficients. The other problems are posed in a small aspect ratio rectangle, and in a T-shaped region.

These tests were carried out on a VAX/785 in single precision (24-bit mantissa) using the experimental interpretive language CLAM (Conversational Linear Algebra Machine) [21]. By providing a convenient symbolic interface to the LINPACK and EISPACK libraries, CLAM allowed relatively quick "breadboarding" of the various algorithms. The tests are not as comprehensive as some of those available in the literature for individual problems and methods (e.g., [2], [5], [16], [17]) because of size, speed, and precision limitations, nor do they embrace as wide a scope of domain geometries or operators. The chief value of these results is tutorial, in that they permit algorithmic comparison on a common set of problems from common initial iterates with common convergence criteria and measures, all of which may vary or be left unstated from paper to paper.

3.1. Conventions in conducting tests and reporting results. To complete the specification of Algorithm PCG of § 2.1, which is the basis for all of the experiments, the initial iterate is always taken to be zero everywhere, and convergence is based on the relative size of the unnormalized Euclidean norm of the true residual. Since these practices are not uniform in the testing of such algorithms, we comment briefly upon them. In practical applications of PCG, the most conveniently monitored convergence criterion is the norm of the preconditioned residual, $(r, \mathcal{B}^{-1}r)^{1/2}$, since the square of this quantity is already required to advance the algorithm. However, when comparisons across a variety of preconditioners $\mathcal{B}$ are carried out, the convergence criterion should not be affected by the type of preconditioner. Therefore the norm of the unpreconditioned residual was calculated at every iteration of the serial tests, as well. We declare convergence when $(r^k, r^k)^{1/2} < \varepsilon (r^0, r^0)^{1/2}$, as opposed to the absolute criterion used in some of the early domain decomposition literature, in an attempt to remove dependence on the resolution of the problem. In our test problems the shape of the right-hand side f is generally such that its domain average decreases by an appreciable factor as the uniform mesh is refined over several powers of two and points further from the symmetrically located maximum of f are brought in. This is reflected in a reduced initial residual, since the initial iterate is zero, and fewer iterations are required to reach an absolute residual tolerance. If anything, we should insist that an iterative method work *harder* as the resolution increases in order to realize the potential of the lower truncation error of the discretization, otherwise the additional resolution is wasted from the continuous viewpoint. As a minimum requirement, we insist that the residual be decreased by a constant factor. In all of the tables to follow, $\varepsilon = 10^{-4}$.

The principal results that we report for each experiment are the number of iterations to convergence, I, the estimated condition number of the preconditioned system, κ, and the average reduction per iteration of the residual, ρ. These are complementary indications of the rate of convergence of the method. As the only one of these three quantities which depends solely upon the operator, the true condition number is an attractive measure. However, a large condition number may lead to an overly pessimistic appraisal of a method if the eigenvalues are unevenly distributed, and an exact condition number is expensive to compute. The iteration count is the most useful "bottom line" convergence measure for use in conjunction with cost-per-iteration complexity estimates to determine overall algorithmic complexity. However, this is convergence criterion-dependent. The average rate of reduction per iteration, defined by $((r^I, r^I)/(r^0, r^0))^{1/(2I)}$, where I is the number of iterations to convergence, is a more reliable estimator of the convergence rate than the condition number, without being as strongly dependent upon the particular convergence criterion as I, and it does not exhibit the threshold effect that I does. However, ρ still retains a dependence on the initial iterate. Since none of these three measures is ideal, we report all of them.

The condition number estimate in all of our tables is obtained as a by-product of the PCG iterations by the method of Lanczos [27], as implemented in [28], at a small computational overhead. For each k in the loop (PCG.6)–(PCG.14), the diagonal and subdiagonal elements of a symmetric tridiagonal matrix are formed according to

$$d_k = \frac{1}{\alpha^k} + \frac{\beta^{k-1}}{\alpha^{k-1}}, \qquad s_{k+1} = -\frac{\sqrt{\beta^k}}{\alpha^k},$$

respectively. The extreme eigenvalues of this matrix often accurately approximate those of $\mathcal{B}^{-1}\mathcal{A}$ even if terminated with k considerably less than n. We have checked these estimates against the true condition numbers for the $h^{-1} = 16$ row of the examples in Tables 1 and 7. Very close agreement obtains in Table 1, where at least the first two significant figures of κ_{true} and κ_{Lanczos} agree for all of the methods. In Table 7 the Lanczos-derived estimates shown overestimate the true condition number by 11–46%.

Finally, we note that although the finite element formulation has been chosen throughout this article in order to provide a uniform theoretical background for the different methods, the results in Tables 5, 6, and 7 were actually generated using the standard second-order finite difference method to construct the discrete A and $\tilde{A}$. (These alternative formulations do not generally coincide at the discrete level when the operator is not piecewise constant.)

3.2. Stripwise decomposition tests. The first test problem is Poisson's equation

$$\nabla^2 u = f,$$

in the unit square divided symmetrically into two strips, where f is chosen so that $u = 16xy(1 - x)(1 - y)$. This problem is essentially the same as the first example in [16], [17]. It may be solved conveniently by an SCM. Surface plot comparisons of the preconditions in Table 1 with C were given in Fig. 3.

For this domain geometry, and for all but one to follow, the Schur complement matrix preconditioners M_C and M_B are identical, so there is no need for separate tabulation. The optimality properties of M_C, M_G, and M_D are in evidence, with the number of iterations independent of problem size. As the mesh is refined, ρ actually shows a slight improvement for M_G and M_D, but this is not regarded as significant. The MSC preconditioners are inferior, and exhibit steadily deteriorating ρ. The last

TABLE 1

$\nabla^2 u = f$ on the unit square, divided symmetrically into two strips. Results for SCM as a function of problem size and interface preconditioner.

h^{-1}		M_C	M_G	M_D	$M_{S(0)}$	$M_{S(1)}$	$M_{S(2)}$	I
16	I	1	2	3	5	5	4	8
	κ	1.00	1.09	1.30	1.76	1.49	1.30	13.1
	ρ	3.7 (−6)	9.0 (−4)	3.2 (−2)	1.5 (−1)	8.8 (−2)	4.2 (−2)	1.1 (−1)
32	I	1	2	3	7	6	6	12
	κ	1.00	1.09	1.32	2.47	2.07	1.76	26.1
	ρ	1.4 (−5)	8.0 (−4)	2.7 (−2)	2.4 (−1)	2.0 (−1)	1.4 (−1)	4.4 (−1)
64	I	1	2	3	9	8	7	17
	κ	1.00	1.09	1.34	3.52	2.94	2.48	52.4
	ρ	8.4 (−5)	8.0 (−4)	2.2 (−2)	3.3 (−1)	3.0 (−1)	2.5 (−1)	5.7 (−1)

TABLE 2

$\nabla \cdot (a \nabla u) = 0$ on the unit square, divided symmetrically into two strips, where $a = 1.0$ in one subdomain and 0.1 in the other. Results for SCM as a function of problem size and interface preconditioner.

h^{-1}		M_C	M_G	M_D	$M_{S(0)}$	$M_{S(1)}$	$M_{S(2)}$
16	I	1	3	4	5	4	4
	κ	1.00	1.09	1.35	1.76	1.48	1.29
	ρ	4.3 (−6)	2.8 (−3)	8.7 (−2)	1.3 (−1)	9.4 (−2)	4.8 (−2)
32	I	1	2	4	6	6	5
	κ	1.00	1.09	1.36	2.47	2.07	1.76
	ρ	9.0 (−6)	9.0 (−4)	9.1 (−2)	2.0 (−1)	1.6 (−1)	1.2 (−1)
64	I	1	2	4	7	7	6
	κ	1.00	1.09	1.37	3.28	2.93	2.48
	ρ	5.0 (−5)	7.9 (−3)	9.3 (−2)	2.5 (−1)	2.3 (−1)	1.9 (−1)

TABLE 3

$\nabla^2 u = f$ on a low aspect ratio rectangle, divided asymmetrically into two strips. Results for SCM as a function of problem size and interface preconditioner.

h^{-1}		M_C	M_B	M_G	M_D	$M_{S(0)}$	$M_{S(1)}$	$M_{S(2)}$
32	I	1	3	3	3	5	4	4
	κ	1.00	1.27	2.10	2.00	1.63	1.45	1.28
	ρ	7.6 (−6)	1.6 (−2)	2.2 (−2)	3.3 (−2)	1.1 (−1)	9.4 (−2)	6.6 (−2)
64	I	1	3	3	3	6	6	5
	κ	1.00	1.27	2.09	2.05	2.24	1.96	1.64
	ρ	4.3 (−5)	1.6 (−2)	2.2 (−2)	2.6 (−2)	1.9 (−1)	1.7 (−1)	1.3 (−1)

TABLE 4

$\nabla^2 u = f$ on an asymmetric T-shaped region, divided into two strips. Results for SCM as a function of problem size and interface preconditioner.

h^{-1}		M_C	M_G	M_D	$M_{S(0)}$	$M_{S(1)}$	$M_{S(2)}$
16	I	3	2	4	4	4	3
	κ	1.08	1.07	1.43	1.41	1.21	1.12
	ρ	9.5 (-3)	9.9 (-3)	9.3 (-2)	7.4 (-1)	5.2 (-2)	2.4 (-2)
32	I	3	3	5	5	5	4
	κ	1.11	1.11	1.47	1.72	1.60	1.38
	ρ	1.7 (-2)	1.9 (-2)	1.1 (-1)	1.2 (-1)	1.0 (-1)	7.3 (-2)
64	I	3	3	5	6	6	5
	κ	1.14	1.14	1.49	2.49	2.26	1.91
	ρ	3.3 (-2)	3.3 (-2)	1.1 (-1)	2.2 (-1)	1.9 (-1)	1.5 (-1)

TABLE 5

$\nabla \cdot (\underline{a}\nabla u) + ku = f$ on the unit square, divided symmetrically into two strips, where $a_{11} = e^{xy}$, $a_{22} = e^{-xy}$, $a_{12} = a_{21} = 0$, and $K = (1 + x + y)^{-1}$, with subdomain preconditioning by the Laplacian. Results for PMM as a function of problem size and interface preconditioner and for GMM as a function of problem size.

h^{-1}		M_C	M_G	M_D	$M_{S(0)}$	$M_{S(1)}$	$M_{S(2)}$	GMM
8	I	7	7	7	7	7	7	7
	κ	2.42	2.42	2.53	2.41	2.41	2.41	2.42
	ρ	2.2 (-1)	2.2 (-1)	2.4 (-1)	2.3 (-1)	2.2 (-1)	2.2 (-1)	2.2 (-1)
16	I	8	8	8	8	8	8	8
	κ	3.25	3.24	3.23	3.15	3.24	3.24	3.25
	ρ	3.0 (-1)	3.1 (-1)	3.1 (-1)	3.2 (-1)	3.1 (-1)	3.1 (-1)	3.0 (-1)
32	I	9	9	10	10	10	10	9
	κ	3.92	3.89	4.04	4.57	3.99	4.03	3.92
	ρ	3.6 (-1)	3.6 (-1)	3.6 (-1)	4.0 (-1)	3.8 (-1)	3.7 (-1)	3.6 (-1)

TABLE 6

$\nabla \cdot (\underline{a}\nabla u) + ku = f$ on the unit square, divided symmetrically into two strips, where $a_{11} = e^{xy}$, $a_{22} = e^{-xy}$, $a_{12} = a_{21} = 0$, and $K = (1 + x + y)^{-1}$, with subdomain preconditioning by a locally averaged separable variable-coefficient operator. Results for PMM as a function of problem size and interface preconditioner and for GMM as a function of problem size.

h^{-1}		M_C	M_G	M_D	$M_{S(0)}$	$M_{S(1)}$	$M_{S(2)}$	GMM
8	I	5	5	6	5	5	4	5
	κ	1.47	1.47	1.98	1.46	1.37	1.31	1.52
	ρ	1.1 (-1)	1.2 (-1)	1.8 (-1)	1.2 $(-\intercal)$	9.9 (-2)	8.6 (-2)	1.2 (-1)
16	I	5	5	6	6	6	5	5
	κ	1.52	1.52	2.09	1.90	1.71	1.54	1.66
	ρ	1.3 (-1)	1.3 (-1)	1.9 (-1)	2.0 (-1)	1.5 (-1)	1.3 (-1)	1.5 (-1)
32	I	5	5	6	8	7	7	6
	κ	1.52	1.51	2.14	2.64	2.33	2.06	1.81
	ρ	1.4 (-1)	1.4 (-1)	1.9 (-1)	2.9 (-1)	2.6 (-1)	2.0 (-1)	1.8 (-1)

TABLE 7

$\nabla \cdot (a\nabla u) = f$ on the unit square, divided symmetrically into two strips, where $a = 1 + b\tan^{-1}(x - \frac{1}{2}) + c\tan^{-1}(d(y - \frac{1}{2}))$, with subdomain preconditioning by a locally averaged separable variable-coefficient operator. Results for PMM as a function of problem size and interface preconditioner and for GMM as a function of problem size.

h^{-1}		M_C	M_G	M_D	$M_{S(0)}$	$M_{S(1)}$	$M_{S(2)}$	GMM
8	I	6	6	7	6	5	5	7
	κ	1.87	1.89	2.41	2.00	1.79	1.81	2.79
	ρ	1.7 (−1)	1.7 (−1)	2.2 (−1)	1.7 (−1)	1.5 (−2)	1.5 (−2)	2.5 (−1)
16	I	6	6	7	7	6	6	8
	κ	1.94	1.97	2.59	2.69	2.31	2.09	3.47
	ρ	2.0 (−1)	2.0 (−1)	2.5 (−1)	2.6 (−1)	2.1 (−1)	1.8 (−1)	2.9 (−1)
32	I	7	7	7	9	8	7	9
	κ	2.10	2.12	2.62	3.80	3.25	2.78	3.85
	ρ	2.2 (−1)	2.2 (−1)	2.6 (−1)	3.6 (−1)	3.1 (−1)	2.7 (−1)	3.3 (−1)

column, for which $\mathcal{B} = I$, shows the proportionality of the condition number to the number of degrees of freedom in the unpreconditioned system.

The second problem involves a physical interface which coincides with the subdomain boundary. The equation is:

$$\nabla \cdot (a\nabla u) = 0$$

where the diffusion coefficient a is 1.0 in one of the subdomains and 0.1 in the other, and where u obeys the Dirichlet condition $u = xy$ on the boundary of the unit square. By partitioning the domain so that each subdomain has a uniform diffusion coefficient, fast solvers may be exploited. Again, an SCM is appropriate for this problem, the results of which are shown in Table 2.

The optimal methods perform well in spite of the jump discontinuity. (The decrease in the number of iterations required with M_G between $h^{-1} = 16$ and 32 is not regarded as significant in this sub-asymptotic range.) The MSC methods fare slightly better than in the featureless case, but still cannot compete with the optimal methods on so ideal a problem.

The third problem is again Poisson's equation, a compressed version of the first problem posed in the rectangle $(0, 1) \times (0, 3/8)$, with an interface at $y = \frac{1}{4}$ and f chosen so that $u = (1024/9)x(1 - x)y(3/8 - y)$. At $h^{-1} = 32$, the upper subdomain is only three interior grid points high. Table 3 contains the results.

The subdomain aspect ratios in this problem are more typical of those in multistrip decompositions of domains of roughly unit aspect ratio. This is the only problem to exhibit a distinction between M_C, which is again exact, and M_B.

As our only example of a geometry which is unsuitable for an undecomposed fast Poisson solver, we consider the asymmetric T-shaped domain problem from [2]. The domain is the unit square with two rectangles removed, as shown to scale in Fig. 1(b). The equation is Poisson's equation with inhomogeneous Dirichlet boundary data and right-hand side chosen so that $u = x^2 + y^2 - x e^x \cos y$. Though the overall geometry is nonseparable, the subdomains can each be handled by a fast Poisson solver, so an SCM is appropriate, as shown in Table 4.

The optimal methods have no trouble handling geometrical irregularity such as this. The MSC methods are more competitive than before due to the spoiling of symmetry which prevents the use of any exact preconditioning, but they continue to be inferior for sufficiently fine resolution.

The fifth problem involves generalization in another direction: a nonseparable operator. We consider ELLPACK problem #1 [34]:

$$\nabla \cdot (a\nabla u) + Ku = f$$

where $a_{11} = e^{xy}$, $a_{22} = e^{-xy}$, $a_{12} = a_{21} = 0$, $K = -(1+x+y)^{-1}$, and where f is chosen so that $u = \frac{3}{4} e^{xy} \sin(\pi x) \sin(\pi y)$.

For this problem, we use a PMM and present results for two different forms of the partitioned matrix preconditioner $\mathcal{B}$ in two separate tables. The condition number estimates pertain to $\kappa(\tilde{B}^{-1}A)$, where $\tilde{B}$ is constructed according to (2.7), by using the different M-blocks shown at the head of the table columns. Results for the preconditioning arising from taking $\tilde{A}$ of (2.7) to be the Laplacian operator are shown in Table 5. (CLAM's capacity is exceeded by our modular implementation of the PMM at $h^{-1} = 64$, so results for the very coarse problems with $h^{-1} = 8$ are added to Tables 5, 6, and 7 in order to provide a third stage for comparison.) The Laplacian is a rather coarse-grained preconditioner, which does not take advantage of the sensitivity of the domain decomposition technique to local operator properties. We also consider a more conventional use of the PCG technique, the GMM of preconditioning a nonseparable problem by one which can be implemented by a fast Poisson solver over the entire domain. The results, displayed in the last column, are identical to those of M_C, which is, of course, the decomposed equivalent of the Laplacian.

The problem is a difficult one for all of the methods, as evidenced by the fact that for the coarsest mesh case, the number of iterations for all methods is fully equal to the number of unknowns on the interface. (Of course, we are now iterating on vectors with length $O(h^{-2})$, but recall that for the first four problems considered, the PMM and SCM implementations have identical iteration counts much lower than the number of interfacial unknowns.) For problems of this difficulty, the MSC preconditioners do not fare appreciably worse than the optimal ones, and achieve comparable condition numbers even at the moderate resolutions investigated. However, the performance of the MSC preconditioners deteriorates with increasing resolution more rapidly than the optimal ones by any of the three measures in the tables. Furthermore, in comparing iteration counts, it should be recalled that the construction of $M_{S(k)}$ requires $k+1$ solves per subdomain, the arithmetic complexity of which is roughly equivalent to that of $k+1$ extra iterations which make no appearance in the tables.

Table 6 shows the improvement possible by generating the preconditioner blocks $\tilde{A}_k$ by subdomain averaging the original operator A, giving a PMM finer granularity than a GMM. Let $\langle a_{11}\rangle_y(x)$ and $\langle K\rangle_y(x)$ denote subdomain averages of the respective coefficients with respect to y and $\langle a_{22}\rangle_x(y)$ and $\langle K\rangle_x(y)$ the same with respect to x. In each subdomain k, $\tilde{A}_k$ has the separable form

$$[\tilde{A}_k]_{ij} = \int_{\Omega_k} \left(\langle a_{11}\rangle_y \frac{\partial \psi_j}{\partial x} \frac{\partial \psi_i}{\partial x} + \frac{1}{2}\langle K\rangle_y \psi_j \psi_i + \langle a_{22}\rangle_x \frac{\partial \psi_j}{\partial y} \frac{\partial \psi_i}{\partial y} + \frac{1}{2}\langle K\rangle_x \psi_j \psi_i \right) d\mathbf{x}.$$

With the local averaging, the best of the optimal PMMs begin to break away from the GMM even though only two subdomains are employed. A more graphic illustration of the improvements offered by the PMM in the many subdomain case is given in Example 3 of [5].

Our final stripwise decomposition example is

$$\nabla \cdot (a\nabla u) = f$$

on the unit square, where $a = 1 + b \tan^{-1}(x - \frac{1}{2}) + c \tan^{-1}(d(y - \frac{1}{2}))$, using the values for b, c, and d listed in § 2.4, where surface plots of the Schur complement matrix and various approximations thereto were given. In this problem there is a significant difference in the subdomain averages of a, which would tend to favor the PMMs over a GMM, and a significant variation of a along the interface, $y = \frac{1}{2}$, which would tend to favor MSC preconditioning.

A separable subdomain-averaged PMM preconditioner was constructed in the manner described above. In this example, the results of which appear in Table 7, all of the PMMs are better than or comparable to the GMM; however, the MSC advantage begins to disappear even at fairly coarse resolution.

3.3. Boxwise decomposition tests. We carried out serial tests of the two decomposition strategies involving crosspoints on the first problem of the previous subsection, namely Poisson's equation on the unit square. Table 8 contains the results for the uncoupled crosspoint version of the algorithm, and Table 9 contains the results for the coupled crosspoint version. Since there is only one crosspoint in this example, the two algorithms differ only in the assembling of the right-hand side of the crosspoint equation, as described in § 2.7.

TABLE 8

$\nabla^2 u = f$ on the unit square, divided into four equal boxes. Results for PMM without vertex coupling, as a function of problem size and interface preconditioner.

h^{-1}		M_C	M_G	M_D	$M_{S(0)}$	$M_{S(1)}$	$M_{S(2)}$
16	I	5	5	6	9	7	8
	κ	8.60	8.59	8.89	12.8	12.5	12.1
	ρ	6.9 (−2)	6.9 (−2)	2.0 (−1)	2.7 (−1)	2.4 (−1)	2.2 (−1)
32	I	6	6	7	10	10	10
	κ	12.4	12.4	12.1	24.4	22.7	21.9
	ρ	1.1 (−1)	1.1 (−1)	2.2 (−1)	4.4 (−1)	3.3 (−1)	4.4 (−1)
32	I	6	6	7	15	13	13
	κ	15.1	15.1	15.9	45.4	40.4	37.0
	ρ	2.0 (−1)	2.0 (−1)	2.4 (−1)	5.3 (−1)	4.8 (−1)	4.8 (−1)

TABLE 9

$\nabla^2 u = f$ on the unit square, divided into four equal boxes. Results for PMM with vertex coupling after Bramble et al., as a function of problem size and interface preconditioner.

h^{-1}		M_C	M_G	M_D	$M_{S(0)}$	$M_{S(1)}$	$M_{S(2)}$
16	I	5	5	6	8	7	7
	κ	6.38	6.38	5.77	10.4	9.96	9.52
	ρ	6.7 (−2)	6.8 (−2)	1.9 (−1)	2.8 (−1)	1.9 (−1)	2.4 (−1)
32	I	5	5	6	11	9	11
	κ	7.13	7.23	8.20	19.8	18.3	16.7
	ρ	1.2 (−1)	1.2 (−1)	2.1 (−1)	3.9 (−1)	3.2 (−1)	3.8 (−1)
64	I	6	7	7	15	13	12
	κ	13.4	13.4	12.7	36.5	32.4	29.5
	ρ	2.1 (−1)	1.5 (−1)	2.2 (−1)	5.0 (−1)	4.6 (−1)	4.6 (−1)

Even though there is only a single crosspoint, the difference between employing local and nonlocal basis functions for the crosspoint degree of freedom is evident in comparing the tables. The condition numbers are uniformly smaller in the nonlocal case, though the overall number of iterations is not greatly affected. The growth of condition number for Dryja's interface preconditioner with crosspoint coupling (the third column of Table 9) follows the theoretical bound $c_1(1+\ln{(n/\sqrt{p})^2})$ with a c_1 of approximately 1.

A word is in order concerning the construction of the MSC preconditioners in the case of multiple interfaces (four in these examples). We require that M be block-diagonal as with the other preconditioners, to preserve the independence of the interfacial solves. In order to avoid solving the Dirichlet problems on each subdomain for each degree k of approximation in MSC(k), we economize by varying the components of the vectors v_i of (2.9b) on all interfaces simultaneously, rather than by treating the interfaces one-by-one. The algorithm described in § 2.4 is then applied block-by-block to generate the coefficients of the interfacial blocks of $M_{S(k)}$. The vectors v_i always have zeros corresponding to the crosspoint location and the crosspoint block is unaffected by the choice of interfacial blocks. As in the case of Poisson's equation on two strips, the MSC methods cannot compete with the optimal methods.

3.4. Variational methods tests. The methods of § 2.5 were applied to the model problem of Table 1, with the results shown in Table 10. A two-strip decomposition was used for the saddle-point methods. A decomposition of the type pictured in Fig. 5 was employed for the CG-Schwarz methods. The overlap region was centered on the horizontal bisector of the square and its width was one-eighth of the length of a side. This geometrical width was held constant as the mesh was refined, thus the discrete size of the overlap region increased. Numerical studies of the convergence of Schwarz-type methods which we do not report in detail here show this to be an important consideration. Fixing the discrete size of the overlap region instead, thus allowing the geometrical width to shrink with increasing resolution, causes substantial deterioration of convergence. For instance, the growth of the condition number for the unpreconditioned system CGS/I is superlinear in h^{-1} in this case, as opposed to the linear behavior of κ with h^{-1} in the third column of Table 10.

We note that the $K^{1/2}$ preconditioning is very effective on the CG-Schwarz method, the spectrum of the discrete operator $\mathscr{A}$ of which has not been analyzed theoretically to date. However, it is apparent by comparison with Table 1 that on such simple

TABLE 10

$\nabla^2 u = f$ *on the unit square, divided symmetrically into two strips, with and without overlap. Results as a function of problem size and method/preconditioning combination.*

h^{-1}		Saddle-1	Saddle-2	CGS/I	CGS/$I+\frac{1}{2}K$	CGS/$K^{1/2}$
16	I	4	5	6	4	3
	κ	5.47	4.41	21.5	7.21	1.89
	ρ	8.4 (−2)	1.1 (−1)	1.9 (−1)	4.6 (−2)	1.1 (−2)
32	I	7	7	9	5	2
	κ	10.6	8.65	44.4	14.1	1.49
	ρ	2.1 (−1)	2.3 (−1)	3.2 (−1)	1.5 (−1)	7.0 (−3)
64	I	9	10	12	7	2
	κ	20.5	17.3	89.9	29.0	1.47
	ρ	3.3 (−1)	3.7 (−1)	4.6 (−1)	2.6 (−1)	4.4 (−3)

problems these methods are inferior to the SCM with optimal preconditioning. It should be recalled in comparing iteration counts across these methods that the CGS method requires twice as many subdomain solves per iteration as the SCM.

4. Parallel experiments with domain decomposition algorithms. In order to test the convergence of the methods on a larger number of subdomains and to test the degree of parallelization that is possible in practice, two PMM methods, with and without vertex coupling and with M_D as the interfacial preconditioner, were programmed for the Intel Hypercube. For simplicity and economy of coefficient storage, we considered only Poisson's equation on the unit square. For programming convenience, efficient use of the processors and economy of data transfer between nodes, we wrote a single program to run on each of the nodes, rather than writing special purpose programs to do the major identifiable operations in Algorithm PCG, such as interior solves or edge solves. The same program was used to run both strips and boxes, with different compile-time constants to reshape the arrays. The number of processors was left dynamic.

4.1. Domain-to-processor mapping and dataflow analysis. The square domain is uniformly discretized with n subintervals on a side and divided into p subdomains in one of two ways. In the case of domains consisting of strips, each domain is an $n \times n/p$ rectangle. In the case of boxes, each domain is an $n/\sqrt{p} \times n/\sqrt{p}$ square. For simplicity and efficiency we require n and p to be powers of 2. By restricting ourselves to this limiting case of decomposition regularity, we are able to pass over the complex issue of load balancing. The work per processor is balanced a priori and does not change during the course of the solution process in response to any adaptive mechanism. It should be noted that regular decompositions of this type are the exception in applications. The tradeoffs between load balancing efficiency and communication efficiency in multiprocessor implementations of adaptive algorithms for partial differential equations have begun to receive attention elsewhere [4], [22]. We note however, that some geometrical adaptivity can be accommodated within the context of *logically* uniform decompositions by means of generalized tensor-product gridding (see, e.g., the examples in [5]).

Four types of nodes are to be distinguished in the decomposition, for purposes of keeping track of the data flow: interior nodes, separator set nodes, nodes which are adjacent to a separator, and nodes which are adjacent to an exterior boundary. For the strip decomposition, we associate the gridpoints along each interface with one of the two subdomains it separates so that each processor (except for one) is assigned one of the interfaces of length n. For definiteness in what follows, let the strips run north-south, and let the east face of each subdomain contain the separator nodes, the west face containing nodes which are adjacent to a separator, with the obvious exceptions of the west-most and east-most subdomains. For the box decomposition, we associate the gridpoints along each interface with one of the two subdomains it separates and each vertex with one of the four subdomains it separates so that each processor (except for those along two of the domain boundaries) is assigned two interfaces of length $n\sqrt{p}$ and one crosspoint. For definiteness, let the east face and south faces of each subdomain contain the separator nodes, let the southeast corner contain the crosspoint, and let the west and north faces contain nodes which are adjacent to a separator, again with the obvious boundary exceptions. We map p strips onto the hypercube by labeling the strips from one end of the domain to the other in binary reflected Gray code order [25]. We map p boxes onto the hypercube by forming the tensor-product of two such rings, along the row and column directions of the subdomain "grid." In this way all of the local exchanges in the physical domain are also local exchanges between processors, any two of which are connected if and only if their binary local representations differ in exactly one bit.

We now analyze the data flow in each of the major steps in Algorithm PCG. We concentrate on the boxwise decomposition, since strips may be regarded as a special case thereof.

The operation (PCG.7) of applying the distributed $\mathscr{A}$ matrix consists of: (1) sending the vector of data along each processor boundary not adjacent to a physical boundary to the neighboring processor; (2) computing the interior components of the product from the 5-point star formula; (3) receiving the vector of data coming across each boundary and computing the boundary components of the product. Note that it is not necessary to distinguish between separator nodes and those adjacent to a separator in this step.

The operation (PCG.11) of solving with $\mathscr{B}$ consists of: (1) solving for u^P in the subdomain interior (the subdomain interior includes the processor boundary nodes that are adjacent to a separator); (2) sending the vector of data along each north and west processor boundary not adjacent to a physical boundary to the neighboring processor; (3) receiving the vector of data coming across each south and east processor boundary and forming the right-hand side of the edge separator system and the local summands of the right-hand side of the crosspoint system; (4) sending the appropriate scalar summands to the processors to the north and west, if any; (5) solving the south and east edge systems for u^E on the separator set; (6) receiving the summands coming from the processors to the south and east, if any, and forming the right-hand side of the crosspoint system; (7) scattering the local component of the right-hand side of the crosspoint system to all other processors, and receiving their components in turn; (8) solving an identical global crosspoint system in each processor; (9) extending the crosspoint data linearly along the separator set edges to form u^V; (10) summing u^V and u^E along the separator set to form u^H on the separator set; (11) sending the vector of u^H data along each south and east boundary not adjacent to a physical boundary to the neighboring processor; (12) receiving the vector of data coming across each north and east processor boundary and forming the right-hand side of the interior u^H system; (13) solving for u^H in the subdomain interior and summing u^H and u^P. Steps (4), (6)–(7), and (9)–(10) are unnecessary in the decoupled form of the algorithm, and step (8) is replaced by a scalar divide local to each processor containing a crosspoint in this case.

The operation of performing a dot product in (PCG.7) and (PCG.12) consists of two traversals of a binary spanning tree, arbitrarily rooted in processor "0". First, the local portion of the dot product is computed. These partial sums are then passed from leaf to root, and summed along the way. The root processor performs the final sum and sends the data back from root to leaf.

4.2. Numerical results. We present data obtained on an Intel iPSC-6 for the strip form and the two box forms of the algorithm described above. For simplicity of coefficient generation and economy of storage (as memory proved to be constraining), we considered only Laplace's equation on a square. The problem is the same as that in Tables 1, 8, and 9.

Our conventions for the tests on the iPSC differ from those in § 3 in that the preconditioned residual is used to monitor convergence, rather than the actual residual. This is the practical choice since we are not comparing different preconditioners against each other in this section, but rather carrying out larger scale tests on selected algorithms.

Since monitoring the true residual would require an extra global dot product per iteration, the reported execution times would exhibit an unnatural penalty associated with increased subdivision of the domain. The relative reduction required in this different norm was set to be the same as in § 3, namely 10^{-4}.

The notation employed in the tables follows that of § 3 except that ρ is now defined as $((r^I, \mathscr{B}^{-1}r^I)/(r^0, \mathscr{B}^{-1}r^0))^{1/(2I)}$. T is the actual execution time (computation plus communication) of the domain decomposition algorithm, which does not include the initial distribution of the problem data or the post-convergence analysis of the results. Our timings for various cube dimensions (as reflected in p, the number of processors employed in the calculation) were all obtained on a cube of uniform declared dimension (namely six) with some processors idle, in order to avoid nonuniform host-processor polling rates. Where applicable, s measures the ratio of two execution times: T for the next smaller number of processors on the same size problem divided by the current T. It is thus a local measure of speedup, and a natural one for domain decomposition algorithms, but it is not the *speedup* as it would be defined in a strict sense, since the algorithm changes with the number of processors (see [23]).

We comment briefly on the sparsity of the tables. Our program requires a minimum of 8 subintervals on a side for each subdomain. Therefore, the number of processors that can be employed on a given problem is bounded above by the resolution of the mesh. Unfortunately, the number of processors is also bounded below by the limited local memory of each node. The largest number of degrees of freedom that could be accommodated per subdomain was between 2^{11} and 2^{12}; therefore, our largest problems, involving 2^{14} or 2^{16} nodes, could not be run on small numbers of processors. These two restrictions imposed a banded structure on the region of $h - p$ parameter space in which it was feasible to run experiments.

The results of a series of runs using strips are given in Table 11. The $p = 2$ column of this table is comparable to the M_D column of Table 1. Due to the different, more lenient convergence criterion, one less iteration is required in the more highly refined cases, and the Lanczos estimate of the condition number is obviously sensitive to I for I as small as 2 or 3 in this problem. Note the effect of Theorem 2.2: as the number of processors is increased while the refinement is held constant, κ goes up asymptotically in proportion to the square of the number of processors (subdomains). The number of iterations required does not behave as badly as the condition number. From the limited data, it appears to go up roughly in proportion to the number of processors, with fixed refinements. The increasing number of iterations asymptotically defeats the power of the additional processors as far as s is concerned, however, in that the local speedups do not approach 2.

The results of a series of runs using boxes without crosspoint coupling are given in Table 12. The $p = 4$ column of this table may be compared to the M_D column of Table 8; again the preconditioned residual convergence criterion is more lenient, but the condition number estimates agree almost exactly. In this table d/h is constant along a diagonal; therefore by Theorem 2.3 we would expect to see asymptotically a proportionality between κ and p along a diagonal, which is approximately the case. The number of iterations required goes up sublinearly with the number of processors (subdomains), with fixed refinement. For this table and the next, an "ideal" algorithm would display local speedups s of 4.

The results of a series of runs using boxes with crosspoint coupling are given in Table 13. The $p = 4$ column of this table may be compared to the M_D column of Table 9, subject to the caveats above, and the $p = 16$ column shows close agreement with Table 6.2 of [5]. According to Theorem 2.3, the condition number should be bounded

TABLE 11

$\nabla^2 u = f$ in the unit square, divided into equal strips. Results for PMM *with M_D on the interfaces, as a function of problem size and number of processors.*

h^{-1}		$p=1$	2	4	8	16
16	I	1	3			
	κ	1.00	1.26			
	ρ	5.0 (−6)	2.9 (−2)			
	T	4.85	3.39			
	s	—	*1.43*			
32	I	1	2	5		
	κ	1.00	1.09	3.29		
	ρ	1.7 (−5)	8.8 (−3)	9.9 (−2)		
	T	25.0	13.6	9.60		
	s	—	*1.84*	*1.42*		
64	I		2	4	8	
	κ		1.09	3.29	13.0	
	ρ		4.8 (−3)	8.5 (−2)	2.8 (−1)	
	T		70.8	43.0	27.9	
	s		—	*1.65*	*1.54*	
128	I				8	18
	κ				13.0	51.9
	ρ				2.8 (−1)	5.9 (−1)
	T				150	114
	s				—	*1.32*

by a constant along a diagonal, which appears to be the case. The number of iterations virtually levels off and the condition number actually *decreases* as more processors are added with fixed refinement.

A tendency portrayed by several rows of Tables 11–13 is that adding processors at fixed mesh resolution eventually becomes inefficient. This is due to two factors: increasing the number of subdivisions of the domain tends to increase the iteration count for some methods; and even on a per iteration basis, communication becomes dominant over computation in this limit on message-passing machines such as the Hypercube. However, the tables illustrate that significant overall speedups are obtainable in spite of the inefficient use of processors. Furthermore, high efficiency regions can be found. For a theoretical analysis of the efficiency of domain decomposition algorithms in a much larger region of $h-p$ parameter space, see [23], [26].

5. Conclusions. Several basic algorithmic forms, different decomposition topologies, and a variety of preconditioners for the separator set equations, each with advantages and disadvantages, make the study of domain decomposition surprisingly rich.

Because of its lower computational complexity, the SCM is to be preferred when it is applicable, namely when the subdomain solves can be handled exactly. In this case the full PMM iterates reduce to the SCM iterates and the latter can be obtained more cheaply. The PMM is a more flexible algorithm for general symmetric scalar problems, but many generalizations are needed, especially to nonsymmetric systems of equations, where some generalized form of preconditioned conjugate gradients, such as the generalized minimum residual method, will come into play, and where the optimal preconditioners for the symmetric positive definite version of the algorithm will have less value.

TABLE 12

$\nabla^2 u = f$ in the unit square, divided into equal boxes. Results for PMM with M_D on the interfaces and without vertex coupling, as a function of problem size and number of processors.

h^{-1}		$p = 1$	4	16	64
16	I	1	6		
	κ	1.00	8.89		
	ρ	5.0 (-6)	1.6 (-1)		
	T	4.85	4.02		
	s	—	1.21		
32	I	1	6	11	
	κ	1.00	12.1	25.3	
	ρ	1.7 (-5)	1.8 (-1)	3.6 (-1)	
	T	25.0	19.2	8.86	
	s	—	1.30	2.17	
64	I		6	12	17
	κ		15.9	32.2	94.4
	ρ		1.8 (-1)	4.0 (-1)	5.7 (-1)
	T		94.8	37.6	15.3
	s		—	2.52	2.46
128	I			13	19
	κ			40.5	120
	ρ			4.7 (-1)	6.1 (-1)
	T			192	60.3
	s			—	3.18
256	I				22
	κ				146
	ρ				6.5 (-1)
	T				319

The optimal preconditioners are to be preferred to the MSC preconditioners over the full range of examples contained herein, but the latter offer more possibilities for generalization in conjunction with problems not dominated by a Laplacian-type term, and show at least some promise in dealing with coefficient irregularity.

In terms of convergence properties, boxwise decompositions have been shown preferable to stripwise decompositions for large numbers of processors, and the crosspoint-coupled version of the algorithm is preferable from the point of view of iteration count.

The limited range of parameter space over which parallelized tests can actually be carried out with present hardware does not allow for conclusive experimental comparisons of the algorithms. However, our parallelization analysis [23] reveals the important result that for machine parameters which are reasonably achievable and for reasonably large problems, boxwise decompositions can be made more efficient than stripwise decompositions per iteration. The combination of their better convergence properties, and the fact that when domain decomposition is efficiently parallelizable at all the more implicit crosspoint-coupled version of the algorithm is not much less efficient per iteration than the decoupled version, argues for further research in the direction of more implicit preconditioners.

Acknowledgments. We would like to thank all of the members of the numerical analysis community at Yale for their stimulation during our informal "Reading Group

TABLE 13

$\nabla^2 u = f$ in the unit square, divided into equal boxes. Results for PMM with M_D on the interfaces and with vertex coupling after Bramble et al., as a function of problem size and number of processors.

h^{-1}		$p = 1$	4	16	64
16	I	1	6		
	κ	1.00	5.74		
	ρ	5.0 (−6)	1.3 (−1)		
	T	4.85	4.28		
	s	—	*1.13*		
32	I	1	5	7	
	κ	1.00	7.88	7.01	
	ρ	1.7 (−5)	1.5 (−1)	2.6 (−1)	
	T	25.0	16.6	7.39	
	s	—	*1.51*	*2.25*	
64	I		6	7	6
	κ		10.7	10.2	7.16
	ρ		1.5 (−1)	2.5 (−1)	2.1 (−1)
	T		95.1	24.7	16.7
	s		—	*3.85*	*1.48*
128	I			7	7
	κ			14.1	10.5
	ρ			2.5 (−1)	2.4 (−1)
	T			111	36.3
	s			—	*3.06*
256	I				8
	κ				14.5
	ρ				2.7 (−1)
	T				139
	s				—

for Elliptic System Substructuring," which met during the spring of 1985. We are especially grateful for the contributions of Stan Eisenstat, Tony Chan, and Diana Resasco, which are only incompletely reflected in the bibliography, and for Doug Baxter's tireless assistance with the Hypercube programming. We also thank the referees for their thorough comments and improvements.

REFERENCES

[1] C. R. ANDERSON, *On domain decomposition*, Technical Report, Math. Dept. and Comput. Sci. Dept., Stanford Univ., 1985.

[2] P. E. BJORSTAD AND O. B. WIDLUND, *Iterative methods for the solution of elliptic problems on regions partitioned into substructures*, Technical Report 136, Courant Institute of Mathematical Sciences, New York Univ., September 1984. (See also the 1985 version with an expanded section of numerical examples.)

[3] ———, *Solving elliptic problems on regions partitioned into substructures*, in Elliptic Problem Solvers II, G. Birkhoff and A. Schoenstadt, eds., Academic Press, New York, 1984, pp. 245–256.

[4] M. J. BERGER AND S. BOKHARI, *A partitioning strategy for non-uniform problems on multiprocessors*, Technical Report 85-55, ICASE, November 1985.

[5] J. H. BRAMBLE, J. E. PASCIAK AND A. H. SCHATZ, *The construction of preconditioners for elliptic problems by substructuring*, I, Math. Comp., to appear.

[6] ———, *An iterative method for elliptic problems on regions partitioned into substructures*, Math. Comp., to appear.

[7] B. L. BUZBEE, F. W. DORR, J. A. GEORGE AND G. H. GOLUB, *The direct solution of the discrete Poisson equation on irregular regions*, SIAM J. Numer. Anal., 8 (1971), pp. 722–736.

[8] T. F. CHAN, *Analysis of preconditioners for domain decomposition*, Technical Report 408, Comput. Sci. Dept., Yale Univ., August 1985.

[9] T. F. CHAN AND D. RESASCO, *A survey of preconditioners for domain decomposition*, Technical Report 414, Comput. Sci. Dept., Yale Univ., September 1985. In Proc. IV Coloquio de Matemáticas del CINVESTAV, Workshop in Numerical Analysis and its Applications, Taxco, Mexico, August 18–24, 1985.

[10] ———, *A domain-decomposed fast Poisson solver on a rectangle*, Technical Report 409, Comput. Sci. Dept., Yale Univ., October 1985.

[11] R. CHANDRA, *Conjugate gradient methods for partial differential equations*, Technical Report YALEU/DCS-RR-129, Comput. Sci. Dept., Yale Univ., January 1978.

[12] P. CONCUS, G. H. GOLUB AND D. P. O'LEARY, *A generalized conjugate gradient method for the numerical solution of elliptic partial differential equations*, in Proceedings of the Symposium on Sparse Matrix Computations, J. R. Bunch and D. J. Rose, eds., Academic Press, New York, 1975, pp. 309–332.

[13] Q. V. DINH, R. GLOWINSKI AND J. PERIAUX, *Solving elliptic problems by domain decomposition methods with applications*, in Elliptic Problem Solvers II, G. Birkhoff and A. Schoenstadt, eds., Academic Press, New York, 1984, pp. 395–426.

[14] M. DRYJA, *A capacitance matrix method for Dirichlet problem on polygonal region*, Numer. Math., 39 (1982), pp. 51–64.

[15] ———, *A finite element–capacitance method for elliptic problems on regions partitioned into subregions*, Numer. Math., 44 (1984), pp. 153–168.

[16] M. DRYJA AND W. PROSKUROWSKI, *Fast elliptic solvers on rectangular regions subdivided into strips*, in Advances in Computer Methods for Partial Differential Equations—V, R. Vichnevetsky and R. S. Stepleman, eds., IMACS, 1984, pp. 360–368.

[17] ———, *Capacitance matrix method using strips with alternating Neumann and Dirichlet boundary conditions*, Appl. Numer. Math., 1 (1985).

[18] S. EISENSTAT, personal communication, 1985.

[19] R. GLOWINSKI, Q. V. DINH AND J. PERIAUX, *Domain decomposition methods for nonlinear problems in fluid dynamics*, Comp. Meths. Appl. Mech. Engrg., to appear.

[20] G. H. GOLUB AND D. MAYERS, *The use of pre-conditioning over irregular regions*, 1983. Lecture at Sixth Int. Conf. on Computing Methods in Applied Sciences and Engineering, Versailles, France, December 1983.

[21] W. D. GROPP, *Numerical linear algebra on workstations*, in Proc. Army Research Office Workshop on Microcomputers in Scientific Computing, 1985.

[22] ———, *Dynamic grid manipulation for PDEs on hypercube parallel processors*, Technical Report YALEU/DCS/RR-458, Comput. Sci. Dept., Yale Univ., March 1986.

[23] W. D. GROPP AND D. E. KEYES, *Complexity of parallel implementation of domain decomposition techniques for elliptic partial differential equations*, this Journal, 1986, submitted.

[24] R. W. HOCKNEY, *The potential calculation and some applications*, Meth. Comput. Phys., 9 (1970), pp. 135–211.

[25] S. L. JOHNSSON, *Communication efficient basic linear algebra computations on hypercube architectures*, Technical Report 361, Comput. Sci. Dept., Yale Univ., September 1985.

[26] D. E. KEYES AND W. D. GROPP, *A comparison of domain decomposition techniques for elliptic partial differential equations and their parallel implementation*, Technical Report YALEU/DCS/RR-448, Comput. Sci. Dept., Yale Univ., December 1985.

[27] C. LANCZOS, *An iteration method for the solution of the eigenvalue problem of linear differential and integral operators*, J. Res. NBS, 45 (1950), pp. 255–282.

[28] D. P. O'LEARY AND O. WIDLUND, *Capacitance matrix methods for the Helmholtz equation on general three-dimensional regions*, Math. Comp., 33 (1979), pp. 849–879.

[29] J. OLIGER, W. SKAMAROCK AND W.-P. TANG, *Schwarz alternating procedure and S.O.R. accelerations*, Technical Report, Comput. Sci. Dept., Stanford Univ., 1985.

[30] A. T. PATERA, *A spectral element method for fluid dynamics: Laminar flow in a channel expansion*, J. Comput. Phys., 54 (1984), pp. 468–488.

[31] W. PROSKUROWSKI AND O. WIDLUND, *A finite element-capacitance matrix method for the Neumann problem for Laplace's equation*, this Journal, 1 (1980), pp. 410–425.

[32] J. S. PRZEMIENIECKI, *Matrix structural analysis of substructures*, AIAA J., 1 (1963), pp. 138–147.

[33] D. RESASCO, personal communication, 1985.

[34] J. R. RICE, E. N. HOUSTIS AND W. R. DYKSEN, *A population of linear second order, elliptic partial differential equations on rectangular domains—Part* I, Technical Report 2078, Mathematics Research Center, Univ. of Wisconsin, Madison, May 1980.

[35] G. RODRIGUE AND J. SIMON, *Jacobi splittings and the method of overlapping domains for solving elliptic P.D.E.'s*, in Advances in Computer Methods for Partial Differential Equations—V, R. Vichnevetsky and R. S. Stepleman, eds., IMACS, 1984, pp. 383–386.

[36] H. A. SCHWARZ, *Gesammelte mathematische Abhandlungen*, Springer, Berlin, 2, 1890, pp. 133–134.

[37] P. N. SWARZTRAUBER AND R. A. SWEET, *Efficient* FORTRAN *subprograms for the solution of separable elliptic partial differential equations*, ACM Trans. Math. Software, 5 (1977), pp. 352–364.

SIAM J. SCI. STAT. COMPUT.
Vol. 8, No. 2, March 1987

A PARALLEL ADAPTIVE NUMERICAL SCHEME FOR HYPERBOLIC SYSTEMS OF CONSERVATION LAWS*

BRADLEY J. LUCIER† AND ROSS OVERBEEK‡

Abstract. We generalize the first author's adaptive numerical scheme for scalar first order conservation laws to systems of equations in one space dimension. The resulting numerical method generates highly nonuniform, time-dependent grids, and hence is difficult to execute efficiently on vector computers such as the Cray or Cyber 205. In contrast, we show that this type of algorithm may be executed in parallel on alternate computer architectures. We describe a parallel implementation of the algorithm on the Denelcor HEP, a multiple-instruction, multiple-data (MIMD) shared memory parallel computer. This program dynamically partitions the problem domain so as to achieve effective load balancing among the available processes.

Key words. adaptive grids, MIMD computation, domain decomposition

AMS (MOS) subject classifications. 65M05, 68B99

Introduction. In [22] the first author presented an adaptive numerical scheme for the numerical approximation of the scalar hyperbolic conservation law

(C)
$$u_t + f(u)_x = 0, \qquad x \in \mathbb{R}, \quad t > 0,$$
$$u(x, 0) = u_0(x), \qquad x \in \mathbb{R}.$$

The numerical method used spatial adaptation to refine the grid near singularities in the solution. The novelty of the method lay in the criteria used to adapt the grid, the provision of both a priori and a posteriori stability estimates for the complete adaptive scheme, and the experimental demonstration that asymptotic speed-up results for some problems when compared with a method using the same finite difference operator on a fixed, uniform grid. Although the adaptive method is unsuitable for execution on vector computers such as the Cray or Cyber 205 because it uses a highly nonuniform, time-dependent computation grid, the algorithm may be executed in parallel on alternate computer architectures. In this paper we extend the algorithm for scalar conservation laws to hyperbolic systems of conservation laws, and we describe a parallel implementation of the algorithm on the Denelcor HEP, a multiple-instruction, multiple-data (MIMD) shared memory parallel computer [16]. We employ a dynamic tree partitioning algorithm that achieves approximate load balancing among the tasks presented to the available processes. Because our implementation uses a macro-preprocessor to avoid mention of the specific hardware synchronization primitives provided on the HEP, our programs may be transported to any shared memory multiprocessor on which the synchronization macro package has been installed.

There has been much recent interest in adaptive or moving grid methods applied to evolution equations, and specifically to conservation laws. Papers describing numerical schemes or analyses may be found in [2]-[5], [9], [13]-[14], [15]-[23], [25]-[27], [29], [33], [35]-[36]. Papers making specific mention of data structures for adaptive computation include [1], [4], [5], [22], and [32].

---

* Received by the editors November 27, 1985; accepted for publication (in revised form) May 13, 1986. This article was presented at the Second SIAM Conference on Parallel Processing for Scientific Computing that was held in Norfolk, Virginia on November 18-21, 1985.

† Department of Mathematics, Purdue University, West Lafayette, Indiana 47907. The work of this author was partially supported by the National Science Foundation under grant DMS-8403219.

‡ Mathematics and Computer Science Division, Argonne National Laboratory, Argonne, Illinois 60439. The work of this author was supported by the Applied Mathematical Sciences subprogram of the Office of Energy Research, U.S. Department of Energy, under contract W-31-109-Eng-38.

1. Background: The sequential algorithm for scalar equations. We briefly describe the method for scalar conservation laws presented in [22], to which the interested reader is referred for more details. The numerical method is based on the following algorithm, similar to well-known algorithms for adaptive linear approximation [6]-[7], for choosing a grid on which to approximate a function u defined on an interval $[a, b]$.

ALGORITHM M. This algorithm chooses grid points at which to approximate a bounded function u defined on $[a, b]$ that is constant outside $[a, b]$. Let ε be a small parameter.

(1) The grid points consist only of the points a and b and the centers of admissible intervals. Admissible intervals are defined by (2) and (3) below.
(2) The interval $[a, b]$ is an admissible interval.
(3) For any admissible interval I, let $3I = \{x \,|\, \text{dist}\,(x, I) \equiv \inf_{y \in I} |x - y| < |I|\}$. If $|I| \geqq \varepsilon$ and

$$(1) \qquad |I| \int_{3I} [|u_{xx}| + |f''(u)| u_x^2] \, dx \geqq \varepsilon,$$

then the left and right halves of I are admissible intervals. The above integral is finite if u_{xx} is a finite measure; otherwise, it is to be interpreted as infinite. Note that $3I$ is an *open* interval. The approximation to u is chosen to be the piecewise linear interpolant of u at the given grid points.

This algorithm chooses a grid that satisfies three criteria that we feel are important for adaptive numerical methods that use piecewise linear functions as approximations to solutions of evolution equations:

(1) Under plausible assumptions about the structure of the solution u of (C) (that $u \in BV(\mathbb{R})$, and that between discontinuity curves $u_x \in BV(\mathbb{R})$), it may be shown that u can be approximated well in $L^1(\mathbb{R})$ by continuous piecewise linear functions on this grid.
(2) It may be shown formally that the spatial operator $f(u)_x$ may be approximated well in $L^1(\mathbb{R})$ by piecewise constant functions on this grid.
(3) One observes empirically that the error incurred in the regridding process from one time step to the next is small on this grid; there are heuristic reasons, based on the assumed local smoothness of u away from discontinuity curves, for believing this.

The numerical scheme solves (C) on an interval $[a, b]$ instead of $\mathbb{R}$. To ensure that interactions with the boundaries of the interval $[a, b]$ may be neglected, we assume that the widths of the leftmost and rightmost minimal interval are greater than ε. We also assume that $f \in C^2$ and that $\|f'\|_{L^\infty(\mathbb{R})} \leqq 1$; the latter condition may always be achieved by a change in the time scale. The numerical scheme is as follows:

(1) A grid $\{x_i^0\} = M^0$ and initial approximation U^0 is chosen, based on the initial data $u_0(x)$ ($U^n(x_i^n) = U_i^n$).
(2) For each $n \geqq 0$:
   (a) The approximate solution is advanced from time t^n to t^{n+1} at all the grid points $x_i^n \in M^n$ using, in our case, the Engquist-Osher finite difference operator [10]:

$$(F) \qquad \frac{\overline{U_i^{n+1}} - U_i^n}{\Delta t} + \frac{f^+(U_i^n) - f^+(U_{i-1}^n)}{h_i^n} + \frac{f^-(U_{i+1}^n) - f^-(U_i^n)}{h_{i+1}^n} = 0.$$

The flux f has been separated into its increasing (f^+) and decreasing (f^-) parts, $f = f^+ + f^-$. To maintain the stability of the scheme, the time step for the finite difference scheme (F), Δt, is chosen to be $\varepsilon/4$; $h_i^n = x_i^n - x_{i-1}^n$;

(b) The grid selection algorithm is applied to the piecewise linear function $\overline{U^{n+1}}$ with values $\overline{U_i^{n+1}}$ at the points $x_i^n \in \mathbf{M}^n$ to yield a new grid $\mathbf{M}^{n+1}$ and approximation U^{n+1}.

The greatest difficulty in a sequential implementation of the method is the organization of the data structures and the implementation of Algorithm M (which, strictly speaking, is not algorithmic at all, but definitional). Because the grid selection is based on recursive subdivision of the basic interval $[a, b]$, the natural data structure through which to organize the grid information is a binary tree. Each point in the grid, or equivalently, each admissible interval, corresponds to a node in the tree; therefore, we will speak of nodes, grid points and intervals interchangeably. The information stored in each node is presented in Fig. 2 of [22]; we give a brief discussion here of the main points. The left and right *children* of a node are the nodes corresponding to the left and right halves of the interval associated with that node; the *parent* relation is the inverse of the child relation. Two other pairs of links are needed to calculate the integral in (1). If a point x_i is centered in the interval $I = (x_l, x_r)$, then links are stored in x_i to the points x_l and x_r, which are called the left and right *boundary* points of x_i. As well, if an interval I is not a leaf in the tree (if it has been divided by Step 3 in Algorithm M), links are stored to the adjacent intervals of the same width as I immediately to the left and right of I. We choose to call these links *sibling* links. (Because these links correspond to adjacent nodes at the same depth in the tree representing the grid, *cousins* may be a more appropriate term!) It may be shown that nonleaf nodes *always* have adjacent left and right siblings; this will prove important in the parallel version of the algorithm.

After a calculation that determines the initial grid $\mathbf{M}^0$, the computations of each time step are organized as follows. In the first part of each time step, the finite difference scheme calculates U^{n+1} defined on $\mathbf{M}^n$, as in Step 2(a) above. In the final part of each time step, a new grid is chosen based on the function $U^{n+1} \equiv \overline{U}$. This grid selection algorithm is divided into two phases. In the first phase (which is illustrated in Fig. 4 of [22]), a standard recursive algorithm, similar to algorithms for adaptive quadrature, calculates for each grid point $x_i^n \in \mathbf{M}$ centered in the interval $I = (x_l, x_r)$, the values of *left int*, *right int*, and *int*, which are the values of (1) integrated over the intervals (x_l, x_i^n), (x_i^n, x_r) and (x_l, x_r), respectively. This calculation is considerably simplified by the fact that $\overline{U}$ is piecewise linear. For example, $\overline{U}_{xx}$ consists solely of multiples of delta measures located at each grid point x_i^n, so that if x_i^n is a leaf node,

$$\int_{(x_l, x_r)} |\overline{U}_{xx}| \, dx = |\overline{U}_x^+(x_i) - \overline{U}_x^-(x_i)|,$$

where $\overline{U}_x^+$ is the right-hand limit of $\overline{U}_x$ and $\overline{U}_x^-$ is the left-hand limit of $\overline{U}_x$. The above expression will be denoted by $x_i^n \to uxx$. (In general, a right arrow designates a subsidiary property of a node; it could be a numerical value associated with the node, or a link to another node, such as a node's parent or child.) Similarly, $\overline{U}_x$ is constant between grid points, so that if we define $\overline{f}'(s) = |f''(s)|$ for all s,

$$\int_{(x_i, x_{i+1})} |f''(\overline{U})| \overline{U}_x^2 \, dx = (\overline{f}(\overline{U}(x_{i+1})) - \overline{f}(\overline{U}(x_i))) \frac{\overline{U}(x_{i+1}) - \overline{U}(x_i)}{x_{i+1} - x_i}.$$

After these integrals are calculated, the second phase of the grid modification algorithm begins. The tree associated with $\mathbf{M}^n$ is traversed in a top-down, breadth-first ordering, examining each node in turn. If a node x_i^n is a left child, it is not difficult to see that with the definitions given in the previous paragraph of the various links, the integral in (1) may be calculated as

(2) $x_i^n \to$ parent $\to$ int $+ x_i^n \to$ parent $\to$ left sibling $\to$ right int $+ x_i^n \to$ left boundary $\to$ uxx.

(See Fig. 5 of [22].) The boundary and sibling links are included in the data structure specifically for this computation. A breadth-first traversal is used because this calculation depends on the sibling links of the parent, which must be present. Step 3 of Algorithm M is then applied to decide whether the node x_i^n should have children. If a leaf node x_i^n should have children, they are added to the tree and the appropriate links in the tree are updated; if an interior (nonleaf) node should not be subdivided, then the subtrees headed by its children are removed. It may be shown that at every stage in the calculation all interior nodes have adjacent left and right siblings, so that (2) may be calculated.

2. An adaptive method for hyperbolic systems. We now consider when u in (C) is a vector of unknowns in $\mathbb{R}^m$, and the equation takes the form

$$
\begin{aligned}
u_t + F(u)_x &= 0, && x \in \mathbb{R}, \quad t > 0, \\
u(x, 0) &= u_0(x) \in \mathbb{R}^m, && x \in \mathbb{R}.
\end{aligned}
$$

(S)

We assume that for all u the Jacobian matrix $A(u) = \partial F(u)$ has m real and distinct eigenvalues $\lambda_1(u) < \lambda_2(u) < \cdots < \lambda_m(u)$, with associated right eigenvectors $r_1(u), r_2(u), \cdots, r_m(u)$. Furthermore we assume that each eigenvalue is either *genuinely nonlinear* in the sense of Lax or is linearly degenerate, that is, the eigenvectors $r_k(u)$ may be normalized so that $\nabla_u \lambda_k(u) \cdot r_k(u)$ is either identically 1 (which is a convexity condition) or is identically 0 (see [17]). Again we assume a time scaling such that $|\lambda_i(u)| \leq 1$ for all i and all u that will arise in the computation.

Several finite difference schemes (see [12], [28], [31]) have been devised for such problems that satisfy certain auxiliary conditions, such as having Riemann invariants. In our algorithm we chose a generalization of the Engquist–Osher scheme, introduced by Osher and Solomon in [30], which is based on a method described in [17] for solving the Riemann problem for (S). The Riemann problem has the special initial data

$$
u_0(x) = \begin{cases} u_l & \text{for } x \leq 0, \\ u_r & \text{for } x > 0. \end{cases}
$$

Because the structure of Osher and Solomon's finite difference operator determines the grid selection algorithm (as we believe it should), their scheme is described below.

Near each point $u \in \mathbb{R}^m$ one may find a local covering $\sigma(\cdot, u) : [-S, S]^m \to \mathbb{R}^m$, with $\sigma(0, u) = u$, by solving successively the differential equations:

$$
\frac{d\Gamma_k}{d\tau} = r_k(\Gamma_k) \quad \text{for } \tau \text{ between 0 and } s_k, k = m, \cdots, 1,
$$

with $\Gamma_m(0) = u$ and $\Gamma_k(0) = \Gamma_{k+1}(s_{k+1})$. Set $\sigma(s, u) = \Gamma_1(s_1)$. (The paths $\Gamma_k(\tau)$ are related to the solution of the Riemann problem with $u_l = u$ and $u_r = \sigma(s, u)$.) Because the matrix whose columns consist of the eigenvectors $r_k(u)$ is nonsingular, for small enough S the mapping σ exists, is one-to-one, and covers a local neighborhood of u. In other words, any state v near u may be connected to u by a unique path $\{\Gamma_k\}$. For many physical problems, and for the Euler equations for gas dynamics in particular, it may be shown that any two physically possible states may be connected by such a path. This property is necessary for the finite difference scheme of Osher and Solomon to make sense, and we restrict our attention to systems (S) that have this property.

Note that for the conservation law (C), the spatial difference operator $(f(U_i^n) - f(U_{i-1}^n))/h_i^n$ may be written as

$$(3) \quad \frac{f(U_i^n) - f(U_{i-1}^n)}{h_i^n} = \frac{f^+(U_i^n) - f^+(U_{i-1}^n)}{h_i^n} + \frac{f^-(U_i^n) - f^-(U_{i-1}^n)}{h_i^n}$$

$$= \frac{1}{h_i^n} \int_{U_{i-1}^n}^{U_i^n} (f'(u) \vee 0)\, du + \frac{1}{h_i^n} \int_{U_{i-1}^n}^{U_i^n} (f'(u) \wedge 0)\, du,$$

where $a \vee b = \max(a, b)$ and $a \wedge b = \min(a, b)$. The scheme (F) may be thought of as distributing the first term on the right of (3) to the right endpoint of the interval (x_{i-1}^n, x_i^n) and the second term to the left. The basic idea of the Osher–Solomon finite difference method for systems is to apply the difference scheme (F) along each curve Γ_k^i connecting U_{i-1}^n to U_i^n; i.e., $U_i^n = \sigma(s, U_{i-1}^n)$. For the system (S), the wave speeds $\lambda_k(u)$ correspond to $f'(u)$ and the paths $\{\Gamma_k^i\}$ replace the simple path of integration, so that

$$(4) \quad \frac{F(U_i^n) - F(U_{i-1}^n)}{h_i^n} = \frac{1}{h_i^n} \sum_{k=1}^{m} \int_{\Gamma_k^i} (\lambda_k(u) \vee 0) r_k(u)\, du + \frac{1}{h_i^n} \sum_{k=1}^{m} \int_{\Gamma_k^i} (\lambda_k(u) \wedge 0) r_k(u)\, du.$$

The finite difference scheme for systems, then, consists of distributing Δt times the first sum to U_i^n at the right endpoint of the interval (x_{i-1}^n, x_i^n) and Δt times the second sum to U_{i-1}^n, at the left. Osher and Solomon showed that these integrals may be calculated simply and effectively for many problems of interest.

One may instantly devise an adaptive method for systems, based on Algorithm M, once one finds a suitable substitute for the condition (1). The condition we choose, although heuristic, reduces to (1) in the special case of a scalar conservation law, and may be shown to be effective when solving constant coefficient, linear problems.

We first note that when the flux f of (C) is convex or linear and u is a piecewise linear function defined on a grid $\{x_i\}$, we may write

$$(5) \quad I_1(i) \equiv \int_{x_{i-1}}^{x_i} |f''(u)| u_x^2\, dx = |f'(u(x_i)) - f'(u(x_{i-1}))| \frac{|u(x_i) - u(x_{i-1})|}{h_i};$$

similarly,

$$(6) \quad I_2(i) \equiv \int_{x_i-\delta}^{x_i+\delta} |u_{xx}|\, dx = \left| \frac{u(x_{i+1}) - u(x_i)}{h_{i+1}} - \frac{u(x_i) - u(x_{i-1})}{h_i} \right|$$

in the limit of small δ. We generalize (5) and (6) for systems (with the assumption of genuinely nonlinear or linearly degenerate eigenvalues) by noting that the eigenvalues $\lambda_k(u)$ play the part of the derivative $f'(u)$, and so for systems we set

$$(7) \quad I_1(i) \equiv \sum_{k=0}^{m-1} |\lambda_k(\Gamma_k^i(0)) - \lambda_k(\Gamma_{k+1}^i(0))| \frac{\|\Gamma_k^i(0) - \Gamma_{k+1}^i(0)\|_1}{h_i},$$

and

$$(8) \quad I_2(i) \equiv \left\| \frac{u_{i+1} - u_i}{h_{i+1}} - \frac{u_i - u_{i-1}}{h_i} \right\|_1,$$

where $\|v\|_1 = \sum_{k=1}^{m} |v_k|$ for $v \in \mathbb{R}^m$. When $m = 1$ definitions (5) and (6) coincide with (7) and (8). The adaptive scheme for systems uses Algorithm M to choose the grid, substituting (7) and (8) for (5) and (6) whenever the latter two quantities arise in the scalar computation of (1).

A complete analysis of the adaptive scheme using these substitutes for the integral (1) may be carried out for the constant coefficient, linear case, that is, for

(9)
$$u_t + Au_x = 0, \qquad x \in \mathbb{R}, \quad t > 0,$$
$$u(x, 0) = u_0(x) \in \mathbb{R}^m, \qquad x \in \mathbb{R},$$

where A is a constant matrix. We may write $A = R\Lambda R^{-1}$, where Λ is the diagonal matrix with nontrivial entries λ_k, and R is the matrix whose columns consist of the right eigenvectors of A. The finite difference scheme that we use may now be written as

(10)
$$\frac{U_i^{n+1} - U_i^n}{\Delta t} + \frac{A^+(U_i^n - U_{i-1}^n)}{h_i^n} + \frac{A^-(U_{i+1}^n - U_i^n)}{h_{i+1}^n} = 0,$$

where $A^+ = R\Lambda^+ R^{-1}$ and Λ^+ is the diagonal matrix with diagonal entries $\max(\lambda_k, 0)$; $A^- = R\Lambda^- R^{-1}$, with $\Lambda^- = \Lambda - \Lambda^+$. To analyze the system, we introduce the change of dependent variables $u = Rv$; by this device, the system (9) is transformed to the decoupled system

$$v_t + \Lambda v_x = 0, \qquad x \in \mathbb{R}, \quad t > 0,$$
$$v(x, 0) = R^{-1} u_0(x);$$

the scheme (4) is equivalent to

$$\frac{V_i^{n+1} - V_i^n}{\Delta t} + \frac{\Lambda^+(V_i^n - V_{i-1}^n)}{h_i^n} + \frac{\Lambda^-(V_{i+1}^n - V_i^n)}{h_{i+1}^n} = 0.$$

Because the components of this system are uncoupled, and the system is linear (so that $I_1(i) = 0$), the analysis presented in Theorem 5.2 of [22] may be applied separately to each component of v to prove the following theorem, which we state here without proof.

THEOREM. *Let each component of u_0 have a first derivative that is of bounded variation, and let $u(x, t)$ be the solution of* (9). *Assume, moreover, that Algorithm M is modified so that if an interval is smaller than $\varepsilon^{1/2}$, then it may no longer be divided by Step 3; let $\Delta t = \varepsilon^{1/2}/4$. If $n\Delta t = T$, and U^n is the solution of the adaptive grid algorithm above, then*

$$\|u(T) - U^n\|_{(L^1(\mathbb{R}))^m} \leq 3(T+1)m\Delta t \|R\|_1 \|R^{-1}\|_1 \|u_0'\|_{(BV(\mathbb{R}))^m}.$$

$\|R\|_1$ *is the operator norm of R when applied to $\mathbb{R}^m$ with the $\|\cdot\|_1$ norm.*

The computer implementation for systems of equations is organized somewhat differently than the implementation for a scalar equation. Each time step begins with U^n defined on $\mathbf{M}^{n-1}$. Two passes are then made through the tree. The first pass through the tree calculates the "integral" in (1) over each of the intervals (x_l, x_i^{n-1}), (x_i^{n-1}, x_r) and (x_l, x_r) for every interval $I = (x_l, x_r)$ with $x_i^{n-1} = (x_l + x_r)/2$ in $\mathbf{M}^{n-1}$. In so doing, it calculates for each leaf x_i^{n-1} in $\mathbf{M}^{n-1}$ the values of $\Gamma_k^i(s_k^i)$ and $\Gamma_k^{i+1}(s_k^{i+1})$ and substitutes (7) and (8) for (5) and (6), which are used in the scalar computation. For systems such as the Euler equations, calculating the intersection of the curves Γ_k takes much longer than calculating (7) and (8), so that the supplementary calculations to choose the grid are very cheap. The recursive algorithm used in the scalar computation is again used here to accumulate the value of (1) for interior nodes. The second pass through the tree combines the tree modification part of Algorithm M, which uses the calculation (2) requiring the sibling links, and the calculation of $\overline{U^{n+1}}$ from U^n using the Osher–Solomon finite difference scheme. In this second pass, the tree is traversed in a breadth first ordering, as before, to add and remove nodes where necessary to obtain $\mathbf{M}^n$. The breadth first ordering implies that each node's parent's sibling links are always available when needed in (2). In addition, whenever one discovers a leaf x_i^n in $\mathbf{M}^n$, then one knows that the left and right neighbors (boundaries) of x_i^n cannot be changed by further modifications to the tree. This allows one to calculate the contributions of the sums in (4) on each interval (x_{i-1}^n, x_i^n) and (x_i^n, x_{i+1}^n) to the values of U_{i-1}^{n+1}, U_i^{n+1}, and U_{i+1}^{n+1}. Thus, it is at this time that the finite difference scheme is applied locally to U^n to obtain U^{n+1}.

3. Parallel implementation. Several changes had to be made to the original data structure and computational sequence found in [22] to implement an efficient parallel version of the adaptive algorithm. We will begin our discussion by describing in more detail the recursive calculation of the intergral (1) over each interval (x_l, x_i), (x_i, x_r), and $(x_l, x_r) = I$ associated with a node $x_i = (x_l + x_r)/2$ in the grid.

The basic algorithm is very simple (cf. Fig. 4 in [22]):

```
Calculate Integrals (I) {
        do calculations common to all nodes x_i
        if (I is a leaf) {
                calculate left int, right int, and uxx from basic formulae
                set int := left int + right int + uxx
        } else {
                Calculate Integrals (I → left child)
                Calculate Integrals (I → right child)
                set left int := I → left child → int
                set right int := I → right child → int
                calculate uxx from basic formula
                set int := left int + right int + uxx
        }
}
```

By maintaining a stack of nodes waiting to be processed and introducing in each node I a counter $I \to count$ that keeps track of the number of children of that node that have been processed, the recursion may be removed in a standard way; see, for example, [37, pp. 316ff.]. We include the following algorithm only because we use it as a model for later algorithms. It assumes that the stack has been initialized and that the root of the tree has been pushed onto the stack.

```
while (the stack is not empty) {
        pop I from the stack
        while (I is not a leaf) {
                do calculations common to all intervals
                set I → count := 0
                push I → right child onto the stack
                set I := I → left child
        }
        /* at this point I is a leaf */
        do calculations common to all intervals
        calculate left int, right int, and uxx from basic formulae
        set int := left int + right int + uxx
        set done := false
        while (I is not the root node and not done) {
                set I := I → parent
                if (I → count = 0) {
                        /* only one child of I has been processed */
```

```
                  set I → count := 1
                  set done := true
            } else {
                  /* both children of I have been processed */
                  set left int := I → left child → int
                  set right int := I → right child → int
                  calculate uxx from basic formula
                  set int := left int + right int + uxx
            }
      }
}
```

To implement this algorithm in parallel, we follow the strategy of Lusk and Overbeek [24] (and, obviously, Brinch Hansen [8] and others), and set up a *monitor* to control access to the stack by a fixed number of processes executing identical copies of the above code in parallel. A monitor is a shared data structure that can be accessed by only one process at a time, together with routines that access and modify that structure. In our case, the stack of nodes waiting to be processed has associated with it two routines, *push a node onto the stack*, and *request a node from the stack*. When a process requests a node from the stack, either (a) it is successful and a node is popped from the stack, or (b) all processes are waiting to get a node from the stack and the stack is empty. In the latter case, the *request* monitor routine returns a special code to all processes that indicates that the integral calculation stage of execution is finished because there are no other processes executing that can add a node to the stack. When the special termination code is sent out, one process, the *organizer*, sets up the next part of the computation, while the *worker* processes wait until the stack is nonempty and there is more work to be done. The monitor routines are implemented as macros that are expanded into in-line code by a macro preprocessor, so that little overhead is expended in the synchronization code. It is true, however, that the code in the monitor is executed sequentially, so whenever one routine is pushing a node onto the stack, for example, no other process may enter the monitor.

Because processes may not access the global (shared) stack in parallel, it is important to minimize contention among processes using the stack. This can be accomplished by having each process complete the computation for a subtree if this subtree is smaller than a maximum size. This requires one to keep track of the size of the subtree headed by each node in the tree; this information is stored in a field that we call *subtree size*. The integral calculation algorithm may be further abstracted as follows:

```
while (the global stack is not empty) {
      pop I from the global stack
      while (I → subtree size > max size) {
            do preliminary calculations
            push I → right child onto the global stack
            set I := I → left child
      }
      /* at this point I heads a subtree with max size or fewer nodes */
      process the subtree headed by I
}
```

This strategy works well when the tree is balanced, that is, when the two subtrees headed by the children of a node are roughly of the same size. In this case, each process computes results for about *max size* to (*max size*)/2 nodes. However, the trees that are generated by our grid algorithm are very unbalanced, because the tree is deep and narrow near discontinuities in the solution (see [22, Fig. 3]). This causes some processes to have little work to do between trips to the monitor, thereby decreasing the amount of inherent parallelism. Thus, a dynamic tree partitioning algorithm that breaks up the tree into parts of roughly the same size is necessary to ensure that all processes have about the same work load between trips to the monitor.

We developed the top-down tree partitioning algorithm presented in Fig. 1, which is similar to a bottom-up algorithm noted in [11]. In the tree modification pass of the computation, complete subtrees may be removed by the algorithm, thereby making a bottom-up scheme impractical—it is useless to examine nodes that should have already been removed by a previous part of the calculation. This algorithm ensures that each process works on between (*max size*)+1 and 3(*max size*), inclusive, nodes before returning to the monitor. It also ensures that every node on the global stack heads a subtree of size at least (*max size*)+1. The partitioning algorithm employs a local stack on which to hold unprocessed subtrees. In practice, each worker process executes the code in Fig. 1 imbedded in a loop that repeats endlessly, with the worker processes waiting between time steps when there are no nodes on the shared stack. At the end of the program a special signal is sent to all worker processes that allows them to terminate gracefully.

There are two conflicting requirements when considering the value of the parameter *max size*. *Max size* should be small enough so that the tree is partitioned into many pieces and all processes end work at about the same time; it should be large enough so that little time is spent by processes waiting to enter the monitor. One might find that only for larger trees can these conflicting requirements be met—there may just not be enough inherent parallelism available in the computation of a small tree.

Because the tree partitioning algorithm does not guarantee that the nodes will be processed in any particular order (other than top-down), it was difficult to apply this

```
TREE PARTITION ALGORITHM {
        Let stack size denote the number of nodes in the
            subtrees stored temporarily on the local stack
        pop I from global stack
        set stack size := 0
        while (stack size ≦ max size and stack size + I → tree size > 3 (max size)) {
                process I as an interior node
                let min tree be the smaller of the subtrees of the two children of I
                let max tree be the larger of the subtrees of the two children of I
                if (min tree → tree size + stack size > 3 (max size)) {
                        push min tree onto the global stack
                } else {
                        push min tree onto the local stack
                        set stack size := stack size + min tree → tree size
                }
                set I := max tree
        }
        if (I → tree size + stack size > 3 (max size)) {
                push I onto the global stack
        } else {
                push I onto the local stack
        }
        Process all subtrees on the local stack
}
```

FIG. 1. *Tree partition algorithm.*

algorithm directly to the second pass through the tree in each time step. It was during this pass that we traversed the tree in breadth first order while evolving M^{n-1} into M^n according to Algorithm M and advancing the solution using the finite difference operator. A breadth first traversal of the tree is strongly suggested because the decision whether to modify a node by adding or removing subtrees depends on the calculation in (2), which depends in turn on the availability of the left and right siblings of that node's parent. If one does use a breadth first traversal, however, then the maximum parallelism available during the second pass is limited to the number of nodes at a given depth in the tree. Near shocks the tree is very narrow (cf. Fig. 3 of [22]), and very little parallelism is available. As an indication of this, we note that our first implementation used a breadth first traversal of the tree and could achieve a speed-up of at most a factor of 1.5 independently of the number of processes invoked in the computation. Clearly another strategy is in order.

It is at this point that we use the fact that the grid modification process may be interpreted as a tree transformation, where the initial tree, M^{n-1}, satisfies certain invariants because it has been developed by the same process at the previous time step. In particular, it is known that every node in M^{n-1} has a parent either on the outer edge of the tree structure or with adjacent left and right siblings, so that every node originally in M^{n-1} may be examined in parallel (subject to the condition that the tree be traversed top-down, so that nodes that will be removed during this time step are removed before their children are examined). Thus, if we allow ourselves to remove subtrees at will, but to add only a layer of nodes one node thick to the edge of the tree, all the nodes originally in M^{n-1} may be examined and modified in parallel. Because sibling links are horizontal, and not vertical, we cannot add these links to new nodes until all the nodes in M^{n-1} have been processed; one can show that even under this condition children may be added to leaf nodes in parallel with the processing of the rest of the tree. The tree partitioning algorithm in Fig. 1 may now be used to balance the execution load among the processes.

After the nodes in M^{n-1} have been processed, and the tree has been transformed into a state intermediate to M^{n-1} and M^n, it remains to add the sibling links to the new nodes and to apply Step 3 of Algorithm M and the finite difference operator to the nodes that have been added in this step. This "clean-up" part of the second pass is done sequentially, using a breadth first, top-down traversal of only the nodes that have been added during this time step. Because it is rare that a subtree of height two or more is added to a node during one time step (it was never observed in any computer simulation), this part of the computation, though sequential, takes very little time.

4. Computational results and discussion. Our method was applied to approximate the one-dimensional Euler equations of gas dynamics. The physical quantities in this system are the density ρ, the momentum m and the specific energy e, so that

$$u = \begin{pmatrix} \rho \\ m \\ e \end{pmatrix} \quad \text{and} \quad F(u) = \begin{pmatrix} m \\ \dfrac{m}{\rho}\left(m + (\gamma - 1)\left(e - \dfrac{1}{2}\dfrac{m^2}{\rho}\right)\right) \\ \dfrac{m}{\rho}\left(e + (\gamma - 1)\left(e - \dfrac{1}{2}\dfrac{m^2}{\rho}\right)\right) \end{pmatrix}.$$

To compare the results with experiments by Sod [34], we set $\gamma = 1.4$; the initial values of $\rho(x)$ were chosen to be 1 for $x \leqq 0$ and 1/8 for $x > 0$; the momentum was initially

0 everywhere; and $e(x) = 2.5$ for $x \leq 0$ and $e(x) = 0.2$ for $x > 0$. The grid refinement algorithm was modified slightly for this problem. To make the grid slightly less uniform, Step 3 of Algorithm M was changed for m-dimensional systems so that if $|I| \geq \varepsilon$ and

$$|I| \int_{3I} [|u_{xx}| + |f''(u)||u_x^2|] \, dx \geq m\varepsilon$$

(with the appropriate substitute for the integral when $m > 1$) then the left and right halves of I are admissible intervals. To avoid an artificial time scaling, the time step Δt was set to $\varepsilon/16$. Figures 2(a) through 2(c) show the numerical approximations to the density ρ, the pressure $p = (\gamma - 1)(e - (m^2/2\rho))$, and the internal energy $((e/\rho) - \frac{1}{2}m^2/\rho^2)$ at time 0.15 when solved on the interval $[-1, 1]$ with $\varepsilon = 1/256$. These graphs are drawn with the same horizontal and vertical scales as the graphs in [34]. A total of 193 grid points were used to approximate the solution at the final time; the minimum grid spacing was $1/1024$, while the largest spacing was $1/8$. The results in [34] were obtained with a uniform grid of 100 points, so we use twice the number of grid points in this experiment. Figure 3 shows the node placement superimposed upon a graph of the density ρ; note that the horizontal scale is expanded by a factor of three, so that the contact discontinuity appears much more spread out.

Some comparison should be made between this and other methods. It is the purpose of this paper to illustrate that grid adaptation, developed with careful consideration of the underlying finite difference operator, can be effective when solving problems with moving singularities. The finite difference scheme that we chose, the Osher–Solomon scheme, is a first order scheme that gives relatively good resolution to shocks. If we denote the grid spacing on a uniform grid by h, the scheme has $O(h)$ error where the solution is smooth and smears moving contact discontinuities to a width of $O(h^{1/2})$. An examination of the condition (1) in Algorithm M shows that our adaptive scheme sets the local grid intervals near contacts and shocks to $O(\varepsilon)$ and the local grid intervals in the smooth part of the flow to $O(\varepsilon^{1/2})$, so that the errors in each part of the flow are of the same order of magnitude. (Shocks are resolved to a width of $O(\varepsilon)$, but because the error in the shock speed depends, in general, on the error in the generally smooth flow on each side of the shock, the L^1 error near the shock is again $O(\varepsilon^{1/2})$.) It is our contention that solving the problem more accurately in one area of the flow than in another is generally unnecessary, and so this is the correct balance between local grid sizes in each region of the domain for this finite difference operator.

If a formally second order TVD scheme [12] were used as the underlying finite difference operator, a new set of trade-offs would be implied. The error in the smooth area of the flow would be $O(h^2)$; if the scheme resolved moving contacts in a fixed number of grid points, then the error near contacts would be $O(h)$; the error near shocks would again be $O(h)$. This implies that the local grid spacing near singularities in the flow should be $O(\varepsilon)$, while the grid spacing in the smooth areas of the flow should be $O(\varepsilon^{1/2})$. This would result, however, in an overall error of $O(\varepsilon)$.

The methods of Oliger [3], Bolstad [5] and Berger [4] use locally adapted temporal as well as spatial increments. We maintain that although this technique is useful, it would achieve only a constant factor speed-up over the results presented here because of the first order accuracy of our finite difference operator. This may be seen by counting how many grid intervals of each width are in the grid. Near the contact, there are $O(\varepsilon^{-1/2})$ intervals of width ε that require a time step of order ε. In the smooth part of the flow there are $O(\varepsilon^{-1/2})$ intervals of width $O(\varepsilon^{1/2})$ that require a time step of

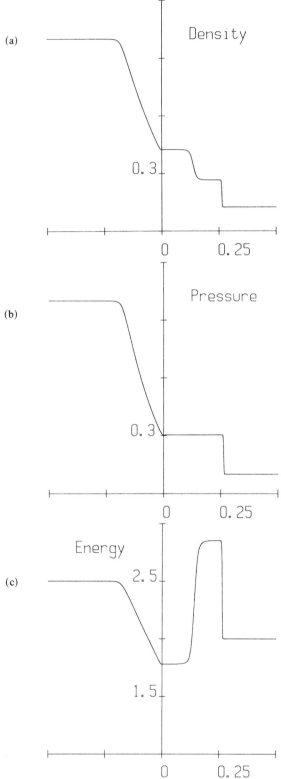

FIG. 2. *Graphs of* (a) *the density* ρ, (b) *the pressure* p, *and* (c) *the internal energy* E *at time* 0.15 *for the example given in text.*

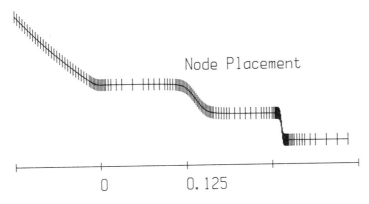

FIG. 3. *The density ρ for x between $-1/8$ and $3/8$. Tics mark the placement of the grid points. Note that the horizontal scale here is three times the horizontal scale in Fig.* 2.

$O(\varepsilon^{1/2})$. Thus, $O(\varepsilon^{-3/2})$ operations are required whether or not we use larger time steps in the smooth part of the flow. This difference in the constant factor is of course an important practical consideration but it does not result in asymptotically greater order CPU times. The situation changes drastically when formally second order difference operators are used. In this case the same analysis shows that locally adaptive time steps *are* effective in reducing CPU times.

The methods of Oliger and his students employ local, uniform spatial subgrids over which the computation can be effectively vectorized. It is easily seen from Fig. 3 that even though we allow an essentially arbitrary grid, in our example the grid naturally organizes itself into subregions of uniform grid spacing. Because of this, it is reasonable to believe that their methods will outperform our method on this problem; i.e., they may achieve a smaller error at a lower computational cost (if their adaptive grid criteria chooses the grid correctly—at least in Bolstad's early work, the ratio of maximum to minimum grid spacing is bounded by a constant, and so the argument used above to estimate the error in various parts of the region is not valid). Based on the "fingering" phenomena documented by Glimm and his co-workers, we suspect that inhomogeneities in media and higher spatial dimension may lead to grids that are not modeled well by small numbers of overlapping, uniform, subgrids. This must be verified experimentally, of course.

The algorithm was implemented in C on the Denelcor HEP using the synchronization macro package described in [24]. The architecture of the HEP is described in [16]; for our purposes each Process Execution Module (PEM) may be seen as a computer with an execution pipeline of length eight that executes instructions from processes in a common execution queue. One instruction from the queue is started every cycle that an instruction is waiting to be executed. When an instruction is completed, the next instruction from the same process is entered into the instruction queue. Processes waiting on semaphores busy-wait in a separate queue. In a one PEM system, all main memory accesses except for accesses to asynchronous variables and indexed stores go through a local memory interface that has a queue length of eight; all other memory accesses go through the general memory switch, which has an effective queue length of 24–30 (see [15]). One HEP may have several PEMs.

The speed-ups resulting from the parallel algorithm are presented in Table 1 and Fig. 4. Table 1 presents the clock times for the execution of the program for the Euler equations with $\varepsilon = 1/256$. Execution times were not directly measurable, and the clock

TABLE 1

Execution times

Number of processes	Time (in seconds) for first pass	Time (in seconds) for second pass
1	165.589419	51.099661
2	86.486981	27.329106
3	60.209457	19.657619
4	48.109058	16.012172
5	40.244957	13.783819
6	35.079278	12.341126
7	32.348853	11.445739
8	29.046026	10.726242
9	27.370288	10.190968
10	25.556640	9.809485
11	24.225887	9.481623
12	23.330546	9.264341
13	22.942822	9.215509
14	22.728492	9.123390
15	22.503358	9.183468

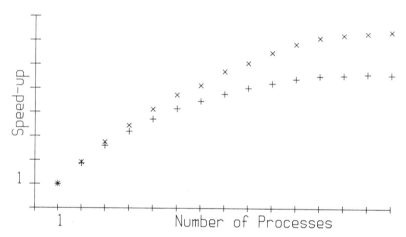

FIG. 4. *Speed-up versus number of processes for the Euler equations example. The points × represent the first pass of each time step, the points + represent the second.*

times were partially vitiated by the periodic execution of a system disk management routine for a fraction of a second. Figure 4 presents the speed-up versus the number of processes for the same problem.

Because of the various queues in the HEP architecture, with their different lengths, it is difficult to estimate the maximum possible speed-up for this algorithm independent of the task synchronization time. However, some indication may be given by an examination of the assembly code for the program. Ignoring synchronization code, fewer than 13% of all nonsynchronization instructions in the main execution path of the program are indexed store instructions. Furthermore, much of the time is spent in the library routines *pow*( ) and *sqrt*( ) (used to calculate the position of the points $\{\Gamma_k^i(s_k^i)\}$), which have mainly register to register instructions. If one assumes that the *sqrt* routine takes about 15 instructions and the *pow* routine takes about 40 instructions (conservative estimates), this further lowers the fraction of instructions that use the general memory switch to an estimated 9%. A crude estimate of the maximum speed-up possible in a program may be obtained by taking an average of the queue lengths of the instructions executed, weighted by the number of instructions that go through each queue. In our case this would be less than $0.91 \times 8 + 0.09 \times 24$, or about 9.44. The final speed-up of 7.36 achieved for the first computational passes of each time step, on a problem of relatively small size, is very good.

The second computational pass of each time step did not speed up as much as the first because of the spatial dimension of the underlying physical problem. When a shock moves along the x-axis, most often only two or four nodes are added in front of the shock in one time step. These nodes are added at the deepest part of the tree, after most of the tree has been processed. There is therefore about a factor of two parallelism available during the latter part of the tree modification and finite difference pass. This effect would disappear for two-dimensional problems, for which approximately $O(N^2)$ nodes would be added along a moving front at each time step, where the average grid size where the solution is smooth is $O(N^{-1})$. Thus, a much greater amount of parallelism would be available in the two-dimensional problem.

5. Conclusions. We present a programming methodology and tree partitioning algorithm that allows us to efficiently compute the solution of a nonlinear partial differential equation with moving discontinuities in parallel on a currently available machine. It has been shown empirically in [22] that in some cases the present adaptive method achieves asymptotic speed-up over uniform fixed grid methods with the same difference scheme. This work shows that even though the fixed grid scheme may be simple to execute on vector machines, parallel processing offers hope of executing adaptive grid methods at supercomputer speeds. The use of these techniques with better difference schemes may improve the approximation schemes for the problems by an order of magnitude. Because the amount of parallelism available depends on tree size, two-dimensional problems, with larger and more complex grids, offer the promise of even more parallel efficiency.

Acknowledgments. Danny Sorensen offered much help and many suggestions during the course of this work. The computer coding was done on the Denelcor HEP at Argonne National Laboratory. The last two references to more recent papers were suggested by a referee.

REFERENCES

[1] R. E. BANK, *The efficient implementation of local mesh refinement algorithms*, in Adaptive Computational Methods for Partial Differential Equations, I. Babuska, J. Chandra and J. Flaherty, eds., Society for Industrial and Applied Mathematics, Philadelphia, 1983, pp. 74–84.

[2] J. B. BELL AND G. R. SHUBIN, *An adaptive grid finite difference method for conservation laws*, J. Comput. Phys., 52 (1983), pp. 569–591.

[3] M. BERGER AND J. OLIGER, *Adaptive mesh refinement for hyperbolic partial differential equations*, J. Comput. Phys., 54 (1984), pp. 484–512.

[4] M. BERGER, *Data structures for adaptive mesh refinement*, in Adaptive Computational Methods for Partial Differential Equations, I. Babuska, J. Chandra and J. Flaherty, eds., Society for Industrial and Applied Mathematics, Philadelphia, 1983, pp. 237–251.

[5] J. H. BOLSTAD, *An adaptive finite difference method for hyperbolic systems in one space dimension*, Ph.D. dissertation, Lawrence Berkeley Lab. LBL-13287 (STAN-CS-82-899), 1982.

[6] C. DE BOOR, *Good approximation by splines with variable knots*, in Spline Functions and Approximation Theory, A. Meir and A. Sharma, eds., ISNM, v. 21, Birkhauser-Verlag, New York, 1973, pp. 57–72.

[7] ———, *Good approximation by splines with variable knots* II, in Lecture Notes in Mathematics 363, Springer-Verlag, New York, 1974, pp. 12-20.

[8] P. BRINCH HANSEN, *Operating System Principles*, Prentice-Hall, Englewood Cliffs, NJ, 1973.

[9] J. DOUGLAS, JR. AND M. F. WHEELER, *Implicit, time-dependent variable grid finite difference methods for the approximation of a linear waterflood*, Math. Comp., 40 (1983), pp. 107-122.

[10] B. ENGQUIST AND S. OSHER, *Stable and entropy satisfying approximations for transonic flow calculations*, Math. Comp., 34 (1980), pp. 45-75.

[11] G. N. FREDERICKSON, *Data structures for on-line updating of minimum spanning trees, with applications*, SIAM J. on Comput., 14 (1985), pp. 781-798.

[12] A. HARTEN, *High resolution schemes for hyperbolic conservation laws*, J. Comput. Phys., 49 (1983), pp. 357-393.

[13] A. HARTEN AND J. M. HYMAN, *Self-adjusting grid methods for one-dimensional hyperbolic conservation laws*, J. Comput. Phys., 50 (1983), pp. 235-269.

[14] G. W. HEDSTROM AND G. H. RODRIGUE, *Adaptive-grid methods for time-dependent partial differential equations*, in Multigrid Methods, W. Hackbusch and U. Trottenberg, eds., Springer-Verlag, New York, 1982, pp. 474-484.

[15] H. F. JORDAN, *HEP architecture, programming, and performance*, in Parallel MIMD Computation: the HEP Supercomputer and its Applications, J. S. Kowalik, ed., MIT Press, Cambridge, MA, 1985, pp. 1-41.

[16] J. S. KOWALIK, Ed., *Parallel MIMD Computation: the HEP Supercomputer and its Applications*, MIT Press, Cambridge, MA, 1985.

[17] P. D. LAX, *Hyperbolic systems of conservation laws and the mathematical theory of shock waves*, SIAM Regional Conference Lectures in Applied Mathematics, Number 11, 1972.

[18] R. J. LEVEQUE, *A large time step generalization of Godunov's method for systems of conservation laws*, SIAM J. Numer. Anal., 22 (1985), pp. 1051-1073.

[19] ———, *Convergence of a large time step generalization of Godunov's method for conservation laws*, Comm. Pure Appl. Math., 37 (1984), pp. 463-478.

[20] ———, *Large time step shock-capturing techniques for scalar conservation laws*, SIAM J. Numer. Anal., 19 (1982), pp. 1091-1109.

[21] B. J. LUCIER, *A moving mesh numerical method for hyperbolic conservation laws*, Math. Comp., 46 (1986), pp. 59-69.

[22] ———, *A stable adaptive numerical scheme for hyperbolic conservation laws*, SIAM J. Numer. Anal., 22 (1985), pp. 180-203.

[23] ———, *Error bounds for the methods of Glimm, Godunov and LeVeque*, SIAM J. Numer. Anal., 22 (1985), pp. 1074-1081.

[24] E. L. LUSK AND R. A. OVERBEEK, *Use of monitors in FORTRAN: a tutorial on the barrier, self-scheduling DO-loop, and askfor monitors*, in Parallel MIMD Computation: the HEP Supercomputer and its Applications, J. S. Kowalik, ed., MIT Press, Cambridge, MA, 1985, pp. 367-411.

[25] K. MILLER, *Alternate modes to control the nodes in the moving finite element method*, in Adaptive Computational Methods for Partial Differential Equations, I. Babuska, J. Chandra and J. Flaherty, eds., Society for Industrial and Applied Mathematics, Philadelphia, 1983, pp. 165-184.

[26] ———, *Moving finite elements, II*, SIAM J. Numer. Anal., 18 (1981), pp. 1019-1057.

[27] J. OLIGER, *Approximate Methods for Atmospheric and Oceanographic Circulation Problems*, in Lecture Notes in Physics 91, R. Glowinski and J. Lions, eds., Springer-Verlag, New York, 1979, pp. 171-184.

[28] S. OSHER AND S. CHAKRAVARTHY, *High resolution schemes and the entropy condition*, SIAM J. Numer. Anal., 21 (1984), pp. 955-984.

[29] S. OSHER AND R. SANDERS, *Numerical approximations to nonlinear conservation laws with locally varying time and space grids*, Math. Comp., 41 (1983), pp. 321-336.

[30] S. OSHER AND F. SOLOMON, *Upwind difference schemes for hyperbolic systems of conservation laws*, Math. Comp., 38 (1982), pp. 339-374.

[31] J. PIKE, *Grid adaptive algorithms for the solution of the Euler equations on irregular grids*, to appear.

[32] W. C. RHEINBOLDT AND C. K. MESZTENYI, *On a data structure for adaptive finite element mesh refinements*, ACM Trans. Math. Software, 6 (1980), pp. 166-187.

[33] R. SANDERS, *The moving grid method for nonlinear hyperbolic conservation laws*, SIAM J. Numer. Anal., 22 (1985), pp. 713-728.

[34] G. A. SOD, *A survey of several finite difference methods for systems of nonlinear hyperbolic conservation laws*, J. Comput. Phys., 27 (1978), pp. 1-31.

[35] A. J. WATHEN, *Mesh-independent spectrum in the moving finite element equations*, to appear.

[36] A. J. WATHEN AND M. J. BAINES, *On the structure of the moving finite element equations*, IMA J. Numer. Anal., to appear.

[37] D. K. KNUTH, *The Art of Computer Programming. Volume* 1: *Fundamental Algorithms*, second edition, Addison-Wesley, Reading, MA, 1973.

[38] W. D. GROPP, *Local uniform mesh refinement on loosely-coupled parallel processors*, Yale Univ. Tech. Report YALEU/DCS/RR-352, 1985.

[39] W. D. HENSHAW, *The numerical solution of hyperbolic systems of conservation laws*, California Inst. of Technology, Ph.D. thesis, 1985.

SIAM J. SCI. STAT. COMPUT.
Vol. 8, No. 2, March 1987

INTERPRETING PARALLEL PROCESSOR PERFORMANCE MEASUREMENTS*

HARRY F. JORDAN†

Abstract. This paper discusses execution time versus number of simultaneous operations in parallel computing systems. The main focus is on shared memory multiprocessors. A model for execution time as a function of the number of processes used in a computation is developed. The model addresses the effect of sequential code, code which can be executed by only a limited number of processes, hardware limits to speedup, critical section synchronization overhead and the influence of task granularity. The model is shown to correspond very closely to experimental measurements of execution time on the HEP pipelined, shared memory multiprocessor. Use of the model as an analysis tool in complex parallel programs is indicated.

Key words. parallel processor, performance, speedup, synchronization, multiprocessor

AMS (MOS) subject classifications. 68A05, 68J10

1. Introduction. Programs written to be executed by a large number of processes are often formulated so that they can be run with different numbers of processes. In addition to the desire to measure speedup by running the program with differing numbers of processes, pressure for process number independence arises from several other sources. Portability considerations and the fact that some processors may be unavailable at a given time in a multiprocessor system argue for making the number of processes a parameter in a parallel program. Furthermore, with large numbers of processes, it is difficult to formulate programs having a detailed dependence on the number of processes executing them. In this paper, evidence is presented that, given a program which can be executed by any number of processes, its execution time as a function of this number gives significant insight into the program structure. It can be used to estimate program parameters such as degree of parallelization, task granularity and synchronization overhead. Some of these parameters may be hard to predict directly from the program code while the known values of others can be used to support the accuracy of the performance models presented below.

2. Effects of sequential code. The simplest model shows the general shape of the execution time versus number of processes curve for an imperfectly parallelized program. The model, discussed by Ware [1] in 1972, can be viewed as separating a program into a perfectly parallelized and a strictly sequential section. For small numbers of processes, many parallel programs exhibit a behavior of execution time versus number P of processes of the form

$$T(P) = c_1 + \frac{c_2}{P}.$$

A simple least squares fit to determine c_1 and c_2 can be applied to a suitable portion of the execution time versus number of processes curve to estimate the degree of parallelization. Sharp corners in this rapidly decreasing portion of the curve can be caused by sections of the program in which parallelism is limited to, say, K processes. The execution time then behaves as

$$T(P) = c_1 + \frac{c_2}{\min(K, P)} + \frac{c_3}{P}.$$

* Received by the editors November 18, 1985; accepted for publication (in revised form) April 18, 1986. This article was presented at the Second SIAM Conference on Parallel Processing for Scientific Computing that was held in Norfolk, Virginia on November 18–21, 1985.

† Computer Science Department, Indiana University, Bloomington, Indiana 47405-4101.

The existence of a sharp change in slope of $T(P)$ is a good indication that a significant portion of the execution time is devoted to a program section which is limited in the number of computations that can be done in parallel.

If multiprogramming or pipelining is used to allow more parallel computations to be specified than there are physical hardware units, the speedup is limited by the number U of hardware units. The denominator in the parallel time term changes from P to min (U, P) much as in the limited program parallelism case. The $T(P)$ curve in this case has a flat section representing the minimum execution time possible with the hardware. Any increase in the number of processes can only increase execution time as a result of extra computation, synchronization or process management associated with more processes. For the purposes of performance measurement it may be quite interesting to observe the $T(P)$ curve for P larger than that giving the minimum execution time, since this gives an indication of overhead associated with each process on parallelization.

The effect of limited parallelism is easier to see in the speedup curve, which shows a predominantly linear behavior with slope changing at $P = K$. An example of this behavior was seen in measurements made on a parallelized version [2] of the MA28 sparse LU-decomposition program originally written by Duff [3]. This program was written for the HEP [4] pipelined multiprocessor. It was known from analysis of the code that the search for an optimal pivot using the Markowitz criterion contained a parallelism limit. A critical section needed to parallelize the pivot search loop had a size which was one sixth of that of the loop body for the matrix size and percent sparsity in the measurement run. Thus, no more than six processes could be productively used in the pivot search. The other large parallel section, the reduction of nonpivot rows, did not have as low a parallelism limit. The speedup curve for this program is shown in Fig. 1. The parallelism limit at six processes is clearly visible. The hardware

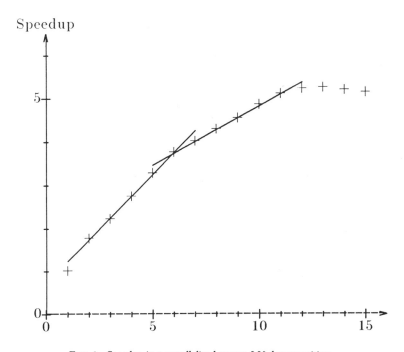

FIG. 1. *Speedup in a parallelized sparse LU-decomposition.*

parallelism limitation, U, on the HEP computer is 10-12, depending on instruction mix, and is also apparent in Fig. 1.

3. Synchronization overhead. Several common synchronization operations can be viewed functionally as critical sections of code, which can be executed by only one process at a time. We can alter the Ware model to allow for this. Assume that a fraction f of the sequential code cannot be parallelized and that the cost of parallelizing the fraction $(1-f)$ of the code is a critical section of length t_c in each process. The amount of useful work done by each process in the parallel section is

$$\frac{(1-f) \times T(1)}{P}.$$

It may be possible for all other processes to complete their critical sections while a given process is doing its fraction of useful work. This can only occur when the amount of useful work exceeds the number $P-1$ of other processes times t_c. Conflict for critical section access can occur in this case, but a justification for using the best case analysis of perfect overlap is that, if the critical section is made up of short segments executed in a loop, the delays occurring on the first pass cause the processes to fall into synchronism. Thus, no delays occur on subsequent passes through the loop, and the best case timing is well approximated. In this case, the total execution time can be written

$$T(P) = f \times T(1) + (1-f) \times \frac{T(1)}{P} + t_c,$$

provided

$$(1-f) \times T(1) \geqq P \times (P-1) \times t_c.$$

When the amount of time a process spends doing useful work is shorter than the total time spent by other processes sequentially passing through their critical sections, the useful work is masked by critical section delay, and the best case time becomes

$$T(P) = f \times T(1) + P \times t_c, \qquad (1-f) \times T(1) < P \times (P-1) \times t_c.$$

Combining the cases, the best case analysis gives

$$T(P) = f \times T(1) + t_c + \max\left((1-f) \times \frac{T(1)}{P}, (P-1) \times t_c\right).$$

This expression has a minimum at

$$P_m \approx \frac{1}{2} + \left(\frac{(1-f) \times T(1)}{t_c}\right)^{1/2}, \qquad \frac{t_c}{(1-f) \times T(1)} \ll 1$$

and rises linearly with P for $P > P_m$.

The above analysis assumes no limit on the number P of processes that may execute in parallel. In a multiprogrammed or pipelined parallel processor the limit U on the number of parallel hardware units must be taken into account. The addition of further processes does not speed the completion of the $(1-f) \times T(1)$ workload which can be parallelized but does increase the number of processes executing critical sections. Taking this limit into account, the execution time model becomes

$$T(P) = f \times T(1) + t_c + \max\left(\frac{(1-f) \times T(1)}{\min(P, U)}, (P-1) \times t_c\right).$$

Thus a linear rise in execution time as P becomes large is an indication of critical section type synchronization, and the length of the critical section can be estimated from the slope of the linear rise.

A parallel program to solve the Laplace equation with Dirichlet boundary conditions on a square was written to test a parallel Successive Over Relaxation (SOR) algorithm [5] on the HEP computer. Multiple processes were used to relax the rows of a 100 by 100 grid, and the maximum change in solution value over the grid was computed cooperatively by processes relaxing different rows by using a critical section. The execution time showed all the salient features of the above formula. An estimate of the model parameters from the data yielded the formula

$$T(P) = 9.15 + 0.73 + \max\left(\frac{215.10}{\min{(P, 10.51)}}, 0.73(P-1)\right).$$

This model is plotted as a continuous line in Fig. 2 along with the measured execution times, marked by "+". The parallelism limit U was determined from the height of the flat section and t_c from the slope of the linearly rising tail while $f \times T(1)$ and $(1-f) \times T(1)$ came from a least squares fit of the simple Ware model formula to data in the range $1 \leq P < U$. The last digits of the estimated parameters were affected slightly by the analysis to be presented in the next section. While the code for the Laplace SOR was not massive, detailed instruction counts were not done, but the estimated parameters are quite consistent with program section sizes estimated from the Fortran source code and from the parallelism limits measured in other HEP programs.

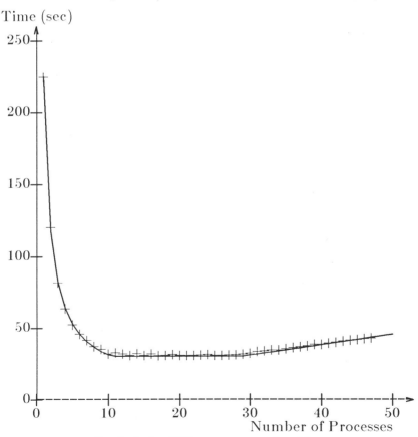

FIG. 2. *Laplace SOR measurements and model.*

4. Task granularity correction. Another measurable effect occurs when the parallel work has a fixed granularity. If a parallel program consists of serial work $T_s = f \times T(1)$ and parallel work of N indivisible units of size t_u, then N is said by Mohan [6] to be the logical parallelism of the program. A simple program with this behavior might be one with some sequential code followed by a DOALL [7] of order N. The machine model for the execution of this program has two parallelism parameters. P is the instruction parallelism and represents, in an MIMD machine, the number of instruction streams used by the program and, in an SIMD machine, the vector length for a single vector instruction (length of vector registers where this applies). U is a limit on the number of hardware units that can operate in parallel on the P "processes" associated with the instruction parallelism. We assume a vanishing "process switch" overhead as occurs in pipelined processing where "process switch" merely corresponds to issuing the next unit of computation into the pipeline. We also ignore the filling and emptying of the pipe which is really a part of process synchronization. It is absent, for example, in vector chaining and in pipelined multiprocessors when there is no interprocess interaction. Since the units t_u are not subdividable, the N units are divided by the process structure into $\lfloor N/P \rfloor$ units, on which P processes work simultaneously, and $N \bmod P$ units, on which at most $N \bmod P$ processes can be active. Including this effect, the execution time is given by a modified version of the hardware limited Ware model

$$T(P) = T_s + \frac{P\lfloor N/P \rfloor t_u}{\min(P, U)} + \frac{(N \bmod P)t_u}{\min(N \bmod P, U)}.$$

For $P < U$, the granularity effect results in flat portions of the execution time curve between successive values of P which divide N evenly, since the addition of further processes does not reduce execution time until the next even divisor is reached. In a hardware limited parallelism situation, it is helpful to view the effect as a difference between the execution times including and ignoring the granularity. The difference between the time with arbitrarily divisible work and that with N indivisible units is

$$\delta(P) = \frac{(N \bmod P)t_u}{\min(N \bmod P, U)} - \frac{(N \bmod P)t_u}{\min(P, U)}.$$

This difference can be viewed as a correction to the hardware limited Ware model. $\delta(P)$ is zero either if P divides N evenly or if $U \leqq N \bmod P$. When nonzero, its value can be written

$$\delta(P) = t_u \left(1 - \frac{N \bmod P}{\min(P, U)}\right).$$

In the range of P where hardware is not a limitation, $P < U$, the correction term is always nonzero except when P evenly divides N. In the hardware limited region, the correction is zero unless $N \bmod P < U$. In this region, deviations from the hardware limited Ware model should be observed whenever the total work divides across processes with a small remainder.

If there is a flat region of minimum execution time, these divisibility corrections can be easily seen. If the logical parallelism of the program is not obvious from the code it may be possible to deduce it from a remainder analysis. Since the size of the correction $\delta(P)$ is a simple fraction of t_u, an even easier parameter to extract is the size, in execution time, of the granule.

Mohan's thesis [6] thoroughly explores the granularity correction as the effect of logical parallelism. His analysis does not cover a hardware parallelism limit and is thus characteristic of the situation for $P < U$. Flat plateaus in execution time are clearly shown in both his models and simulations. The Laplace SOR program for HEP, described above, clearly exhibits the effects of the granularity correction, both in the hardware limited portion and in the rising tail resulting from critical section conflict. Figure 3 shows a detailed view of the measured execution times (again denoted "+") along with a solid line plot of the model equation including the correction term

$$T(P) = 9.15 + 0.73 + \max\left(\frac{215.10}{\min(P, 10.51)}, 0.73(P-1)\right) + \delta(P).$$

The parameter t_u in $\delta(P)$ was not estimated separately but taken to be

$$t_u = \frac{(1-f) \times T(1)}{100},$$

since processes execute 100 tasks corresponding to rows of the grid. It can be seen that the overall fit of the complete equation is quite good. As expected, the positions of the visible granularity peaks are very well predicted since they depend only on remainder analysis. The height of the peaks is somewhat less well predicted.

5. Conclusions. Some fairly simple models have been exhibited above which not only predict the performance of programs with simple structure on parallel processors, but which can also be used to analyze performance measurements on more complex programs for the purpose of estimating parallelism related parameters of the program

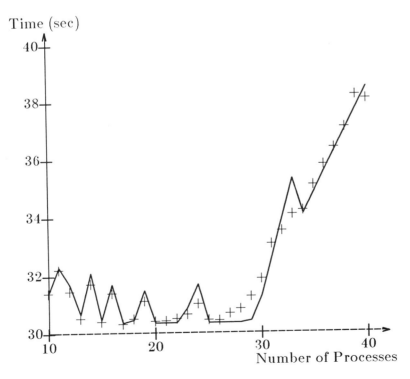

FIG. 3. *Laplace SOR measurements and model with granularity term.*

HARRY F. JORDAN

structure. These models have been observed to be very accurate in practice and, in simple cases, the parameters estimated from the $T(P)$ curve have matched well with values obtained by direct analysis of the code.

The task granularity model is particularly accurate in giving the positions of the resultant peaks. This effect also appears in register based vector machines in programs where vectors are longer than the vector registers. The hardware parallelism limit also shows up as the effect of pipeline length in pipelined vector machines. It is harder to study in the vector case because pipeline startup strongly influences the measurements in the region where this limit takes effect.

The synchronization overhead is particularly interesting because many synchronization mechanisms impose the same type of process waiting involved in the critical section model. The hardware parallelism limit in the pipelined MIMD architecture characteristic of the HEP has the effect of suppressing other influences and making the synchronization overhead apparent at large numbers of processes.

REFERENCES

[1] W. H. WARE, *The ultimate computer*, IEEE Spectrum, March 1972, pp. 84–91.
[2] G. ALAGHBAND AND H. F. JORDAN, *Parallelization of the* MA28 *Sparse Matrix Package for the* HEP, Report CSDG 83-3, Computer Systems Design Group, Electrical and Computer Enging. Dept., Univ. Colorado, Boulder, 1983.
[3] I. S. DUFF, MA28—*A set of* FORTRAN *subroutines for sparse unsymmetric linear equations*, AERE Report R.8730, H.M. Stationery Office, London, 1977.
[4] H.F. JORDAN, *Experience with pipelined multiple instruction streams*, Proc. IEEE, Vol. 72, No. 1, January 1984, pp. 113–123.
[5] N. R. PATEL AND H. F. JORDAN, *A parallelized point rowwise successive over-relaxation method on a multiprocessor*, Parallel Computing, 1, 3, 4, December 1984.
[6] JOSEPH MOHAN, *Performance of parallel programs: Model and analysis*, Ph.D. thesis, Carnegie-Mellon Univ., Pittsburgh, PA, 1984.
[7] D. A. PADUA, D. J. KUCK AND D. H. LAWRIE, *High speed multiprocessors and compilation techniques*, IEEE Trans. Comput., C-29 (1980), pp. 763–776.

SIAM J. SCI. STAT. COMPUT.
Vol. 8, No. 2, March 1987

HYPERCUBE ALGORITHMS AND IMPLEMENTATIONS*

OLIVER A. McBRYAN† AND ERIC F. VAN DE VELDE‡

Abstract. Parallel algorithms are presented for important components of computational fluid dynamics algorithms along with implementations on hypercube computers. These programs, used to solve hyperbolic and elliptic equations, achieve high efficiency on 5- and 7-dimensional hypercubes.

For elliptic equations, a parallel preconditioned conjugate gradient method is described which has been used to solve pressure equations discretized with high order finite elements on irregular grids. A parallel full multigrid method and a parallel fast Poisson solver are also presented. Hyperbolic conservation laws have been discretized with parallel versions of finite difference methods and with the random choice method.

The performance of these algorithms is analyzed in terms of machine efficiency, communication time, bottlenecks and software development costs. A key aspect of this work is the development of a library of parallel operators for distributed vectors and matrices, efficient for both full and sparse data. The implementation of these operators on hypercubes is described along with measurements of communication effects. Using the library, the PDE algorithms mentioned above have been implemented on both serial computers and on hypercubes without *any* code modification. All interprocess communication is hidden in library routines. A general parallel computer simulator is described along with its use in the development of the algorithms.

The relation of the model problems solved here to the more complex physical problems encountered in real fluids is discussed. Techniques are developed for comparing the behavior of an algorithm on different architectures as a function of problem size and local computational effort.

Key words. hypercube, parallel, linear algebra, multigrid, conjugate gradient, PDE, matrix

AMS(MOS) subject classifications. 65W05, 65F05, 65F10, 65M99, 65N99, 65N30

1. Introduction. In this paper we describe the implementation of partial differential equation solvers on hypercube processors, part of an ongoing effort to exploit parallelism in the solution of equations arising in Computational Fluid Dynamics. We present results of computations run on the Caltech Mark II Hypercube parallel processor and on the Intel iPSC d7 processor. These machines have respectively 32 and 128 processors connected on 5- and 7-dimensional hypercube networks. We have previously described the implementation of some of these algorithms on the shared memory Denelcor HEP parallel computer [1]-[8].

Our goal is to develop algorithms that make close to optimal use of available parallelism on a range of realistic problems. Our studies have concerned the development of parallel algorithms for elliptic, parabolic and hyperbolic equations. These algorithms include important components of real fluid dynamics codes. All of our algorithms are for equations with two space dimensions, though extension to three dimensions is straightforward in each case. While most of the computational results described in the paper relate to PDE solution, the techniques used are much more general. The PDE solvers are written entirely in terms of a general-purpose library of parallel operations which automates the construction of distributed data structures and provides parallel operations on them. Much of the paper (§§ 3-6) will concentrate on this library, describing its implementation on hypercubes, and the techniques used to make it efficient for such architectures. In § 1.1 we give an overview of this library,

---

* Received by the editors January 16, 1986; accepted for publication (in revised form) May 22, 1986. This article was presented at the Second SIAM Conference on Parallel Processing for Scientific Computing that was held at Norfolk, Virginia, November 18–21, 1985.

† Courant Institute of Mathematical Sciences, New York University, New York, New York 10012, and Los Alamos National Laboratory, Los Alamos, New Mexico 87545. The work of this author was supported in part by U.S. Department of Energy contract DE-AC02-76ER03077, by National Science Foundation grant DMS83-12229, and by the T-Division, Los Alamos National Laboratory.

‡ Courant Institute of Mathematical Sciences, New York University, New York, New York 10012.

followed in § 1.2 by an introduction to the PDE problems we have solved. Section 1.3 discusses the relation of the model problems solved in this paper to parallelization of complex physical problems and introduces a method for performance analysis that provides useful comparison of parallelization efficiency between different algorithms and machines. In § 1.4 we make some comments relevant to comparison of our studies on the Caltech Hypercube and on the Intel iPSC. Section 1.5 surveys the remainder of the paper in more detail.

1.1. Portable parallel software and libraries. A primary long-range aim of our work is the development of portable programming methodologies for numerical applications. The goal is to be able to use the same code on a wide range of different processors, including serial, SIMD and MIMD machines, with both shared memory and message-passing architectures. We report progress in this area. In particular, we have implemented a library of vector and matrix operations for hypercubes. This library deals with globally distributed vectors and matrices. It includes allocation routines for such objects, standard linear algebra operators such as inner products, vector maximum, vector sums and products, matrix transpose, matrix-vector and matrix-matrix products and rank one updates. The allocation routines allow vectors and matrices to be distributed in various ways across the processors, and routines are provided to convert between different representations. The library is efficient for both sparse matrices such as those encountered in discretizing partial differential equations and for full matrices. A second library involves routines for object-level communication, both between hypercube nodes as well as with the host processor. All of our applications are implemented in terms of these two libraries.

There are several advantages that result from the use of these libraries, beyond the normal improvement in software modularity. Some of the library routines involve substantial and complex inter-process communication on the hypercube—for example the *inner_product, transpose* and *matrix_vector* routines for distributed vectors and matrices. These library routines may be written for different parallel processors as well as for serial and vector processors and represent a powerful mechanism for hiding communication and network dependence in programs. As a result, most of our applications algorithms can be run on both serial machines and hypercubes with *no* code modification. In particular we identify a class of algorithms, which we term *transpose-split algorithms* which have this property. We present a general discussion of such algorithms as well as several applications to hyperbolic and elliptic problems.

We have also observed that a large number of algorithms, when written in terms of our library, take the form of SIMD rather than MIMD programs. In particular the code running in each node is identical and does not refer in any way to location in the network (of course such dependencies are buried in the library routines). Furthermore we do not use cooperating host programs which only tend to complicate the clarity of algorithms, and introduce critical sections into programs. We believe that by casting programs in an SIMD form, portability is greatly enhanced, and programs can be easier to debug and understand.

A critical issue here is the semantics of the vector library routines. We illustrate this with the example of the inner product of two distributed vectors. In our approach, the inner product operation is called simultaneously by all processors, and all return with the same global value. We do not allow the possibility that a single processor requests a global inner product. Consequently all processors compute quantities such as inner products that are used to determine when to terminate an iteration. Each processor independently decides to terminate its iteration, although of course all terminate at the same point since the same inner product value is obtained at all nodes. An alternate approach would be to assign one processor (or the host) as a control processor to monitor convergence. On detecting sufficient accuracy that processor would then notify all others to terminate. This scheme does not have an SIMD form since one processor is distinguished. There is also no real time savings in this scheme because although most processors avoid computing with the inner product, they have to wait while the control processor computes the inner product and notifies them to continue iterating or to terminate.

1.2. Elliptic and hyperbolic equations. Once the parallel libraries are available, implementation of various solution methods for PDE becomes straightforward. All of the basic parallel data structures required for storing data across the processors are automatically generated by calls to library routines. Further library routines are available to perform all operations on these data structures that require any communication. The remaining code is then related to only one processor, and is just standard serial code—we have not developed any new numerical methods for solving PDE. The algorithms we have used include random choice and finite difference methods for hyperbolic equations, multigrid methods for Poisson-type equations and preconditioned conjugate gradient methods for arbitrary-order finite element discretizations of elliptic equations on irregular grids.

The hyperbolic equations are the easiest to parallelize, and in fact we have parallelized various hyperbolic solvers by adding as little as one line of code to the corresponding serial code (see § 8.3). We have used several parallelization strategies for hyperbolic equations and we compare these from the point of view of computational efficiency. The simplest method is not the most efficient. However it is quite sufficient as computation already substantially dominates communication costs even for this method. From a software point of view we prefer the simpler approach—trading a small amount of efficiency for a large decrease in software complexity. Furthermore we have used the same parallelization strategy, which we call *transpose splitting parallelization*, for various other applications, including an FFT-based fast Poisson solver (see §§ 7 and 13). The basic observation underlying this approach is that an efficient parallel matrix transpose can be used to parallelize a numerical algorithm of ADI or operator splitting type.

Another general parallelization technique, which we call *areal decomposition*, is applicable to both hyperbolic equations and to multigrid methods and other relaxation schemes. Here a grid is decomposed into rectangular subgrids which are distributed in an areal (or volume) manner to a set of processors. Extra boundary layers are provided around each subgrid and are used to store duplicate data recording values at grid points in neighboring processors out to a specified distance, typically 1 grid point. A basic library routine is used to globally allocate such data structures and another routine (*shuffle*) can be called to update the boundary duplicates at any time. The combination of the data structure and the *shuffle* operation simulates a shared memory extremely closely—in fact it does simulate one exactly for grid operators whose stencil range does not exceed the buffer range. Efficiency depends on the aspect ratio of the subgrids used and we measure this area-perimeter effect in several applications.

1.3. Real problems and performance comparisons. For the most part we have studied model problems which have simpler governing equations than those for realistic physics. We have studied the issue of how effectively real problems may be parallelized. Real physical equations differ from our model equations in complexity. For example expensive equations of state may need to be solved at every grid point. Because of the resulting increase in computation time per grid point, with little or no increase in communication time, computational efficiency will in general be higher for many realistic problems than for our model problems. Since the model problems already behave extremely well, the prognosis for the real problems looks excellent.

We have studied this question using a model hyperbolic code that does nothing but compute NFLOPS floating point operations per grid point and performs the standard inter-process communication typical of hyperbolic solvers. We then study the computational efficiency of this code as a function of grid size, number of processors and NFLOPS. The conclusion is that attaining high efficiency is extremely easy even on very coarse grids, in fact efficiencies over 90% are attainable on the Intel iPSC with NFLOPS of under 100, on grids so coarse that there are only a few dozen grid points per processor (see § 9 for details). Caltech Hypercube efficiencies are generally even higher. We obtain efficiency performance curves for various grid sizes that essentially characterize the behavior of the hypercube in question for a very wide range of numerical processes. Given an estimate of NFLOPS we can predict performance of an algorithm on various grids or with increasing numbers of processors. Furthermore comparing such curves for different algorithms gives an immediate comparison of the algorithms over the range of parameters. Plotting equivalent curves for different processors would provide a useful way to compare hardware designs over a range of different problems.

Variations in hardware design can play a major role in the behavior of algorithms, even among machines with the same network configuration. Critical parameters include the amount of memory per processor, the network communication rate, the overhead for sending short messages and the overall balance between these quantities and the processor speed. This has shown up very clearly in our work with the Caltech Hypercube and the Intel iPSC. Despite the larger memory and somewhat faster processing speed of the iPSC, the Caltech machine is more successful for most algorithms because there is almost no overhead for short messages, whereas with the iPSC all messages up to 1024 bytes in length take essentially the same time. The question of communication startup cost is closely tied to the available memory. In the current iPSC design, the memory available (about 250K bytes per node) is such that for many algorithms, communication is just beginning to be efficient even in the largest problems that can fit on the processors. For example, if a square subgrid of maximal size is stored on an iPSC processor, it will contain about 2^{16} real-valued grid points and consequently have edges containing about 256 grid points (1024 bytes of data). A communication in which a whole edge is communicated at once to another processor is then barely in the efficient range. In practice, memory is required for program storage and other data so that the situation is actually less favorable. The Caltech Hypercube does not suffer from this problem. In fact on that machine even individual boundary data points of a subgrid may be efficiently transferred to a neighboring processor. It follows that such *areal decompositions* of grids are substantially more favorable on the Caltech machine.

In analyzing algorithms in the sequel we will comment where appropriate on these issues. Such considerations play an especially important role in the asymptotic analysis of algorithms. An otherwise accurate analysis may be seriously flawed in practice if communication startup overhead is omitted. In § 2.3 we introduce three critical parameters α, β and γ which characterize the communication and computation performance of parallel computers. These quantities are used repeatedly throughout the paper.

1.4. Caltech Hypercube vs. Intel iPSC. We have referred above to advantages of the Caltech design over the Intel iPSC. The iPSC has advantages too, such as more memory and processors. The results of our experiments performed on the Caltech and Intel Hypercubes are not for the most part directly comparable. We describe now some of the reasons for this.

We performed all of the Caltech Hypercube experiments prior to any of the iPSC experiments. The former experiments were performed with generally far inferior algorithms to the latter. In part we had learned from the Caltech experiments, and in part we were forced to develop better algorithms by the difficulties of dealing with the iPSC communications overhead. As an example, when we first moved a multigrid code from the Caltech Hypercube to the Intel iPSC it ran 100 times *slower* on the latter machine! Analysis showed that control messages being sent between the host computer and the node processors were dominating all computation. The fundamental problem was that control messages were typically a few words long and were therefore hundreds of times less efficient than on the Caltech cube. Another problem appeared to be that the host is time-shared and may not be ready to interrupt itself immediately on receipt of a message from the cube, effectively increasing communication costs with nodes. A third problem was that boundary data on the edges of subgrids were transferred to neighboring processors one point at a time. The combination of these three effects generated the hundred-fold slow-down. The final form of the iPSC algorithms involve no exchange of messages with the host, and buffer all boundary data to avoid sending single points. This should be taken as a very serious demonstration of the importance of coupling algorithm and hardware design. We have not had an opportunity to return to Caltech to repeat the old experiments with our optimized software. Undoubtedly efficiencies would be much closer to optimal in all cases with the new software. It is also difficult to compare the machines because of the different memory sizes. The largest problems that can fit in the Caltech Hypercube are relatively small iPSC problems, and as a result suffer more from communication startup effects than do larger iPSC problems.

1.5. Overview of contents. In § 2 we review the hardware and software environment of the Caltech and Intel Hypercubes. In § 3 we introduce two hypercube simulators we have developed that were crucial to the work described in this paper. In § 4 we describe the organization of the hypercube network into various topologies, including grids, trees and a hierarchy of canonical rings. Section 5 concentrates on the vector library introducing distributed vector formats and the operations defined on them, in particular, *inner_product* and *shift_vector*. Section 6 describes the various distributed matrix representations and the matrix library, including the important *transpose*, *matrix_vector* and *matrix_matrix* operations.

The second half of the paper deals with applications of the software described in §§ 3–6. In § 7 we introduce the concept of transpose-split algorithms, indicate their implementation on hypercubes and an analysis of their communication vs. computation costs. Section 8 discusses the solution of hyperbolic equations using several parallelization schemes. Section 9 presents the analysis of computational efficiency as a function of work per grid point and of grid size referred to earlier.

Section 10 serves as an introduction to the elliptic equation solvers in the remaining sections. Section 11 presents an implementation of a full multigrid elliptic equation solver for hypercubes. Section 12 describes a parallel preconditioned conjugate gradient solver for arbitrary-order finite element (or finite-difference) equations. Finally § 13 provides an application of transpose splitting to the development of a fast solver for the Poisson equation, which also serves as a parallel preconditioner for the conjugate gradient solver.

In each of the implementation sections we present results of actual hypercube implementations, along with analyses of efficiency and communications overhead.

It is difficult in a paper of this type to provide complete references to related work. The numerical analysis involved is not new, and we have given a few references to the literature in each case. The decomposition of PDE problems on parallel machines has been actively explored in recent years by many groups. For example, areal distribution schemes have been used frequently and we do not attempt to catalogue these. The development of portable linear algebra libraries may be traced back to LINPACK [9] and to related developments such as the BLAS routines [10]. Work on extension of LINPACK to vector and parallel machines has also been underway for some time [11]-[17]. Application of parallel computers to the solution of PDE has been discussed frequently [18]-[23]. Issues of software portability in parallel environments have been addressed by several groups, in particular we reference the work of Lusk and Overbeek [24], and Jordan [25]. A large source of algorithms for hypercubes are found in the many publications of the Caltech/JPL group, in particular see [26] and the annual reports of the CCCP project [27]. Application of hypercubes to linear algebra and to solution of elliptic equations is discussed in several reports from Yale [28]-[32]. For a very complete list of references to related work on parallel numerical algorithms see the excellent review of Ortega and Voigt [33].

2. Architecture and software.

2.1. The Caltech Cosmic Cube.
The Cosmic Cube is a parallel processor developed by Geoffrey Fox and Charles Seitz [26], [34] at Caltech. The Caltech Mark II Hypercube consists of 2^D ($D = 5$ or 6) independent processors, each with its own local memory. There is no shared memory available; the processors cooperate by message passing. Messages are passed over an interconnection network which is a *hypercube* in a space of dimension D, see Fig. 1. Processors are located at the vertices of the D-dimensional hypercube and adjacent vertices of the cube are connected by a communication channel along the corresponding edge. All data exchange between processors occurs in 8-byte packets along these cube edges which are asynchronous full duplex channels. In addition to the 2^D node processors, there is a host processor which acts as a control processor for the entire cube and also provides the interface between the cube and a user. All I/O to and from the cube must pass through the host, which is connected to

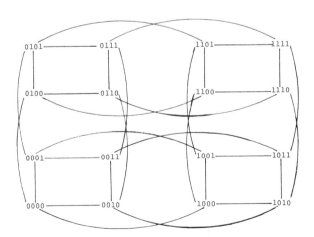

FIG. 1. *Representation of a 4-dimensional hypercube.*

one corner of the cube by an extra communication channel. The original Caltech design consists of a 64-node 6-dimensional hypercube utilizing Intel 8086/8087 processors with 128K bytes of memory at each node. This architecture has the advantage of being easily fabricated from standard components, and may be scaled up to much larger sizes (in powers of 2) with almost no change in design. Because of these features, machines of this type are likely to become widely available in the immediate future, whereas development of highly parallel global memory machines will take substantially longer.

A more advanced Caltech cube called the Mark III is now under development. This will have much faster processors at the nodes (Motorola 68020) and local memory per node will reach several megabytes. Other enhancements will be incorporated based on the experience with the prototype.

2.1.1. Caltech Hypercube programming. There are two fundamentally different communication modes available on the hypercube. In the *interrupt driven mode*, processors are interrupted by messages arriving from the communication channels. These messages are preceded by sufficient identification and destination information so that the processor can either forward them to another channel (if the current processor is not the destination) or process the incoming message (if the message has arrived at its destination). In the *crystalline operating system* messages are not preceded by address information. As a result, each processor has to know in advance exactly what communication pattern to expect. The latter system is unquestionably more efficient, although it is clearly also more restrictive. For the computations described in this paper the crystalline operating system was quite adequate. The parallelization of other algorithms (e.g. the local grid refinement algorithms discussed in our related papers [4], [6]) will likely require some interrupt driven communication protocols. For the remainder of the discussion we will refer only to the crystalline operating system when discussing Caltech Hypercube software.

The software for the cube consists of an operating system kernel, a copy of which resides in each processor, as well as a run-time library providing user access to the communication facilities. Typically, identical copies of a user program are down-loaded to all processors where they execute concurrently. All scheduling is accomplished through communication calls, so that some care is required to prevent locking situations from occurring.

As discussed previously, the D-cube has 2^D vertices with D edges radiating from each. Thus each processor sees D channels connecting it to its neighbors. The cube nodes are numbered in the range $[0, 2^D - 1]$, such that the D-digit binary representations of physically adjacent nodes differ only in 1 bit. The channels emanating from a node may then be numbered $0, 1, \cdots, D-1$ according to which bit differs in the binary node representations at either end of the channel. There is also an extra channel from node 0 to the intermediate host (referred to as the *IH* below) through which all communications to and from the cube pass. Data to be communicated between processors is sent in 8-byte packets, which are sufficient to encode all scalar data types. A set of system calls are available to node-resident programs which implement the required communication primitives for these packets. Similar system calls are available on the host to provide communication with the cube. In order to give the flavor of these system calls, we list some of the most important ones, along with their functions, in Table 1. In the table the notation *IH* and *ELT* are used, respectively, for the intermediate host and for the nodes, *data* represents an 8-byte item, *CUBE* denotes the channel to or from the *IH* to the hypercube and P is the number of processors.

TABLE 1
Crystalline cube communications.

wtIH(data,CUBE)	Write a data packet from the IH to node 0
rdsig(data)	Data sent from the IH is read by each node
wtres(data)	Data is sent from a node to the IH
rdbufIH(data, CUBE,P)	Read the union of data sent by all nodes to the IH into array datas
wtELT(data,chan)	Send data to the cube neighbor on channel chan
rdELT(data,chan)	Read data from the cube neighbor on channel chan
shift(ind,inc,outd,outc)	Write buffer outd onto channel outc, then read from channel inc into buffer ind

The *shift* operator allows either the in or out channel to be specified to be a nonexistent channel, denoted *NULLCHAN*. In this case *shift* simply omits the corresponding read or write operation. This feature is especially useful in the treatment of nonperiodic grid boundaries where a read or write beyond the boundary is not desired. We have found that most hypercube communication may be written in terms of the *shift* operator alone. In part this is because the *shift* operator actually includes the *rdELT* and *wtELT* operations which are special cases corresponding to setting *outc* = *NULLCHAN* and *inc* = *NULLCHAN*, respectively.

One additional routine is very useful in the simulation of many physically interesting problems, such as those derived from discretizations of partial differential equations on regular grids. An important feature in such discretizations is that there is typically only nearest-neighbor connectivity among the variables of interest. For efficient use of the hypercube, it is then very desirable to map the grid onto the cube in such a way that neighboring grid points (in 2- or 3-dimensional space) are mapped onto adjacent nodes of the cube. Communications overhead will be minimized by such a mapping. Accomplishing such a mapping is nontrivial and in general impossible. For example, there is no such mapping of a 3-dimensional grid onto a 5-cube since the grid requires a local connectivity of 6 at each node. A general purpose routine called *whoami* has been developed by John Salmon at Caltech [35] based on *binary gray codes*, which generates a suitable mapping of the above type in most cases where one is possible. The *whoami* call is usually executed at the start of any grid-oriented program, and in addition to creating a suitable mapping of the grid to the cube nodes it returns communication channel information for each of the *grid-neighbors* of each processor. This allows the programmer to think entirely in *grid space* rather than in the less intuitive *edge space* of the cube.

A hypercube program consists of two separate programs: an *intermediate host program* and an *element program*. The intermediate host program initiates the computations and returns the results to the user, but does not interfere with the core of the computations. These are described by the element program, identical copies of which are executed in all processors of the hypercube simultaneously.

2.2. The Intel iPSC computer. The Intel Corporation has recently marketed the first commercial realization of the hypercube design, based largely on the Caltech cosmic cube. The machine, known as the iPSC, comes in three models—the d5, d6 and d7. These have, respectively, 32, 64 and 128 processors. The individual processors are the Intel 80286/80287 with up to 512Kb of memory, and the interconnections are provided by high-speed Ethernets, using an Intel Ethernet chip. The intermediate host machine, which is both the control processor and the user interface, is an Intel 310 microcomputer running a UNIX system (Xenix). In addition to the Ethernets along cube edges, a global communication channel is provided from the intermediate host machine to the individual processors. This feature is useful for debugging and to a limited extent for control purposes. Besides the UNIX system on the host, software for the system consists of a node-resident kernel providing for process creation and debugging along with appropriate communications software for interprocessor exchanges, and for host to processor direct communication. Combined computing power of a 128-node system can be over 5 MFLOPS, which along with the 64 Mbytes of memory available, provides a relatively powerful computer.

2.2.1. iPSC programming. The software environment for the Intel iPSC is distinctly different from the crystalline operating system described above. To begin with, the operating system supports multiple processes at each cube node, identified by their process identity number *pid*. All communication primitives can address an arbitrary process on an arbitrary node. The underlying message passing system includes automatic routing of messages between any two processes. This frees the user from developing complex routing schemes in his software, but at the expense of some extra communication overhead. We present a list of the iPSC communication calls in Table 2.

A further flexibility is the availability of both synchronous and asynchronous communication modes. The system supports a concept of *virtual channel*, unrelated to the physical channels connecting nearest neighbor nodes. A process can communicate with several other processes simultaneously by opening several virtual channels (using the routine *copen*()) and then exchanging messages using asynchronous communication calls. All messages have a user-defined integer attribute, called *type*, which is assigned by the sender. A receiver may request messages by type, but not by source process or source node. Fortunately the range of the type attribute is large enough ($[0,32767]$) to allow the source of a message to be encoded in its type. Messages of any size up to 16384 bytes may be sent, although the overhead for message transmission severely discourages sending small messages, a point which we return to in a later section. To send a message, the message pointer and length are supplied along with the destination node and process and the *type* attribute (*send*() and *sendw*()). To receive a message, a type and a message buffer and desired length are supplied, and on receipt of the message the actual length, source node and source process identity (*pid*) are returned

TABLE 2
iPSC communication routines.

Node routines:

chan = copen(pid)	open a virtual channel for process *pid*
send(chan,type,mesg,len,node,pid)	send a *type* message to *pid* on *node*
recv(ci,type,msg,len,cnt,node,pid)	read message of type *type*
length = probe(chan,type)	are there messages of type *type*?
status(chan)	is channel free yet?
flick()	nonbusy wait
sendw(chan,type,mesg,len,node,pid)	blocking send to *pid* on *node*
recvw(ci,type,msg,len,cnt,node,pid)	blocking read of *type type*
syslog(pid,string)	print a message on the host

Host routines:

sendmsg(chan,type,mesg,len,node,pid)	blocking send to *pid* on *node*
recvmsg(ci,type,msg,len,cnt,node,pid)	blocking read

(*recv*() and *recvw*()). To support asynchronous transmissions, it is possible to determine if a previous message has completed on a specific virtual channel (with *status*()), and to determine if there is a message of a specific type pending at a node (with *probe*()). One very unfortunate feature of the system is that the host communication primitives are less powerful. For example it is not possible to request receipt of a message at the host by *type* and in fact one is forced to read messages in totally arbitrary order. As a consequence, it is usually necessary to develop a software buffering scheme for messages at the host so that incoming messages may be stored until one of an appropriate type arrives. This is a serious inconvenience and will hopefully be remedied in future versions of the iPSC software.

2.2.2. Computation and communication costs.

Two characteristics of the current iPSC design are the slow communication rate and the high overhead for short messages. In fact messages of length 1 and 1024 bytes take essentially the same time. As a measure of the slowness we note that a message of length 16384 bytes takes 12 seconds to traverse a nearest-neighbor ring of 128 processors, or over 17 seconds using a ring in random (sequential) order. The cost of sending a message of length 1 byte to a neighboring processor is approximately 5.3 ms while longer messages require about 5.5 ms per 1024 byte segment. Figure 2 displays the cost of sending packets as a function of packet size. These numbers are approximate and were obtained by sending 30 consecutive messages from node 0 to its 6 neighbors on a 6-dimensional cube. An uncertainty is involved because the system clock is accurate only to 16 ms. Larger numbers of messages could not be sent to obtain better statistics without a time delay due to an operating system bug. Messages were sent using both the asynchronous *send* routine and the synchronous *sendw* routine, though there was little difference as indicated by the pair of curves in Fig. 2. This slow communication speed is way below the hardware limits of the Ethernet connections and suggests that much time is wasted in operating system overhead. Despite this fact we have found that the iPSC can be used with high efficiency on a wide range of problems because of the substantial memory available per node. To indicate the processor speed, we note that a *C for* loop with no body requires about 11 μs per point, while a loop with a typical floating point computation such as $a = a + b * c$ requires about 67 μs per point. Thus we rate the

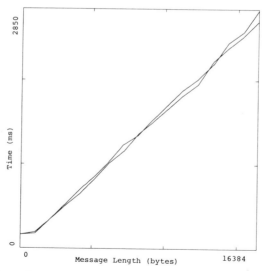

FIG. 2. *Synchronous and asynchronous message sending time as a function of the message length on the iPSC.*

processor at about .03 Mflops though this estimate might vary by a factor of about 2 in different situations. We summarize processor speed characteristics in Table 3.

We present a study of timing costs for messages of different sizes on a 128 processor d7 in Fig. 3. The times measured are for passage of messages of various sizes around a complete ring of 128 processors. Each processor reads a message from its clockwise neighbor on the ring, then sends the message to its anti-clockwise neighbor. The sequence starts and ends at processor 0 which records the time between sending the message and final receipt. The upper curve is for a ring of nonnearest neighbor processors, ordered as $0, 1, \cdots, 127$, while the lower curve is for a nearest-neighbor ring. Superimposed on the lower curve is a second curve, generated on the iPSC using Caltech Hypercube communication calls. The latter calls were implemented using a simulator we have written for the Caltech Hypercube on the iPSC hardware (see § 3.2). As can be seen, overhead for using the simulator is completely negligible.

2.3. Basis for communication cost analyses. In subsequent sections, we analyze communication costs for many algorithms. Generally we assume that the cost to transfer

TABLE 3
iPSC *performance.*

C **for** loop: empty body	10.9 μs per point
C loop to copy real numbers	15.7 μs per point
C **for** loop $a = a + b * c$	67.4 μs per point
send 0 bytes	5.3 ms
send 1024 bytes	5.9 ms
send 2048 bytes	11.2 ms
send 16384 bytes	90 ms
clock() system call	155 μs
clock() time unit	16 ms

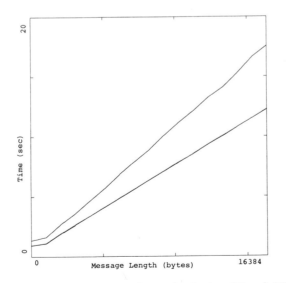

FIG. 3. *Time for different size messages to travel around a ring in a 128 node iPSC. The top curve is for the ring in which the processor numbers are increasing. The bottom curve is a nearest neighbor ring (based on binary reflected gray codes). Superimposed on the lower curve are the times obtained by using the Caltech simulator on the iPSC for the nearest neighbor ring.*

a segment of k real numbers between two neighboring processors is of the form:

$$ST(k) = \alpha + \beta k.$$

This is accurate for the Caltech Hypercube, but is a simplification for the Intel iPSC since the formula does not model the communication cost correctly over the whole range of permissible message lengths. From Fig. 3 we notice that messages shorter than 1024 bytes (256 reals) all take essentially the same time. This is an important case which we have included in our analyses by using different values α_{long} and β_{long} for long messages, and α_{short} and β_{short} for short messages.

We have derived estimates for the coefficients α and β from the data displayed in Fig. 3. The data for the lower curve in this figure was obtained by measuring the time necessary to send a message around a 128 node nearest neighbor ring. The timing represented there is then the curve $T = 128\, ST(k)$. From this we have deduced that, with times measured in microseconds,

$$\alpha_{short} = 6625, \qquad \beta_{short} = 8.28,$$
$$\alpha_{long} = 3477, \qquad \beta_{long} = 22.5.$$

These numbers are in sharp contrast with the cost γ to perform a typical arithmetic operation, which from Table 3 is seen to be of order $30\ \mu s$. In particular the ratio $\alpha_{short}/\gamma = 220$ indicates that communication of single data items is hundreds of times slower than a corresponding computation. Another parameter that appears in the analysis of some algorithms is the length λ words of a buffer used to accumulate short messages for communication in a single packet. Ideally λ should be chosen such that $\alpha/\lambda < \beta$. On the iPSC we have used $\lambda = 4096$.

For comparison we present here the corresponding data for the Caltech Hypercube. In that case a single value of α and β suffice to cover the whole range, and we find:

$$\alpha = 92, \qquad \beta = 40.$$

Thus message startup overhead becomes small as soon as even a few words are communicated between nodes, although communication rates for very long messages are about twice as slow as on the iPSC. Computation rates γ for the Caltech Hypercube are comparable to those for the iPSC. The buffer of length λ is not required at all.

The four parameters α, β, γ and λ appear in efficiency estimates throughout the paper without further comment. We also use γ as a measure of integer computation speed, for example, it is used to measure the cost of copying arrays. In addition we use N to denote the size of vectors or the dimension of arrays and we use $P = 2^D$ to denote the number of processors.

3. Hypercube simulators. An important aspect of our hypercube work was the development of a hypercube simulator for the Intel iPSC. It is difficult to develop programs for a parallel computer such as a hypercube in a reasonable period of time without access to a simulator for the machine. A simulator allows programs to be developed on faster and more robust computers, tested under conditions of moderate parallelism (we have used 4 to 16 processor simulations) and then moved to the target hardware with reasonable assurance that issues of synchronization and control are correct. One can then concentrate on the many remaining issues that can prevent successful execution, such as faulty node compilers, defective processor hardware or bad communication lines. In addition, by instrumenting a simulator one can obtain useful statistics when real codes are run. We have instrumented all of our codes, and statistics on a per-processor basis are collected on many items such as numbers and sizes of messages sent and received, amount of memory used and so on. This information is extremely helpful in pinpointing communication bottlenecks in the code. These statistics are collected by each node separately and are automatically sent on program termination to the host machine for storing in a history file. We have also instrumented the standard communication calls used on the real hypercube so that history files are obtained during actual runs as well. In § 3.3 we present a set of higher level communication routines that we have found especially useful on the Caltech Hypercube, where messages are normally of length 8 bytes.

We describe now two hypercube simulators we have developed, one for the Intel iPSC, and one for the Caltech Hypercube. These simulators may be run across a series of machines, with sets of nodes assigned to different machines. This allows for much faster simulations. We have also simulated the Caltech Hypercube on the Intel iPSC, which allows Caltech Hypercube programs to be ported directly to the iPSC without any code modification.

3.1. An Intel iPSC simulator for UNIX. We have developed an Intel iPSC simulator that uses the UNIX operating system to simulate both hypercube processes and inter-process communication. The simulator actually represents a general model of message-based parallel computation and can be used to simulate various different architectures. We use the operating system to implement processes, the directory tree to implement nodes and the file system to implement message passing. Each hypercube node is assigned a subdirectory of the running directory, with the directory name being the hypercube node number. The hypercube host is assigned to a host subdirectory. Each process running on that node is assigned to a subsubdirectory, again numbered in relation to the number of processes on the node. Thus process *pid* on node *node* resides in directory *./node/pid*.

The simulator starts by creating all of the relevant directories and starting up the requested programs in the appropriate directories. The processes then communicate with each other, and with the host, by exchanging files containing their messages. The procedure here is simple: a process creates a message in a message file with a name *source.seq_num* that identifies its source and also a *sequence number* from the source to the destination. The sequence number is incremented each time the source sends a message to that destination. Each process records the sequence number of the last message sent to each of the other processes, initialized to 0. Furthermore each process remembers the next expected message sequence number from each of the other processes, again initialized to 0. Once a message is complete it is moved to the appropriate destination directory. The receiving node looks for appropriately named files in its directory and on reading a file, adds the message to a linked list of messages. This list is ordered by source node, and within that by sequence number. When a message is requested of a particular type (by a *recv* or *recvw*), the list is searched for a message of that type whose sequence number is the next expected one from its source. This ensures that messages from the same source are received by programs in the order sent. If no such message is found, the process continues reading and storing incoming messages until a suitable one appears.

The simulator is independent of the mechanism for message routing. Thus various message routing systems may be added to simulate actual hardware designs. The simplest message routing uses file renaming to transmit a file to its destination directory. This simulates a fully connected network hardware in that all processes are connected to each other in a completely equivalent fashion. We have also used the *socket*-based interprocess communication facilities of 4.2bsd UNIX to implement message transmission as an alternative to file passing. However the file mechanism has the advantage of working over networks of heterogeneous systems and with various flavors of UNIX. In addition to the fully connected network, we have also simulated a hypercube network. In this case messages are passed through a sequence of *nearest-neighbor directories* in order to reach a target. We stress that for most purposes this is completely unnecessary and significantly slows the simulation since most messages must be handled several times. In fact the fully interconnected network is perfectly adequate for iPSC simulations since the iPSC software supports symmetrical communication among all processes, completely hiding the hardware.

3.2. A Caltech Hypercube simulator on the Intel iPSC. Developing a Caltech Hypercube simulator for the iPSC also proved to be useful. This allows identical codes (i.e. Caltech Hypercube codes) to be run on both machines, with a software overhead that we have measured to be under 1%.

Caltech processes are implemented as iPSC processes, with only one per node allowed. Since Caltech processes work with channel numbers, we first create a mapping of channel numbers to node numbers. The basic communication primitives such as *rdELT* and *wrtELT* (see Table 1) are then implemented using the iPSC *recvw* and *send* primitives (see Table 2). Note that Caltech protocols of reading and writing channels imply that when receiving a message the message is requested from a specific source, the node at the other end of the requested channel. On the other hand iPSC protocols do not allow for requesting receipt of messages by source location, but only by message type. We overcome this problem by using the iPSC message type to encode the source node of a message when sent. A receiver then requests a message with type equal to the desired source node number. The only complexity encountered is at the host processor. At the host, the iPSC protocol does not even allow asking for messages of a specific type; one simply reads messages as received. This issue is dealt with using a complicated buffering scheme where incoming messages are stored and ordered with respect to both sequence number and type. A Caltech Hypercube simulator for UNIX was previously written at Caltech [27] but the one developed here is different in that it is targeted at another parallel machine—the iPSC. By combining the Caltech Hypercube simulator for the iPSC with the iPSC simulator for UNIX, we have created a new Caltech Hypercube simulator for UNIX.

3.3. An object-level communication library. The Caltech Hypercube communication software deals with messages in terms of 8-byte units. This tends to lead to unpleasant code where 4 integers, or 2 floating point numbers or the like are stored into an 8-byte array for transmission. Resulting code is hard to read and prone to bugs, especially if the receiver decodes the bytes differently from the sender's encoding. On the Intel iPSC we have seen that sending lots of short messages is extremely inefficient.

We have developed a simple higher-level interface to these routines that allows objects (data-structures) of arbitrary size to be communicated between nodes and with the host with essentially optimal efficiency. In Table 4 we indicate the calling sequence of some of these routines. In addition to sending linear arrays and structured types (as in C) between processors, this library also supports communication of vectors and matrices between processes and with the host. In particular there are routines to send a globally distributed vector or matrix to the host, frequently used in printing the final results of a program. The *send_local_vectors* routine allows r vectors $v_1, \cdots, v_r$, with addresses stored in the array v and with lengths $n_1, \cdots, n_r$ stored in the array n to be sent to a neighbor. On the Caltech Hypercube this routine simply sends each vector in short segments, whereas on the Intel iPSC the vectors are first copied and concate-

TABLE 4
Communication routines.

send_structure_to_node(chan,struct,size)
recv_structure_from_node(chan,struct,size)

send_local_vectors_to_node(chan,r,n,v)
recv_local_vectors_from_node(chan,r,n,v)

send_matrix_to_node(chan,mat)
recv_matrix_from_node(chan,mat)

nated into an array of length 4096 bytes which is sent each time it fills with a single *send* call. The last segment sent may of course be shorter. Unless all of the vectors are already over 1024 bytes, this results in much more efficient iPSC communication, at the cost of copying the vectors. If some of the vectors supplied to the routine are already long, then they are sent directly to avoid the extra copying overhead. The *recv_local_vectors* routine just splits and copies incoming 4096-byte segments into r local vectors. Similarly the *send_matrix_to_node* routine buffers the rows of the matrix into large messages on the iPSC. These two routines are actually part of the vector library described in § 5.

The only nontrivial issue in the other routines is the handling of quantities whose size is not a multiple of 8 bytes. In these cases it is necessary to send a last packet containing some zero data in order that the full communication be a multiple of 8 bytes. On receiving messages this can require buffering the message first, and then copying it to its destination. In particular this occurs on reading the union of messages sent by all nodes to the host, if the messages are not a multiple of 8 bytes.

4. Hypercube interconnection topologies. The interconnection network of the hypercube can be organized in a variety of ways depending on the application. In the following subsections we consider some of these topologies since they are essential for many of the later algorithms. The cases of most importance to us are mappings of grids, trees and rings to the cube network.

4.1. Grids on hypercubes. Grids are mapped onto the hypercube using the *whoami* facility developed by J. Salmon [35]. The routine uses Binary Gray Code (BGC) sequences [36], [37] to number processors. These are sequences of numbers such that consecutive terms in the sequence differ by only one bit in their binary expansions. For example, one 4-bit BGC is the sequence (by rows):

$$0000 \ 0001 \ 0011 \ 0111 \ 1111 \ 1110 \ 1100 \ 1000$$
$$1001 \ 1011 \ 1010 \ 0010 \ 0110 \ 0100 \ 0101 \ 1101.$$

As mentioned earlier, nodes on the hypercube with processor numbers that differ in only one bit in their binary expansion are physical neighbors. If we interpret the terms in a BGC sequence as processor numbers, then nearest neighbors in the sequence will also be physical neighbors. This allows 1-dimensional grids to be mapped onto the hypercube using only nearest-neighbor connections. The generalization to higher dimensional grids is done by mapping each dimension to a suitable subcube and using the 1-dimensional mappings for those subcubes.

Certain applications require periodic grids to be mapped to the cube. The above BGC sequence is not suitable for this purpose because its last element is not a neighbor of the first one. A subclass of Gray codes, the Binary Reflected Gray Codes (BRGC), have the desired property [35]. In the sequel we will always use a canonical BRGC defined recursively as follows. With one bit the BRGC sequence is 0 1. With d-bits we take the $d-1$ bit sequence, followed by the same sequence reversed in order and with each dth bit set. Thus with two bits we have the sequence 00 01 11 10 and with four bits the sequence is:

$$0000 \ 0001 \ 0011 \ 0010 \ 0110 \ 0111 \ 0101 \ 0100$$
$$1100 \ 1101 \ 1111 \ 1110 \ 1010 \ 1011 \ 1001 \ 1000.$$

This is the standard processor ordering used by the Caltech Hypercube research group [27]. With a BRGC ordering the subcubes used for a grid whose dimensions are each a power of 2 will all be periodic, allowing periodic grids of such dimensions to be mapped to the cube. The BRGC sequence also has the property that two elements that are a power of 2 apart differ in at most two bits [38].

4.2. Trees on hypercubes. There are several ways to embed a tree onto a hypercube. The most natural trees are either binary trees or D-ary trees where D is the cube dimension. In the following discussion we choose the root of the tree to be at node 0, but any other point can be used as easily.

The observation that allows a balanced binary tree to be mapped to the hypercube, is that a D-cube may be regarded as two $(D-1)$-cubes with corresponding processors from each connected by an extra channel. Numbering the processors in the two $(D-1)$-cubes as $p_0, \cdots, p_0+2^{D-1}-1$, and $p_0+2^{D-1}, \cdots, p_0+2^D-1$, respectively, we connect processor p_0+p in the first subcube with processor p_0+p+2^{D-1} in the second subcube. The binary tree on the D-cube is then defined recursively as having the lowest numbered processor as its root and the two $(D-1)$-cubes as its left and right subtrees. Note that this is a logical binary tree only—some processors occur several times at tree nodes. For example, processor 0 occurs D times, being the root of D subtrees. Each processor is located exactly once at a leaf of the tree.

An alternative tree mapping is to represent the network as an unbalanced D-ary tree. This mapping is based on the obvious fact that D connections emanate from every node. This tree is a physical tree—each node in the tree corresponds to a unique processor. The tree may be defined either by giving the children of each node, or by specifying the parent of each node. The children of a node are the processors whose node numbers are obtained by setting in turn each of the low-order unset bits in the D-digit binary representation of the node number. Alternatively, the parent of a node is located by unsetting the lowest-order set bit in the binary representation of the node number.

These two logical trees are in reality two different ways of representing the same set of connections. Depending on the application it can be helpful to consider trees from either viewpoint. Figure 4 represents the 4-cube as a tree from these two points of view.

4.3. The hypercube network as a hierarchy of rings. As indicated above, it is possible to map a ring structure onto the hypercube by giving the processors the position of their processor number in a Binary Reflected Gray Code sequence. As a property of the binary gray codes, processors that are neighbors in this ordering (logical neighbors) are also neighbors on the Hypercube (physical neighbors). We will use the terms *logical distance* and *physical distance* in this sense throughout the rest of the paper. As noted in § 4.1, the BRGC ordering has the further property that two processors at logical distance 2^d, $d = 1, \cdots, D-1$, in the ring are at a physical distance 2. For each d in the range $1, \cdots, D-1$ there is then a collection of subrings of processors such that processors at logical distance 2^d in the subring are at physical distance 2. We call these the *level d subrings* of the hypercube. Every processor is on exactly one subring of level d. A subring connecting processors at logical distance 2^d in the main ring contains

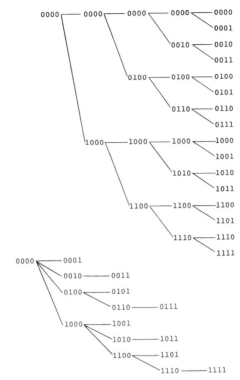

FIG. 4. *Nodes of a 4-dimensional hypercube as a balanced binary tree and as an unbalanced tree of order 4.*

2^{D-d+1} nodes, and hence there are $2^D/2^{D-d+1} = 2^{d-1}$ such subrings covering the hypercube. In Fig. 5, we display on the left the 4 logical hierarchies of rings in a 16 node (4-dimensional) hypercube which has been ordered with the BRGC. On the right, we show the actual physical communication channels used to implement the logical structures. Note that except for the level 0 ring, logical neighbors on the subrings always are separated by distance 2. We see that the main ring structure is used for the rings at levels 0 and 1. Level 2 consists of 4 logical subrings. The physical links at level 2 however form only 2 subrings, corresponding to the fact that 1 logical link requires 2 physical links. It should be noted that parallel communication is possible on all subrings at the same level.

We have implemented a library subroutine that, analogously to the *whoami* routine mentioned earlier, returns the channel information needed to use the hypercube as a hierarchy of rings. This routine starts by creating a level 0 ring, by calling the *whoami* routine to construct a 1-dimensional periodic grid. From this ring the other levels can then easily be constructed. On the Caltech Hypercube, the information returned consists of $D-1$ pairs of channels: a left and a right channel for each physical ring level. This gives a complete description of the subring hierarchy since each processor is a member of just one physical subring at each level.

5. Parallel vector operations. We describe the development of a library of vector operations on a hypercube. This description is valid for a wide range of parallel processors, including shared memory and even serial machines. All that we assume is that the processors may be organized into a 1-dimensional *ring* of processors in which each processor can communicate efficiently with its neighbors on either side. On a hypercube there are many ways to imbed such a ring onto the processor network in

LOGICAL STRUCTURE   PHYSICAL STRUCTURE

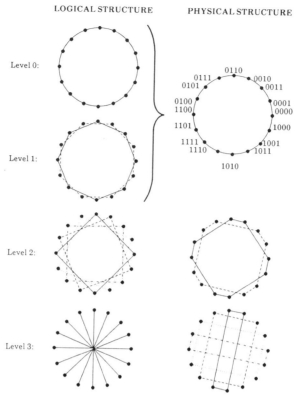

FIG. 5. *The logical hierarchies of rings in a* 16-*node hypercube and the communication channels used to implement them.*

such a way that only nearest-neighbor connections are involved (see § 4). In order to simplify notation, we assume in the following that the processor ordering $0, 1, \cdots, P - 1, 0$ is already such an optimal ring.

An important feature of this library is that individual processors work entirely with a local vector and are never aware of the location of other parts of the distributed vector. This is true even with operations such as *inner_product* which involve communication between different processors. Furthermore the operations on local vectors are themselves vector operations. Thus the library could take full advantage of an available vector processor on each node.

5.1. Distributed vectors. We use a consistent scheme for distributing all vectors over the P processors. We consider here only vectors of length $N \geqq P$. We divide the vector into P contiguous and roughly equal-length segments. It is then possible to distribute a segment to each of the P processors. We will call a vector stored in this way, a *distributed vector*. We will assume that every distributed vector of the same length is distributed in the same way over the processors, i.e. segments of different vectors residing in the same processor have the same length. The actual distribution formula we have used is as follows. We divide the vector length N by the number of processors:

$$N = hP + r, \qquad 0 \leqq r < P.$$

The first r processors will be assigned segments of length $h + 1$ elements and the remaining $P - r$ processors will be assigned segments containing h elements. In the case that P divides N exactly, all segments are then of size $h = N/P$.

To create a distributed vector of length N, all processors call an allocation routine:

$$v = allocate\_vector(N, type).$$

Several types of vector representation are supported, of which the most important types are called SIMPLE and SHIFT. The SIMPLE form represents each vector segment as an array of length h or $h + 1$. In addition to performing the above computation for the segment length in each processor, this routine allocates storage for the array and returns a pointer to a data structure v which represents the vector. The data structure records the type, local segment length and a pointer to the start of the vector. In the SHIFT format, each vector segment is located in a buffer of length $2h$ within which it is allowed to slide around (see the following section on shifting vectors). Initially the segment is centered in the buffer. In this case, the data structure v records the type and local segment length, pointers to the start of the segment both before and after shifting, as well as the buffer extremities. Whenever it is intended to apply the *shift_vector* operation to a vector, the vector should be allocated of type SHIFT. A library routine *convert_vector* is available to convert a vector from one type to another.

5.2. Operations on distributed vectors. We have implemented a large set of operations on such distributed vectors. Application of any such operation is accomplished by having all of the processors call the appropriate routine simultaneously, with the appropriate vector data structures as arguments. Vectors of different types may be freely mixed, as appropriate conversions are applied when needed. We list sample routines from the library, along with their purpose, in Table 5.

TABLE 5

Basic vector routines.

allocate_vector	allocate local segment of a vector
delete_vector	deallocate storage for a vector
convert_vector	change type of vector
zero_vector	$v_i = 0$
shift_vector	$v_i = v_{(i-s) \bmod N}$
max_vector	$\max_{0 \le i < N} v_i$
sum_vector	$\sum_{i=0}^{N-1} v_i$
inner_product	$\sum_{i=0}^{N-1} u_i v_i$
copy_vector_to_vector	$v_i = u_i$
add_scalar_times_vector_to_vector	$u_i = u_i + s v_i$
add_vector_to_scalar_times_vector	$u_i = s u_i + v_i$
add_vector_times_vector_to_vector	$u_i = u_i + v_i w_i$

Most of these routines are trivial to parallelize. However *shift_vector, inner_product, max_vector* and *sum_vector* involve communication between processors. We discuss these four routines in more detail in the following subsections. The remaining routines involve no communication and are optimally parallel: the corresponding operation is performed in each processor on the local segments of the vector arguments, using the standard serial code. Thus we will not discuss routines such as

$$add\_vector\_times\_vector\_to\_vector$$

any further.

5.3. The vector shift algorithm. The *shift_vector* operation consists of sliding each element of the distributed vector forward by s elements, placing the last s elements of the vector at the start. It is essential that this operation be very efficient since it is used by many of our other algorithms. For this operation we require that each vector segment is of at least length one, or, in other words, that each processor contains at least one element of the vector.

We discuss first the simple case of a short shift of length 1. Most of the shifting will occur internal to a processor. If there are h elements in a segment, the cost of sliding the segment forward is $O(h)$. In addition, each segment has to execute communication calls to send its last segment component to the following processor and to receive the last component from the previous processor. All of the internal shifting within nodes may be done in parallel, and similarly for the shifting of the segment ends, so that overall the cost of the operation appears to be $O(h)$, which is unacceptable.

We have implemented the shift operation as an $O(1)$ operation at the cost of using some extra memory in each node. The idea is to imbed the local segment of each vector in a larger buffer which extends a distance $O(h)$ (for example $h/2$) on either side of the segment. For this purpose, vectors are allocated by the *allocate_vector* routine using type *SHIFT*, see the previous section. Vectors are then shifted by simply leaving them in place, adding the new end element from a neighboring processor to the appropriate end of the local vector. The effect of this is to cause the vector to slide around in its buffer with successive shifts. The pointer to the start of the vector in the corresponding vector data structure is incremented for each shift. After $O(h)$ elementary shifts, the vector may have slid to the end of its buffer in each node. At this point an $O(h)$ operation is required to copy it back to its initial point in each processor. However one can regard this $O(h)$ operation as amortized over the $O(h)$ shifts that preceded it, so that the overall cost of a shift is still effectively $O(1)$. This copy back to the original position is automatically detected and performed by the software. When shifted vectors are involved in other vector operations, the appropriate offsets are automatically used for each vector.

The shift operation for large shifts, consisting of many one element shifts in succession, can be made even more efficient by using the full hypercube hierarchy of rings at many levels in addition to the top level ring used above. As this optimization is somewhat complex we assign the discussion to a separate section.

5.4. The optimized vector shift algorithm. Based on previous observations, we can optimize the *shift* operation for the case in which the number of shifts is large. In fact we will show that large shifts may be performed $P/\log P$ times faster than if the simple shift algorithm above were used. In the notation of the previous section, we require that $r=0$ for this algorithm, so that the length N of the vector is an exact multiple of the number of processors: $N = hP$. Thus every processor contains a segment of length h of the vector.

We introduce some useful terminology. An *element shift* will denote the logical operation that shifts a vector by one element. An *element transfer* will denote the physical communication operation between two processors required to transfer a vector element from one processor to another. Analogously, we call a *segment shift* the logical operation of shifting a vector h times. A *segment transfer* is then the communication operation between processors to transfer a segment. Note that a segment shift results in each processor transmitting its complete segment to the following processor in the ring, receiving in turn the complete segment of the preceding processor. We assume that an element transfer takes time $O(1)$ while a segment transfer takes time $O(h) = O(N/P)$. We will show that any shift can be performed in time at most $O(N \log P/P)$.

Suppose we need to shift a vector by m element shifts, where without loss of generality we assume $m > 0$. If we write

$$m = m_s h + m_e, \qquad 0 \le m_e < h,$$

we can reduce the m element shifts to m_s segment shifts and m_e element shifts. Note that if $m_s \geq P$, we can reduce it further by letting $m_s = m_s \bmod P$, since a shift of P segments is a shift of $N = hP$ elements and thus is equivalent to not shifting at all. A further immediate savings is possible by observing that when $m_s > P/2$, it is better to shift the segments in the opposite direction $m_s - P$ times. Suppose that all these reductions are done on m_s. Then the resulting m_s will be in the range $-P/2 + 1, \cdots, P/2$.

The m_e element shifts are performed separately as in the previous section. In fact they may be lumped together into one for the internal shift, which then becomes an $O(1)$ operation using the buffering mechanism described earlier. Because of the need, mentioned earlier, to occasionally copy a shifted segment back to its initial position, a better estimate of the cost of m_e internal shifts would be that it is $O(m_e)$. The m_e last elements of each segment will be sent to the following segment, resulting in a communication cost that is $O(m_e)$. Therefore the total cost of m_e element shifts is $O(m_e)$.

We now use the hierarchy of rings to speed the segment shifts. Consider the binary representation $b_{D-2} \cdots b_1 b_0$ of m_s. For each $i > 0$ such that b_i is set, we need to perform 2^i segment shifts, which reduce to just one segment shift on the logical subrings of level i. As discussed in § 4.3 this may be accomplished with just 2 shifts on the physical subrings of level i. This has the effect of performing 2^i segment shifts while taking the time of only 2 segment transfers. Bit 0 is an exception because if set it requires only one segment shift of the main ring, taking the time of one segment transfer. Thus even in the worst case, where all $D - 1$ bits in m_s are set and where the number of element shifts is $h/2$, the total time is at most:

$$T_{shift} = \{2(D-2) + 1\}T_{segment} + h/2 T_{element}$$

$$= O(\log P)O(N/P) + O(N/P).$$

Note that these estimates neglect any overhead related to sending short messages. In § 6.6.1 we present a more complete analysis of these costs. We summarize these results as two theorems:

THEOREM 1. *The time $T_{shift}(m)$ to shift a vector of length N by a distance m on a hypercube with P processors satisfies*

$$T_{shift}(m) \leq \alpha(1 + d(m)) + 2\beta d(m)N/P + (\beta + \gamma)m \bmod (N/P),$$

where $d(m)$ is the number of set bits in the binary expansion of m div N/P.

THEOREM 2. *Upper bounds for the maximum time T_{shift}^{max} and average time T_{shift}^{ave} to shift a vector of length N by a distance m on a hypercube with P processors are:*

$$T_{shift}^{max} \leq (2\beta \log P + \gamma)N/P + 2\alpha \log P,$$

$$T_{shift}^{ave} \leq (\beta \log P + \gamma)N/P + \alpha \log P.$$

The algorithm above fails if the length of the vector is not a multiple of the number of processors. In this case there are r segments of length $h + 1$ and $P - r$ segments of length h. With segment shifts, the segments of length $h + 1$ are transported to arbitrary processors. To bring the vector back to its original form (with the longer segments in the logically early processors) requires $O(N)$ element transfer operations, destroying any efficiency obtained by using segment shifts. One solution in such cases is to solve a slightly larger problem such that the length of the vectors is a multiple of P.

5.4.1. Timings for the optimized vector shift. We have measured the effectiveness of the optimized vector shift by timing shifts of various sizes for vectors of varying

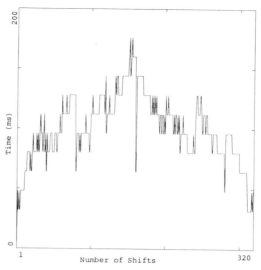

FIG. 6. *Time to shift a vector of length* 320, *distributed over the* 32 *node* iPSC (10 *elements per processor*), *as a function of the number of element shifts.*

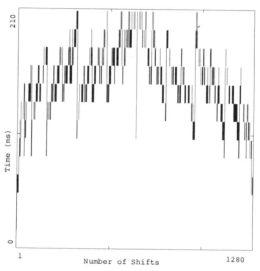

FIG. 7. *Time to shift a vector of length* 1280, *distributed over the* 128 *node* iPSC (10 *elements per processor*), *as a function of the number of element shifts.*

length and with different numbers of processors. Figure 6 shows the time required to shift a vector of length 320 on a 32-node iPSC. The graph shows the shift time as a function of the shift length, which varies from 1 to 319. Figure 7 presents the same statistics for a vector of length 1280 on a 128 node iPSC, again shifted by distances 1 through 1279. These two cases are useful to compare since the number of elements h per node segment is the same in each case, namely 10. We note that the cost of performing shifts on the larger cube is only slightly more than on the 32-node cube. Specifically the slowest shift in the 128 node case is only about 10% slower than in the 32 node case. Furthermore the variation from longest to shortest shift is comparable. Finally in Fig. 8 we present shift statistics for a vector 100 times longer, i.e., of length

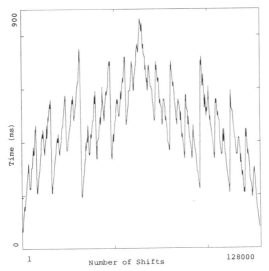

FIG. 8. *Time to shift a vector of length* 128000, *distributed over the* 128 *node* iPSC (1000 *elements per processor*), *as a function of the number of element shifts.* (*Only representative sample is displayed.*)

128000 so that there are 1000 elements per node. The shift times for the shorter vectors are dominated by the high message start-up cost of the iPSC.

5.5. Inner product. The semantics of the inner product operation in our library needs careful discussion. Each processor calls the *inner_product* routine simultaneously, providing as arguments the two vector segments local to the processor. The *inner_product* routine returns in *every* processor with the value of the inner product of the two complete distributed vectors. No processor is distinguished in these semantics.

The implementation of the routine does of course distinguish processors. The inner product operation is complicated because it involves communication between the processors to sum inner products of the segments local to each processor, and further communication to broadcast the final sum back to all of the nodes. On cube architectures, this should be done by summing over a *tree* of processors, since if one processor is used to accumulate all partial inner products, it will result in a critical section. A D-ary tree is mapped onto the processor network with node 0 as the root. The parent of a node is defined by zeroing the lowest nonzero bit of the node number while the children of a node are obtained by setting in turn exactly one of the low-order zero bits of the node number. The inner product routine then takes the form:

```
real inner_product (v1, v2):
mysum = local_inner_product(v1, v2)
for each child
      read child_sum from child
      mysum = mysum + child_sum
end for
if (node ≠ 0) send mysum to parent
if (node ≠ 0) read sum from parent
for each child
      send sum to child
end for
return sum
```

With this implementation the cost of an inner product will be $O(N/P) + O(\log P)$, with the $O(N/P)$ reduced further if vector hardware is available on the nodes. Clearly all of the local sums may be computed in parallel in time $O(N/P)$, proportional to the local segment length $h = N/P$. The sum of the partial sums over the D-ary tree may be computed in time D, if the unit of time consists of 1 real addition plus communication of a real number to a neighbor. To see this, note that the unbalanced D-ary tree rooted at node $000 \ldots 0$ contains $(D-1)$-ary, $(D-2)$-ary, $\cdots$, 0-ary subtrees rooted at its children $100 \ldots 0$, $010 \ldots 0$, $000 \ldots 1$, respectively. Assume as an induction principle that the result is true for each subtree of fanout $0, 1, \cdots, (D-1)$. The hypothesis is clearly true for $D = 0$ and $D = 1$. By the induction hypothesis, the sum from node $100 \ldots 0$ will arrive at $000 \ldots 0$ at time $D - 1$, from node $010 \ldots 0$ will arrive at time $D - 2$ and so on. Each partial sum can then be added to the total in $000 \ldots 0$ while the next partial sum arrives. It follows that all summation will be completed by time D, completing the induction. The broadcast of the result to the individual processors reverses the above steps and also requires time $O(D)$.

Following the steps in the proof in detail and using the formulation in § 2.3 for the cost of sending messages, we arrive at the result:

THEOREM 3. *The cost of performing an inner product of two vectors of length N on a hypercube with P processors satisfies*

$$T_{inner\_product} \leqq 2\gamma N/P + (2\alpha_{short} + 2\beta_{short} + \gamma) \log P.$$

We assign the same semantics to other related operations such as *max_vector* and *sum_vector*. Again *max_vector* will be called by each node with the local segment of the vector as argument and returns with the maximum component of the corresponding *global* vector in time $O(\log P)$.

In Fig. 9 we display the execution time of the *inner_product* routine for vectors of increasing size, from 1 to 950 elements per processor, on the 128 processor iPSC. The initial point on the curve is related to the high startup cost for short messages on the iPSC. Since the communication cost is independent of vector size, the curve is essentially linear, reflecting the time taken to compute the local inner products within

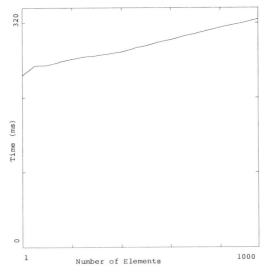

FIG. 9. *Time to compute the inner product of a distributed vector on the 128 node iPSC as a function of the number of elements per processor.*

each node. As can be seen, even for vectors of length over 120000 elements the inner product is dominated on the iPSC by the communication cost.

6. Parallel matrix operations. Distributed matrices are of special importance in numerical algorithms and we use several different representations for them depending on the application. By far the most important routines in this library are the *transpose* and *matrix_vector* operations. The library also contains routines to allocate and print matrices, to exchange submatrices among nodes, and to convert matrices from one representation to another. We summarize in Table 6 the basic matrix operations of importance. Higher level operations such as addition and multiplication of matrices are easily constructed from the basic set.

TABLE 6
Basic matrix routines.

allocate_matrix	allocates global matrix in each node
delete_matrix	deletes an allocated matrix
convert_matrix	convert between matrix formats
send_matrix_to_cube	host sends a matrix to the nodes
recv_matrix_from_host	host reads a global matrix
send_matrix_to_node	send piece of matrix to another node
recv_matrix_from_node	receive piece of matrix from another node
transpose	transpose a matrix in place
matrix_vector	global matrix times distributed vector
matrix_matrix	product of global matrices
rank1_update	rank 1 update of matrix
areal_parameters	set areal decomposition parameters
shuffle	exchange areal boundaries with neighbors

As with distributed vectors, distributed matrices are represented by small data structures in each processor that encode the location of the data, the type of the matrix representation, the array dimensions and other relevant information. This allows matrices of different types to be handled consistently. Since each processor is aware of the data representation it is working with, it is not necessary to depend on some control processor to handle flow control for matrix operations. The most important representation types are CONTIGUOUS_ROW, DISTRIBUTED_ROW, CONTIGUOUS_COLUMN, DISTRIBUTED_COLUMN, DIAGONAL and AREAL. The allocation routine has the form:

$$mat = allocate\_matrix(rows,cols,type,nsparse,sparse).$$

If *nsparse* is nonzero it indicates that the matrix is sparse, and the value of nsparse then indicates the number of nonzero rows, columns or extended diagonals according to the value of *type*. The argument *sparse* is a pointer to an array of *nsparse* integers indicating which rows, columns or extended diagonals are nonzero. Sufficient storage is set aside to store the matrix, and the data structure *mat* when returned includes the sparsity information as well as the size of and pointer to the local matrix segment stored in each processor. The sparse format supported here does not include general sparse matrices, but is adequate for a large class of matrices whose sparsity structure has a diagonal form. For type AREAL matrices the sparsity information is ignored, but certain other information is obtained in this case from the *areal_parameters* routine which must be called before any matrix of this type is allocated, see § 6.3.

6.1. Row and column matrix formats. The simplest representations of an $N \times N$ matrix are row or column oriented. We make use of two different row representations. As usual we decompose N as: $N = hP + r$, $0 \leq r < h$. In the CONTIGUOUS_ROW representation, each row is stored entirely in one processor. The first r processors contain $h + 1$ consecutive rows of the matrix, which we store contiguously as an $(h + 1) \times N$ matrix, while the remaining $P - r$ processors contain h rows of the matrix, stored as an $h \times N$ matrix. In the DISTRIBUTED_ROW representation, each row is stored as a distributed vector, with the vector segments in each processor from consecutive rows stored contiguously. This representation is fully defined by the distributed vector format discussed previously and we say no more about it here as a result. We note that the N vector segments stored in one processor form an $N \times (h + 1)$ or $N \times h$ matrix. The corresponding column representations are obvious.

The two representations are in fact closely related. Given a CONTIGUOUS_ROW representation we can convert it to the DISTRIBUTED_COLUMN form by simply transposing each of the submatrices stored in individual processors. Similar transpositions convert a DISTRIBUTED_ROW format to CONTIGUOUS_COLUMN format. Since no communications are involved, and all local transpositions may occur in parallel, the time to effect these transformations is $O(N^2/P)$.

6.2. The diagonal form of a matrix. The third representation of a matrix we call the DIAGONAL form. This form is especially convenient for matrices which have a small bandwidth or which contain only a few nonzero diagonals. We consider an $N \times N$ matrix A with rows indexed by i, columns by j, both i and j in the range $0, \cdots, N - 1$. The kth diagonal of A, where k is in the range $-(N-1), \cdots, (N-1)$, consists of those elements $A_{i,j}$ such that $j - i = k$. This diagonal contains $N - |k|$ elements. We construct *extended diagonals* D_m indexed by m in the range $0, \cdots, (N-1)$ as follows. For each $k > 0$, consider the diagonals k and $k - N$ which have, respectively, $N - k$ and k elements. It is therefore possible to construct a vector of length N, which we will index by $m = k$ and call an extended diagonal, consisting of diagonal $k - N$ in the first k components of the vector and diagonal k in the last $N - k$ components. The complete matrix A is uniquely represented by the N extended diagonals of length N. For the rest of the paper we will refer to these extended diagonals simply as diagonals.

It is convenient to introduce a matrix D whose rows are the extended diagonals of A (ordered by the index m introduced above). More compactly, we can describe D as an *index transformation* of the matrix A:

$$A_{i,j} = D_{(j-i) \bmod N, j}.$$

This notation will be used frequently in the sequel without further comment. Figure 10 displays a 6×6 matrix A and its diagonal form D.

The diagonal form of a matrix is stored on a parallel machine by representing each extended diagonal as a distributed vector. In other words the matrix D is stored in DISTRIBUTED_ROW form.

$$
A = \begin{bmatrix}
00 & 01 & 02 & 03 & 04 & 05 \\
10 & 11 & 12 & 13 & 14 & 15 \\
20 & 21 & 22 & 23 & 24 & 25 \\
30 & 31 & 32 & 33 & 34 & 35 \\
40 & 41 & 42 & 43 & 44 & 45 \\
50 & 51 & 52 & 53 & 54 & 55
\end{bmatrix}
\quad
D = \begin{bmatrix}
00 & 11 & 22 & 33 & 44 & 55 \\
50 & 01 & 12 & 23 & 34 & 45 \\
40 & 51 & 02 & 13 & 24 & 35 \\
30 & 41 & 52 & 03 & 14 & 25 \\
20 & 31 & 42 & 53 & 04 & 15 \\
10 & 21 & 32 & 43 & 54 & 05
\end{bmatrix}
$$

FIG. 10. *Conversion of a matrix A to diagonal form D.*

An important aspect of the diagonal form is that it can be constructed from the simple *CONTIGUOUS_COLUMN* or *DISTRIBUTED_ROW* form without any communication. To see this, note that from the expression above for the elements of D, the jth column of the diagonal form is a permutation of the jth column of the matrix A. Since D is stored in *DISTRIBUTED_ROW* form, each column of D is entirely within one processor (see § 6.1). As seen previously, a *CONTIGUOUS_COLUMN* or *DISTRIBUTED_ROW* matrix also has its columns local to processors. It follows that if A is in *DISTRIBUTED_ROW* form, conversion of A to the *DIAGONAL* form D involves only in-column permutations internal to each processor.

6.3. The areal form of a matrix. The *AREAL* form of a matrix is used to distribute a rectangular $N_x \times N_y$ matrix in a block-rectangular form to processors assigned to a logical rectangular $p_x \times p_y$ grid. Each block is surrounded by a dummy boundary of width b rows or columns. The boundary allows the matrix to be treated as if stored in a global memory, provided operations on it have a stencil of radius at most b. Figure 11 displays a typical areal matrix distribution in which the submatrices are chosen to be square and are surrounded by boundaries of width 1. Prior to allocating matrices of type *AREAL* the logical grid dimensions and the boundary width must be specified by a call to the library routine *areal_parameters*:

$$areal\_parameters(\,p_x,\,p_y,\,per_x,\,per_y,\,b\,).$$

This routine constructs the logical grid mapping into the hypercube and stores the resulting connectivity information and boundary width b. The routine returns an error value if the logical grid cannot be mapped to the hypercube using only nearest neighbor connections. The grid is periodic in the x or y direction according as per_x or per_y is nonzero. The mapping of a logical grid to the hypercube network has been discussed in § 4.1. Subsequent calls to *allocate_matrix* with type *AREAL* use the information stored during the last *areal_parameters* call, and this information is copied and stored in the matrix data structure returned by the allocation call.

For simplicity we assume in this section that we can factor the number of processors as $P = p_x p_y$ and that N_x and N_y are multiples of p_x and p_y, respectively: $N_x = n_x p_x$,

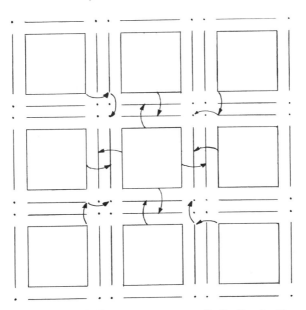

FIG. 11. *The shuffle operation on an areally distributed grid.*

$N_y = n_y p_y$. The processors may be labeled by a grid index as P_g, $g = (i, j)$ with $0 \leq i < p_y$, $0 \leq j < p_x$. The required matrix A is then conceptually split into P equal sized rectangular $n_x \times n_y$ submatrices A_g, with each assigned to a separate processor. Matrix element $a_{I,J}$ is assigned to processor $P_{I/n_y, J/n_x}$. The *allocate_matrix* routine allocates storage for these arrays in the processors along with storage for the boundary. Each submatrix is centered in an allocated matrix of size $(n_x + 2b) \times (n_y + 2b)$. Thus the block A_g is indexed as $A_{g;i,j}$ where $-b \leq i < n_y + b$, and $-b \leq j < n_x + b$. The rows and columns in the ranges $[-b, -1]$ and $[n_x, n_x + b - 1]$ or $[n_y, n_y + b - 1]$ correspond to the dummy boundary rows or columns.

The primary purpose of the boundary points is to allow copies of some matrix elements stored on neighboring processors to be available locally. The *shuffle* library operation:

$$shuffle(matrix, width, sides),$$

updates the boundary data for a submatrix by exchanging boundary rows or columns with all neighboring processors. Only the outer *width* boundary rows or columns are exchanged, although generally *width* will be chosen to coincide with the boundary width b of the matrix. The *sides* parameter specifies which of the 4 sides of the rectangles to exchange. Four symbolic constants NORTH, SOUTH, EAST, WEST are used, with values 1, 2, 4 and 8. Any set of sides may be specified by orring together the corresponding symbolic constants.

An important point to note is that the shuffle operation on the EAST or WEST sides involves sending noncontiguous data, assuming the submatrices are stored by rows. Sending the individual boundary elements is too expensive on the Intel iPSC and so these elements are first copied to a buffer of appropriate size before sending. Similarly *shuffle* receives buffered sides from neighbors, then copies the data to the appropriate noncontiguous boundary locations. We have observed that the cost of these copy operations can be a substantial fraction of the communication time; see for example Table 3.

Applications of the areal distribution of a matrix will be encountered in §§ 8 and 11. In these applications almost all communication is handled by the *shuffle* operation. An important issue is the aspect ratio of the submatrices A_g allocated to each processor. Figure 12 represents mappings of logical 8×4, 16×2 and 32×1 grids onto a 32-node hypercube, and their effect on the aspect ratio of submatrices of a distributed matrix. In principle, the shuffle operation is proportional in cost to the perimeter of a subgrid, and can be minimized for fixed subgrid area by ensuring that the subgrids are near square. We remark that on the Intel iPSC, where short messages are as expensive as those of length 1024 bytes, the shuffle operation is actually a fixed (large) cost operation. The largest real square submatrix that can be stored in an iPSC processor has about 64K elements (256K bytes) and consequently sides of length 256 elements or 1024 bytes. Thus a shuffle operation on one side consumes exactly one send and receive communication call, no matter how small the matrices are. This seriously affects the behavior of many algorithms, and also makes it essentially impossible to measure area/perimeter effects. On the Caltech Hypercube on the other hand such area/perimeter effects are readily observed, see for example Fig. 24. We summarize the overheads for *shuffle* communication in:

THEOREM 4. *The shuffle operation on a matrix of dimension $N_x \times N_y$, distributed areally on a $p_x \times p_y$ 2-dimensional mesh of processors takes time:*

$$T_{shuffle} \leq 2\beta(N_x/p_x + N_y/p_y) + 2\gamma N_y/p_y + 4\alpha,$$

where the γ term represents the cost of copying noncontiguous boundary columns.

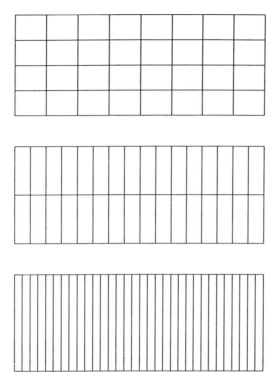

FIG. 12. *Assignment of equal area grid blocks to* 32 *processors but with different area-perimeter ratios.*

6.4. Matrix-vector multiplication. In the case of the distributed-row matrix format, matrix-vector multiplication is essentially trivial. In this case the multiplication reduces to a set of standard inner products of distributed vectors. Some communication may be saved by defining processor r to be the root of the inner product tree (rather than processor 0) when multiplying row r of the matrix with the vector—this saves the broadcast of the result to many processors that do not really need it. The time required for the matrix-vector operation is $O(N^2/P + N \log P)$. This algorithm may be extended to provide a matrix multiplication algorithm for distributed matrices. The row representation is only sensible for matrices that are more or less full, so we move on now to a discussion that is appropriate also for many sparse matrices.

We will show that the diagonal representation of a matrix, combined with the *shift_vector* operation, allows the matrix multiplication to be performed efficiently and in a highly portable fashion. To introduce the algorithm, we consider first the case of a dense matrix A where we wish to compute the product $Y = AX$:

$$Y_i = \sum_{j=0}^{N-1} A_{i,j} X_j$$

$$= \sum_{j=0}^{N-1} D_{(j-i) \bmod N, j} X_j$$

$$= \sum_{m=0}^{N-1} D_{m,(i+m) \bmod N} X_{(i+m) \bmod N}.$$

Denote by D_m the mth diagonal of A in diagonal form, by V^k the vector obtained by shifting a vector V, k times, and by $*$ the vector product of two vectors: $(u * v)_i = u_i v_i$.

Then the above equations can be written in vector form as:

$$Y = \sum_{m=0}^{N-1} D_m^m \ast X^m.$$

In the mth term of this sum both D_m and X are shifted m times. Instead of shifting both the diagonals and the vector X by the same amount, we can more efficiently shift the result vector Y by m in the opposite direction. This leads to the final form of the matrix-vector algorithm:

$$Y = 0$$
$$\text{for } m = 0, \cdots, N-1$$
$$\quad Y = Y + D_m \ast X$$
$$\quad Y = Y^{-1}$$
$$\text{end}$$

The first line in the loop of this procedure is nothing but the *add_vector_times_vector_to_vector* procedure, the second line is the *shift_vector* procedure. Parallelization of both of these operations has already been discussed above. Thus in order to parallelize this procedure is suffices to store the extended diagonals, D_m, X and Y as distributed vectors. The computation time of the matrix-vector operation consists of $O(N^2/P)$ arithmetic operations, as is usual for a full matrix, and the time for N shift operations on the vector Y, which is $O(N)$. Communication overhead—the time spent in shifts— will be negligible compared to that in computation for large matrices, defined as those with $N \gg P$.

This algorithm is perfectly acceptable for full matrices. In the case of a sparse matrix with fill-in along diagonals, such as occurs frequently in PDE discretizations, considerable savings can be accomplished. One obvious saving is that it is unnecessary to multiply with zero diagonals. However the right-hand side still must be shifted once for every diagonal. This results in savings on the number of arithmetic operations. The communication cost however remains N shift operations, although many of these can now be grouped together into longer shifts.

If the bandwidth b of the matrix A is limited, we can save on the communication cost by reducing the number of necessary shifts from N to $3b$. Matrices with bandwidth b are characterized in their diagonal forms by having a cluster of extended diagonals with indices in the range $0, \cdots, b$ and a cluster of diagonals with indices in the range $N-b, \cdots, N-1$. In this case we split the loop of vector operations describing the matrix times vector operation into two parts in the order $m = N-b, \cdots, N-1$ followed by $m = 0, \cdots, b$. We start by initializing Y to zero, which we regard as implicitly shifted $N-b-1$ times. The first loop requires $b-1$ shifts, the second b shifts. Finally, in order to get the right-hand side to its correct (unshifted) place we need to shift b times in the opposite direction. Thus we obtain the algorithm:

$$Y = 0$$
$$\text{for } m = N-b, \cdots, N-1$$
$$\quad Y = Y + D_m \ast X$$
$$\quad Y = Y^{-1}$$
$$\text{end}$$
$$\text{for } m = 0, \cdots, b$$
$$\quad Y = Y + D_m \ast X$$
$$\quad Y = Y^{-1}$$
$$\text{end}$$
$$Y = Y^b$$

This brings the total communication cost to $3b - 1$ shifts which is a very substantial saving over the full matrix case. Note that many diagonals within these nonzero bands may vanish. Shifts associated with zero diagonals should again be combined into larger shifts.

As an example, in typical planar PDE discretizations over an $M \times M$ grid the resulting matrices are of size $M^2 \times M^2$ so that $N = M^2$. Usually there are $O(1)$ nonzero diagonals and the bandwidth b is $O(M)$. Thus time spent on communication will be $O(M)$, against time $O(M^2/P)$ spent on computation. For large problems, defined as those with $M \gg P$, communication time will be dominated by computation time.

Extending the analysis above to include communication startup costs we obtain:

THEOREM 5. *On a P-processor hypercube, matrix-vector multiplication for a matrix of dimension N, with bandwidth b and with d nonzero diagonals, requires time:*

$$T_{matrix\_vector} \leq 2d\gamma N/P + \alpha d + 3\beta b.$$

In case the matrix is symmetric some savings can obviously be accomplished in memory required. However, this will result in increased communication since the diagonals have to be shifted as well as the right-hand side in one part of the calculation.

6.5. Matrix-matrix multiplication. The diagonal form is also very well suited to matrix multiplication:

$$C \leftarrow C + A * B,$$

with A, B and C square matrices of dimension N. In describing the algorithm, we will use a simplified notation in which lower case characters refer to elements of the matrix, while upper case characters refer to elements of the diagonal form. Thus, we have that:

$$a_{i,j} = A_{(j-i) \bmod N, j}.$$

We will further simplify expressions by performing all index arithmetic modulo N for the rest of this section, so that the above formula reduces to:

$$a_{i,j} = A_{j-i,j}.$$

As in the previous section, we use singly subscripted capital letters to represent the extended diagonals. We also use the superscript notation introduced above for vector shifts and $*$ for element-wise vector products.

With the above notation, the classical matrix multiplication formula becomes:

$$C_{j-i,j} = \sum_{k=0}^{N-1} A_{k-i,k} B_{j-k,j}.$$

With $p = j - i$, and $q = j - k$ we have:

$$C_{p,j} = \sum_{q=0}^{N-1} A_{p-q,j-q} B_{q,j}.$$

In vector form, using diagonals of A and B and the vector product, this formula reduces to:

$$C_p = \sum_{q=0}^{N-1} A_{p-q}^{-q} * B_q.$$

It is now easily shown that the following algorithm implements the operation, using only fully parallel operations:

$$
\begin{aligned}
&\text{for } q = 0, \cdots, N-1 \\
&\quad \text{for } p = 0, \cdots, N-1 \\
&\quad\quad C_p \leftarrow C_p + A_{p-q} * B_q \\
&\quad\quad A_{p-q} \leftarrow A_{p-q}^{-1} \\
&\quad \text{end for} \\
&\text{end for}
\end{aligned}
$$

The first line in the loop is the *add_vector_times_vector_to_vector* procedure, which is trivially parallel. The second line is the *shift_vector* procedure. Note that after the operation, all matrices, including A, are in their original form. Only the diagonals of A need to be stored as distributed vectors of type *SHIFT*.

For full matrices, this operation requires one communication operation (time to transfer one floating point variable) for every $2N$ floating point operations. More precisely, the following theorem is valid:

THEOREM 6. *On a P-processor hypercube, matrix-matrix multiplication for full matrices of dimension N, takes time*

$$
T_{matrix\_matrix} \lesseqgtr \gamma N^3 / P + (\alpha + \beta) N^2,
$$

where the γ term represents the combined cost of a floating point multiply and addition.

For $N \gg P$ this algorithm is therefore asymptotically optimally parallel. For sparse matrices with fill-in along diagonals the loops can be easily adapted so that shifts can be grouped together when zero diagonals of B are encountered and to skip the loop body entirely whenever A_{p-q} is zero. Another refinement is possible, important even for full matrices on machines like the iPSC with high message startup cost. Shifts on all diagonals should be done within the same vector shift operation so that all values can be transmitted in one communication operation after appropriate buffering. This requires a modification to the *shift_vector* routine allowing a list of vectors to be specified.

6.6. Rank one update. The diagonal form also is suitable for implementation of rank one updates:

$$
A \leftarrow A + xy^T.
$$

The elements of the matrix $B = xy^T$ are $b_{i,j} = x_i y_j$. It follows that the diagonal form of B has elements $B_{k,j} = x_{j-k} y_j$, where we have used the notation of the previous section as well as indexing modulo N. This may be expressed in terms of vector shifts and element vector products as:

$$
B_k = x^{-k} * y.
$$

This immediately implies the following algorithm for a rank one update:

$$
\begin{aligned}
&\text{for } k = 0, \cdots, N-1 \\
&\quad A_k \leftarrow A_k + x * y \\
&\quad x \leftarrow x^{-1} \\
&\text{end for}
\end{aligned}
$$

This algorithm requires one shift for every $2N$ floating point operation. All of the arithmetic operations are optimally parallel, hence we have the following:

THEOREM 7. *On a P-processor hypercube, the rank one update of an $N \times N$ matrix takes time*

$$T_{rankone} \leqq \gamma N^2/P + (\alpha + \beta)N$$

where the γ term represents the combined cost of a floating point multiply and addition.

6.7. Parallel matrix transpose. The matrix transpose operation allows parallelization in a portable and efficient way for many 2-dimensional numerical methods, see §§ 7, 8 and 13. The goal of this operation is to convert a row distributed matrix into a column distributed matrix. We present two transpose algorithms and their implementations. The first algorithm uses the diagonal form of the matrices introduced above and the vector shift operation. For this algorithm to be efficient, the optimized vector shift algorithm which we discussed previously is crucial. The second algorithm we call the block transpose method. Both algorithms presented require a communication time proportional to $N^2 \log P/P$ floating point number transfers, where N is the dimension of the matrix and $P = 2^D$ is the size of the hypercube. These estimates are based on the assumption that the cost of communications is linear in the amount of data transferred. As discussed previously this assumption is not valid for the iPSC. In particular the transpose based on the shift algorithm is strongly affected by the startup cost for communication, and consequently appears much slower on the iPSC than the block transpose.

6.8. The shift transpose algorithm. There are two key points to understanding this transpose algorithm. First, it is easy, and requires no communication between processors, to convert a matrix from the row distributed form to the diagonal form. This issue has already been addressed in § 6.2 where the diagonal form was introduced. Secondly, it is straightforward to transpose the diagonal form. We now examine the second point in greater detail.

The element $A_{i,j}$ of the matrix A is equivalent to element $D_{(j-i) \bmod N, j}$ of the diagonal form D. The transpose A^T of the matrix A, has a diagonal form DT such that

$$DT_{(j-i) \bmod N, j} = A^T_{i,j} = A_{j,i} = D_{(i-j) \bmod N, i}.$$

From this it follows that

$$DT_{k,j} = D_{N-k,i} = D_{N-k,(j-k) \bmod N}.$$

This means that the kth diagonal of DT is the $(N-k)$th diagonal of D, shifted by k. Note that once $k > N/2$ it is cheaper and equivalent to shift by $N - k$. As a result, the cost of this algorithm, using the simple shift operation (see § 5.3), is $N(N-1)/4$ element transfers, which makes it comparable in cost to transposing the whole matrix on a serial machine. Thus this algorithm makes no effective use of parallelism! It is therefore essential to use the optimized shift operation. We show in the next subsection that the number of communication operations is then reduced asymptotically to $(\log P - 1)N^2/P$, which, apart from the $\log P$ factor, indicates almost optimal use of parallelism. For a 5D cube this is about a factor of 2 better than using the straight shift while for a 7D cube the gain is about a factor of 5.3. We will assume from now on that the shift transpose only uses the optimized version of the shift vector operation. Note however that the length of vectors must then be a multiple of the number of processors.

In the implementation of this transpose algorithm for a matrix A of DIS-TRIBUTED_ROW type, we never actually store the matrix D. Instead of storing the whole diagonal form, we allocate two distributed vectors of type SHIFT. At the kth step, extended diagonals k and $N - k$ of A are constructed in these vectors and respectively shifted by k and $-k$. Once these shift operations are performed, the diagonals are copied back to the matrix, taking care that the diagonals are interchanged correctly.

6.8.1. Communication cost for shift transpose.

THEOREM 8. *The shift transpose of an N by N matrix on a P-processor hypercube takes time*:

$$T_{shift\_transpose} \leq (\beta \log P + \gamma) N^2/P + \alpha N \log P.$$

Proof. The communication cost for transposing an $N \times N$ matrix using this algorithm is incurred by shifting the mth (extended) diagonal m times, with m taking on the values $0, \cdots, N-1$. For each m, we can find m_s and m_e such that $m = m_s h + m_e$ ($0 \leq m_e < h$), where $h = P/N$. The m element shifts required for diagonal m can be obtained by performing m_s segment shifts and m_e element shifts. As m ranges from 0 through $N-1$, m_e assumes each of the values $0, \cdots, h-1$, P times and m_s assumes each of the values $0, \cdots, P-1$, h times.

From the range of values assumed by m_e, we can determine the total cost T_e associated with the element shifts:

$$T_e = P \sum_{k=1}^{h-1} ST(k),$$

where we have used notation introduced in § 2.3. $ST(k)$ is the cost of communicating a segment of length k to a neighbor processor.

We focus our attention now on the segment shifts. Since segment shifts over more than $P/2$ processors are better done as segment shifts in the opposite direction, we can divide the set of values assumed by m_s into three subsets: $[1, P/2-1]$, $[-P/2 + 1, -1]$ and the single value $P/2$. As indicated earlier in discussing the optimized shift algorithm, the actual number of segment transfers to be performed to complete a segment shift over m_s processors is most easily determined by considering set bits in the binary representation of m_s: bit 0 represents 1 segment transfer, the other bits represent 2 physical segment transfers. Since $P = 2^D$, the values in the first range are represented by $D-1$ bits and as the range is traversed each bit is set half of the time, i.e., in $P/4$ cases. It follows that the total number of physical segment transfers for the first range of values of m_s is: $(2D-3)P/4$. The second range of m_s values requires by symmetry an identical number of segment transfers, while the final value $m_s = P/2$ requires 2 segment transfers. Since each value m_s is assumed h times and the cost of a segment transfer is $ST(h)$ it follows that the total cost of all segment shifts required in the transpose algorithm is:

$$T_s = ((D-1.5)P + 2)hST(h).$$

Adding together the quantities T_e and T_s derived above, and using the relation $ST(k) = \alpha + \beta k$ introduced in § 2.3, we obtain as the total time for the shift transpose of a full matrix:

$$T_{shift} = ((D-1.5)P + 2)h(\alpha + \beta h) + P(h-1)(\alpha + 0.5\beta h)$$

$$\leq \beta N^2 \log P/P + \alpha N \log P.$$

The term proportional to α gives the effect of message startup costs and can dominate for small N on machines such as the iPSC where $\beta \ll \alpha$. To complete the proof of the theorem we add in the computation cost related to the copying of data internal to processors.

The shift transpose algorithm is well suited to diagonally sparse matrices, whereas in the matrix-vector multiplication algorithm only the nonzero diagonals actually require shifting.

6.9. The recursive block transpose algorithm. An algorithm for transposing a matrix in a time of order $N^2 \log P/P$ is possible without requiring that the size of the matrix be a multiple of the number of processors (as was necessary for the optimized shift operations used in the previous section). Note that a 2×2 matrix is transposed by exchanging its upper right and lower left elements. This leads to the following serial algorithm to transpose a matrix [39], [28]:

$$Transpose(M):$$

$$M = \begin{bmatrix} M_{00} & M_{01} \\ M_{10} & M_{11} \end{bmatrix}$$

$$M_{01} \leftrightarrow M_{10}$$

$$Transpose(M_{00}) \qquad Transpose(M_{01})$$
$$Transpose(M_{10}) \qquad Transpose(M_{11})$$

A matrix with dimension $N = 2^L$ can be transposed by recursive application of this procedure through L levels. At the final level all matrices are 1×1 and so are trivially transposed. We indicate the first three levels in this procedure in Fig. 13, where the arrows represent block interchanges.

To implement this algorithm on a hypercube we store the matrix M in contiguous-row form and assume that its dimension N is divisible by the processor number $P = 2^D$: thus $N = h2^D$. The case where the size of the matrix is not a multiple of the number of processors does not pose significant problems. We may order the processors either according to their natural order or according to the BRGC ordering. With the natural ordering, we give up nearest neighbor connectivity of adjacent rows; however processors that are a distance 2^d apart in processor numbers differ in only one bit in their binary representation and are therefore nearest neighbors on the network. With the BRGC ordering, nearest neighbor connectivity is preserved at the cost of doubling the communication cost between such processors. As discussed in §§ 4.1 and 4.3, with BRGC order the physical distance between processors at logical distances of a power of 2 is only 2. The experiments we present in later sections were performed with the natural ordering.

At level L in the algorithm the matrices are of dimension $h2^{D-L}$ and are stored as contiguous-row distributed matrices over 2^{D-L} processors. Furthermore these processors are a contiguous sequence of processors and form a $(D-L)$-dimensional subcube of the hypercube. At level D all submatrices are local to one processor and may then be transposed by the normal serial algorithm. Thus we terminate the recursion at level D.

The crucial point in analyzing this algorithm is that the interchange of the upper right and lower left subblock at level L involves communication between processors with processor numbers differing by 2^{D-L-1}; hence the two communicating processors are at a physical distance of 1 (or 2 if BRGC ordering is used). In principle the transpose of the 4 subblocks can be done in parallel. However since the 4 blocks are distributed over only 2 subcubes, the effective parallelism is only 2. Equivalently, the two upper blocks span the same set of processors; the two lower blocks also span a common set of processors. The total time for this algorithm is asymptotically $O(N^2 \log P/P)$ as shown in the following subsection.

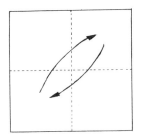

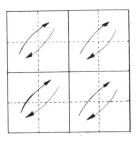

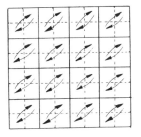

FIG. 13. *Schematic representation of the block transpose algorithm as it would be executed on a 2-dimensional hypercube (4 processors).*

6.9.1. Communication cost for the block transpose algorithm.

THEOREM 9. *The block transpose of an N by N matrix on a P-processor hypercube takes time:*

$$T_{block\_transpose} \leqq ((\alpha/\lambda + \beta + \gamma) \log P + 1.5\gamma) N^2/P + 2(\alpha + \beta\lambda) P.$$

Proof. The fundamental communication taking place in the block transpose algorithm is the transfer of a block of k rows of length l (the submatrices) from one processor to a nearest neighbor processor (assuming natural ordering). The cost associated with this transfer, which we denote by $BT(k, l)$, depends on the implementation details of the transfer, and we consider three possibilities. The most efficient solution is to send a contiguous array of kl elements, entailing a block transfer cost of:

$$BT^1(k, l) = ST(kl),$$

where $ST(k)$ is the segment transfer cost introduced in § 2.3. The rows of the individual submatrices are not stored contiguously however. This makes it more convenient to send over individual rows of the matrix one by one, in which case we obtain

$$BT^2(k, l) = kST(l).$$

Because of the high cost of sending short messages, this procedure is very expensive on the iPSC. We avoid this by using a buffering scheme to collect the noncontiguous rows before transmission. In practice this is accomplished by calling the *send_local_vectors* routine from the vector library, see § 3.3. With a limited buffer length λ, and including time necessary to copy the data into the buffer, the estimated communication time is:

$$BT^3(k, l) = (kl)/\lambda ST(\lambda) + \sigma ST((kl) \bmod \lambda) + \gamma kl,$$

where in the first term integer division by λ is assumed and σ is 0 if kl is a multiple of λ and is 1 otherwise.

Consider now a $2^d h \times 2^d h$ matrix on a d-dimensional hypercube. To exchange the upper right submatrix with the lower left submatrix we use the above transfer operation. Both submatrices have dimensions $2^{d-1}h \times 2^{d-1}h$, each distributed over 2^{d-1} processors. Thus each processor contains a block of h rows of length $2^{d-1}h$. Thus the total interchange of the two submatrices requires time $2BT(h, 2^{d-1}h)$.

Let B_d be the *communication* time required to block transpose a matrix of dimension $2^d h \times 2^d h$ on a d-dimensional hypercube, which we call a level d transpose. As indicated above, the level d transpose is reduced to a block exchange plus four level $(d-1)$ transpose operations. Using the block transfer time introduced above, and the fact that the effective parallelism in the submatrix transposes is 2, we therefore obtain the following recursion relation:

$$B_d = 2B_{d-1} + 2BT(h, 2^{d-1}h),$$

with an initial value $B_0 = 0$. It follows that:

$$B_D = P \sum_{i=0}^{D-1} 2^{-i} BT(h, 2^i h).$$

We can now substitute the appropriate expression for BT^i in terms of ST and use the relation $ST(k) = \alpha + \beta k$ from § 2.3. We obtain as bounds for communication cost in transposing an $N \times N$ matrix, where $N = Ph = 2^D h$:

$$B_D^1 \leqq 2\alpha P + \beta N^2 \log P/P,$$

$$B_D^2 \leqq 2\alpha N + \beta N^2 \log P/P,$$

$$B_D^3 \leqq 2(\alpha + \beta \lambda) P + (\alpha/\lambda + \beta + \gamma) N^2 \log P/P.$$

We notice that for asymptotically large N, the buffered mechanism is the most expensive as expected since for large enough N the individual rows exceed the buffer length. Since the first method is not practical due to the matrix storage scheme, the second method is therefore indicated for large matrices. For smaller matrices on a machine like the iPSC the third method has a great advantage because of the smaller coefficient of the term proportional to α, the message startup cost. In fact using actual iPSC measurements we find that for all but the largest matrices that will fit on the hardware, the term proportional to α plays a dominant role, making the buffered scheme a necessity. To complete the proof of the theorem, we add the computation cost involved in performing P serial transposes of $N/P \times N/P$ matrices in each processor, which consumes time $3/2\gamma N(N/P - 1)$.

6.10. A comparison of transpose algorithms on the iPSC. We now compare the best block transpose method with the shift transpose. From the higher order terms in

N it would seem that both methods are equivalent as far as communication time is concerned. The linear term in the shift transpose cost however dominates for practical problems on the iPSC. Even for the largest matrix that can be stored on the iPSC (2048×2048), the segment length of the distributed vectors used in the algorithm is only 16. This means that all communications taking place are well under the effective minimum message length of 1024 bytes or 256 floating point variables. For the block transpose, the number of floating point variables per message is proportional to N^2/P^2. For the largest problem this is 256 elements per smallest submatrix encountered. Therefore only the values of α and β for long messages play a role if the buffering scheme described above is used. For smaller problems, the short message values influence timings in the exchange of the smaller submatrices. These remarks are borne out by the coefficient of the term proportional to α in Theorems 8 and 9. In the shift transpose case this coefficient is proportional to N while in the block transpose case it is proportional to P and is in fact therefore independent of matrix size.

For clarity, we have neglected the "computation" cost in some formulae above, although this is included in the theorem statements. The basic computation unit for the transpose algorithms is the assignment of an indexed floating point variable, i.e., a statement of the form: $x = y_i$. Assuming this statement takes time γ, we have expressed the computation time as a multiple of γ in Theorems 8 and 9. For the algorithms studied, executed on the iPSC, these costs turn out to be negligible. For example we find that the "computation" cost on a 128 node iPSC for a 2048×2048 matrix is about 10% of the measured transpose time. Thus the transpose is dominated by communication.

6.11. Results and timings. In the figures for this section we always display times as a function of matrix *size*, i.e., of the number of elements N^2. On a serial machine the cost of matrix transpose is a linear function of its size. In Fig. 14 we display the cost of transposing a matrix on the 5D Caltech Hypercube as a function of the size of the matrix. The timings displayed use the transpose algorithm based on the diagonal form and the nonoptimized vector shift operation.

Figure 15 presents corresponding timings for the optimized shift transpose algorithm and the block transpose algorithm as a function of matrix size N^2 on the 128 processor iPSC. Note that, for the largest matrix that can be stored on the iPSC (dimension 2048), the block transpose is much faster than the shift transpose, despite the fact that the latter is asymptotically slightly faster. The linear form of the block transpose curve indicates that that algorithm has already attained its asymptotic behavior. In Fig. 16 we display the timing for the block transpose on a better scale where it becomes clear that the curve has in fact approached its asymptotic rate after an initial high startup overhead for small matrices.

7. Transpose splitting algorithms. We introduce here a general class of algorithms which may be solved on parallel machines with almost no modification to an appropriate serial program. We term these algorithms *Transpose Splitting Algorithms* because the application of a grid point operation is split into two parts: one applied to the x-direction and one to the y-direction. Examples are operator-splitting hyperbolic methods and ADI methods, though many other algorithms may be recognized to be of this type.

Consider a 2-dimensional function $M(x, y)$ on a grid, where x, y label the rows and columns of grid points. We store the values of M as a contiguous-row distributed matrix (see § 6.1), with one or more complete rows of points per processor. Many numerical algorithms amount to applying one or more operations $O(x, y)$ successively

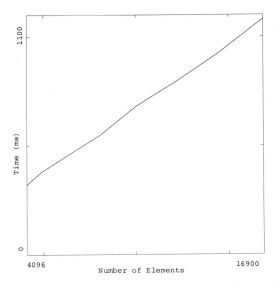

FIG. 14. *Cost of transposing a matrix on the 32 node Caltech Hypercube as a function of the number of elements. Transposing using the nonoptimized vector shift algorithm.*

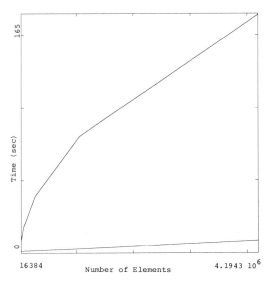

FIG. 15. *Time to transpose a matrix with the shift transpose (upper curve) and the block transpose (lower curve) algorithm, respectively, on the 128 node iPSC as a function of the number of elements.*

to M at each point x, y, which we denote by the notation $O() \cdot M()$. This would be represented in code as a loop of the form:

$$\text{for } each \ x, y: \ O(x, y) \cdot M().$$

Suppose that the operation O may be split into x and y parts which we represent schematically as:

$$O(x, y) = B(y) \cdot A(x), \ x, y \ in \ grid.$$

Now assume that $A(x) \cdot M(x, y)$ applied at point x, y uses only values $M(x, y)$ from the same row y containing the point. Similarly we assume that $B(y)$ applied at x, y

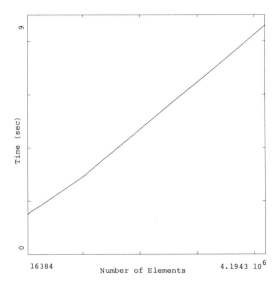

FIG. 16. *Time to transpose a matrix with the block transpose algorithm on the* 128 *node* iPSC *as a function of the number of elements.*

uses only values $M(x, y)$ from the same column x. An equivalent code segment for application of O would then be:

for *each y*
    for *each x*: $A(x) \cdot M()$
for *each x*
    for *each y*: $B(y) \cdot AM()$

Note that in the application of A the inner loop is along a row, and since $A()$ involves only elements from the same row, and since each row is entirely in one processor, it follows that the inner loop involves no communication whatever. The outer loop, the loop over rows, also involves no communication and is furthermore completely parallelized. Thus A may be applied to M without communication and in an optimally parallel fashion.

Unfortunately the loop with B is not so nice. Here there is communication every time that B involves adjacent column elements that happen to be in different processors. However there is a trivial trick that removes all communication from the B loop and also parallelizes it. The idea here is first to apply a transpose to M, or rather to the matrix $A \cdot M$. Then the roles of x, y in the B loop are reversed and the relevant code becomes:

$N = transpose(A \cdot M)$
for *each y*
    for *each x*: $B(x) \cdot N()$

All communication between processors in the application of O to M is now hidden in the transpose operation. Outside of this the code is optimally parallel.

Even for situations in which $A(x)$ applied at point x, y uses values of $M(x, y)$ from another row, this algorithm can still provide a useful approach to parallelism. To accomplish this one stores the matrix M in AREAL form but in the extreme case where the processors are assigned as a $1 \times P$ matrix. Then a vertical *shuffle* is used to ensure that the data required by $A(x)$ when operating on boundary rows of subgrids are available as needed. After a transpose and *shuffle* the data required for B will also be available as needed.

8. Hyperbolic equations. The hyperbolic equations we have studied are of the form of conservation laws:

$$\frac{\partial u}{\partial t} = -\nabla \cdot F(u).$$

The nonlinearity of the function $F(u)$ may result in the formation of discontinuities (shocks) in a finite time. Hence, the numerical methods used to solve such equations must also be able to handle discontinuities of the solution. The random choice method [40] is one solution method that is sensitive to shocks. We have also implemented simple finite-difference schemes such as the Lax–Wendroff method [41].

We have parallelized the hyperbolic solution in several different ways. In one approach, the parallelization of these methods is a typical application of the transpose splitting strategy, which we have discussed as a general method in § 7. The application to hyperbolic equations will be given in § 8.3. Another approach is based on decomposition of the rectangular grids into rectangular subgrids of near-square aspect ratio, with each subgrid assigned to a separate processor, see §§ 6.3 and 8.2. We have implemented the first approach on the Caltech Hypercube. We compare both methods on the Intel iPSC and conclude that the former involves substantially less development effort, while yielding comparable efficiency to the latter approach.

Our test problems have been model hyperbolic equations—scalar equations with simple nonlinearities. Real physical problems involve complex equations of state and may require substantial amounts of numerical computation per grid point. Real problems typically involve only the same communication costs as the model problems however, unless they are discretized using very high-order schemes. To assess the behavior of hypercubes on such codes, we use the same hyperbolic solvers mentioned above, but with a dummy nonlinear function that simply executes n floating point operations. We preserve all communication operations exactly as they would be in the hyperbolic solver. This allows us to measure efficiency as a function of work done per grid point, and of the number of grid points. The results of these studies are very favorable. If significant amounts of work are done per grid point, hypercubes can provide near optimal efficiency even on very coarse grids, down to a few dozen points per processor. The crucial point here is that the model problems already perform well. This ensures that real problems will perform even more successfully. In these studies we use the *computational efficiency* of a program, defined as the ratio of computation time to execution time of the program, as a measure of communication performance. These results are discussed in detail in § 9, although the methods used to parallelize the programs are developed in this section.

8.1. Discretization methods. We have developed parallel hyperbolic equation solvers based on both finite difference and random choice methods. While standard difference schemes vectorize easily, this may not be so for the random choice method since different random sequences may be used in different spatial locations and because the underlying Riemann solutions generally involve complex logic. However random choice parallelizes as easily as do difference methods. In addition, realistic physical problems involve complex equations of state which may be difficult to vectorize, but

again these parallelize readily. These are examples where MIMD parallelism has a
real advantage over SIMD parallelism.

The random choice method (RCM in the sequel) is a general purpose solution
method for hyperbolic conservation laws, allowing formation of shocks without affect-
ing convergence of the method. A fundamental building block of the method is the
1-dimensional Riemann solver for the conservation law under consideration. Given a
step function at time t describing two constant states connected with each other through
a shock, the Riemann solver returns the solution for the given conservation law at time
$t + \Delta t$.

The RCM uses a Riemann solver to construct approximate solutions of 1-
dimensional conservation laws for all time. The function describing the state at time
t is approximated by a sequence of step functions. At each jump of the step function
a Riemann problem is solved, resulting in a solution that is no longer piecewise constant.
The process is then repeated. To extract a step function from an approximate solution,
a random point is chosen in each of the elementary Riemann solutions. It can be
shown [40], [42] that this method converges to the correct solution even in the case
that shocks are present in the system. In two dimensions, the RCM can still be applied
using operator splitting, first performing 1-dimensional random choice solutions along
each row, and then along each column.

In parallelizing this method we have distributed the state variables $u(x, y)$ in
several ways. We have represented the solution as both an areal-distributed grid
function, using a distributed matrix of type AREAL, and as a row-distributed grid
function, using a distributed matrix of type CONTIGUOUS_ROW—see §§ 6.1 and 6.3 for
discussion of these matrix types. The communication pattern varies with the distribution
scheme and we analyze the communication costs of each scheme in the following
subsections. In the areal case communication is provided by the *shuffle* operation
whereas for the row case the *transpose* operation is used. There is one further issue
involved in the parallelization. As is normal for explicit hyperbolic solution methods,
the length of the time-step Δt is constrained by a Courant condition based on the
maximum wave speed. The computation of the maximum wave speed uses the *max_vec-
tor* routine to compute the global maximum of the local processor maxima and
broadcast the results back to the individual processors. Because of the semantics of
the *max_vector* routine, all processors can compute the new time step independently
of each other, although of course they obtain the same result. As a result the algorithm
is completely independent of node location in the network. With both distribution
methods all communication is handled entirely by the vector and matrix libraries.

The same parallelization schemes can be applied to finite difference schemes. In
addition to random choice we have used the Lax–Wendroff method [41]. The key
point is that both methods involve only local stencils of a few grid points. For the
row-distribution method it is also important that the discretization scheme be amenable
to operator splitting.

8.2. Areal decomposition. In the areal decomposition, a logical $p_x \times p_y$ rectangular
grid is mapped onto the hypercube network as discussed in § 4.1. Thus the processors
may be labeled by a grid index as p_g, $g = (i, j)$ with $0 \leq i < p_y$, $0 \leq j < p_x$. For simplicity
we assume in this section that we can factor the number of processors as $P = p_x p_y$ and
that the computational domain is a rectangular $N_x \times N_y$ grid where $N_x = p_x n_x$ and
$N_y = p_y n_y$. A grid function $U = \{U_g\}$ representing the solution values of the hyperbolic
equation on the $N_x \times N_y$ grid is now allocated as a distributed matrix of AREAL type
with boundary width 1 as described in §§ 6.1 and 6.3. Thus the component U_g is

indexed as $U_{g;i,j}$ where $-1 \leq i \leq n_y$, $-1 \leq j \leq n_x$, with the rows and columns numbered -1 and n_x or n_y being the extra boundary rows. To perform the hyperbolic time step computation on the grid, a *shuffle* operation, see § 6.3, is first performed in order to fill the boundary perimeter of each U_g with the appropriate values from the neighboring subgrids. Following this, the standard sequential hyperbolic method is performed in the interior of each subgrid, i.e., for rows and columns in the range $[0, n_y-1] \times [0, n_x-1]$. In the course of this computation the maximum wave speed within that subgrid is computed, and is stored into the local component of a distributed vector of length P. The final phase in the solution is the computation of a new time step, which is based on a Courant condition involving the maximum wave speed. To compute the maximum wave speed, the *max_vector* operation is applied to the vector of local maxima, which provides the global maximum value to all of the processors (see § 5.5 for the semantics of *inner_product* and *max_vector*). This allows all of the processors to compute the next time step simultaneously, using only vector/matrix library routines for all communication activities, and ensuring an SIMD form for the computation in cases where the local discretization operation is translation independent.

8.2.1. Communication costs. For simplicity of analysis, we begin by assuming that the number of processors is a perfect square, $P = p^2$, and that the computational domain is a square grid of N points, with $N = n^2 p^2$. Thus there are n^2 grid points per processor. For any hyperbolic scheme, the computation to be performed per grid point is a local operation in grid space and thus we regard the basic computation per grid point as an $O(1)$ operation. We stress that it may in fact be a large number if the physics or the discretization method is complex. Consequently the cost of the hyperbolic sweep over a subgrid is $O(n^2)$, proportional to the area of the subgrid. Since all subgrids are computed in parallel, this is also the cost of the sweep over the whole grid. The cost of the shuffle exchange operation at the start of the time step is $O(n)$, since the amount of data to be transferred is proportional to the perimeter of the subgrids, and the communications for different subgrids are performed in parallel. Finally the time step computation involves a cost of $O(\log P)$, which is essentially negligible since the maximum is evaluated over a tree. It follows that the computation time per time step for the complete hyperbolic solution is $O(n^2)$, i.e., $O(N/P)$, and that communication costs are negligible compared to computation costs provided only that sufficiently many grid points are stored in each processor, *independent* of the number of processors. Equivalently, the computational efficiency of the algorithm is given by:

$$E = T_{computation} / T_{execution} = \frac{1}{1 + O(1/n)}.$$

If the time step had been evaluated by accumulating the maxima in a single processor, then the time step computation would be $O(P)$ and might actually dominate for problems such that $N < P^2$. We remark that machines which involve a high overhead for sending short messages provide especially poor performance for the areal algorithm on coarse grids, since the subgrid perimeters may be smaller than the effective minimum packet size. In particular, on the Intel iPSC the effective minimum packet size is 1024 bytes, so that a subgrid edge must contain at least 256 points for fully efficient communication. Thus a subgrid would contain 65536 grid points, close to the maximum available user memory (about 275K bytes including the program). Below this size the above analysis is not strictly accurate, since the cost of a boundary shuffle should be taken as $O(\alpha + \beta n)$ in the notation of § 2.3, resulting in a much lower efficiency for small n when α is large as in the iPSC case. In this case the efficiency has the asymptotic form:

$$E = \frac{1}{1 + O(\alpha/n^2 + \beta/n)}.$$

Returning to the more general case of rectangular subgrids, we now study the behavior of the computational efficiency as a function of the aspect ratio $a = n_x/n_y$, the ratio of height to width of the subgrid, where we assume without loss that $n_x \leq n_y$. The computation cost is $O(n_x n_y)$, whereas the communication cost is $O(n_x + n_y)$, ignoring the time step cost. It follows that the computational efficiency of the algorithm is:

$$E = T_{computation}/T_{execution} = \frac{1}{1 + O(1/n_x + 1/n_y)}.$$

This expression is maximized for fixed subgrid size $n_x n_y$ when $n_x = n_y$, which corresponds to the case of square subgrids. The efficiency is minimized by allowing n_x to be as small as possible, which occurs if $p_x = P$ and $p_y = 1$ corresponding to the bottom configuration in Fig. 12. This corresponds to a linear decomposition in which whole columns are distributed to each processor, so that the state variables are effectively represented as a contiguous-column matrix. Assuming that the overall grid is square so that $N_x = N_y$, it follows that $n_x = \sqrt{N}/P$, and $n_y = \sqrt{N}$. Correspondingly the minimal efficiency may then be expressed as:

$$E = \frac{1}{1 + O(P/n_x n_y)^{1/2}},$$

where we note that $n_x n_y$ is the number of grid points per processor. The efficiency may no longer be close to 1 if the number of processors exceeds the number of grid points per processor. In particular, for fixed processor memory size (which limits the subgrid size $n_x n_y$), the efficiency goes to 0 as larger problems are solved with correspondingly more processors.

8.3. Linear decomposition + transpose. For this section we assume that the hyperbolic discretization method is of operator splitting type and consists of a grid sweep with a horizontal stencil operator in the x direction, followed by a grid sweep with a vertical stencil operator in the y direction. We are then in a position to apply the transpose splitting parallelization discussed in § 7. Thus the state variables are distributed as a matrix in CONTIGUOUS_ROW form, in the notation of § 6.1. In particular, N/P rows of grid points are assigned to each processor. The hyperbolic sweep (1-dimensional) is now applied to each row, involving no communication cost since all required stencil values are in a single row and are thus local to a processor. Following this, the matrix of state values is transposed, so that effectively it is now in CONTIGUOUS_COLUMN form. Then the hyperbolic sweep is applied in the y-direction, which now means along rows, and thus again no communication is required. Finally the time step is computed using the max_vector routine. In the following time step we perform the y-sweep before the x-sweep which saves on performing one transpose per time-step. This algorithm differs from the corresponding algorithm on a shared memory machine or on a serial machine only in one line—the presence of the matrix transpose. Indeed, even on a serial machine there may be an advantage in performing the transpose if there is a hardware cache present.

8.3.1. Communication costs. As usual, the computation cost is proportional to the number of grid points per processor and is thus $O(N/P)$. The only communication costs in this version of the algorithm are the transpose and the negligible $O(\log P)$ cost of the *max_vector* routine. As discussed in § 6.7, the transpose may be performed using the block transpose algorithm in $O(N \log P/P)$ time. It appears that communication is comparable to computation on all size machines. In fact communication is always small compared to computation, because the stencil operation performed per grid point in a nonlinear conservation law is typically nontrivial, i.e., has a large value for its $O(1)$ cost compared to the corresponding $O(1)$ cost for the communication. We note that since the block transpose communicates matrix elements in long sequences (see § 6.7), this algorithm behaves well even on machines with a high overhead for communicating short messages. This is borne out in the iPSC experiments reported below.

8.4. Timing and results for hyperbolic equations. In Fig. 17, the time used on the 32 node Caltech Hypercube to perform a random choice method iteration step is given as a function of the size N of the problem. The method used was the operator splitting algorithm with transpose. The lower curve in this figure is the time needed to transpose the solution matrix. The transpose algorithm in these timings used the nonoptimized vector shift operation. Even in this case, the communication cost (transpose) is already dominated by the computation cost.

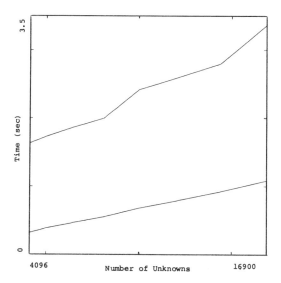

FIG. 17. *Iteration time for the random choice method on the 32 node Caltech Hypercube versus size of the problem. The lower curve is the time necessary to transpose the matrix (shift transpose with nonoptimized vector shift).*

Analogously, Figs. 18 and 19 give the iteration time and the computational efficiency of the random choice method as a function of the size of the problem on the 128 node iPSC. In these iPSC calculations the recursive block transpose algorithm was used instead of the shift transpose used in the Caltech calculations. In Fig. 18 we note that as the grid becomes large both the computation and transpose times are converging to straight lines as expected from the previous discussion—times proportional to the number of grid points N. However the transpose time has a smaller slope, ensuring that it will always be dominated by computation time. For very small grid sizes however one can clearly see from Fig. 18 that the transpose cost dominates the

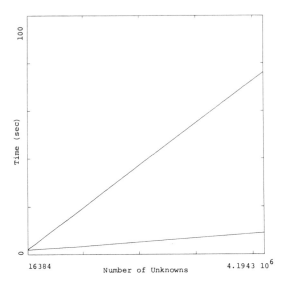

FIG. 18. *Iteration time for the random choice method on the* 128 *node* iPSC *versus size of the problem. The lower curve is the time spent in communication (transpose time with block transpose algorithm and computation of global maximum speeds for the Courant condition).*

computation due to the high communication startup cost on the iPSC. This shows up more clearly in Fig. 19 where computational efficiencies are poor for very coarse grids. For the Lax–Wendroff method using either of the transpose algorithms, we obtained equivalent results.

We have also used the areal decomposition technique for each of the methods, with rectangular subgrids ranging in shape from near square to thin strips. As an example, we display in Fig. 20 the scaled time step cost for the areal-distributed Lax–Wendroff method on a 32 node iPSC as a function of the number of unknowns in the problem. Here the time per time step has been divided by the number of grid

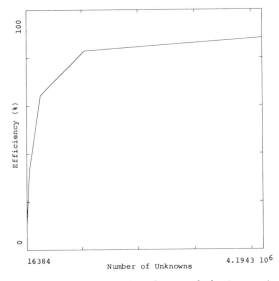

FIG. 19. *Computational efficiency of the random choice method using matrix transpose versus size of problem on the* 128 *node* iPSC.

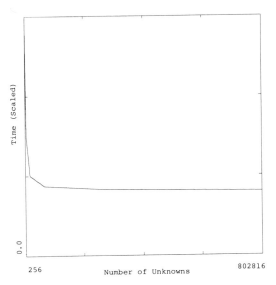

FIG. 20. *Effective processing time per grid point as a function of the problem size (number of unknowns) for the areal decomposition Lax–Wendroff method on the 32 node iPSC.*

points to arrive at a measure of effective processing time per grid point and to allow comparison of different grid sizes. The areal decomposition in this case corresponded to mapping the 32 processors onto an 8×4 rectangular grid. The scaled time decreases rapidly to a limiting value as the grid size increases, corresponding to increasing computational efficiency. The scaled time is proportional in fact to the inverse of computational efficiency.

Table 7 indicates the effect of the area-perimeter law as a function of subgrid rectangle shape on the iPSC for a fixed-size solution. The 128 processors are mapped to logical rectangular $p_x \times p_y$ grids of dimensions 16×8, 32×4, 64×2 and 128×1, respectively, and the 4,096,000 unknowns are then distributed to the processors as indicated previously. As discussed above it is extremely difficult to measure the area-perimeter effect on the iPSC because startup time dominates communication. This is borne out clearly in the table. The near-square 16×8 grid is slightly faster than the following two more rectangular mappings, but the linear distribution is fastest. The explanation is that the linear distribution is a limiting case and involves special effects. For example, no communication is required across two of the sides in a linear distribution. Thus only the first three entries in the table are really relevant and the observed area-perimeter effect is small. For comparison with the Caltech Hypercube, we refer to the corresponding Fig. 24 where aspect ratio effects are quite pronounced.

TABLE 7

iPSC area-perimeter effect.

p_x	p_y	Time (secs/iteration)
16	8	94.576
32	4	95.248
64	2	95.376
128	1	91.968

9. Comparison of algorithms and architectures. In this section we discuss the amount of computational work per grid point that is necessary to maintain efficient use of the hypercube in typical numerical procedures. For this purpose we define the *computational efficiency E* of a program running on a parallel computer as the ratio of computation time to total execution time:

$$E = \frac{T_{computation}}{T_{execution}}.$$

This ratio has the desirable property that efficiency increases if communication time can be overlapped with computation. It does not however measure efficiency relative to the best serial algorithm for the same problem. Note that the classical definition for efficiency is the speedup obtained divided by the number of processors in a system. Assuming that the computation time using one processor is approximately equal to P times the parallel computation time, then the above computational efficiency and the classical efficiency are approximately equal. The above assumption is valid for most algorithms in this paper.

The computational efficiency of a program with localized communication will generally depend strongly on the grid size. As the number of grid points per processor increases, so does efficiency. The efficiency will also depend on the number of floating point operations performed per grid point; if more computation is performed, efficiency will be increased. In § 9.1 we describe measurements we have performed of efficiency as a function of work per grid point for the hyperbolic solvers described in § 8 with both areal and transpose algorithms. Section 9.2 discusses the general applicability and utility of these measurements for the comparative evaluation of architectures and algorithms.

9.1. Efficiency and work per grid point. To measure these effects, we have used the basic transpose-based hyperbolic solver described previously. We replaced the low-level two or three point hyperbolic difference step by a call to a subroutine that executes some number (NFLOPS) of floating point multiplications. By running the resulting program with different grid sizes and values of NFLOPS we obtain performance curves for the iPSC that measure efficiency with respect to both grid size and work per point. We summarize these results with the curves in Fig. 21, obtained on a 128 processor iPSC.

We conclude that computational efficiency is excellent in almost all cases ($E \geqq 50\%$). Even on very coarse grids, such as 128×128 grids where there are only 128 grid points per processor, reasonable efficiencies may be achieved by executing less than a hundred operations per grid point. (In fact we have had excellent efficiencies with even 32 points per node.)

The hyperbolic equations we have solved in this paper have been model problems, where the cost of computation at a grid point is just a few multiplications. From the graphs in Fig. 21 it is clear that the solution of realistic physical equations using real equations of state or other material properties will be extremely efficient, even on very coarse grids. We stress again that there are three other factors that are likely to further increase computational efficiency:

(a) the current iPSC design has a very high communication overhead;
(b) future machines will have much larger memories, and so many more grid points per processor;
(c) the transpose algorithm is far from optimal with respect to communication.

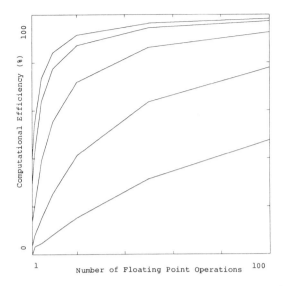

FIG. 21. *Computational efficiency on the* 128 *node* iPSC *for an areal sweep with block matrix transpose versus number of floating point operations executed per grid point. The curves from top to bottom are for grid sizes:* 2048 * 2048, 1024 * 1024, 512 * 512, 256 * 256, 128 * 128.

As an illustration of point (c) we repeated the above experiment using the areal decomposition approach discussed in § 8.1. The resulting efficiency curves are presented in Fig. 22 and are seen to be substantially better than in the transpose case.

We conclude therefore that the vast majority of regular-grid hyperbolic methods will parallelize with an efficiency close to 1, provided only that the memory available on each processor is large enough to store the code, associated data and results needed by that processor for a reasonably large number of grid points. It is important to note that for methods such as random choice where the computational work varies from

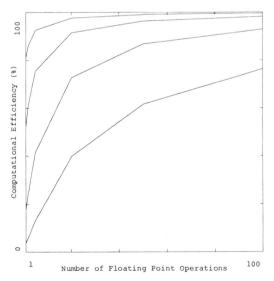

FIG. 22. *Computational efficiency on the* 128 *node* iPSC *for an areal sweep with areal decomposition technique versus number of floating point operations executed per grid point. The curves from top to bottom are for grid sizes:* 1024 * 1024, 512 * 512, 256 * 256, 128 * 128.

point to point in a grid, the efficiency as described above will be misleading in that some processors may in fact be idle while others are completing their locally expensive computations. Thus unless load-balancing or time-sharing of processors is employed, efficiencies for such methods will be lower than predicted unless the value of NFLOPS used in the predictions corresponds to the worst case possible at any grid point.

9.2. Architecture comparisons. There are many criteria that may be used to compare various parallel algorithms and architectures. The efficiency curves introduced in the previous section are one such mechanism which allow computational efficiency of each of a number of relevant algorithms to be compared across a range of machines. We intend to repeat the measurements described in this section for other parallel computers to provide a basis for comparison between machines. We have already measured the curves for two different algorithms, as seen in Figs. 21 and 22, and those graphs allow immediate comparison of the algorithms across a wide range of problem characteristics (NFLOPS and grid sizes). In fact the graphs are applicable to just about any situation where an areal sweep is performed over a rectangular grid and where only nearest-neighbor connectivity is involved between points. As an example, Fig. 22 is directly applicable to the areal multigrid relaxation discussed in § 11—one simply computes the number of floating point operations per grid point in the relaxation, and can then read off the expected efficiency on different grid sizes from the graph.

10. Elliptic equations and solution methods. The basic elliptic equation we have studied is of the form:

$$\nabla \cdot (-\vec{\vec{K}} \cdot \nabla P)(x, y) = F(x, y).$$

Here K has discontinuities, possibly of order a thousand or more, across a given set of curves and in typical applications may represent a fluid density, permeability or dielectric constant. The quantity of most interest is not the pressure or potential P but the velocity or flux $-\vec{\vec{K}} \cdot \nabla P$. The right-hand side F may contain arbitrary point and line sources. Boundary conditions may be Dirichlet, Neumann or mixed. We also allow a parabolic term on the left, provided an implicit time discretization is used. In the latter case, the following discussion will apply to the individual time steps.

Discontinuities of coefficients imply discontinuities in the solution gradient. Discretization of the equation on a rectangular grid leads to bad pressure and velocity solutions due to such discontinuities. For this reason it is essential to adapt the grids locally. In the resulting grids, discontinuities lie only along edges of triangles. The cost of grid generation is negligible compared to equation solution. We allow the use of curved edged triangles (isoparametrics) to provide high order boundary fitting. In In general, our grids consist of unions of rectangles and triangles, with triangles primarily used to fit boundaries and interior interfaces. For details of the grid construction methods used, we refer to our papers [43], [44], [45].

We have used finite element methods to discretize these equations, though similar studies could be applied to finite difference methods. To provide sufficient accuracy, we allow high order elements up to cubics (on triangles) or bicubics (on rectangles). We have discussed the solution of singular elliptic equations by these techniques in [43], [45] and the use of parallelism in the context of a tree of refinement grids elsewhere [6]. We have also previously described the solution of such systems on a parallel machine with global shared memory [4], [6]. We discuss here the implementation of fast solution methods on hypercube parallel processors. We describe the implementation of the *conjugate gradient method* and an *FFT-based fast Poisson solver* which we have used as a preconditioner for the conjugate gradient method. We have also implemented a *full multigrid method* based on a 5-point operator discretization of the equations. Using either of these methods, the solution cost in total operations performed is essentially proportional to the number of unknowns, while at the same time allowing near optimal use of parallelism.

Execution time is strongly dominated by the solution phase and it is the parallelization effort for this which we describe in the following sections. We point out however that the finite element construction is also easily parallelized: the construction of the element matrices can proceed essentially independently on each element, fully utilizing available parallelism. Vectorizing such code is difficult, because the operations to be performed at individual finite element nodes are complicated, and because the elements are neither regular nor homogeneous (rectangles and triangles intermixed). Thus we will focus on parallel solution of the resulting equations and refer to our papers for details of the numerical analysis and of the discretization approach [43]–[47].

11. Parallel multigrid. We have developed a parallel multigrid algorithm and tested it on both the Caltech and Intel Hypercubes. Multigrid methods are near-optimal for a wide range of computations on serial or vector processors. Our test problem was a Poisson equation with Dirichlet boundary conditions on a square, discretized with a 5-point finite difference operator, but the implementation is considerably more general. A multigrid algorithm for the Poisson equation in 3 dimensions on the Caltech Hypercube has been developed independently by Clemens Thole [48].

The basic multigrid idea [49]–[51], [47], [20], [22] involves two aspects: the use of relaxation methods to dampen high-frequency errors and the use of multiple grids to allow low-frequencies to be relaxed inexpensively. A simple *Two-grid Iteration* involves a number of relaxations on a fine grid to reduce high-frequency errors in an initial guess of the solution, a projection of remaining errors to a coarser grid where they are solved for exactly, and then an interpolation back to the fine grid and addition to the solution there. This solution would now be exact but for errors introduced by the projection and interpolation processes. The solution is then improved by repeating the procedure.

The Two-grid Iteration is converted to the *Multigrid Iteration* (MGI) by recursively applying the two-grid iteration in place of the exact solution on the coarse grid. The number of times that the coarse grid iteration is repeated before returning to the fine grid is important for convergence rates—typical values used are once, known as *V-cycles*, or twice, known as *W-cycles*.

Improved convergence can be obtained by choice of a good initial guess for the solution. A simple strategy would be to solve the equations on a coarse grid using the Multigrid Iteration, and interpolate the solution to the fine grid as the initial guess for the Multigrid Iteration there. Recursively applying this idea leads to the *Full Multigrid Iteration* (FMG) which performs a sequence of Full Multigrid solutions on increasingly finer grids, using the solution of each as an initial guess for the next.

Our studies are concerned with the case where there are many fine grid points per processor and we will assume this to be the case throughout the exposition. The algorithms presented in this section are valid for any architecture in which the processors can be arranged as a 2-dimensional periodic or nonperiodic array, depending on the nature of the boundary conditions of the elliptic problem. We have developed both a parallel Red-Black Gauss–Seidel relaxation operator and a parallel alternating line relaxation algorithm. The latter relaxation is important for problems which have variable coefficients, and is implemented using the parallel transpose operation.

Computational efficiency of the multigrid relaxation decreases with coarser grids because the perimeter to area ratio becomes less favorable as the number of grid points is reduced. Consequently we find that V-cycles are somewhat more favored than W-cycles on a hypercube compared to a serial computer. Figure 23 shows a comparison of V- and W-cycle speedup curves for the same sized grid which clearly demonstrates the superior computational efficiency of the V-cycle with respect to communication overhead. Similarly it is advantageous to terminate grid subdivision at a somewhat finer grid than one might use on a serial machine. Note that in Fig. 23 the curves begin only at speedups of 2 or 4. We were unable to solve the problem with that grid size on only one processor due to memory limitations. If the smallest number of processors that could be utilized was p then we arbitrarily assigned speedup p to the p-processor time.

11.1. Distributed grids for multigrid. Having discretized the PDE using finite differences, the resulting equations on any grid level involve the solution or error on a rectangular grid of points. Parallelizing multigrid amounts to distributing these grids over the processors and implementing the communications needed as a result between processors. We accomplish the distribution by representing the solution (or error) on each grid level as a distributed matrix of type AREAL, see §§ 6.1 and 6.3. In particular the hypercube is organized as a fixed rectangular mesh of $P = p_x p_y$ processors for all grid levels, using the matrix library call:

$$areal\_parameters(p_x, p_y, 0, 0, 1),$$

which provides a boundary of width 1 surrounding all sides of each subgrid allocated in subsequent *allocate_matrix* calls for type AREAL, as well as nonperiodic boundary conditions. We will use the term *extended subgrid* to denote such a subgrid with boundary, and will refer to the nonboundary points of the subgrid as its *interior*. We assume that the grids to be used are of dimensions $2^{l_x}p_x \times 2^{l_y}p_y$ for some l_x, l_y. With this choice, the interior of a level l subgrid assigned to a processor may be identified with a subset of the extended level $l+1$ subgrid assigned to that processor. Similarly

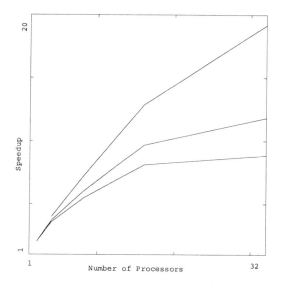

FIG. 23. *The top curve is speedup versus number of processors for V cycle multigrid on a 128 by 128 grid with 4 levels on the Caltech Hypercube. The two lower curves are for V and W cycle multigrid on a 64 by 64 grid with 3 levels.*

the interior of the level $l+1$ subgrid in a processor is contained in the extended subgrid of level l.

11.2. Inter-process communication. Along the boundary of the subgrids at any level some communication will be required by the multigrid relaxation operation. For example, a relaxation at boundary points of a subregion will require the boundary data of the adjoining subregion. The *shuffle* operation from the matrix library, also described in § 6.3, provides exactly the required interchange of boundary data. By calling *shuffle* one can assure that each boundary edge at the start of any operation (relaxation or intergrid transfer) holds a copy of the closest interior edge of the adjacent subgrid. For a 5-point operator, a boundary width of 1 suffices. The only possible problem here is the updating of corner nodes which a priori have to be copied from a nonneighboring processor. These are not actually needed in a five-point problem, but in more general situations are accommodated by adding an extra corner node shuffle. The *shuffle* operation is thus seen to be the basic communication routine necessary for multigrid to work on distributed grids.

Intergrid transfers between multigrid levels (injection and interpolation) are entirely local to each processor because of the containment relationships between the grids presented in the previous section. Thus no communication is involved in these steps. However before any updated grid values are used it is essential to perform a *shuffle* operation to preserve the integrity of the duplicate boundary data. Thus we use the *shuffle* operation not only before each relaxation but also before every intergrid transfer.

It is in fact possible to choose a slightly different areal distribution of a matrix which avoids most of the shuffle operations at the cost of a small amount of memory. In this representation the interior edges of subgrids are actually duplicated in neighboring processors, as well as having a further boundary edge as above. With this choice, the interior of the level $l+1$ subgrid contains all points of the interior of the level l subgrid, obviating any need to perform shuffles after intergrid transfers. In this case a *shuffle* is required only before every relaxation, resulting in a substantial decrease in communication.

To control termination of iteration in adaptive multigrid algorithms, norms of error values need to be calculated. These are evaluated by computing a local inner product in each processor, storing it in the local component of a distributed vector of length P, and then calling *sum_vector* on this distributed vector, which computes the squared norm and distributes it to the processors (see the discussion of the semantics of *inner_product* in § 5.5). If the alternate areal representation of the previous paragraph is used, it is important to assign a weight of 0.5 to interior edge points and a weight of 0.25 to interior corner points in computing local norms since these points are duplicated as interior points in neighboring subgrids.

11.3. The relaxation operation. The relaxation operation is straightforward to implement in each of the subregions. Standard Gauss–Seidel relaxation is discarded on numerical grounds of slower convergence. It introduces artificial discontinuities along the boundaries of the subregions as the parallel version uses the original values of the boundary duplicates. Note that in the limit of subregions consisting of only one grid point, this would reduce to a Jacobi relaxation. Instead we utilize a Red-Black ordering of the grid points. This can be implemented such that the parallel algorithm will, after each iteration step, give the same result as the corresponding serial algorithm. The procedure consists of shuffling, relaxing the red points, shuffling again and then relaxing the black points.

11.4. Intergrid transfers. The error (the residual equation to be precise) is projected to the coarse grid using half-injection—the errors at the black grid points are identically zero after the previous relaxation step. For this step as discussed previously, it is necessary that the extended fine grid subregions contain the nonextended coarse grid regions.

Having solved the error equation on the coarse grid the solution on the fine grid has to be updated by addition of a suitable interpolation of the computed coarse grid error. We have used linear interpolation at this point. To do this in parallel without communication, the extended coarse grid subregion must contain the nonextended fine grid subregion. We update the boundary duplicates in the fine grid subregions following the interpolation using a *shuffle* operation.

11.5. Results and timings for multigrid. In Fig. 23 we compare timings for 3-level V-cycle and W-cycle multigrid iterations with finest grid of dimension 64×64, and also a 4-level V-cycle iteration on a 128×128 grid. These computations were performed on the Caltech Hypercube with from 2 up to 32 nodes. The curves represent speedup attained with increasing number of processors (the 128 grid problem would not fit on 2 processors). We notice that the speedup for the W-cycle is worse than that for the V-cycle. This is due to the fact that in the W-cycle algorithm, one spends a larger segment of the computation time on the coarser grids. In spite of this, it can be expected that for some equations it may be profitable to use the W-cycle instead of V-cycle because of its faster convergence rate. This issue however is too dependent on the particular type of equations solved to be discussed in this context. The V-cycle curve for the finer grid shows substantially improved performance compared to the coarser grid. All of these curves correspond to relatively very coarse grids since the number of grid points per processor is at most 512 on the finest grid.

In Fig. 24 we illustrate the effect of Area/Perimeter considerations on the Caltech Hypercube with 32 processors. The hypercube was organized as logical rectangular grids of dimensions 32×1, 16×2 and 8×4 (see Fig. 12) and we display the resulting

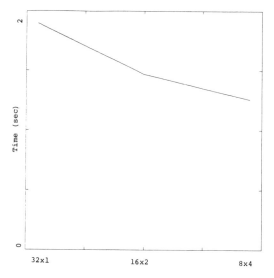

FIG. 24. *Area-perimeter considerations for multigrid on the 32 node Caltech Hypercube. We compare times for a V cycle multigrid iteration on a 128 by 128 grid with 2 levels, when the domain is split in 32 by 1, 16 by 2 and 8 by 4 rectangles, respectively.*

computation time for a multigrid iteration on a 128×128 grid with 2 grid levels. The improvement in timing as the subregions approach squares is obvious. The success of this demonstration is related to the fact that even for short messages communication costs on the Caltech Hypercube are strictly proportional to message length.

To illustrate that communication overhead decreases with an areal distribution as problem size increases, we compare in Fig. 25 the scaled time of a multigrid iteration as a function of grid size. The scaled time is obtained by dividing the iteration time by a quantity proportional to the number of grid points and is therefore proportional to effective work per grid point for multigrid *including* communication overhead. Specifically we compare the times for 16 iterations on a 64 by 64 grid, 4 iterations on a 128 by 128 grid and 1 iteration on a 256 by 256 grid on the 32 node Caltech Hypercube. Scaled time is over twice as small for the finest grid as for the coarsest.

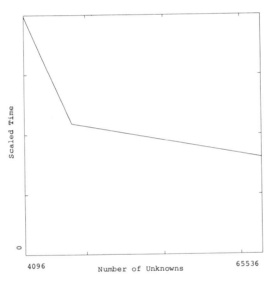

FIG. 25. *Multigrid, 3 levels, V cycle on the Caltech Hypercube. We compare execution times of different sized problems by scaling the times by the number of floating point operations executed.*

Our multigrid results for the Intel iPSC, are cast in a somewhat different form. We solved problems with varying grid sizes on a 128 node iPSC. To compare the iteration times, we calculated the number of *useful* floating point operations (additions or multiplications, but not memory accesses) that were executed in each of the runs. We divided these by the time it took for an iteration to complete. This defines an attained *floprate* for each run. In Fig. 26 we plot the attained floprate for *V*-cycles as a function of grid size, going from 4096 unknowns to over 1.6 million unknowns. We see that for the largest problems we attained about 3.75 megaflops.

12. Parallel conjugate gradient. Discretization of elliptic partial differential equations in two dimensions by finite element or finite difference methods leads to systems of equations with sparse coefficient matrices. The fill-in of the matrix tends to follow diagonals and the bandwidth is about $dN^{1/2}$, where N is the dimension of the matrix and d is the degree of the finite elements used for the discretization. Furthermore typically only $O(1)$ diagonals have nonzero elements. The parallel conjugate gradient method we have developed on the hypercube solves systems of equations with such

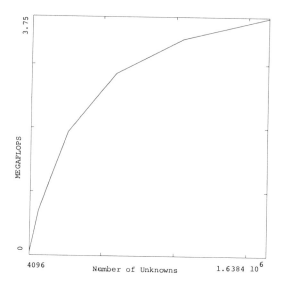

FIG. 26. *Performance of 2 level V cycle multigrid method on the* 128 *node* iPSC. *Number of floating point operations executed per second as function of problem size.*

coefficient matrix structures. This allows us to parallelize the solution of finite element discretizations of arbitrary and even variable degree with high efficiency.

12.1. The serial algorithm. The preconditioned conjugate gradient method [52]–[55] finds the solution of the system of equations $Ax = f$, to a specified accuracy ε by performing the following iteration on the vector x, which has been appropriately initialized:

$$r = f - Ax$$
$$p = Br$$
loop
$$\qquad s = \langle r, Br \rangle / \langle p, Ap \rangle$$
$$\qquad r = r - s \cdot Ap$$
$$\qquad x = x + s \cdot p$$
$$\qquad rbr = \langle r, Br \rangle$$
$$\qquad s = \langle r, Br \rangle / old \langle r, Br \rangle$$
$$\qquad p = Br + s \cdot p$$
until *converged*

Here B is an approximate inverse of A, which is assumed to be positive definite symmetric, and $\langle x, y \rangle$ denotes the inner product of vectors x and y. The *preconditioning* operator B can be effective in improving substantially the convergence rate of the algorithm. In § 13, we will describe a parallel preconditioner for the conjugate gradient algorithm, concentrating in this section on the unaccelerated conjugate gradient method where B is just the identity operator.

12.2. Parallelism in conjugate gradient. We parallelize the algorithm by exploiting parallelism in every operation of the iteration. We have discussed previously how to parallelize each operation in the algorithm above (with the identity preconditioning). All of the vectors in the algorithm are allocated using the *allocate_vector* library routine (see § 5) with type *SHIFT*. The matrix A is allocated using the *allocate_matrix* library routine (see § 6) with type *DIAGONAL* and with the sparsity structure of the nonzero extended diagonals explicitly specified. Each line in the algorithm above is expressed with the corresponding vector or matrix library routine. In particular the communication-intensive operation $p \rightarrow Ap$ is implemented directly using the *matrix_vector* library routine, so that all communication is performed by the optimized *shift_vector* routine. It then suffices to compile the above program with the vector and matrix libraries introduced earlier. Note that the resulting program shows no dependence on a control processor. Each processor obtains the required inner products for convergence control using only a local subroutine call. All processors make the decision to stop iterating, and they will all do so simultaneously since they all receive the same value for the inner products.

12.3. Timing and results for conjugate gradient. In Fig. 27 we display the execution time per iteration step as a function of the number of processors used for the conjugate gradient method on a 64×64 grid on the Caltech Hypercube with from 2 up to 32 nodes. In Fig. 28 we compare the floprates attained in the execution of the conjugate gradient iteration on a 5D Caltech cube for different size grids. The floprates are determined by dividing the actual number of floating point operations executed by the time to perform the iteration. We counted the number of multiplications in the algorithm to be about (*number of diagonals* + 5)N per iteration and about an equal number of floating point additions take place. These computations were performed with the nonoptimized vector shift algorithm, and are for relatively coarse grids.

In Fig. 29 we display the analogous graph for the 128 node iPSC for problems with 4096 up to 409600 unknowns. These computations were performed with the optimized shift algorithm and so are not directly comparable to the Caltech Hypercube results. Counting all useful floating point operations (multiplications and additions), the 128 node iPSC attained about 2.5 megaflops in conjugate gradient iteration. The

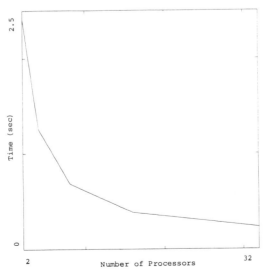

FIG. 27. *Conjugate gradient on a 64 by 64 grid. Time per iteration step versus number of processors used on the Caltech Hypercube.*

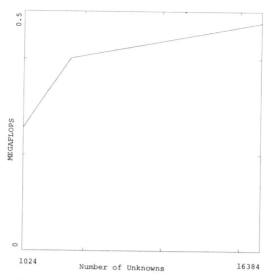

FIG. 28. *Performance of the conjugate gradient method on the* 32 *node Caltech Hypercube. We display the number of floating point operations executed per second for problems with* 1024 *up to* 16384 *unknowns.*

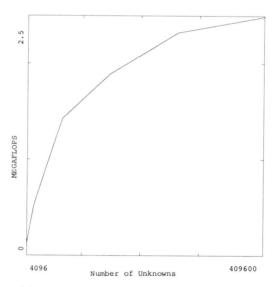

FIG. 29. *Performance of the conjugate gradient method on the* 128 *node iPSC. We display the number of floating point operations executed per second for problems with* 4096 *up to* 409,600 *unknowns.*

matrix used for the purpose of timings had 5 diagonals corresponding to linear finite elements.

13. A parallel fast Poisson solver. We have developed a parallel preconditioner for use in conjunction with the parallel conjugate gradient algorithm described in § 12. The algorithm is based on the Fast Fourier Transform and reduces the solution of the Poisson equation:

$$-\Delta\Phi(x, y) = F(x, y),$$

on a rectangle to Fourier transforms and tridiagonal solvers [56]. This is a standard method frequently used on serial computers and the interest here is entirely in how to parallelize it. An attraction of our parallelization method is that neither the FFT nor the tridiagonal solvers need to be parallelized. Assuming a 5-point discretization of the Poisson equation in a rectangle on an $m \times n$ grid, the solution may be obtained on a serial machine in three steps using the algorithm:

$$
\begin{aligned}
&\text{for col in } 1, \cdots, m \quad \mathit{fft}(n, F(\,\cdot\,, col)) \\
&\text{for row in } 1, \cdots, n \quad \mathit{tridiag}(m, t(row, \cdot\,), F(row, \cdot\,)) \\
&\text{for col in } 1, \cdots, m \quad \mathit{fft}(n, F(\,\cdot\,, col))
\end{aligned}
$$

This algorithm returns the exact solution of the discrete Poisson equation in $O(nm \log n)$ operations on a serial computer. Here the matrix $F = F(\,\cdot\,, \cdot\,)$ is a discretization of the source function $F(x, y)$, while $F(row, \cdot\,)$ and $F(\,\cdot\,, col)$ denote the vectors corresponding to the indicated row or column of the matrix F. The matrix $t(\,\cdot\,, \cdot\,)$ contains the coefficients of the tridiagonal systems, obtained analytically by Fourier transforming the 5-point matrix. The routine $\mathit{fft}(n, v)$ computes a real (sine or cosine) Fast Fourier Transform of a vector v of length n. Similarly the routine $\mathit{tridiag}(m, t, v)$ solves a tridiagonal system $Tu = v$, overwriting the m-component vector v with the solution u.

We have found that such a solver is a useful preconditioner even for higher-order finite elements on logically rectangular grids—one can use the Poisson solver for a rectangular grid corresponding in dimensionality to the nodal points of the finite elements, see McBryan [43], [47].

Vectorization of this algorithm involves considerable effort because it requires vectorizing the FFT routine which is nontrivial especially if the grid dimension n is more general than a power of 2. However parallelization is straightforward. The matrix F is stored as a distributed matrix of type CONTIGUOUS_COLUMN, while the matrix t is precomputed and stored as a distributed matrix of type CONTIGUOUS_ROW, see § 6.1. Each fft and $\mathit{tridiagonal}$ operation is assigned to an individual processor with each processor executing the normal serial code for that operation on one or more columns or rows, respectively. This allows the full available parallelism to be applied effectively.

As we have noted in our previous Denelcor HEP studies, to complete the parallelization of this algorithm on a shared memory parallel computer it suffices to place a *barrier* between the first and second step, and again between the second and third step since it is necessary that all processors complete work on each step before any processor proceeds to the following step. There is a complication however on a hypercube stemming from the fact that the memory on the hypercube is not shared among the processors. In the fft steps it is necessary to distribute the matrix F in contiguous-column form, so that the fft operations are local to individual processors. Similarly in the tridiagonal step it is necessary to distribute the matrix F in contiguous-row form so that each tridiagonal solution involves only values from one processor. To get from a row-distributed matrix to a column-distributed matrix requires a matrix transpose.

It follows that the above algorithm may be parallelized on a local-memory processor by distributing F in contiguous-column form and by inserting an extra *transpose*(F) step between the first and second step and between the second and third step. This along with the *barrier* described previously are the only modifications required to the serial algorithm and in fact all communication for the Poisson solution is hidden in the two transpose operations. On shared memory computers the *transpose* steps are not needed. However on machines with fast data caches there may be an advantage to using the transpose anyway, since it ensures that the fft and $\mathit{tridiagonal}$ solutions work entirely on contiguous data. Another approach to parallelizing the fast Poisson solver, more cumbersome from a programming point of view, would be to adapt the Fourier transform algorithm to handle distributed vectors. This is nontrivial to perform unless the grid dimension is a power of 2.

Acknowledgments. We wish to thank Geoffrey Fox at Caltech for providing access to the Caltech Hypercube and Shirley Enguehard at Caltech for much helpful advice. We also express our appreciation to Los Alamos National Laboratory and to Intel Scientific Computers for access to their iPSC Hypercube systems. In particular we would like to thank Ralph Brickner (Los Alamos National Laboratory) for his patience through many late night and weekend system reboots and Cleve Moler (Intel) for providing documentation and other useful information.

REFERENCES

[1] O. McBRYAN AND E. VAN DE VELDE, *Parallel algorithms for elliptic equations*, Proc. 1984 ARO Novel Computing Environments Conference, Stanford University, Society for Industrial and Applied Mathematics, 1986.

[2] O. McBRYAN, E. VAN DE VELDE AND P. VIANNA, *Parallel algorithms for elliptic and parabolic equations*, Proc. Conference on Parallel Computations in Heat Transfer and Fluid Flows, Univ. Maryland, Baltimore, MD, November 1984.

[3] O. McBRYAN, *State of the art of multiprocessors in scientific computation*, Proc. European Weather Center Conference on Multiprocessors in Meteorological Models, EWCMF, Reading, England, December 1984.

[4] O. McBRYAN AND E. VAN DE VELDE, *Parallel algorithms for elliptic equation solution on the* HEP *computer*, Proc. Conference on Parallel Processing using the Heterogeneous Element Processor, Univ. Oklahoma, Tulsa, OK, March 1985.

[5] ——, *Elliptic equation algorithms on parallel computers*, Comm. Appl. Numer. Math., 2 (1986), pp. 311–318.

[6] ——, *Parallel algorithms for elliptic equations*, Comm. Pure Appl. Math., 38 (1985), pp. 769–795.

[7] ——, *The multigrid method on parallel computers*, Proc. 2nd European Multigrid Conference, Cologne, October 1985, GMD Studie Nr. 110, J. Linden, ed., GMD, July 1986.

[8] ——, *Hypercube algorithms for computational fluid dynamics*, Proc. Oak Ridge meeting on Hypercube Architectures, August 1985, Society for Industrial and Applied Mathematics, to appear.

[9] J. DONGARRA, J. BUNCH, C. MOLER AND G. STEWART, LINPACK *User's Guide*, Society for Industrial and Applied Mathematics, Philadelphia, PA, 1979.

[10] C. LAWSON, R. HANSON, D. KINCAID AND F. KROUGH, *Basic linear algebra subprograms for* FORTRAN *usage*, ACM TOMS, 5 (1979), pp. 308–323.

[11] J. J. DONGARRA, J. DU CROZ, SVEN HAMMARLING AND R. J. HANSON, *A proposal for an extended set of Fortran basic linear algebra subprograms*, ACM SIGNUM, January 1985.

[12] D. B. GANNON AND J. PANETTA, *The systolic level 2 BLAS*, in New Computing Environments: Parallel, Vector and Systolic, A. Wouk, ed., Society for Industrial and Applied Mathematics, Philadelphia, PA, 1986.

[13] J. J. DONGARRA AND R. E. HIROMOTO, *A collection of parallel linear equations routines for the Denelcor* HEP, Parallel Computing, 1 (1984).

[14] D. P. O'LEARY AND G. W. STEWART, *Data-flow algorithms for parallel matrix computations*, Univ. Maryland Tech. Report 1366, January 1984.

[15] J. J. DONGARRA, A. H. SAMEH AND D. C. SORENSEN, *Some implementations of the* QR-*factorization on an* MIMD-*machine*, in Parallel Computing, October 1985.

[16] M. T. HEATH AND D. C. SORENSEN, *A pipelined Givens method for computing the* QR-*factorization of a sparse matrix*, in Proc. Workshop on Parallel Processing using the HEP, S. Lakshmivarahan, ed., Univ. Oklahoma, Tulsa, OK, March 1985.

[17] D. C. SORENSEN, *Buffering for vector performance on a pipelined* MIMD *machine*, MCS-TM-29, Argonne National Laboratory, Argonne, IL, April 1984.

[18] C. GROSCH, *Performance analysis of Poisson solvers on array computers*, in Infotech State of the Art Report: Supercomputers, R. Hockney, ed., vol. 1, Infotech Int. Ltd., 1979, pp. 147–181.

[19] Y. SAAD, A. SAMEH AND P. SAYLOR, *Solving elliptic difference equations on a linear array of processors*, SIAM J. Sci. Statist. Comput., 6 (1985), pp. 1049–1063.

[20] A. BRANDT, *Multi-grid solvers on parallel computers*, ICASE Technical Report 80-23, NASA Langley Research Center, Hampton, VA, 1980.

[21] L. ADAMS, *Iterative algorithms for large sparse linear systems on parallel computers*, NASA Report CR-166027, NASA Langley Research Center, Hampton, VA, 1982.

[22] D. GANNON AND J. VAN ROSENDALE, *Highly parallel multi-grid solvers for elliptic PDEs: An experimental analysis*, ICASE Technical Report 82-36, NASA Langley Research Center, Hampton, VA, 1982.

[23] L. ADAMS AND H. F. JORDAN, *Is SOR Color-Blind?*, ICASE Report No. 84-14, NASA Langley Research Center, Hampton, VA, 1984.

[24] E. L. LUSK AND R. A. OVERBEEK, *Implementation of monitors with macros*, Technical Memorandum ANL-83-97, Argonne National Laboratory, Mathematics and Computer Science Div., Argonne, IL, December 1983.

[25] H. E. JORDAN, *Structuring parallel algorithms in an MIMD, shared memory environment*, Univ. Colorado CS Report, Denver, CO, September 1984.

[26] C. L. SEITZ, *The cosmic cube*, Comm. ACM, 28 (1985), pp. 22–33.

[27] *Caltech/JPL concurrent computation project annual report* 1983-1984, Caltech Report, December 1984.

[28] L. JOHNSSON, *Data permutations and basic linear algebra computations on ensemble architectures*, Yale Univ. Research Report DCS/RR-367, New Haven, CT, February 1985.

[29] T. F. CHAN AND R. SCHREIBER, *Parallel networks for multi-grid algorithms: architecture and complexity*, Yale Univ. Research Report, New Haven, CT, DCS 262, 1983.

[30] Y. SAAD AND M. H. SCHULTZ, *Data communication in hypercubes*, Yale Univ. Research Report, New Haven, CT, DCS/RR-428, October 1985.

[31] ———, *Direct parallel methods for solving banded linear systems*, Yale Univ. Technical Report, CS Dept., New Haven, DCS/RR-387, CT, 1985.

[32] S. L. JOHNSSON, *Communication efficient basic linear algebra computations on hypercube architectures*, Yale Univ. Research Report, New Haven, CT, DCS/RR-361, September 1985.

[33] J. M. ORTEGA AND R. G. VOIGT, *Solution of partial differential equations on vector and parallel computers*, ICASE Report 85-1, January 1985.

[34] G. C. FOX AND S. W. OTTO, *Algorithms for concurrent processors*, Phys. Today, 37 (1984), pp. 50–59.

[35] J. SALMON, *Binary gray codes and the mapping of a physical lattice into a hypercube*, Caltech Concurrent Processor Report (CCP)Hm-51, 1983.

[36] E. N. GILBERT, *Gray codes and paths on the n-cube*, Bell System Tech. J., 37 (1958), p. 915.

[37] M. GARDNER, *Mathematical games*, Scientific American, August 1972, p. 106.

[38] T. CHAN, Copper Mountain, Colorado, April 1985. Remark at 2nd Multigrid Conference.

[39] J. O. ECKLUNDH, *A fast computer method for matrix transposing*, IEEE Trans. Comput., C-21 (1972), pp. 801–803.

[40] A. CHORIN, *Random choice solution of hyperbolic systems*, J. Comput. Phys., 22 (1976), pp. 517–533.

[41] R. RICHTMYER AND K. MORTON, *Difference Methods for Initial Value Problems*, Wiley-Interscience, New York, 1952.

[42] J. GLIMM, *Solutions in the large for nonlinear hyperbolic systems of equations*, Comm. Pure Appl. Math., 18 (1965), pp. 697–715.

[43] O. MCBRYAN, *Computational methods for discontinuities in fluids*, Lectures in Applied Mathematics, vol. 22, American Mathematical Society, Providence, 1985.

[44] ———, *Elliptic and hyperbolic interface refinement in two phase flow*, in Boundary and Interior Layers, J. J. H. Miller, ed., Boole Press, Dublin, 1980.

[45] ———, *Shock tracking for 2d flows*, in Computational and Asymptotic Methods for Boundary Layer Problems, J. J. Miller, ed., Boole Press, Dublin, 1982.

[46] J. GLIMM AND O. MCBRYAN, *A computational model for interfaces*, Adv. Appl. Math., 6 (1985), pp. 422–435.

[47] O. MCBRYAN, *Fluids, discontinuities and renormalization group methods*, in Mathematical Physics VII, Brittin, Gustafson and Wyss, eds., North-Holland, Amsterdam, 1984, pp. 481–494.

[48] C. THOLE, *Experiments with Multigrid on the Caltech Hypercube*, GMD Internal Report, October 1985.

[49] A. BRANDT, *Multi-level adaptive solutions to boundary-value problems*, Math. Comp., 31 (1977), pp. 333–390.

[50] W. HACKBUSCH, *Convergence of multi-grid iterations applied to difference equations*, Math. Comp., 34 (1980), pp. 425–440.

[51] K. STUDEN AND U. TROTTENBERG, *On the construction of fast solvers for elliptic equations*, Computational Fluid Dynamics, Rhode-Saint-Genese, 1982.

[52] M. R. HESTENES AND E. STIEFEL, *Methods of conjugate gradients for solving linear systems*, J. Res. Nat. Bur. Standards, 49 (1952), pp. 409–436.

[53] J. K. REID, *On the method of conjugate gradients for the solution of large sparse systems of linear equations*, in Large Sparse Sets of Linear Equations, J. K. Reid, ed., Academic Press, New York, 1971, pp. 231–254.

[54] P. CONCUS, G. H. GOLUB AND D. P. O'LEARY, *A generalized conjugate gradient method for the numerical solution of elliptic partial differential equations*, in Sparse Matrix Computations, D. J. Rose, ed., Academic Press, New York, 1976.

[55] G. H. GOLUB AND C. F. VAN LOAN, *Matrix Computations*, John Hopkins Press, Baltimore, 1984.

[56] P. SWARZTRAUBER, *The methods of cyclic reduction, Fourier analysis and the FACR algorithm for the discrete solution of Poisson's equation on a rectangle*, SIAM Rev., 19 (1977), pp. 490–501.